Donated by

Tony
and
Heather
Pitts

June 2018

Greening Post-Industrial Cities

City greening has been heralded for contributing to environmental governance and critiqued for exacerbating displacement and inequality.

Bringing these two disparate analyses into conversation, this book offers a comparative understanding of how tensions between growth, environmental protection, and social equity are playing out in practice. Examining Chicago, USA, Birmingham, UK, and Vancouver, Canada, McKendry argues that city greening efforts were closely connected to processes of post-industrial branding in the neoliberal economy. While this brought some benefits, concerns about the unequal distribution of these benefits and greening's limited environmental impact challenged its legitimacy. In response, city leaders have moved toward initiatives that strive to better address environmental effectiveness and social equity while still spurring growth. Through an analysis that highlights how different varieties of liberal environmentalism are manifested in each case, this book illustrates that cities, though constrained by inconsistent political will and broader political and economic contexts, are making contributions to more effective, socially just environmental governance.

Both critical and hopeful, McKendry's work will interest scholars of city greening, environmental governance, and comparative urban politics.

Corina McKendry is Associate Professor of Political Science and core faculty of the Environmental Program at Colorado College.

Cities and Global Governance
Edited by Noah J. Toly
Wheaton College

The Routledge series *Cities and Global Governance* is composed of contributed volumes covering key areas of study at the intersection of urbanism and global governance. Each title explores dimensions of the relationship between the local and the global, between urban landscapes and global dynamics. Authors in the series make empirical and theoretical contributions that advance our understanding of the role of cities as sites and actors in global governance.

For a full list of titles in this series, please visit www.routledge.com/Cities-and-Global-Governance/book-series/CGG

Cities, Networks, and Global Environmental Governance
Spaces of Innovation, Places of Leadership
Sofie Bouteligier

The Power of Cities in International Relations
Edited by Simon Curtis

Global Cities and Climate Change
The Translocal Relations of Environmental Governance
Taedong Lee

The Urban Climate Challenge
Rethinking the Role of Cities in the Global Climate Regime
Edited by Craig Johnson, Noah Toly, and Heike Schroeder

The Global City 2.0
From Strategic Site to Global Actor
Kristin Ljungkvist

Greening Post-Industrial Cities
Growth, Equity, and Environmental Governance
Corina McKendry

Greening Post-Industrial Cities

Growth, Equity, and Environmental Governance

Corina McKendry

Routledge
Taylor & Francis Group

NEW YORK AND LONDON

First published 2018
by Routledge
711 Third Avenue, New York, NY 10017

and by Routledge
2 Park Square, Milton Park, Abingdon, Oxon, OX14 4RN

Routledge is an imprint of the Taylor & Francis Group, an informa business

Library of Congress Cataloging-in-Publication Data
A catalog record for this book has been requested

ISBN: 978-1-138-77613-5 (hbk)
ISBN: 978-1-315-77340-7 (ebk)

Typeset in Sabon
by Out of House Publishing

This book is dedicated to my grandparents, Rev. Dr. T. William Hall and Ruth Fisher Hall M.Ed., for their century of living with gratitude and curiosity.

Contents

Figures

Preface

Work on this book began nine years ago. When the project began, with only Chicago, Illinois and Birmingham, England as case studies, both cities were at the pinnacle of their efforts to use greening as a post-industrial branding strategy. Environmental amenities had transformed their once fading city centers, and elected officials were proclaiming their commitment to becoming leaders in climate governance. My original analysis of what I called "green urban entrepreneurialism" was fairly critical.[1] Though the cities were making some steps toward greater environmental sustainability, their efforts paled in comparison to their rhetoric. Even more disturbing was the distributional implications of green urban entrepreneurialism. The cities were focusing on city center prestige projects, and the transfer of public funds to beautification and away from social welfare was obfuscated by city leaders' claims of the supposedly universal benefits of the greener city. This led me to argue that the promise of cities making a contribution to global environmental governance was at best overstated and at worst a distraction from the larger political changes that needed to occur to achieve social and environmental sustainability.

As the years have passed, I returned to Chicago and Birmingham and began to investigate the city of Vancouver, British Columbia. What has transpired in these cities has led me to a more nuanced analysis of the environmental effectiveness and equity potential of city greening. I have become more convinced that cities, though significantly limited by the broader regulatory and political-economic processes of which they are a part, are nevertheless able to undertake policies with environmental merit. I have also seen a shift toward a greater incorporation of equity into the practices of city greening. Though gentrification, a prioritization of the green consumption preferences of the middle class, and use of scarce public funds for green amenities all remain serious concerns, important steps have been taken by city officials toward a more holistic understanding of the relationship between social and environmental sustainability. The power of globalized capital and of national environmental and urban policies remains pronounced, but local social movements and the political will of city leaders has increasingly challenged the greener city to also be a more equitable one. This is not to say that any of the three cities examined here are equitable, or that they could not be doing more to contribute to effective environmental governance. But the shift in both discourse and practice toward a more inclusive green city has been notable.

Data for this book have come from a variety of sources. Most important has been interviews conducted over the years with elected officials, current and former city staff, local business leaders, and environmental advocates and activists. With interviewees' permission, interviews were recorded, transcribed, and analyzed for recurring themes. If the location of the interview was inappropriate for recording (usually because of noise in a public meeting space), detailed notes were taken of the conversation. Though only a few interviewees requested anonymity, in the chapters that follow I have made all interviews anonymous. Other important data sources are government documents and reports, press releases, news coverage of key events, and peer reviewed studies of the case cities.

As anyone who is familiar with Chicago, Vancouver, or Birmingham will quickly realize, this book does not cover everything that has happened in the three cities since the emergence of green urban entrepreneurialism more than two decades ago. These cities are large, complex, and have many political and social challenges that have nothing to do with greening. I readily admit that much that is important to each city's politics is excluded from this book. Indeed, even the environmental policies of these cities are not exhaustively examined in the pages that follow. Choosing what aspects of the cities' greening agendas to include has been difficult, and there is certainly much more that could be said about environmentalism in each city. In narrowing the focus to a few key issue areas, I have tried to highlight those aspects of city greening that most clearly illuminate the question under investigation of how city leaders negotiate the relationship between environmental effectiveness, equity, and economic development. As such, the discussions that follow should be taken not as analyses of the entirety of the sustainability programs of Chicago, Birmingham, and Vancouver but rather as a series of vignettes that illustrate the major debates and controversies around greening that I encountered in each city.

The past nine years have led me to change my analysis of city greening as shifts have occurred in the practices and discourses of my case cities. Undoubtedly, the next nine years will see further changes in city policies and, correspondingly, in my analysis of them. Yet the underlying challenges of reconciling growth, environmental effectiveness, and equity that are discussed in this book are likely to persist. I therefore hope that this book's analysis of the complexity of the relationship between these elements of city greening will continue to offer insight into the potential for cities to further just, effective environmental governance even as the details of their contestations change.

Note

1 Corina McKendry. Smokestacks to Green Roofs: City Environmentalism, Green Urban Entrepreneurialism, and the Regulation of the Postindustrial City. (PhD Dissertation: University of California Santa Cruz, 2011.)

Acknowledgements

An almost unrecognizable version of this book was my PhD dissertation, completed for the Department of Politics at the University of California, Santa Cruz in 2011. For help with that project, and therefore the roots of this book, I thank my dissertation committee members Ronnie Lipschutz, Julie Guthman, Daniel Wirls, and Barbara Epstein. I also thank the Benjamin and Ruth Hammett Award for Research on Climate Change and the UCSC Department of Politics for funding my dissertation research. For the parts of this research conducted while at Colorado College, I thank Dean Sandi Wong and the Mrachek family for their support. I am also grateful to the Colorado College Crown Faculty Center for funding a two-day manuscript workshop on this book. The generosity of Noah Toly, Michele Betsill, and Dimitris Stevis for participating in the workshop and sharing their insights on my draft manuscript undoubtedly made this a better book. All errors are, of course, my own. For the maps included in this book, I offer my deep appreciation to the Colorado College GIS lab staff Matt Cooney and Noah Villamarin-Cutter. Thanks also to Nik Janos for the years of conversation and collaboration around the politics of urban greening. Finally, my endless love and gratitude to my family: to my parents and sister for always believing in me, Jaime for her love, unwavering support, and editing brilliance, and to Cedar and Rosie for being their wonderful selves.

Acronyms

BES	Birmingham Energy Savers
BMAP	Birmingham Mobility Action Plan
BMHT	Birmingham Municipal Housing Trust
CAC	Community Amenity Contribution (Vancouver)
CCAP	Chicago Climate Action Plan
CDOT	Chicago Department of Transportation
CHA	Chicago Housing Authority
CHP	Combined Heat and Power
D4E	Divvy for Everyone (Chicago)
DECC	Department of Energy & Climate Change (UK)
DERA	Downtown Eastside Residents Association (Vancouver)
DTES	Downtown Eastside (Vancouver)
DVBIA	Downtown Vancouver Business Improvement Association
ECC	European Economic Community
ECO	Energy Company Obligation (UK)
EIA	U.S. Energy Information Administration
ESAG	Eastside Sustainability Advisory Group (Birmingham)
GCAP	Greenest City 2020 Action Plan (Vancouver)
GHG	Greenhouse gas
ICC	International Convention Center (Birmingham)
ICI	Inner City Inclusive Commitment Statement (Vancouver)
LVEJO	Little Village Environmental Justice Organization (Chicago)
MSCs	Multi-Stakeholder Consultations (Canada)
NIA	National Indoor Arena (Birmingham)
NPA	Non-Partisan Association (Vancouver political party)
PEF	Property Endowment Fund (Vancouver)
SRO	Single-Room Occupancy (low-income housing units)
TEAM	The Elector's Action Movement (Vancouver political party)
TOD	Transit-Oriented Development
VANOC	Vancouver Organizing Committee

1 Local Politics of Global Environmental Governance

From belching smokestacks to congested freeways, from cramped tenement housing to high-rise condominiums, cities have a long history of being seen, not without reason, as the antithesis of nature. They are places of concrete and steel, not trees and fields. The cities of the global North in particular are the sites of incredibly high levels of consumption, the extensive production of waste, and intense greenhouse gas (GHG) emissions. Their environmental impact is inevitably huge, extending out well beyond the city limits through their immediate hinterlands as well as through the extensive commodity chains that are at the heart of the globalized economy. For many, cities represent all that is wrong with humanity's control over and separation from nature.[1]

Over the past few decades this assumption has begun to change, with a growing chorus heralding the importance of cities in furthering environmental governance and sustainable development. In the early 1990s this shift was most clearly articulated by the policy document Agenda 21 that emerged from the United Nations Conference on Environment and Development.[2] Agenda 21 highlighted cities as vital players in promoting sustainable development, an argument that international bodies have since made with increasing frequency.[3] In contrast to assumptions that cities are antithetical to nature, many are coming to see them as forerunners in the policy experimentation necessary to address intractable global problems.[4] Cities are, it is argued, where the impacts of climate change are felt most directly and therefore the places where people will be most likely to take action to reduce emissions.[5] Indeed, countless cities around the world have made environmental protection an explicit part of their development agendas. From new transit and bicycle infrastructure, to parks and green roofs, to ambitious waste reduction efforts, to high efficiency building standards, the wide range of environmental initiatives cities are undertaking have led some to claim that "our cities offer [hope] for re-shaping the way we live and the impact we have on the planet."[6]

Green economic development is seen as particularly important, with the prospect that cities will engage in green industry and green job creation a promising alternative to the dirty industries of the past and to the low wage jobs of the service economy.[7] The benefits to cities of green economic growth have been promoted by the United Nations, the European Union, and the World Bank, among others. The World Bank has been especially enthusiastic, asserting that city environmental initiatives have "huge potential rewards in terms of international recognition and competitive advantage."[8] This is a remarkable shift from the long-held idea that urban pollution was the necessary price to pay for economic growth. For proponents of city environmentalism, the increasing urbanization of the planet presents the opportunity "to lock new urban expansion into a new development model towards climate-resilient and low-carbon societies at large scale, leap frogging the old patterns of urban life for a growing population," while creating a new, green economy.[9] Enthusiasm for greening as an economic development strategy has helped justify the incorporation of environmental issues onto the city policy agenda, and many city leaders have embraced the economic potential of city environmentalism.

Not everyone is as sanguine about the benefits of city greening, however. Some critics highlight the extent to which supposedly greener cities may simply be displacing their dirty industries to other regions and countries, thereby reducing the levels of pollution within the city but not the actual environmental impact of city residents and their high levels of consumption.[10] Others note that the green economy is selectively adopted, and it remains hard for even the greenest city leaders to reject a new industry or new development because of its environmental impact.[11] Another concern regarding city environmentalism focuses on the social justice impacts of city greening, with evidence suggesting that it may exacerbate gentrification and displacement.[12] The provision of depoliticized environmental amenities, such as parks and bike lanes, are often seen as particularly culpable in this phenomenon, their appeal to young professionals and the creative class increasing property values and driving lower-income urban residents from their neighborhoods.[13]

This book strives to put the celebrations and the critiques of city greening into more explicit conversation by recognizing both that cities have an important role to play in global environmental governance *and* that greening efforts that exacerbate inequality are not truly sustainable. To do so, it investigates the rise and implementation of environmental initiatives in three post-industrial Anglosphere cities: Birmingham, England; Vancouver, British Columbia, and Chicago, Illinois. Examining how greening has unfolded in these cities, it is clear that the discourse of liberal environmentalism predominates in each city, shaping the environmental and social equity impacts of the cities' contributions to environmental governance in a way that prioritizes economic growth and development. However, concerns about the distribution of the benefits of the greener city and the environmental effectiveness of city initiatives are also present. These issues have pushed city leaders to expand their focus on greening as a development strategy toward efforts that also strive to further environmental effectiveness and social well-being. Indeed, in each of the three cities tensions between greening, growth, and equity are increasingly being recognized and negotiated. Even as this raises promising potential that cities will further just, effective environmental governance, their ability to achieve these three goals remain circumscribed, shaped by local political will and changing global and national regulatory environments.

Chicago, Vancouver, and Birmingham offer an interesting comparison for a number of reasons. The similarities between the three cities are numerous. The economy of each city has been transformed with the rise of globalization and each is part of a country that embraced neoliberalism with considerable enthusiasm in the 1980s and 1990s. Furthermore, each of these cities has explicitly used environmentalism as a strategy to transform its image and economy to promote economic development and flourish in the post-industrial era. The cities have also each declared their commitment to being a global leader in urban environmental sustainability, and have taken important steps toward realizing this commitment. Finally, each city is socioeconomically and ethnically diverse, providing an opportunity to look at issues of equity and environmental justice in relation to the cities' environmental agendas.

There are also important differences between the cities and their greening efforts. Vancouver is widely considered one of the greenest cities in the world. It is frequently celebrated for its urban planning achievements that combine density and livability, for its natural beauty, and for its overall commitment to creating the smallest possible urban environmental impact. Despite its accomplishments, locally the city's environmental achievements are overshadowed by a severe crisis of housing affordability and local conflict around new development. Chicago, particularly under the former Mayor Richard M. Daley, has also received extensive accolades for its greening initiatives and their contribution to transforming Chicago from a fading industrial powerhouse to a vibrant global city. His successor, Rahm Emanuel, has taken Daley's greening efforts even further. Though he has been less successful at maintaining greening as a defining part of the city's post-industrial image, under Emanuel there has been greater political space for local groups to demand a more equitable distribution of the benefits of the greener city. Birmingham, unlike Vancouver and Chicago, has only partially rebranded itself as a leading green city. Though undergoing a remarkable physical transformation in the 1990s and making numerous proclamations as to its commitment to sustainability and climate mitigation, Birmingham has struggled to transform its public image and to revitalize its economy through greening. Furthermore, though Birmingham has done more than either Chicago or Vancouver to make social equity an explicit part of its climate and environmental agenda, a lack of consistent political will and rapidly changing national regulation has left the city struggling to achieve its ambitious social justice and environmental goals.

In all three cities, the form of greening that emerged in the 1990s was closely intertwined with city officials' efforts to brand their city in order to attract investment, tourists, and middle class residents.[14] As they did so, there is evidence that this green urban entrepreneurialism often led to exclusion, displacement, and the diversion of scarce municipal funds toward green ventures and away from meeting the needs of the cities' poorer residents (see Chapter 3). However, what can also be seen in a comparison of Birmingham, Vancouver, and Chicago is a more complicated relationship between greening and social justice. Despite their differing legal, financial, and political contexts, there is an increasing incorporation of social equity into the core of their environmentalism. Though this move remains contested and at times in tension with both environmental and economic development goals, this expanding understanding of the sustainable city is beginning to create possibilities of more equitable and effective contributions to environmental governance.

Legitimacy, Equity, and Effectiveness: Environmental Governance and the Green City

At its core this book is about environmental governance, "the set of regulatory processes, mechanisms and organizations through which political actors influence environmental actions and outcomes."[15] While recognizing that governance is much broader than the state, and that in practice corporations, transnational environmental organizations, global civil society, and other non-state actors are a vital component of governance,[16] as the only body that can make legally binding social rules, the state remains vital to shaping human–environment interactions. Energy systems, the design of cities and suburbs, and the production processes that shape the environmental impacts of consumption are all deeply influenced by the rule-making capacity of the state on multiple political levels. The state, specifically the local state, is therefore the focus of this book.

Much of the literature on environmental governance has examined the global arena.[17] International treaties play an important role in these discussions, as do transnational corporations and global civil society. Other work has begun to analyze the local–global connections within processes of environmental governance.[18] Increasingly, the role of cities is being investigated, with much of this work focused on climate governance.[19] This literature has offered valuable insights into city environmental efforts as well as the complex multiscalarity of environmental governance. The examination of the transmunicipal nature of urban climate governance has been particularly rich, with a growing body of work examining how cities around the world are networking, joining global transmunicipal organizations, sharing best practices, and inspiring GHG reduction efforts in others.[20] All of this calls for a rethinking of how political scales are understood in global environmental politics. National states and international negotiations remain important, but such research points out that much more is happening in the realm of global environmental governance than may appear from an examination of the slow processes of international treaty negotiations.

Synthesizing the vast literature on environmental governance, Bernstein et al. assert that environmental governance should be constituted of three key factors: legitimacy, equity, and effectiveness.[21] Not without criticism,[22] and arguably a normative analysis alongside a descriptive one, this offers a useful starting place for understanding city environmental governance. Looking through the lens of these three aspects of environmental governance enables a conversation between the celebratory literature that sees city environmentalism as vital to a more sustainable global future and critiques of city greening initiatives that see them as exacerbating inequality. Understanding the emergence of cities as legitimate actors in environmental governance and the connection this has with broader trends of neoliberal urbanism, the equity impacts of these policies, and their environmental effectiveness can offer insight into the politics of city greening – who decides, who wins, who loses. In so doing, it can help illuminate the potential and limitations of cities' contributions to just, sustainable global environmental governance.

Legitimacy

Legitimacy is foundational to governance. Legitimacy means that those who are impacted by changing social rules first of all accept the new rules and, secondly, see those who are making the new rules as in an appropriate position to do so.[23] In the case of legitimacy in city environmentalism, the past several decades have seen a shift in the understanding of the appropriate governing role of the municipality. The move from the managerial work of city governments – plowing roads, filling potholes, etc. – to cities being accepted as appropriate actors for addressing environmental problems, including global environmental problems such as climate change, represents a marked transformation in how good urban governance is perceived.[24] As will be discussed in detail in the following chapters, this shift was enabled by a confluence of two important changes. The first was the emergence of liberal environmentalism and the accompanying belief that environmental protection and economic growth could be compatible. The second was the rise of neoliberal urbanism and the changing economies of formerly industrial cities toward the service sector and knowledge-based economies. In this confluence, greening and environmental protection became a way for city leaders to bolster the legitimacy of broader processes of neoliberalization through promises of green growth and amenities that would benefit all.

As has been widely argued, cities were particularly impacted by the rise of neoliberalism and have been both victims and vanguards of neo-liberal policies.[25] As neoliberal national governments withdrew from the Keynesian welfare state and globalization made capital increasingly mobile, the legitimacy of city governments came to be defined by the success of their efforts to attract investment, industry headquarters, tourists, and middle-class residents. Through the late twentieth century and into the twenty-first this belief in markets, place promotion, and urban competitiveness, which came to be known as urban entrepreneurialism, dominated city policymaking.[26] Key to this was transforming the built environment of the city to make it more attractive to the creative class and tourists, often at the expense of cities' lower income communities.[27]

Urban entrepreneurialism certainly could and was enacted without any commitment to greening and to the environment. However, the 1990s also saw the birth of liberal environmentalism, and this was to have an important impact on urban entrepreneurial endeavors. This new global norm of environmental governance rejected earlier assumptions that environmental problems represented the limits to the growth of capitalism. Under liberal environmentalism, an uneasy acceptance of the trade-off between economic growth and environmental protection was replaced with a belief that markets and economic growth, if done correctly, were the solutions to environmental problems.[28] This belief in the compatibility of environmental protection and economic growth legitimized city greening initiatives within the dominant social norm of neoliberal urbanism, particularly by increasing profit for property owners and attracting capital and the well-to-do to urban cores. As it did so, environmental amenities from parks to green condos became part of cities' "green urban entrepreneurial" efforts to attract skilled labor and the creative class.[29]

The ability of greening to further local state legitimacy went beyond its compatibility with urban entrepreneurialism and the urban development agenda, however. To the extent that neoliberal urbanism remained a contested norm, particularly as it furthered displacement and inequality, city greening helped to soften the more exclusionary edges of urban transformation. In so doing it helped to "obscure political conflict" in the neoliberal city and to secure "broad consensus about the sorts of governance practices that can and cannot be imagined and accepted."[30] Greening expanded urban entrepreneurial endeavors away from merely a focus on sites of elite consumption such as theaters and high-end housing developments to environmental amenities that would supposedly benefit everyone, such as parks, better transit, and green jobs. The discursive priority given to greening benefiting "all" residents and the claim that city environmentalism would create more livable and attractive urban areas furthered the legitimacy of these projects. It did this by making city environmental governance "understandable and justifiable to the relevant audience in society,"[31] in this case the growing urban middle class but also, if imperfectly, those who were being left behind by the neoliberal city. In this way, green urban entrepreneurialism helped to create the consent that is requisite of legitimate environmental governance.

This connection between city environmentalism, neoliberalism, and social regulation have led many critical scholars to be highly skeptical of city greening. For some, preexisting power relations and modes of production define which new social norms can be secured, thereby shaping "who can engage in what types of governance and who can use which types of legitimating discourse."[32] This, then, necessarily closes off both social and ecological alternatives to the green entrepreneurial city that challenge these underlying structures of power.[33] In this context, the green city is little more than a "sustainability fix" to the social and environmental contradictions of neoliberalism that "is capable of holding for a time, though not necessarily resolving, tensions between capital and labour, and economic development and collective consumption."[34]

Others have offered an even more scathing analysis of the relationship between sustainability discourse (of which greening is a key aspect) and capitalism.[35] From this perspective, efforts to promote sustainability in general, and to address climate change in particular, represent a technocratic, post-political approach to environmentalism. This post-political consensus is problematic in that it names no names, asserts that "all of us" are in this together in the quest to save the planet from impending (though never realized) apocalyptic doom. Since power and politics are ignored in the articulation of the causes of climate change and other environmental problems, they are also ignored in the proposed solutions, and the same tools of capitalism which got us into the problem of climate change are heralded as the answers for getting us out of it. In failing to recognize power, distribution, and inequality, this depoliticization of climate change closes off spaces of contestation, of challenges to the underlying structures of power that are at the root of environmental problems. This makes sustainability fundamentally reactionary, as the ultimate goal of reducing carbon emissions and managing climate change becomes to "sustain" the current unjust system and to avoid the changes in lifestyle and social structure that climate change threatens to bring.[36]

There is much that is compelling about this critique. As already argued, key to the legitimation of the role of city governments in furthering environmental goals has been the proclaimed compatibility of such efforts with neoliberal development. Furthermore, in each of the cities investigated here, the belief in technical and planning solutions to environmental problems, and the predominance of liberal environmentalism within the justifications of such initiatives, certainly shows moves toward depoliticizing city sustainability.[37] City leaders clearly hope that their environmental efforts will further economic growth in the context of neoliberalism. And even as they strive to reconcile this goal with equity and effectiveness, the promise that "everyone" benefits diverts attention from potential trade-offs between these priorities and the conflict and displacement that has marked the neoliberal city.

This insight is important, yet some of the claims regarding the post-political nature of sustainability discourse ring false.[38] Especially in the United States and Canada but also increasing in Britain, there is nothing remotely consensual or post-political about environmental politics. In the United States, for example, a frighteningly large percentage of elected officials do not even recognize the science of climate change, let alone see carbon reduction as fundamental to the continuation of capitalism. Even in the UK, where such a post-political consensus could arguably be seen for some time, climate change and the environment became increasingly re-politicized under the government of Prime Minister Cameron.[39]

Additionally, just because a governance mechanism is designed in a way that is compatible with the hegemony of neoliberalism does not mean that such logics fully define it. Indeed, though "particular governance institutions may emerge out of particular historical situations, ... the rationalities they entail emerge out of the messy interactions that produce a specific governmental regime."[40] This can be seen in city greening efforts where, though shaped and inspired by the need to establish legitimacy in neoliberal governance, they also include other rationalities besides that of neoliberalism. These co-existing, inconsistent rationalities ask for a more nuanced understanding of the transformative possibility of greener capitalism. As Goldstein posits, "the very idea of green capitalism is too often summarily rejected by critical scholars as a contradiction in terms – at best a naive instance of false consciousness, at worst a diabolical ideological veneer allowing business as usual to continue apace. Instead, what if we explored these contradictions, not as a sign of conceptual failure, but as constitutive elements of a generative and imaginative popular discourse?"[41] In other words, spaces of green capitalist discourse may serve as a legitimation strategy for neoliberal urban governance, but they may also challenge some of the logics of neoliberal capitalism, offering narratives of different socio-ecological futures that could lay the foundation for re-envisioning our relationships with non-human nature and with each other.

This debate has important implications for city greening. In each of the three cases discussed in this book there is evidence both of the depoliticizing tendencies of sustainability discourse and of its transformative potential. Even as a depoliticized "win–win" discourse around green urban entrepreneurialism emerged as a way to help justify and soften broader urban neoliberalism, the success of this discourse as a way to further local state legitimacy was only partially successful. Some aspects of the greening of each city were widely accepted, while at other times challenges to the legitimacy of these efforts emerged, focused most notably on the equity impacts of the supposedly universal benefits of the greener city but also on the effectiveness of city environmental policies. As will be seen, if politics is contention and conflict over distribution, production, and participation, there is much that remains political about the urban politics of environmental governance.

The role of cities in environmental governance, then, emerged as legitimate because of its intersection with already existing understandings of the appropriateness of cities under globalization to engage in entrepreneurial endeavors, of which greening became an important part. Leaders tried to promote greening as apolitical, as holding universal benefits, and as a way to establish both their commitment to good governance and to enhance the legitimacy of neoliberal urbanism. But even as such efforts were undertaken in a way that was supposedly beyond politics, greening led to notably political questions. Issues of the distribution of local state resources, of participatory justice, and of equity have all emerged in the greening of post-industrial cities. This raises the possibility that city environmental governance "might be viewed as a space of contestation between hegemonic and counter-hegemonic forces,"[42] even within the dominant discourse of liberal environmentalism and green urban entrepreneurialism. In none of the cities examined in this book has the primacy of growth and development been rejected, but these spaces of contestation have created what will be called here "varieties of liberal environmentalism."[43] Discussed at greater length below, this concept suggests that even within the confines of neoliberalism, city leaders can take steps to enhance the extent to which equity and environmental effectiveness shape their greening initiatives.

Equity

The issue of social equity is the second key element of environmental governance, and where the counter-hegemonic potential of urban greening can be seen most clearly. The "three pillars" approach to sustainability and sustainable development, which despite decades of criticism and deconstruction remains the foundational definition of sustainability in international environmental and development politics, assumes that environmental protection, economic growth, and social well-being can be compatible.[44] Some have claimed that this is wishful thinking or a failure to challenge the underlying contradictions of capitalist growth, but for others sustainable development, like the idea of greener capitalism discussed above, holds within it the opportunity to rethink vital relationships between people, nature, and each other. For some proponents of sustainability with justice, if taken seriously "the 'triple bottom line' – economy, environment, and equity – is not an abstract principle of accounting, nor is it simply a new turn of phrase. Rather, a commitment to the three e's results in politics aligned with conditions that improve the quality of life for all citizens in the future as well as in the present."[45]

Taking the social pillar of sustainable development seriously will require a decisive move toward social and environmental justice.

The argument that true sustainability cannot be achieved without addressing social equity and ensuring that all benefit from protecting the environment is the crux of Julian Agyeman's concept of "just sustainability." Agyeman defines just sustainability as "ensur[ing] a better quality of life for all, now and into the future, in a just and equitable manner, whilst living within the limits of supporting ecosystems."[46] For Agyeman, a just and sustainable community will improve quality of life and well-being; meet the needs of current and future generations; achieve multiple forms of justice including the justice of recognition, procedure, and outcome; and will live within environmental limits.[47] As such, this concept challenges environmentalists to consider the short- and long-term justice implications of their efforts and for an explicit incorporation of a diversity of voices and perspectives into work to achieve sustainability.

Unfortunately, in the context of city environmentalism this has often not been the case. City greening focuses specifically on the environmental quality and impact of urban areas. But if equity is an essential aspect of environmental governance, the above arguments about sustainability, which strives to combine environmentalism with equity and growth, also apply. Despite claims that all would benefit from the greener city, green urban entrepreneurialism could not obfuscate the growing inequality of the neoliberal city. As cities faced increasing disparities between the rich and poor, crises of housing affordability and displacement, and the pressures of austerity from neoliberalized national governments, some have argued that the greener city at best does nothing to address these pressing concerns of social sustainability and, at worst, exacerbates them.[48]

The relationship between physical beautification and gentrification has been the focus of much of this concern. The complexity of processes of gentrification make it methodologically difficult to draw clear causality between displacement and greening initiatives, but in many instances there is strong evidence suggesting such a relationship exists.[49] Furthermore, there is a widespread perception among many social justice activists and lower income urban communities that new parks, bike lanes, and other green amenities are creating processes of "eco-gentrification"[50] or "environmental gentrification,"[51] displacing existing residents by making their neighborhoods more appealing to the middle class. Concerns about displacement often lead to a distrust of the motivations behind a city's proclaimed commitment to environmental improvements, many seeing them as a forerunner to gentrification.[52] The phenomenon of environmental gentrification raises questions regarding for whom the city is being greened, with many asserting that such efforts are not aimed at enhancing the well-being of the urban poor, who, often having suffered decades of environmental injustices, are now deprived of the benefits of the greener city.

Investigation into the connection between physical greening (parks, trees, etc.) and displacement is expanding, but much more research is needed to understand the justice implications of city climate initiatives.[53] The research that has been done indicates that social justice is peripheral to, if not totally ignored by, most city climate mitigation efforts around the world.[54] That justice is not addressed in the majority of urban climate experiments does not mean that these projects do not have justice impacts, of course. Indeed, as climate change becomes the defining feature of city environmental governance in the twenty-first century, it will be vital to recognize that "decisions about low-carbon restructuring raise important questions of social equity and distributional justice – i.e. who gains and who loses – between and within cities across the world."[55] Transformations in infrastructure, production, and urban design that are emerging as cities' contributions to a "low-carbon transition" will have important implications for social equity and environmental justice that need to be more carefully examined.[56]

In Birmingham, Vancouver, and Chicago, though physical greening and livability emerged as part of their branding and economic developments strategies in the 1990s, climate change soon became a predominant element of each city's environmental agenda. This shift built on the same justifications that had enabled green urban entrepreneurialism, namely that a climate friendly city was also a more economically vibrant one and that a commitment to climate governance could contribute to economic growth.[57] Interestingly, and in contrast to the majority of urban climate experiments examined by Bulkeley,[58] each of these three cities has undertaken efforts to incorporate social equity into their climate initiatives. The successes and challenges they have faced in doing so offer a glimpse into how cities may wrestle with the relationship between the imperative of climate regulation, the ongoing economic pressures of globalization and austerity, and call for global and local climate justice.[59]

Indeed, in local climate efforts and within other aspects of city environmentalism, the past several years have seen growing dissatisfaction with the equity and local justice impacts of city greening initiatives that were too focused on branding and on providing benefits to the well-to-do. In response, demands for environmental justice, for low-income communities to receive their fair share of environmental amenities, and for efforts to break the link between greening and displacement have all begun to re-shape city environmentalism. Part of the success of the social justice challenge to city greening can be linked to the ways city officials have tried to legitimize green urban entrepreneurialism. As argued above, green urban entrepreneurialism served as a legitimation strategy for the neoliberal city, softening its more exclusionary edges with the promise that all would benefit from the greener, more beautiful, more economically vibrant city. To a limited extent this occurred, and many of the new environmental amenities green entrepreneurial cities built have indeed been enjoyed by a wide cross-section of city residents. However, deep inequalities remain, creating spaces for communities to call for the promised benefits of the greener city to actually be delivered.

These challenges have emerging in different forms. In Chicago, environmental justice organizations and grassroots community development groups have called attention to the maldistribution of environmental goods in the city, demanding a more equitable distribution of the benefits of the greener city and real community input into the process of green urban development. In Vancouver, calls for social sustainability have come, on the one hand, from lower-income communities that challenge the utility of the city's housing policies in creating affordable housing and, on the other hand, from middle-class residents who resist the creation of lower-income homes in wealthier areas. Sometimes contradictory, local actions around development in Vancouver have forced issues of affordability and social sustainability into conversation with the city's ambitious greening agenda. In Birmingham, there has been less direct public push-back against the equity impacts of the green transformation the city has attempted. Partly this can be attributed to the fact that Birmingham, facing deep problems of deprivation, has gone farther than the other two cities in incorporating poverty alleviation into its overall climate and environmental goals. Inconsistent political will has led many of these goals to be neglected, however, and in Birmingham the major contestations are between those city officials and staff who want sustainability to be prioritized and those for whom it remains of secondary importance.

As will be seen in greater details in the chapters that follow, even though greening has served as a legitimation strategy for the neoliberal city, it has also created spaces in which challenges to the inequitable distribution of public resources, displacement, and poverty can be made. This has the potential to change what it means for a city to be sustainable, with equity coming to play an increasingly important role. This budding transformation in city environmentalism also illustrates the extent to which even within the hegemony of liberal environmentalism, contestation is creating spaces for the redefinition of the legitimate goals of environmental governance.[60]

Effectiveness

Legitimacy and equity are vital elements of environmental governance. However, if those are the only goals and norms upon which the success of governance arrangements are based, they may not do anything to improve environmental quality.[61] To the extent that environmental governance is, or should be, about changing the relationship between human and non-human nature to be less destructive of ecosystems, people's health, other species, and the stability of the atmosphere, it matters whether or not governance arrangements are able to further these goals. Effectiveness must therefore be included as the third vital standard by which environmental governance is measured.

In the context of national government austerity and the slow pace of international environmental efforts, many see cities as the political scale best able to achieve concrete progress toward environmental protection. For proponents, cities are where "the 'rubber hits the road' [because] problems caused by imbalances between the environment and economy often result in resource drains at the local level, leaving local government officials to devise solutions to address such imbalances."[62] Facing the immediacy of the impact of environmental problems on urban areas, city leaders may be able to overcome political polarization and engage in the policy experimentation necessary to find creative, cost-effective solutions.[63] In addition to heightened responsiveness to the environmental needs and problems facing communities, being the political scale closest to people may also make municipal governments "uniquely placed to provide vision and leadership to local communities by raising awareness and [influencing] behaviour change,"[64] thereby engaging in the process of changing social norms that contributes to effective environmental governance.[65]

For some, however, the very idea that a city could be environmentally sustainable is an oxymoron. Wackernagel and Rees's now famous concept of the ecological footprint, for example, suggests that such an accomplishment is indeed impossible.[66] Wackernagel and Rees attempt to combine a wide variety of environmental indicators, from waste to consumption to energy use, in order to determine the amount of land, or the "footprint," that all of these processes would consume. Doing so, they find that cities' footprints are significantly larger than the physical area they cover, and therefore they are not sustainable (though the authors do recognize there can be environmental benefits from the efficiencies enabled by cities).[67]

The footprint metaphor may be useful in thinking through ecological debt and the global maldistribution of consumption, but for understanding cities this analysis is problematic because it conflates sustainability with geographic self-sufficiency. In highly urbanized countries and, indeed, as the entire world becomes increasingly urbanized, self-sufficiency is far too narrow a metric by which to define a sustainable city. The ecological footprint model implies that a low-density, suburban development may be more environmentally sustainable than a dense urban center because the ecological footprint of the area will be closer to the size of the physical footprint. But this may very well not be the case. Per capita, and accounting for income, residents of dense urban areas may actually have a much small environmental impact than their rural or suburban peers. Access to public transportation, proximity to work and amenities, and smaller homes may all contribute to lower per capita consumption of environmental resources in urban areas, even if the combined footprint of a city's residents is quite large.[68] This is not to deny that the concentration of people and economic activity in dense urban areas has the potential to create regional environmental problems. But to dismiss the sustainable city as an impossibility ignores the potential environmental benefits of well-conceived urbanization.

If we reject the implication of the ecological footprint model that a truly sustainable city must be self-contained, we are still left striving to define what a sustainable city is and how to know if a city's environmental efforts are effective. To some extent it seems that measuring the effectiveness of city environmental initiatives should be straightforward. Does the city have more green space and tree cover than it did before adopting its policies? Has water use decreased? Has air or water pollution abated? Are more trips taken by modes other than the personal car? Does it have lower greenhouse gas emissions? Indeed, there is a substantial set of literature that examines city greening efforts along these lines, as something of a check-list of best practices.[69] These ideas of what an environmentally sustainable city is or should be generally include some combination of parks, recycling, energy conservation programs, bike lanes, walkability, green space, and public transportation, with more recent studies tending to focus on efforts to reduce GHG emissions and other pollution. Relatedly, there have been a number of efforts by scholars and by environmental organizations to quantify and rank how green cities are and which are the greenest or most sustainable.[70]

The problem with any of these visions of a sustainable city, particularly attempts to rank cities to determine which is the greenest, is that cities are very different from one another. They are dealing with different histories of industry or resource extraction, with older industrial cities having to address legacies of pollution in a way that younger cities are not forced to do. Cities are also embedded in different ecosystems, changing which environmental issues are most pressing. Vancouver, which is located in a temperate rainforest with nearly sixty inches of rain a year, for example, faces quite different concerns regarding water use and supply than Phoenix, Arizona, located as it is in a desert with an average annual rainfall of about eight inches and where water travels hundreds of miles through man-made infrastructure to reach the city. The differing environmental contexts of cities mean that, arguably, there is no one metric that can be used to determine whether or not a city is environmentally sustainable.

One solution to this is offered by Portney who, rather than measuring how sustainable cities are, tries to determine "how seriously" they take their commitment to environmental sustainability.[71] This recognizes that city environmental efforts are still emerging as well as considers the different starting points and challenges that cities face. For Portney, one of the key signs that cities are indeed taking their commitments seriously is the presence of clear, measurable indicators by which they can track their environmental progress. Indicators help institutionalize city efforts, hold city leaders accountable to their stated commitments, and reduce the possibility that city environmentalism is mere greenwashing, with no corresponding change in the environmental impact of city activities. With all this in mind, rather than trying to determine how close a city is to an ideal of sustainability, one way to see if a city is effectively contributing to environmental progress is to examine if it is engaging in development trajectories that are less "profoundly exploitative [of the environment] than those that preceded them."[72]

The obvious critique of this approach is that even if cities are taking sustainability seriously and are adopting less exploitative forms of development than they had been, this by no means indicates that cities are doing enough to contribute to solving environmental problems. For localized issues such as water pollution and green space, where it is easier to link specific policy changes with environmental improvements, such causal connections may be apparent. However, if, as many claim, cities are also contributing to global environment governance, their effectiveness in addressing global problems is much harder to determine.[73]

Furthermore, even as evidence begins to emerge that cumulatively city environmental efforts may indeed have global impact,[74] it remains clear that cities' efforts alone will not be sufficient to solve many pressing environmental problems. The political and financial constraints faced by cities, including the economic development pressures discussed above, may limit their ability to make environmentally beneficial choices that sacrifice economic growth in any significant way, circumscribing which environmental initiatives cities will undertake.[75] This was an important limitation to green urban entrepreneurialism. As a way to rebrand fading industrial centers, the greener city meant, first and foremost, a city that was literally greener – more trees and parks, hanging baskets of flowers, and taking advantage of urban waterfronts as sites of recreation and consumption. These initiatives often beautify a city, and they may have some local environmental benefits (trees reduce the urban heat island effect, for example), but it is not clear that they contribute to broader environmental governance or sustainability in any substantial way. Furthermore, the need for city environmentalism to support economic growth necessarily took some environmental actions, like limiting airport expansion, off the table. This has changed somewhat in recent years, with the cities examined in this book at times accepting a longer and less direct payoff for their environmental initiatives. For the most part, however, the need for urban environmentalism to further local economic growth continues to shape and limit their initiatives.

Another of the major challenges to the effectiveness of city environmental efforts is their embeddedness in other political levels. Without excessively reifying the cascade model of government wherein each political scale sits clearly within the next like a set of Russian dolls,[76] it remains the case that in most countries cities are the legal creations of larger levels of government and that their power over policies with important environmental impacts are often limited. Effective city environmental sustainability initiatives therefore require both a local commitment to such efforts and "depend on the ability of cities to support policy initiatives that work with a wider range of state and non-state actors whose diverse interests, actions and institutions have important bearing on the ability to engage in [environmentally effective policies] at wider scales of interaction."[77] As will be seen throughout this book, the need for wider political and economic contexts that are conducive to furthering effective environmental governance can make it difficult for ambitious cities to achieve many of their goals. It also adds an additional layer of complexity to understanding cities' accomplishments and failures.

The limitations of the political scale of the city in enacting effective environmental policies highlight the potential shortcomings of research that focuses too closely on this political scale. Such a focus can, for example, lead "to an emphasis on household recycling activities without addressing the fundamental issues of how an economic system produces modes of production that are not environmentally sound. ... [It can be] problematic in that it can easily leave out global economic and ecological systems that are deeply involved, yet cannot be addressed at the level" of individual cities.[78] Few studies of the effectiveness of city environmentalism go so far as to fully ignore the importance of cities' relationships to other political levels, but dismissing the importance of global economic systems in shaping such efforts is much more common. This book strives to avoid this lacuna by situating city greening efforts explicitly within their broader policy and political economic contexts, while still emphasizing the importance of local politics in relation to the adoption and implementation of such initiatives.

This recognition of the structural constraints to city environmentalism, combined with a growing emphasis on clear indicators of environmental achievements, are important for analyzing the effectiveness of urban greening. But there may be another way to look at the effectiveness of cities' contributions to environmental governance. It may be equally valuable to examine whether these efforts "are having a lasting impact on ... the wider notion of development within which adaptation to climate change [or other environmental issues] are framed."[79] Because infrastructure lasts for many decades, city policies that change the development trajectory of an urban area through well-designed densification, improved transportation options, altering land use patterns to protect green space, etc. may have important implications for the long-term environmental impact of a city, even if the short-term benefits are less clear.[80] Such a perspective also raises the possibility that engaging in processes of environmental governance, and making sustainability an issue that is more strategically incorporated into wider municipal agendas, will change what city leaders see as appropriate and normal activities for local government.[81] If city environmentalism, even if framed in the narrow discourse of liberal environmentalism, can "change ... the terms of the debate as well as establish ... new norms and means of conduct,"[82] over time cities may become even more crucial players in improving humanity's relationship with non-human nature.

Varieties of Liberal Environmentalism

Liberal environmentalism assumes that when done correctly environmental protection and economic growth are compatible. This idea has come to dominate international as well as local environmental policies and governance.[83] However, even within the assumption that protecting the environment can be good for the economy there is variation in what this means in practice. This variation is closely tied to how much the state is willing to intervene in the market and private activities to achieve environmental effectiveness and to enhance the equity impacts of its environmental agenda. As has already been suggested, the legitimacy of liberal environmentalism may increasingly depend on achieving equity and effectiveness as well as growth, and local activists and others are calling to task those aspects of city greening that underplay these goals. The result has been the emergence of what will be called in the chapters to follow "varieties of liberal environmentalism." The differences within the varieties of liberal environmental governance that have emerged in Vancouver, Birmingham, and Chicago offer important insights into the unsettled relationships between growth, equity, and environmental protection that define the green city and shape the legitimacy of city greening efforts.

The key factors that vary between the varieties of liberal environmentalism are (1) the extent of state intervention in the market to secure goals other than economic growth, (2) the effectiveness of environmental protections, and (3) the importance given to enhancing social equity. Liberal environmental governance can therefore be thought of as a spectrum between ideal-type varieties (see Figure 1.1). On one end is *neoliberal environmentalism*. Neoliberal environmentalism is manifested on the level of the city as green urban entrepreneurialism (see Chapter 3 and above). This variety of liberal environmental governance is focused overwhelmingly on promoting and adopting greening initiatives that enhance growth and economic development. Environmental effectiveness and social equity, though they may be given discursive nods, are not seriously prioritized. An example of this would be an expensive downtown park that is promoted as providing green space to everyone but that disproportionately benefits city center property owners and the tourist industry. Neoliberal environmental governance therefore offers support for the claim that city greening is little more than a way to secure capital accumulation while greenwashing the ecological and social harms of capitalism.

Neoliberal environmentalism is but one variety of liberal environmental governance. Indeed, as will be discussed in Chapter 4, it is the tokenization of both environmental effectiveness and social equity within neoliberal environmentalism that opens up spaces of contestation through which other varieties of liberal environmentalism may emerge. In response to neoliberal environmentalism's unfulfilled promise to reduce the environmental impact of the city and to enhance social and environmental equity, challenges to the legitimacy of neoliberal environmentalism have emerged, along with growing demands that its promised social and environmental benefits be realized. These contestations may lead in three different directions, toward three different varieties of liberal environmental governance: progressive liberal environmentalism, ecoliberalism, or social liberalism. Though still operating within the overall premises of the liberal market economy and the growth imperative, each of these varieties entail more significant efforts to achieve concrete environmental and/or social equity goals.

The variety of liberal environmental governance furthest from neoliberal environmentalism will be called here *progressive liberal environmentalism*. Within progressive liberal environmentalism, the state actively intervenes in the market and in actions of the private sector to further social and environmental goals. To be sure, this by no means entails rejecting the importance of the market, economic growth, and cooperation with the private sector that define liberal environmentalism more broadly. However, progressive liberal environmentalism is marked by the local state's balancing of the growth imperative with equity and environmental effectiveness. For example, a legally mandated energy efficiency program that saves businesses money, reduces greenhouse gas emissions, and directly reduces the cost of heating and energy use for low-income households would fall under the category of progressive liberal environmentalism in that it would sit in the intersection of the goals of economic benefits (saving businesses money), environmental effectiveness (reducing GHG emissions), and enhancing social equity (reducing the cost of energy for low-income households). Progressive liberal environmentalism therefore goes the furthest toward fulfilling the win–win–win promise of sustainable development.

As can be seen in Figure 1.1, going from neoliberal environmentalism toward progressive liberal environmentalism is not the only move the local state can make to enhance the legitimacy of urban greening.[84] It could also move toward *ecoliberalism* or toward *social liberalism*. Ecoliberalism entails enacting policies that synthesize the goals of economic growth and environmental protection while continuing to downplay issues of social inequity within the greener city. Increased state intervention in market activities to achieve greener building standards

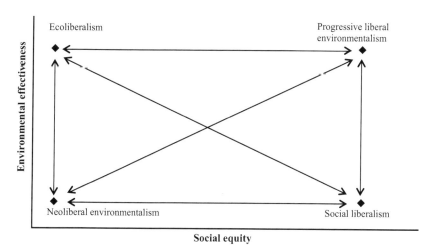

Figure 1.1 Varieties of liberal environmentalism.

without paying attention to how this impacts housing affordability would be such a policy. Ecoliberalism may be effective in reducing the environmental impact of an urban area and achieving the promise of green growth. It may do so at the expense of lower-income residents, however, and therefore fail to create a more inclusive, sustainable city.

Conversely, social liberalism emphasizes economic growth that enhances social equity, with environmental issues being subsumed by these other considerations. For social liberalism to remain a variety of liberal environmental governance, greening would still have a role to play in city efforts. However, conflict between social and environmental goals would be heavily weighted in favor of the former. An example of social liberalism would be subsidies for fuel consumption for lower-income families that are not also accompanied by efficiency and weatherization measures. Such a policy reduces the burden of fuel poverty, an environmental injustice, but it also increases overall GHG emissions (see Chapter 5). As with ecoliberalism, social liberalism may lead to important improvements in urban governance. However, it too fails to fully engage with the intersection of growth, equity, and greening.

As will be illustrated in Chapters 4–7, there is evidence that cities are moving beyond neoliberal environmentalism toward varieties of liberal environmental governance that take effectiveness and equity more seriously. But this is by no means a linear path. Cities moving toward progressive liberal environmentalism may make a shift, prioritizing either social or environmental goals more the other, thereby moving toward ecoliberalism or social liberalism rather toward the synthesis of all three goals. Cities may also reverse direction, a serious effort to enhance equity and/or effectiveness moving back toward neoliberal environmentalism in the face of changing regulatory environments, economic pressures, or new political leadership. Therefore, instead of implying necessary progression, this schema strives to offer a way to think through variations in the ways green cities may or may not address social and environmental goals within the confines of the liberal market economy.

Structure of the Book

The rest of this book proceeds as follows. Chapter 2 discusses the historical context out of which cities' role in global environmental governance emerged. It begins with the economic boom of the decades following World War II and ends with the rise of liberal environmentalism in the early 1990s. Over these decades there was an important shift in national urban and environmental policies away from national state intervention toward a focus on competitiveness and the market to achieve social goals. For environmental policy, this era saw a move from the assumption that there was a trade-off between environmental protection and economic growth toward a belief that, if done correctly, the needs of the economy and the needs of the environment could be compatible. The changing political economy of these decades and the changing ideas of effective environmental policy had significant impacts on Birmingham, Chicago, and Vancouver.

Chapter 3 looks at how the retrenchment of the welfare state under neoliberalism and the increasing mobility of capital under globalization inspired city leaders to find new ways to compete for investment, tourism, and well-to-do residents, marketing themselves through processes of urban entrepreneurialism. Greening soon became an important part of this. Examining how green urban entrepreneurialism played out differently in Vancouver, Birmingham, and Chicago, this chapter shows how greening was framed and promoted as an economic development strategy that would benefit all. This enabled green urban entrepreneurialism to soften some of the harsher edges of neoliberal urbanism, even if in practice green urban entrepreneurial endeavors were heavily focused on the well-to-do and creative class workers and tourists that the cities were explicitly trying to attract.

Chapter 4 examines the early twenty-first century in which city greening in Birmingham, Vancouver, and Chicago increasingly came to incorporate a commitment to sustainable development and environmental governance. The chapter investigates whether or not this shift represented a move beyond the green urban entrepreneurialism that defined the early days of cities' greening agendas. It argues that as calls for a recognition of the equity implications of city environmentalism emerged with greater force and as greening efforts were increasingly promoted as addressing global environmental issues, moves toward other varieties of liberal environmentalism could be seen. Yet even as equity, effectiveness, and contributions to wider environmental governance became incorporated into city greening, the prioritization of growth and development that marks neoliberal environmentalism continued to shape the cities' environmental initiatives.

Chapter 5 begins what can be considered part two of the book. Whereas Chapters 2–4 offer a big picture, historically situated narrative about the emergence and transformation of greening in Chicago, Birmingham, and Vancouver, Chapter 5 begins an investigation into how their moves beyond green urban entrepreneurialism have played out in particular issue areas. The deeper investigation into energy, housing and development, and green amenities enables a closer examination of how the tensions and synergies between growth, equity, and effectiveness have been grappled with in each city. What will be seen are both important attempts and failed opportunities to make contributions to environmental governance in a socially just way. In the case of energy, each city was able to find win–win solutions that reduced energy consumption and GHG emissions, while saving businesses and the city money. Promisingly, climate justice and social equity began to be incorporated into cities' climate agendas. However, the cities' abilities to reduce their emissions in a socially just way varied significantly, depending heavily on local political will and changing national regulatory contexts.

Housing and urban development and its intersection with a socially and environmentally sustainable city are the focus of Chapter 6. The chapter examines the tension that has emerged in each city between green building efforts, displacement, and municipal leaders' dependence on private developers. The differences in housing and development policies between Birmingham, Vancouver, and Chicago are substantial. However, officials in all three cities wrestle with how much to demand from developers in terms of affordable housing and green buildings, with inconsistent national regulatory frameworks, and with difficult questions about the desirability of neighborhood change. This chapter illustrates that although urban greening may certainly exacerbate displacement, from a comparative perspective the relationship between the greener city and gentrification is not always the defining feature of this issue. Achieving the potential social and environmental benefits of urban development is heavily dependent on the ability and willingness of local leaders to manipulate development interests to achieve these goals.

Chapter 7 looks at green amenities beyond neoliberal environmentalism, particularly green space and bicycling. It illustrates how the move to a more comprehensive approach to the sustainable city has enhanced equitable access to these important pieces of green infrastructure. The successes all three cities have had in expanding green transit and open space, and the extent to which equity has increasingly been incorporated into these efforts, is notable. But the slow pace of change and the challenges of achieving greater equity in access to environmental amenities illustrate the difficulty of transforming the built environment in a way that is more ecologically benign and socially inclusive. Taken together, the issues examined in Chapters 5–7 show the shift that has occurred away from neoliberal environmentalism to an explicit recognition of equity and effectiveness in city greening. They also show the pronounced limitations of this shift, limitations that help illustrate the imperfect negotiations between city contributions to effective environmental governance, social equity, political will, and policies beyond the purview of the local state.

Finally, the Conclusion elaborates upon the insights these three cases offer on the role of cities in furthering effective environmental governance. On one hand, the growing emphasis on cities as key to addressing global environmental problems needs to be tempered and contextualized. Arguments that cities are able to experiment with environmental best practices, are the level of government closest and therefore most responsive to people, and that they are able to take up action on climate change when international action is insufficient, are all compelling. However, the research presented here implies that such celebration of urban sustainability needs to be examined with a more nuanced understanding of the multiple frameworks in which city leaders operate and make decisions about pursuing environmental initiatives. On the other hand, this study of Chicago, Vancouver, and Birmingham also shows that the hope invested by many in the progressive potential of cities is not unfounded. Increasingly ambitious greening efforts and a growing awareness of how these efforts impact the intersection of social and environmental sustainability are enabling these cities to contribute, albeit imperfectly, to more socially just and environmentally effective development.

This book's examination of the unfolding of the environmental agenda of Birmingham, Chicago and Vancouver supports Whitehead's assertion that, despite its problems, we should not give up on the idea of the sustainable city. "We have far more to lose than we have to gain from the demise of sustainable urbanism. ... Rather than starting this discursive battle all over again, armed perhaps with a new paradigm of urban eco-development, the principles of urban sustainability could provide a grid of legitimation against which to hold urban authorities and communities who claim to be acting sustainably to account."[85] Though having potential to sugarcoat the status quo or to exacerbate urban inequality, the green city also has transformative potential in that it questions some of the root assumptions of neoliberal capitalism. Efforts to achieve a just, sustainable city can challenge the primacy of private property over public goods, of development that favors the elite at the expense of working-class and poorer communities, and it can ask us for a deeper rethinking of the relationship between human societies and non-human nature.[86] As such, the concept of a green or a sustainable city remains a space of contestation through which alternative futures can yet be imagined and created.

Notes

1 See Paul Wapner, *Living through the End of Nature: The Future of American Environmentalism* (Cambridge, MA: MIT Press, 2010).
2 United Nations, "Agenda 21: The United Nations Programme of Action from Rio" (New York: United Nations, 1992).
3 E.g. United Nations Centre for Human Settlements, *Sustainable Cities Programme: Approach and Implementation*, 2nd edn. (Nairobi, Kenya: UNCHS: UNEP, 1998); UN-HABITAT, "Hot Cities – Battle Ground for Climate Change," in *Global Report on Human Settlement 2011* (Nairobi, Kenya: United Nations Human Settlements Program, 2011); Hiroaki Suzuki et al., *Eco2 Cities: Ecological Cities as Economic Cities* (Washington, DC: The World Bank, 2010); Stephen Hammer et al., "Cities and Green Growth: A Conceptual Framework," *OECD Regional Development Working Papers* 2011/08" (OECD Publishing, 2011).
4 Benjamin Barber, *If Mayors Ruled the World: Dysfunctional Nations, Rising Cities* (New Haven, CT: Yale University Press, 2013).
5 Devashree Saha, "Empirical Research on Local Government Sustainability Efforts in the USA: Gaps in the Current Literature," *Local Environment* 14, no. 1 (2009).
6 Sadhu Aufochs Johnston, Steven S. Nicholas, and Julia Parzen, *The Guide to Greening Cities* (Washington, DC: Island Press, 2013), 1–2.
7 Joan Fitzgerald, *Emerald Cities: Urban Sustainability and Economic Development* (New York, NY: Oxford University Press, 2010).
8 Quoted in Peter Brand and Michael J. Thomas, *Urban Environmentalism: Global Change and the Mediation of Local Conflict* (New York, NY: Routledge, 2005), 28.
9 UNFCCC, "Cities & Regions Launch Major Five-Year Vision to Take Action on Climate Change," http://newsroom.unfccc.int/lpaa/cities-subnationals/lpaa-focus-cities-regions-across-the-world-unite-to-launch-major-five-year-vision-to-take-action-on-climate-change/. (2015). (Accessed February 24, 2016).
10 David Sattherwaite, "How Urban Societies Can Adapt to Resource Shortage and Climate Change," *Philosophical Transactions of the Royal Society* 369 (2011).
11 Nik Janos and Corina McKendry, "Globalization, Governance, and Re-Naturing the Industrial City: Chicago, IL and Seattle, WA," in *The Power of Cities in International Relations*, ed. Simon Curtis (New York: Routledge, 2014).
12 Sarah Dooling, "Ecological Gentrification: A Research Agenda Exploring Justice in the City," *International Journal of Urban and Regional Research* 33, no. 3 (2009); Melissa Checker, "Wiped out by the 'Greenwave': Environmental Gentrification and the Paradoxical Politics of Urban Sustainability," *City & Society* 23, no. 2 (2011); Noah Quastel, "Political Ecologies of Gentrification," *Urban Geography* 30, no. 7 (2009).
13 See Stephen Zavestoski and Julian Agyeman, eds., *Incomplete Streets: Processes, Practices, and Possibilities* (New York, NY: Routledge, 2015).
14 See Miriam Greenberg, *Branding New York: How a City in Crisis Was Sold to the World* (New York, NY: Routledge, 2008) and Eleanora Pasotti, *Political Branding in Cities: The Decline of Machine Politics in Bogotá, Naples, and*

Chicago (Cambridge, UK: Cambridge University Press, 2009) for discussions of the phenomenon of urban branding.

15 Maria Carmen Lemos and Arun Agrewal, "Environmental Governance," *Annual Review of Environment and Resources* 31 (2006): 298.

16 Ibid.; J.P. Evans, *Environmental Governance* (New York, NY: Routledge, 2012).

17 Lemos and Agrewal.

18 For example, Gabriela Kutting and Ronnie Lipschutz, eds., *Environmental Governance: Power and Knowledge in a Local-Global World* (New York, NY: Routledge, 2009).

19 Harriet Bulkeley, *Cities and Climate Change* (London, UK: Routledge, 2013); Craig Johnson, Noah Toly, and Heike Schroeder, eds., *The Urban Climate Challenge: Rethinking the Role of Cities in the Global Climate Regime* (New York, NY: Routledge, 2015); Harriet Bulkeley and Michele M. Betsill, *Cities and Climate Change: Urban Sustainability and Global Environmental Governance* (New York, NY: Routledge, 2003).

20 Sofie Bouteligier, *Cities, Networks, and Global Environmental Governance* (New York, NY: Routledge, 2013); Taedong Lee, *Global Cities and Climate Change: The Translocal Relations of Environmental Governance* (New York, NY: Routledge, 2015).

21 Steven Bernstein, Jennifer Clapp, and Matthew Hoffman, "Reframing Global Environmental Governance: Results of a CIGI/CIS Collaboration" (Center for International Governance Innovation, 2009).

22 Hayley Stevenson and John S. Dryzek, "The Legitimacy of Multilateral Climate Governance: A Deliberative Democratic Approach," *Critical Policy Studies* 6, no. 1 (2012).

23 Steven Bernstein, "Legitimacy in Intergovernmental and Non-State Global Governance," *Review of International Political Economy* 18, no. 1 (2011).

24 David Gibbs, Andy Jonas, and Aidan While, "Changing Governance Structures and the Environment: Economy–Environment Relations at the Local and Regional Scales," *Journal of Environmental Policy & Planning* 4 (2002).

25 Neil Brenner and Nikolas Theodore, eds., *Spaces of Neoliberalism: Urban Restructuring in North America and Western Europe* (Malden, MA: Blackwell, 2002); Gene Desfor and Roger Keil, *Nature and the City: Making Environmental Policy in Toronto and Los Angeles* (Tucson, AZ: University of Arizona Press, 2004); Jason R. Hackworth, *The Neoliberal City: Governance, Ideology, and Development in American Urbanism* (Ithaca, NY: Cornell University Press, 2007); Nik Heynen, Maria Kaika, and Erik Swyngedouw, eds., *In the Nature of Cities: Urban Political Ecology and the Politics of Urban Metabolism* (New York: Routledge, 2006).

26 David Harvey, "From Managerialism to Entrepreneurialism: The Transformation in Urban Governance in Late Capitalism," *Geografiska Annaler, Series B, Human Geography* 71, no. 1 (1989); Tim Hall and Phil Hubbard, eds., *The Entrepreneurial City: Geographies of Politics, Regime, and Representation* (Chichester, UK: Wiley, 1998).

27 Hackworth.

28 Steven Bernstein, *The Compromise of Liberal Environmentalism* (New York, NY: Columbia University Press, 2001); see also Maarten A. Hajer, *The Politics of Environmental Discourse: Ecological Modernization and the Policy Process* (New York: Oxford University Press, 1995).

29 Corina McKendry, Smokestacks to Green Roofs: City Environmentalism, Green Urban Entrepreneurialism, and the Regulation of the Postindustrial

City. (PhD Dissertation: University of California Santa Cruz, 2011).; Janos and McKendry.

30 Harriet Bulkeley et al., *Transnational Climate Change Governance* (Cambridge, UK: Cambridge University Press, 2014), 141.

31 Weber 1994, cited in Bernstein, "Legitimacy in Intergovernmental and Non-State Global Governance," 25.

32 Bulkeley et al., 139, citations omitted.

33 Vincent Beal, "Urban Governance, Sustainability and Environmental Movements: Post-Democracy in French and British Cities," *European Urban and Regional Studies* 19, no. 4 (2012).

34 Aidan While, Andrew EG Jonas, and David Gibbs, "The Environment and the Entrepreneurial City: Searching for the Urban 'Sustainability Fix' in Manchester and Leeds," *International Journal of Urban and Regional Research* 28, no. 3 (2004): 551.

35 Erik Swyngedouw, "Impossible 'Sustainability' and the Postpolitical Condition," in *The Sustainable Development Paradox: Urban Political Economy in the United States and Europe*, ed. Rob Krueger and David Gibbs (New York, NY: Guilford Press, 2007); "Apocalypse Forever? Post-Political Populism and the Spectre of Climate Change," *Theory, Culture & Society* 27, no. 2–3 (2010).

36 Peter Newell and Matthew Paterson, *Climate Capitalism: Global Warming and the Transformation of the Global Economy* (Cambridge, UK: Cambridge University Press, 2010).

37 See Corina McKendry, "Participation, Power, and the Politics of Multiscalar Climate Justice," in *The Social Ecology of the Anthropocene*, ed. Richard Matthew, et al. (World Scientific Publishers, 2016).

38 James McCarthy, "We Have Never Been 'Post-Political'," *Capitalism Nature Socialism* 24, no. 1 (2013).

39 See Guardian, "David Cameron at Centre of 'Get Rid of All the Green Crap' Storm," *Guardian*, November 21, 2013.

40 Bulkeley et al., 175.

41 Jesse Goldstein, "Appropriate Technocracies? Green Capitalist Discourses and Post Capitalist Desires," *Capitalism Nature Socialism* 24, no. 1 (2013): 26.

42 Bulkeley et al., 155.

43 I thank Dimitris Stevis for his suggestion of the phrase "varieties of liberal environmentalism."

44 See Jeremy L. Caradonna, *Sustainability: A History* (Oxford, UK: Oxford University Press, 2014) for a thorough history of the concept of sustainability.

45 M. Paloma Pavel, "Introduction," in *Breakthrough Communities: Sustainability and Justice in the Next American Metropolis*, ed. M. Paloma Pavel (Cambridge, MA: MIT Press, 2009), xxxii.

46 Julian Agyeman, Robert D. Bullard, and Bob Evans, eds., *Just Sustainabilities: Development in an Unequal World* (London: Earthscan, 2003), 5.

47 Julian Agyeman, *Introducing Just Sustainabilities: Policy, Planning, and Practice* (New York, NY: Zed Books, 2013).

48 E.g. Checker; Rob Krueger and David Gibbs, eds., *The Sustainable Development Paradox: Urban Political Economy in the United States and Europe* (New York, NY: Guilford Press, 2007); Zavestoski and Agyeman.

49 Quastel; Noah Quastel, Markus Moos, and Nicholas Lynch, "Sustainability-as-Density and the Return of the Social: The Case of Vancouver, British Columbia," *Urban Geography* 33 (2012).

50 Noah Quastel, "Political Ecologies of Gentrification," *Geography* 30 (2009).

51 Checker.
52 For example, Ibid.; Ann Dale and Lenore L. Newman, "Sustainable Development for Some: Green Urban Development and Affordability," *Local Environment* 14, no. 7 (2009); Philip Nyden, Emily Edlynn, and Julie Davis, "The Differential Impact of Gentrification on Commuities in Chicago" (Chicago, IL: Loyola University Chicago Center for Urban Research and Learning, 2006).
53 Harriet Bulkeley and Michele M. Betsill, "Revisiting the Urban Politics of Climate Change," *Environmental Politics* 22, no. 1 (2013); Gordon Walker, *Environmental Justice: Concepts, Evidence and Politics* (New York, NY: Routledge, 2012); Aidan While, "Carbon Regulation and Low-Carbon Urban Restructuring," in *After Sustainable Cities?*, ed. Mike Hodson and Simon Marvin (New York, NY: Routledge, 2014).
54 Vanesa Castan Broto and Harriet Bulkeley, "A Survey of Urban Climate Change Experiments in 100 Cities," *Global Environmental Change* 23 (2013); Harriet Bulkeley et al., "Climate Justice and Global Cities: Mapping the Emerging Discourse."
55 While, 41.
56 Harriet Bulkeley et al., eds., *Cities and Low Carbon Transitions* (New York, NY: Routledge, 2011).
57 Corina McKendry, "Environmental Discourse and Economic Growth in the Greening of Postindustrial Cities," in *The Economy of Green Cities: World Compendium on the Green Urban Economy*, ed. R. Simpson and Zimmermann. M. (New York, NY: Springer, 2012).
58 Bulkeley et al.
59 See Corina McKendry, "Cities and the Challenge of Multiscalar Climate Justice: Climate Governance and Social Equity in Chicago, Birmingham, and Vancouver," *Local Environment* 21, no. 11 (2016); "Participation, Power, and the Politics of Multiscalar Climate Justice."
60 Harriet Bulkeley, *Accomplishing Climate Governance* (Cambridge, UK: Cambridge University Press, 2016).
61 Bernstein, Clapp, and Hoffman.
62 Saha, 20.
63 Craig Johnson, Heike Schroeder, and Noah Toly, "Introduction: Urban Resilience, Low Carbon Governance and the Global Climate Regime," in *The Urban Climate Challenge: Rethinking the Role of Cities in the Global Climate Regime*, ed. Craig Johnson, Noah Toly, and Heike Schroeder (New York, NY: Routledge, 2015).
64 Defra 2008, quoted in Brenda Boardman, *Fixing Fuel Poverty: Challenges and Solutions* (London, UK: Earthscan, 2010), 200.
65 Bernstein, *The Compromise of Liberal Environmentalism*.
66 Mathis Wackernagel and William E. Rees, *Our Ecological Footprint: Reducing Human Impact on the Earth* (Gabriola Island, BC; Philadelphia, PA: New Society Publishers, 1996).
67 William E. Rees and Mathis Wackernagel, "Urban Ecological Footprints: Why Cities Cannot Be Sustainable and Why They Are a Key to Sustainability," *Environmental Impact Assessment Review* 16 (1996).
68 Edward Glaeser, *Triumph of the City: How Our Greatest Invention Makes Us Richer, Smarter, Greener, Healthier, and Happier* (New York, NY: The Penguin Press, 2011); David Owen, *Green Metropolis: Why Living Smaller, Living Closer, and Driving Less Are the Keys to Sustainability* (New York, NY: Riverhead Books, 2009).
69 For example, Stephen Coyle, *Sustainable and Resilient Communities: A Comprehensive Action Plan for Towns, Cities, and Regions* (Hoboken, NJ:

John Wiley & Sons, Inc., 2011); Steffan Lehmann, *The Principles of Green Urbanism: Transforming the City for Sustainability* (Washington, DC: Earthscan, 2010); Sarah James and Torbjorn Lahti, *The Natural Step for Communities: How Cities and Towns Can Change to Sustainable Practices* (Gabriola Island, BC: New Society Publishers, 2004); Timothy Beatley, ed. *Green Cities of Europe: Global Lessons on Green Urbanism* (Washington, DC: Island Press, 2012).

70 For example, Marina Alberti, "Measuring Urban Sustainability," *Environmental Impact Assessment Review* 16 (1996); Warren Karlenzig, *How Green Is Your City?* (Gabriola Island, B.C.: New Society Publishers, 2007); Ken Regelson, "Sustainable Cities: Best Practices for Renewable Energy & Energy Efficiency" (Sierra Club, 2005); Sustainlane, "2008 U.S. City Rankings," www.sustainlane. com/us-city-rankings/overall-rankings (accessed December 16, 2010; please note: this URL is now inaccessible).

71 Kent E. Portney, *Taking Sustainable Cities Seriously: Economic Development, the Environment, and Quality of Life in American Cities, 2nd Edition* (Cambridge, MA: MIT Press, 2013).

72 Ian Drummond and Terry Marsden, *The Condition of Sustainability* (New York, NY: Routledge, 1999), 21.

73 Bulkeley et al.

74 For example, Lucas de Moncuit, "Carbonn Cities Climate Registry: 2013 Annual Report" (2014).

75 See Janos and McKendry.

76 See Harriet Bulkeley and Michele Betsill, "Rethinking Sustainable Cities: Multilevel Governance and the 'Urban' Politics of Climate Change," *Environmental Politics* 14, no. 1 (2005) for a critique of this model.

77 Johnson, Schroeder, and Toly, 5.

78 Saskia Sassen, "Bringing Cities into the Global Framework," in Johnson, Schroeder, and Toly, 30.

79 Bulkeley et al., 172.

80 David Gordon and Michele Acuto, "If Cities Are the Solution, What Are the Problems? The Promise and Perils of Urban Climate Leadership," in *The Urban Climate Challenge: Rethinking the Role of Cities in the Global Climate Regime*, ed. Craig Johnson, Noah Toly, and Heike Schroeder (New York, NY: Routledge, 2015).

81 Bulkeley et al.

82 Ibid., 175–6.

83 See Bernstein, *The Compromise of Liberal Environmentalism* and above.

84 There are, of course, numerous possibilities of urban governance outside of this schema. This could include the neoliberal city in which greening plays no part or, on the other end of the spectrum, socialist governance beyond market liberalism. The former is outside the scope of this study. As for moving beyond liberalism, in this historical moment it does not appear possible for Anglosphere cities to move fully beyond the demands of the market economy. I am therefore interested in how they negotiate other goals within this constraint.

85 Whitehead 2012, quoted in While, 56.

86 Pavel, Julian Agyeman, *Sustainable Communities and the Challenge of Environmental Justice* (New York: New York University Press, 2005).

2 From Keynesianism to Liberal Environmentalism

Understanding the emergence of cities as sites of environmental governance requires looking at the broader political shifts that led to this phenomenon. This chapter examines two interconnected changes that were particularly important. The first was changing urban policy as the United States, Canada, and Britain moved from the Keynesianism of the post-World War II era to neoliberalism. The second was the move from the widely held assumption that environment protection would hurt the economy to liberal environmentalism's assertion that protecting the environment can spur economic growth. Together these two shifts set the stage for cities to engage in greening as part of their development strategies. This history therefore offers valuable insight into cities' embrace of liberal environmentalism and into the roots of the tensions between growth, the environment, and equity that continue to define the politics of city greening.

Cities in the Golden Age of Capitalism

The decades following World War II saw rapid economic growth, capitalist states that were increasingly willing to intervene in the economy, and, eventually, some national efforts to address the environmental harms of industrial society. The underlying premise of the post-war Keynesian political economy was that the national government should take a proactive role in maintaining economic growth through active monetary policy, generous government spending to maintain consumption, and the welfare state. So successful were the sustained growth and broad-based prosperity of this "Golden Age" that leading economists of the day insisted that the problem of the business cycle had been eliminated.[1] Though discontent remained within this system, both from those who were excluded from the consumption opportunities promised by it and from factory workers frustrated by the rigidity of manufacturing jobs, the Keynesian era saw material standards of living expand dramatically for large segments of the population of the industrialized countries.[2]

During this time the governments of Canada, the United States, and Britain adopted a number of policies to redistribute the prosperity of the era between and within cities. The British government was especially ambitious. In addition to a cradle to grave welfare state, it was actively involved in housing provision. Between the end of World War I and 1980 both Labour and Conservative governments oversaw the construction of over six million council (i.e. public) housing units, housing that served middle- and working-class residents as well as the poor.[3] The British government also intervened in urban economic development, and the welfare state and housing construction were accompanied by industrial planning initiatives that attempted to distribute industries around the country.[4] Spatial inequality certainly remained, but for the most part there was political consensus in Britain "that inequality (social and geographical) was both economically inefficient and socially regressive."[5] Furthermore, starting in the 1960s the government began targeting poor populations within cities for services beyond the already generous welfare state, and the national government maintained a commitment to addressing urban poverty and inequality.[6]

The United States emerged from World War II as the world's most powerful industrial state. Government intervention in the macroeconomy was widely accepted, and the country saw the rise of an historically unprecedented middle class. Cities and suburbs expanded as the GI Bill provided subsidized homes for returning war veterans and developers raced to fill the housing demand of the baby boom. The American welfare state remained the weakest of the three countries, however, and the growing prosperity of the era also saw social polarization and political fragmentation, accompanied by some federal initiatives to address urban poverty.[7]

Discriminatory housing policies were especially problematic, excluding people of color, particularly African Americans, from the financial benefits of home ownership even while access to home ownership by middle- and working-class whites expanded.[8] This led to a concentration of poverty in many urban areas that was exacerbated as white people with access to government-subsidized home loans left cities for the suburbs, leaving decreased tax bases and fewer resources to provide for cities' remaining populations. In response, as in the UK, "cities were treated as special cases in federal domestic policy," receiving grants, subsidies, and aid through the 1950s Urban Renewal Programs, President Johnson's War on Poverty, and housing and job training efforts by the Nixon and Carter administrations.[9] Though none of these policies was sufficient to alleviate urban poverty or to ameliorate institutionalized racism, they did illustrate a belief that urban inequity was a problem that the federal government had a responsibility to directly address.

In Canada minimum basic income, universal healthcare, a strong trade union movement, and generous provision of housing marked the robust welfare state.[10] Constitutionally, much of the country's social policy was under the purview of the provinces, but growing provincial–federal cooperation enabled broadly consistent welfare policies across the country, particularly universal health care.[11] Such cooperation could be seen in the housing sector as well, which, despite technically being the responsibility of the provinces, came to be heavily supported by the federal government. As with the GI Bill in the United States, the government's Central Housing and Mortgage Corporation worked with private housing markets to help middle-income Canadians move into single-family suburban homes. The goals of this policy were to get the middle class into better housing and to open up more housing stock for the poor through "filtering," wherein apartments and less expensive housing become available as the middle class move elsewhere.[12] The federal commitment to a comprehensive housing policy, along with social planning and public welfare more broadly, expanded throughout the 1960s with an increase in subsidized social housing along with direct federal loans and grants.[13] The government also encouraged non-profit and cooperative housing, funding community groups to construct such homes and rent them out to lower-income residents.[14]

As the governments of Britain, the United States, and Canada engaged in policies to distribute and enhance the wealth of the post-war boom, Birmingham, Chicago, and Vancouver all underwent important changes. Before the war Birmingham, the city in which James Watt and colleagues invented the steam engine and one of the first major industrial cities in the world, was known for its large variety of high-skilled, small manufacturers producing a wide range of products. In the years following World War II, the economy of the city flourished, and Birmingham saw its booming industry become increasingly consolidated and focused on the automobile. Labor unions were powerful, unemployment was often under 1 percent, wages in the Birmingham area were some of the highest in the country, and the West Midlands region produced 40 percent of the country's exports by value.[15]

The prosperity of the region, along with the severe damage that had been inflicted on the city center by bombing during the war, inspired city leaders to adopt an ambitious development agenda. Planners embraced "redevelopment projects with a zeal unwitnessed in any other British city," radically reinventing Birmingham's built environment.[16] New malls, freeways, and office buildings were constructed, and by 1970 55,000 homes had been demolished and 81,000 new homes had been built, many of which served the growing number of immigrants from the New Commonwealth countries drawn to Birmingham by its plentiful employment opportunities.[17]

In a decision that would have a lasting impact on Birmingham's environmental agenda, as the city center was rebuilt it was constructed to serve the automobile, the driver of the city's economy. Facing rapid economic and population growth, Birmingham City Council lobbied for massive national investment in new roads. A major new inner ring road for Birmingham received funding from the Department of Transport in 1950, with city councilors of both major political parties heralding it as the "complete solution to Birmingham's ... traffic problems."[18] Such faith was invested in this road that when funding for it was received, the City began to dismantle its extensive tram network, a project that would by the 1990s make Birmingham the largest city in Europe without a subway or an electrified public transportation system. In addition to reducing public transportation, the new roads destroyed many old neighborhoods and small industries and cut the city center off from surrounding areas. In this new, modern Birmingham pedestrians were seen as an impediment to vehicles, and dozens of pedestrian underpasses (called "subways") were built beneath roads to minimize pedestrian disruption to the flow of traffic. The ring road and the subways, the latter of which were unappealing if not downright dangerous, made downtown largely inaccessible to pedestrians, turning "central Birmingham [into] a diesel-choked, economic wasteland."[19] Yet for a time, the wealth of the city overshadowed the downsides of its rapid, car-centric development.

Chicago, like Birmingham, was long a manufacturing powerhouse, its concentration of railroad lines and industries making it by the late 1800s the most powerful Midwest city and one of the most important in the United States.[20] The south side of Chicago was especially important, its extensive rail and water transportation infrastructure facilitating Chicago's emergence by the early twentieth century as one of the country's primary steel-producing regions. This inspired other industries to settle in the area, particularly those that relied on large amounts of heavy, expensive to transport steel such as railway cars (Pullman being the most well-known), agricultural machinery, and automobiles. Unlike Birmingham whose economy flourished after the World War II, however, industrial production stabilized rather than expanded in Chicago in the years following the war, and by the late 1960s Chicago's industrial heyday had already passed.[21]

In Chicago, the boom of the Keynesian era was focused on the suburbs, and these decades saw the region, like America as a whole, become increasingly suburbanized.[22] This shift can be seen in the area's changing population distribution. In 1920, the City of Chicago contained about 80 percent of the region's population. By 1960 the population of the city was roughly equal to that of the surrounding suburbs.[23] This population shift happened partly because Chicago was largely built out, meaning space for new home construction was mostly in the suburbs. Even more important was white flight, with suburban growth "an overreaction ... to the city's long-standing racial animosities."[24] Chicago's African American population, facing pervasive housing discrimination but also drawn to the areas closest to industrial jobs, concentrated in the south and west sides of the city. Tens of thousands of public housing units were eventually constructed in part to alleviate overcrowding of these areas. However, the Truman administration's decision to keep costs to a minimum by building high-rises rather than the lower-density housing requested by city officials, and the refusal of white aldermen (Chicago's version of city councilors) to allow mixed-race public housing in their wards,[25] furthered the racial segregation of Chicago.[26] Eventually 38,000 families came to live in the massive, city-managed housing developments.[27]

Vancouver never had the manufacturing might of Birmingham or Chicago, but it too saw important changes during the global boom of the post-war Golden Age. The core of Vancouver's economy was British Columbian resource extraction, and from its founding in the late 1800s the city's economy was based primarily on providing the administrative hub for BC's timber, coal, and mineral production. Vancouver's manufacturing was likewise linked to resource development, with such industries as sawmills, barrel factories, and machine shops growing up around False Creek, the inlet that divides downtown Vancouver from the rest of the city.[28]

The increasing world demand for minerals and raw materials after World War II greatly benefited BC's extractive industries, particularly the timber, pulp and paper industries but also its fisheries and mining sectors. To support these sectors, the provincial government invested heavily in railroads, roads, hydroelectric dams, and other infrastructure.[29] As extractive industries grew and consolidated after the war, related service-sector employment necessary to support these industries grew rapidly in Vancouver. The expanding public-sector employment that accompanied the rise of the Canadian welfare state was also concentrated in the city. Reflecting this growth, and strongly encouraged by the commitment to real estate development of the Non-Partisan Association (NPA) – the municipal political party that dominated Vancouver politics from before the war until the early 1970s – gross office space in the city core tripled between 1957 and 1980.[30] Housing likewise expanded rapidly throughout the region, mostly consisting of suburban-style single-family homes.

Environmentalism, Economic Growth, and Its Limits

In the midst of the prosperity of the Golden Age, increased industrialization, road construction, suburbanization, urban development, and the pollution that accompanied these phenomena, the modern environmental movement emerged. As concentrated industrial and economic centers, cities were a focus of much environmental concern. Although the particularly egregious aspects of nineteenth century urbanization had been lessened through the provision of municipal water and sewer services, many cities still struggled with significant water pollution. Air pollution was a serious problem as well, exacerbated by expanding freeways and automobile use. Garbage disposal remained an issue in many areas, and the loss of woodlands and green space to sprawl grated on middle-class sensibilities and the increasing recreational use of nature.[31]

In the United States, extensive media coverage of environmental disasters such as the 1969 Cuyahoga River fire and an oil spill on the beaches of Santa Barbara, California brought environmental issues, and the downsides of post-war technology and economic growth, powerfully into people's living rooms. The fear that the era of prosperity had led to serious impacts on the planet and human health, and that therefore the trajectory of growth had to be curtailed, could be seen in the seminal environmental works of this era such as *Silent Spring, The Population Bomb, Limits to Growth*, and others.[32] Although in the radicalism of the time some called for a rejection of capitalism as inherently inconsistent with ecology, others were more moderate, promoting pollution control, recycling centers, and greener consumer products.[33] Either way, all presumed a trade-off between economic growth and environmental protection, the major disagreement being how much growth and prosperity should be sacrificed for the needs of the planet.

Responding to the upwelling of environmental protest and concern, the United States led the first round of broad-scale Keynesian environmentalism, wherein the national state took the lead in regulating industry in order to reduce pollution. The far-reaching environmental legislation adopted in the U.S. in the 1960s and 1970s addressed problems ranging from endangered species protection to air pollution, and created a complex legal and administrative structure (most notably the Environmental Protection Agency) to flesh out and enforce the new regulations. With some important exceptions, such as President Nixon's veto of the Clean Water Act of 1972 because of its estimated price tag (a veto which was overridden by Congress), concern about the cost of these regulations or their potential economic impact was downplayed at this time. The new laws identified problems of pollution as being "caused primarily by callous and unthinking business and industry" and therefore saw industry as being responsible for bearing the cost of clean-up.[34] The most extreme example was the Endangered Species Act of 1973 that stated that economic factors should not be considered when deciding whether or not a species would be protected. Most laws were not as explicit in their disregard for the cost of implementation. Overall, however, it was widely assumed that there was a trade-off between industry profits and environmental protection but that the costs were necessary for eliminating pollution and enhancing the nation's quality of life.

The federal government was seen as the appropriate venue for enacting environmental regulation for a number of reasons. First of all, this was compatible with the prevailing spirit of Keynesianism which saw national government regulation of industry and intervention in the economy as necessary to securing social goods. Though for Keynesians these social goods generally meant economic growth, full employment, and a social safety net, it was not a stretch to see the appropriateness of federal government intervention in the activities of industry to secure a cleaner environment. Another reason was the growing complexity and danger of industrial production, with the expanding manufacture of plastics and chemicals raising special concern. For the most part local governments, and even most states, lacked the technical and administrative skills to regulate these industries. Of even greater significance was the political power of, and city government financial dependence on, the local industries that needed to be regulated, making it exceedingly unlikely that they would do so.[35] State governments, though having more resources and political power than cities, were also often unwilling to risk job loss by seriously challenging polluting industries.[36] In these years before globalization and the idea of an international "race to the bottom," the federal government was therefore the least vulnerable to economic reprisal.

The emergence of modern environmentalism in the UK was somewhat different than in the United States. Though the UK lays claim to having the oldest system of pollution control in the world, with laws adopted to address specific problems of industrial processes as early as 1863, these laws did not represent a coordinated, nationwide effort at environmental protection or reducing pollution in general.[37] As in the United States, a number of environmental disasters in the 1960s raised the British public's concern about pollution, including an oil tanker crash off the coast of Cornwall that spilled 60,000 tons of crude into the Atlantic and onto England's beaches in early 1967 and the discovery of upwards of 100,000 dead birds along the British coast, killed by the dumping of PCB into the country's rivers and oceans. As these and other environmental issues came to the forefront of people's consciousness, membership in conservation organizations increased significantly and media coverage of environmental issues jumped 281 percent between 1965 and 1973.[38]

Unlike the increase in environmental regulation that occurred during the 1970s in the United States, however, the growth in public awareness of environmental issues in Britain did not translate into a notable change in national environmental policy. One reason for this may have been that the existing system of environmental controls made it harder for the environmental movement to articulate a straightforward legislative agenda, even though the system was seen by many environmentalists as inadequate. Whereas American regulation (the gold standard by the late 1970s) established set standards for pollution reduction and hefty fines for noncompliance, the British approach to pollution control was marked by "an absence of statutory standards, minimal use of prosecution, a flexible enforcement strategy, considerable administrative discretion, decentralized implementation, [and] close cooperation between regulators and the regulated."[39] Another reason why public dissatisfaction with the UK's system of environmental protection did not lead to greater changes was that compared to the relatively open political system in the U.S., British environmental groups and other non-industry members of society had little access to environmental decision making and enforcement processes.[40] This limited activists' ability to translate dissatisfaction with the regulatory process into successful demands for stronger policies. In the midst of the perceived trade-off between industry and the environment, the British government was not willing to sacrifice the former for the latter.

The environmental movement in Canada, as in the United States and Britain, was inspired by critiques of the excesses and dangers of postwar industrial society.[41] As in the other two countries, environmental crises close to home, including the running aground of an oil tanker in Chedabucto Bay, Nova Scotia in 1970 and extensive fishing bans due to mercury contamination of the nation's waterways, led to a growth in public concern about the environment. The environmental organization Greenpeace was founded in Vancouver in 1971, and during this time the Sierra Club and the Canadian Wildlife Federation grew in membership and expanded the focus of their work from conservation to pollution control.[42] Yet as in the UK, the environmental movement's success at translating the growing concern of the Canadian public into concrete policies to reduce pollution proved to be limited.

In the late 1960s, as environmental issues first came onto the public agenda, the Canadian government insisted that it was outside of its constitutional jurisdiction to address such concerns, as the provinces have control over natural resources, public lands, and property.[43] The groundswell of public support for environmental protection was eventually able to overcome this constitutional excuse for inaction. In the early 1970s the federal government adopted a few important environmental laws, particularly the Canada Water Act and Fisheries Act Amendments in 1970 and the Clean Air Act in 1971.[44] Despite their similar titles, these laws did not represent the strong form of environmental regulation being passed in the United States. The Canadian legislation was much less ambitious in scope, and concern about the financial burden these regulations would have on industry remained paramount. For example, though the Canada Water Act enabled the federal government to establish water resource management plans, there was no legal authority to enforce them.[45] The Fisheries Act Amendments created uniform effluent standards for polluting industries, but these were weakened by gradual implementation and individually negotiated compliance schedules for industries in order to mitigate "the harsh consequences of uniform national standards" on their bottom line.[46] To critics, the regulations adopted by Canada were seen as merely symbolic, attempting to illustrate federal commitment to protecting the environment without ever having to undertake the challenge of implementation. Furthermore, when public concern about pollution was overtaken by worries about inflation, unemployment, and other issues, politicians, who assumed a trade-off between jobs and environmental regulation, "err[ed] on the side of the public's higher priority – jobs."[47] By the mid-1970s environmental regulation had fallen off the Canadian political agenda, and there was little political interest in aggressively administering the newly passed laws.

The End of the Golden Age

Even as the burgeoning environmental movement in the global North began to challenge the environmental ills that accompanied post-war prosperity, the Keynesian economic order began to collapse. The reasons for the end of the Golden Age are numerous and much debated. They included an overcapacity of global manufacturing, the rigidity of Fordist mass production, and inflation exacerbated by spending on the Vietnam War and the welfare state.[48] As investment slowed and industries shut down, inflation was accompanied by growing unemployment, challenging the economic underpinnings of the Keynesian decades. The oil shocks that exacerbated the economic crisis are particularly important for the story at hand. In addition to having a major economic impact on affected countries, the oil embargo of 1973 and the accompanying shortages facing consumers at the gas pump seemed to offer proof for environmentalists' claims that the world would soon be reaching the ecological limits to the expansion of capitalism. Some began to feel that the fossil fuel that had underpinned a century of wealth would run out within their lifetime.[49] As U.S. President Carter donned sweaters, installed solar panels on the White House, and called energy conservation the "moral equivalent of war,"[50] the idea that there were limits to economic growth and the increasing consumption of resources gained prevalence.

The major cities of the U.S., Canada, and Britain were deeply impacted by the recession. Chicago, already struggling, saw accelerated deindustrialization. The last of Chicago's stockyards closed in 1971, followed by most of its steel mills and other heavy manufacturing. In the few short years between 1977 and 1981, 10 percent of all manufacturing establishments in Chicago closed while many that remained drastically slashed their payrolls. By 1982 the city had seen a 46 percent decline in manufacturing jobs; by the mid-1990s this number would be up to 60 percent.[51] Many displaced workers were unable to find new employment, and a majority of those who did find new full-time work saw their pay cut by 20 percent or more.[52] The unemployment rate in some of the worst hit areas of the city rose to nearly 50 percent, houses were abandoned, and the high school dropout rate soared.[53] The 1980 census showed Chicago to have 10 of the 16 poorest neighborhoods in the United States, most of which were predominantly black.[54]

As manufacturing collapsed, services did not quickly emerge as a major source of employment. A 1986 study of Chicago's economy highlighted not only the city's major loss of manufacturing jobs but also its anemic growth in the service sector, with 2 percent growth in services between 1976 and 1981 compared to 18 percent in the Chicago region and 23.5 percent nationwide.[55] As the decade progressed, service jobs continued to avoid the city, and by 1993 the Loop, Chicago's downtown business district, had a 21 percent vacancy rate, the highest since the Great Depression.[56] Meanwhile white flight accelerated, and between 1970 and 1990 the number of white, non-Hispanic residents of the city dropped by 43 percent. A 1991 report by the Urban League found that the Chicago region, with its impoverished, black and Latino city and flourishing white suburbs had the greatest income disparity between racial groups of any region in the United States.[57]

Deindustrialization was equally dramatic in Birmingham. In 1969, the influential urbanist Jane Jacobs cited Birmingham as one of only two British cities (the other being London) that remained "economically vigorous and prosperous."[58] This was about to change. In the 1970s when recession, labor struggles, and government efforts to control inflation hit the region's massive auto conglomerate British Leyland with substantial losses, the company closed many of its factories, creating a ripple of job loss throughout the region.[59] After decades in which unemployment had been virtually unknown, between 1971 and 1987 Birmingham lost nearly 200,000 jobs, 29 percent of the city's total employment.[60] As jobs disappeared the region "shifted from being one of the most prosperous in the UK to being an economy in crisis and decline," and Birmingham become the poorest free-standing city in England.[61]

Like in Chicago, there was a notable racial and ethnic element to Birmingham's unemployment patterns. Birmingham's immigrant population had grown rapidly in the post-war decades as people from the Commonwealth, particularly the Caribbean and the Indian subcontinent, were drawn to the area for its plentiful and well-paying jobs. As Birmingham's population grew, city housing policies had led to segregation, with many immigrant communities concentrated near the city center. Because most of the factories that survived the recession were the larger, newer facilities in the outer areas of the region, this concentrated housing pattern meant that city center industrial job loss hit immigrant communities particularly hard. By the mid-1980s seven wards in inner Birmingham had unemployment rates around 40 percent, and throughout the decade unemployment among the city's immigrant and non-white ethnic populations was three times that of the white British population.[62] The city government was largely unresponsive to the needs of its immigrant and ethnic minority communities, and the decade saw growing tensions between immigrant youth and city police.[63] Birmingham, once a leader of British industry, faced a severe economic and social crisis.

Vancouver, with a more service-oriented economy than Birmingham and Chicago, experienced this time period differently. Indeed, while the

1970s saw Birmingham and Chicago reeling from deindustrialization, Vancouver emerged as a leading progressive city. A campaign by Chinese-Canadian activists to stop a freeway from destroying their neighborhood left Vancouver as one of the few North American cities without freeway access to downtown and "launched the assault on growth boosterism … [that] proved to be a significant and lasting success for urban conservation and an inspiring example for anti-growth, pro-neighbourhood coalitions."[64] Resistance to "large-scale unsympathetic redevelopment of the downtown" came both from low-income residents being displaced by 1960s urban renewal and from middle-class progressives, some of whom worked in solidarity with those being displaced and others whose concern was with quality of life, environmental protection, and the threat of high-rise apartments to their nicer residential neighborhoods.[65] Led by a center-left municipal party – The Elector's Action Movement (TEAM), first elected in 1972 – the city embraced livability, environmental protection, and community planning as focal points of Vancouver municipal politics.[66]

Even as livability and a challenge to downtown boosterism began to define Vancouver, the city could not avoid the economic upheaval of the changing global economy. Initially the oil shocks of the early 1970s benefited British Columbia, increasing demand for the region's coal. However, as global recession spread, the accompanying downturn in demand for the region's minerals and timber, combined with the consolidation and mechanization of the extractive industries, led to skyrocketing unemployment in the province.[67] Many of BC's unemployed found their way to Vancouver, particularly to a neighborhood known as the Downtown Eastside (DTES). The DTES is an older part of the city whose low-cost residential hotels and access to goods and services had long made it attractive to low-income workers, the unemployed, seniors, people with disabilities, and others.[68] By the early 1980s, Vancouver's unemployment rate had risen to over 14 percent, with much of this concentrated in the DTES.[69]

Neoliberalism and Retrenchment

It is conceivable that the intersection of environmentalists' critique of perpetual growth and the hardships of the recession could have led to support for a greater state role in ensuring an ecologically sound and socially just economy. Instead, the difficulties of the decade came to be attributed not to the limits of capitalism but to Keynesianism's excessive regulation and government intervention in the workings of the market. From the welfare state to environmental protection, the government came to be seen as the problem rather than as the solution to market failures. This economic philosophy would eventually come to be known by many as neoliberalism.

The story of the emergence of neoliberalism has been told in detail elsewhere, and need not be repeated in depth here.[70] Briefly, as a theory of political economy, neoliberalism sees minimally regulated markets as the best way of achieving economic growth and securing individual freedom. It "proposes that human well-being can best be advanced by liberating individual entrepreneurial freedoms and skills within an institutional framework characterized by strong private property rights, free markets, and free trade."[71] The role of the state is only to facilitate this framework through providing a legal structure to secure property rights and contracts, guaranteeing the integrity of money, and providing for national defense.[72]

In theory neoliberals call for minimal government. In practice the government has played a vital role in instituting neoliberalism, either through rolling back regulations seen as onerous to the workings of the market or by implementing "new forms of institution-building and government intervention" consistent with the neoliberal priorities of competitiveness, individualism, and the primacy of the market.[73] This move away from the Keynesian welfare state to neoliberalism, though playing out differently in the UK, the U.S., and Canada, transformed the fortunes of the cities being examined here. Of particular importance was a retrenchment of the welfare state and a move away from social policies targeting urban poverty toward a focus on urban competitiveness.

UK Prime Minister Margaret Thatcher, elected in 1979, replaced postwar policies aimed at addressing uneven urban and regional development with a new emphasis on competition between cities for private investment and government funds. Public–private partnerships became foundational to local governance under Thatcher, as did policies that transferred power to non-elected and private-sector bodies.[74] Casting local authorities "as leftwing and inefficient,"[75] the Thatcher government tightened central government control over local authorities' finances, limiting their ability to spend money on redistributive efforts or to engage in alternatives to the neoliberal development strategies promoted by the government.[76] Policies supporting struggling areas and furthering geographical equity were replaced by policies that focused on regional and industrial "winners" rather than "lame ducks."[77] Instead of redistribution, markets would be the preferred method of addressing urban problems and regenerating local communities. The promotion of "an 'enterprise culture' … would liberate marginalized populations from their [supposedly] demoralizing dependencies."[78] In practice what this meant was an almost 20 percent reduction in fiscal resources to local governments between 1979 and 1983. This hit the poor in struggling cities such as Birmingham hard, resulting in "price increases, rent increases, and cuts in services" at the same time the need for such support was growing.[79]

Thatcher's effort to weaken left-leaning local governments also included a sharp increase in national government control over publically owned council housing, including decisions about levels of investment, pricing, and maintenance.[80] In addition, as part of Thatcher's larger privatization agenda, local governments were forced to relinquish ownership of much of their housing stock, selling units to tenants or transferring ownership to housing associations and independent landlords. Thatcher's Right to Buy scheme, codified in the Housing Act of 1980, benefited those tenants who were able to buy their homes at a substantial discount. However, these sales, in combination with severe limits put on local authorities' ability to invest in or expand their housing stock led to "the contraction and impoverishment of the public housing sector [in which] the poor and the powerless lost out."[81] Furthermore, many of the large redevelopment schemes undertaken during this time, such as the London Docklands, led to the outright displacement of poor populations by luxury condominiums for the well-to-do. Indeed, the term gentrification, widely adopted in the United States and elsewhere, was coined in Britain to refer to this phenomenon.[82]

U.S. President Ronald Reagan also set out to dismantle federal wealth transfers and development assistance to cities. Reagan's first budget requested a 44 percent cut in a large set of urban programs including community development grants, employment training, mass transit, and social services block grants. The Democratic Congress resisted some of these measures, but Reagan was able to achieve cuts of over 35 percent.[83] The administration continued to chip away at this funding and by 1990 total federal aid, much of which had been targeted toward older cities such as Chicago, had been cut by 64 percent.[84] To some extent Reagan's elimination of federal funds that principally benefited urban areas can be seen as brazenly political – his support came overwhelmingly from suburbs while cities, particularly those with large African American populations, skewed heavily Democratic.[85]

The Reagan Administration's cuts to federal support for cities were also consistent with the broader neoliberal goals of lessening government income redistribution to the poor and promoting competitiveness. Such was the language of the administration's 1982 National Urban Policy Report. The report asserted that cities, like firms, should compete with one another for economic growth and that "instead of vying for federal grants, state and local governments should recognize that 'it is in their interest to concentrate on increasing their attractiveness to potential investors, residents and visitors.' "[86] Tax reductions, enterprise zones, and the removal of legal restrictions to development were offered by the report as keys to attracting investment and unleashing the entrepreneurial spirit of local small businesses. Cities could achieve economic growth and gain control over their own destinies, the administration argued, not by insulating themselves or their residents from market forces but by successfully competing in the global economy. As budgets were cut and devolution put the burden for welfare provision onto subnational states, the Keynesian buffer between local governments and the increasingly volatile global economy evaporated.

Canada followed the trend toward neoliberalism observable in the U.S. and Britain, including an emphasis on international competition for investment capital, deregulation, privatization, a reduction in social services, and an attack on the power of labor unions. Though Brian Mulroney, Canada's Prime Minister from 1984 to 1993, was arguably less ideologically driven than his U.S. and British counterparts, the outcome was for the most part the same, "the entrenchment of neoliberalism as the normative economic policy paradigm" of the country.[87] As Canada moved away from its historical skepticism about economic integration with the United States toward an acceptance of regional free trade, income taxes, unemployment insurance and other aspects of the welfare state were "harmonized downward so that they ... correspond[ed] closely to the minimalist post-Reagan American standards."[88] For example, although federal support for housing had been on the decline for some time in response to public disapproval of failed urban redevelopment projects, in 1994 the Canadian government announced it was ending all federal funding for housing development.[89]

Important to Canada's neoliberalization was a strengthening of the role of provinces in promoting economic development. This created "an intensification of uneven development, as the relative fortunes of regions increasingly depend[ed] on how each [was] integrated into the continental and global markets."[90] This reliance on global markets had always been pronounced for the export-dependent economy of British Columbia. But neoliberal retrenchment was seen by BC leaders, particularly Premier Bill Bennett who had been elected in 1975, as crucial to overcoming the province's recession. Bennett's policy of neoliberal "restraint" included an insistence on a balanced budget despite widespread unemployment across the province, the weakening of trade unions, cuts to education and social services, and attacks on public-sector employment.[91] The widespread opposition that erupted in response to Bennett's proposals led to modification of some of the restraint legislation, but most of his agenda passed intact, weakening social welfare supports and the power of public-sector unions in BC.[92] Vancouver, its economy heavily reliant on being the administrative hub for social services and the public sector, was significantly impacted by these cuts.

Roll-backs to Liberal Environmentalism

Neoliberalism also transformed environmental policy. The United States, perhaps because Keynesian environmentalism had gone farthest in reining in industrial pollution, saw the most pronounced backlash against environmental regulation. The federal environmental laws of the 1970s that forced changes in the behavior of industry were quite effective at improving environmental quality and protecting natural resources. They were also expensive, costing businesses billions of dollars in clean-up and pollution control.[93] From a societal perspective, these costs were probably more than compensated for by improvements in public health and general well-being, but by the 1980s businesses had begun loudly decrying the cost of environmental protections as "strangulation by regulation."[94]

Responding to industry's concern, the rolling back of environmental policies was high on Reagan's agenda.[95] His efforts met with stiff resistance from Congress, and his attempts at outright elimination of widely popular environmental protections were a failure. Yet Reagan was able to use cabinet appointments, funding allocations, and simple refusal to enforce the law to weaken the regulations' impacts. The Environmental Protection Agency, for example, lost 26 percent of its budget and a quarter of its staff during Reagan's first two years in office. For his appointments to the head of the EPA, the Bureau of Land Management, and other agencies responsible for enforcing environmental laws, he chose people who were unabashedly critical of the regulations they were supposed to enforce. Reagan's actions flew in the face of the broad support still held by the public for the country's environmental achievements, and membership in environmental organizations working to stop his rollbacks soared.[96]

Prime Minister Thatcher was likewise hostile to environmental concerns. Early in her administration an anti-environmentalist was appointed Secretary for the Environment and security services began to harass increasingly vocal environmental activists.[97] Like Reagan, Thatcher saw environmental protection as a barrier to economic growth and in conflict with Conservatives' "ideological commitments to deregulation and rolling back the state [and] their emphasis on industrial competitiveness."[98] The support of the business community to Britain's accommodating and consensus-oriented environmental regulations meant that the laws themselves were not targeted as particularly burdensome, so Thatcher's efforts centered on weakening enforcement and trying, as a leaked cabinet memo put it, to reduce the public's "over-sensitivity to environmental considerations."[99]

This soon led to conflict with the European Economic Community (ECC). The ECC's rule-oriented environmental regulatory approach was resisted by the UK government, which defended its style of voluntary regulation and its desire to "avoid the imposition of policy solutions" on the nation's industry.[100] As tensions between the Conservative government and the rest of Europe over environmental protections escalated in the second half of the 1980s, and as Britain's own environmental movement branded the UK "the Dirty Man of Europe,"[101] membership in British environmental groups continued to grow. In the 1989 European parliamentary elections the UK Green Party received nearly 15 percent of the vote, not gaining any seats but making it clear to the major political parties that environmental issues were important to the British public.[102]

The vocal public support for environmental protection, and the public push-back Reagan and Thatcher received when they attempted to weaken environmental laws and their enforcement, illustrate one of the limitations of this first era of "roll-back" neoliberalism.[103] In democratic countries, neoliberalism was often met with public resistance to attempts to do away with popular elements of state regulation. This raised political problems for proponents of this agenda, and maintaining the legitimacy of the project required a rebranding of neoliberalism. Thus began the "roll-out" phase of a softer, gentler form of neoliberal governance.[104] Rather than efforts to merely weaken and shrink the state, active neoliberal state-building would create new regulations that would bring as much of society as possible into the logic of the market.[105]

For environmental issues, the emergence of liberal environmentalism was at the core of this change. In the international arena, the idea that environmental protection and growth could be compatible began to emerge in 1987 with the Brundtland Commission's now classic articulation of the concept of sustainable development.[106] This strove to overcome the long-standing tension in international environmental negotiations between the countries of the global North and the global South, the latter of which saw environmentalism as a thinly veiled way to prevent their economic development.[107] Formally adopted by the international community at the 1992 Rio Earth Summit, sustainable development and liberal environmentalism turned this argument on its head, asserting that growth was the solution to environmental problems rather than their cause.[108] In so doing, liberal environmentalism institutionalized new norms of environmental regulation, particularly market and economic mechanisms to achieve environmental protection while spurring growth and development.[109] Within the broader context of roll-out neoliberalism, this enabled political leaders to address public concerns about the environment in a way that was consistent with their primary commitment to business-friendly regulation and economic growth.

Domestically, the beginning of this shift in the UK could be seen at the end of the 1980s when Thatcher had an apparent change of heart on the environment. This appears to have been inspired by a combination of Thatcher's desire to re-establish leadership in European economic integration negotiations, growing sophistication of the domestic environmental lobby, and the need of the government to enhance its legitimacy with an increasingly environmentally conscious public and media.[110] In 1988 Thatcher gave her first major environmental speech in which she "spoke of the importance of sustainable development and the need to nurture the environment."[111] At the 1989 Conservative Party Conference it was declared that "Conservatives were 'not merely friends of the Earth' but also 'its guardians and trustees for generations to come.' "[112] In the election that followed, all major parties were quick to brandish their green credentials.[113] Similarly, George H. W. Bush, Reagan's vice-president and successor, ran for president calling himself the "environmental candidate," claiming that if elected he would be "a Republican president in the Teddy Roosevelt tradition. A conservationist. An *environmentalist.*"[114] These shifts from the anti-environmentalism of the early 1980s were notable. However, both Bush and Thatcher's Conservative successor John Major promoted environmental protection in a way that was consistent with roll-out neoliberalism's "purposeful construction and consolidation of neoliberalized state forms, models of governance, and regulatory relations."[115] This included market-based regulations such as cap and trade programs, voluntary corporate pollution reduction efforts, and cost-benefit analysis.

In 1997 when Tony Blair and the Labour Party won the British national election, the new government strengthened the country's commitment to environmental sustainability and to liberal environmentalism. Labour's platform asserted that the environment needed to be "at the heart of policy-making, so that it is not an add-on extra, but informs the whole of government, from housing and energy policy through to global warming and international agreements."[116] To achieve this, the government called for "a range of market-based measures ... [such as] eco-taxes, government purchasing initiatives, consumer education campaigns and instituting voluntary eco-labeling schemes."[117] These were accompanied by incentive programs to encourage corporate and individual environmental responsibility. In the early 2000s Blair argued that "tackling climate change or other environmental challenges need not limit greater economic opportunity ... economic development, social justice and environmental modernisation must go hand in hand."[118] Liberal environmentalism, framed as compatible with neoliberal ideas of competitiveness and the primacy of economic growth, along with a nod to furthering social justice, had become official government policy.

In the United States, liberal environmentalism was codified by the most important environmental initiative passed during the Bush Administration, the 1990 Clean Air Act Amendments. The amendments introduced two novel practices into pollution reduction efforts. These were the requirement that the EPA conduct a cost-benefit analysis of the Act and the creation of a market-based emissions trading program ("cap and trade") for sulfur dioxide.[119] The importance of this shift was not lost on President Bush. Assessing his own environmental record, Bush claimed that his administration "crafted a new common-sense approach to environmental issues, one that honors our love of the environment and our commitment to growth."[120] Henceforth, cost-benefit analysis would be used to determine whether any particular environmental action was worth the burden it would place on industry, and the standards and enforcement, or so-called "command and control" policies of early environmental laws would be supplanted by market-based arrangements between businesses and the state. New markets would be created for pollutants, creating economic incentives for emissions reduction and enabling some businesses to profit from their ability to sell pollution credits.[121] The commodification of the environment, it was claimed, would serve to protect it.

The move toward market-oriented environmentalism in the United States continued under President Clinton. In contrast to changes occurring in Britain in the mid-1990s, however, under Clinton the environment became an increasingly partisan issue. When Republicans gained a majority in Congress in 1994 and began a legislative attack on environmental laws, Clinton, who started his presidency as "only a lukewarm supporter of environmental policy reform initiatives,"[122] saw an opportunity to garner support among the large number of Americans still quite concerned with environmental issues. It also helped him maintain support among liberal Democrats as he pushed for other policies they found distasteful, particularly the North American Free Trade Agreement (NAFTA). Clinton defeated Congress's efforts to roll back environmental laws, but in doing so he also further institutionalized liberal environmentalism. Echoing President Bush before him, Clinton asserted that environmental "concerns would ... be weighed in the balance against competing social needs and the pressures for (near-term) economic development."[123] When possible, voluntary win–win arrangements with business to reduce their emissions would be promoted over government mandates.[124] Clinton did use his executive powers to further environmental goals in ways that George H.W. Bush did not, particularly to expand the acres of public lands off limits to extractive activities. For the most part, however, the similarities between the policy solutions offered by Clinton and Bush illustrate the extent to which the assumed effectiveness of market tools in furthering social goods such as environmental protection had become ubiquitous.[125]

Canada had a more ambiguous move toward liberal environmentalism, vacillating between liberal regulatory efforts and roll-backs of environmental standards in the name of economic growth. In early 1987, an open-ended poll found that a majority of Canadians thought that the environment was the most pressing concern facing the country.[126] In response, Prime Minister Mulroney took some important steps to control pollutants that caused acid rain and to phase out problematic substances like PCBs and ozone depleting substances.[127] He also instituted multi-stakeholder consultations (MSCs) that brought together representatives of different interests with the purpose of achieving a consensus on how to address both economic and environmental concerns.[128] Participants in MSCs included multiple levels of government, different administrative agencies, and industry representatives. They were used in formulating a wide variety of Canadian environmental policy both at the federal and provincial levels, including the Canadian Environmental Protection Act, the Federal Pesticide Registration Review, federal pulp and paper regulations, and the National Pollutant Release Inventory.[129] Such initiatives certainly represented the potential for more effective pollution control in Canada. However, even as stronger laws slowly made their way onto the books, they were not always stringently enforced, often relied on voluntary compliance, and were limited by tensions between the federal government and the provinces regarding legal authority to enact such laws.[130]

Though consistent with neoliberalism's belief in minimum government regulation of industry, the extensive use of voluntary instruments was strongly critiqued by environmentalists. They raised concerns that voluntary pollution reduction initiatives would encourage free riders and would "reintroduce the closed door, industry-government bipartite bargaining model that defined the early stages of Canadian environmental policy formation, with industrial actors preempting the establishment of more vigorous policy goals by 'volunteering' to pursue less ambitious goals."[131] Many of these concerns were realized in the early 2000s when drinking water regulated by such voluntary initiatives in Walkerton, Ontario and in North Battleford, Saskatchewan killed seven people and made thousands sick.[132]

Along with establishing MSCs and implementing some new environmental regulations, in 1990 the Mulroney government announced the $3 billion Green Plan, the five-year goal of which was to promote creative new initiatives within Canadian environmental policy. Though launched with much fanfare, the Green Plan itself contained a "surprising paucity of measures to directly protect the environment."[133] Instead of fostering new policy approaches to prevent or regulate pollution, it focused on funding and education designed to minimize opposition from the provinces and other stakeholders.[134] With a change of government in 1993 the Green Plan was terminated early, having spent less than a third of its allocated funds.[135]

In part the Green Plan's failure reflected public concern for the environment being replaced once again by "a widespread and intense sense that government budget deficits had been too high for too long."[136] Following the termination of the Green Plan, between 1995 and 1998 the federal government reduced environmental spending by 32 percent.[137] The provinces, particularly Alberta and Ontario, quickly followed suit, reducing their budget deficits through cuts to monitoring, enforcement, and funding of environmental regulations. Natural resource ministries also bore a disproportionate share of the cutbacks to public spending.[138] Some provinces did take more ambitious stances on environmental protection than the federal government, but for the most part going into the 2000s "both the federal and some provincial governments … opted to raise barriers to employing regulation in the name of competitiveness and under the guise of 'reducing the red tape' that businesses face."[139] In Canada, as in the United States, the assumed trade-off between economic growth and environmental protection was not fully displaced by liberal environmentalism. Yet those environmental regulations that were adopted were consistent with liberalism environmentalism's prioritization of growth, voluntarism, and benefits to industry.

Conclusion

The move toward liberal environmentalism represented an important shift in how the relationship between environmental protection and economic growth were understood. The shift was not uncontested, but overall the idea that the environment could be protected in a way that also furthered economic interests created a new set of tools for environmental regulation. These tools undoubtedly varied in effectiveness, with, for example, cap and trade under the U.S. 1990 Clean Air Act amendments successfully reducing emissions whereas voluntary clean water efforts in Canada led to deadly contamination. But in a notable change from the beginnings of the modern environmental movement, by the 1990s sacrifice and limits to growth vanished from mainstream environmental discourse. For cities reeling from deindustrialization, unemployment, and the volatility of an increasingly globalized economy, this change would prove to be vital to city leaders' efforts to use environmentalism as a catalyst for economic growth.

Notes

1 Robert Brenner, *The Economics of Global Turbulence* (New York, NY: Verso, 2006).
2 David Harvey, *The Condition of Postmodernity: An Enquiry into the Origins of Cultural Change* (New York, NY: Blackwell, 1989).
3 Peter Malpass and David Mullins, "Local Authority Housing Stock Transfer in the UK: From Local Initiative to National Policy," *Housing Studies* 17, no. 4 (2001); Brian Wheeler, "A History of Social Housing," www.bbc.com/news/uk-14380936 (accessed January 15, 2016).
4 Neil Brenner, "Urban Governance and the Production of New State Spaces in Western Europe, 1960–2000," *Review of International Political Economy* 11, no. 3 (2004); Craig Johnstone and Mark Whitehead, "Horizons and Barriers in British Urban Policy," in *New Horizons in British Urban Policy: Perspectives on New Labour's Urban Renaissance*, ed. Craig Johnstone and Mark Whitehead (Burlington, VT: Ashgate, 2004).
5 Jamie Peck and Adam Tickell, "Local Modes of Social Regulation? Regulation Theory, Thatcherism, and Uneven Development," *Geoforum* 23, no. 3 (1992): 355.
6 Michael Parkinson, "The Thatcher Government's Urban Policy, 1979–1989: A Review," *The Town Planning Review* 60, no. 4 (1989).
7 Andrew E.G. Jonas and Kevin Ward, "A World of Regionalisms? Towards a US-UK Urban and Regional Policy Framework Comparison," *Journal of Urban Affairs* 24, no. 4 (2002).

8   Robert A. Beauregard, *When America Became Suburban* (Minneapolis, MN: University of MN Press, 2006).

9   John L. Palmer and Isabel V. Sawhill, "Foreword," in *Reagan and the Cities*, ed. George E. Peterson and Carol W. Lewis (Washington, DC: Urban Institute Press, 1986), xv; Frank Gaffkin and Barney Warf, "Urban Policy and the Post-Keynesian State in the United Kingdom and the United States," *International Journal of Urban and Regional Research* 17, no. 1 (1993).

10 William K. Carroll and Williams Little, "Neoliberal Transformation and Antiglobalization Politics in Canada: Transition, Consolidation, Resistance," *International Journal of Political Economy* 31, no. 3 (2001).

11 James J. Rice and Michael J Prince, *Changing Politics of Canadian Social Policy*, 2nd edn. (Toronto: University of Toronto Press, 2013).

12 Roberto Leone and Barbara W. Carroll, "Decentralisation and Devolution in Canadian Social Housing Policy," *Environment and Planning C: Government and Policy* 28 (2010).

13 Ibid.

14 Rice and Prince.

15 Kenneth Spencer et al., *Crisis in the Industrial Heartland: A Study of the West Midlands* (Oxford, UK: Clarendon Press, 1986).

16 Liam Kennedy, "The Creative Destruction of Birmingham," in *Remaking Birmingham: The Visual Culture of Urban Regeneration*, ed. Liam Kennedy (New York: Routledge, 2004), 1.

17 Christopher Upton, *A History of Birmingham* (Chichester, Sussex, UK: Phillimore, 1993); T.R. Slater, "Birmingham's Black and South-Asian Population," in *Managing a Conurbation: Birmingham and Its Region*, ed. A.J. Gerrard and T.R. Slater (Studley, Warwickshire: Brewin Books, 1996).

18 Frank Hendriks, *Public Policy and Political Institutions: The Role of Culture in Traffic Policy*, New Horizons in Public Policy (Cheltenham, UK: Edward Elgar, 1999), 101.

19 Ben Flatman, *Birmingham: Shaping the City* (Birmingham, UK: RIBA Publishing, 2008), 28.

20 See William Cronon, *Nature's Metropolis: Chicago and the Great West*, 1st edn. (New York, NY: W. W. Norton, 1991).

21 Janet L. Abu-Lughod, *New York, Chicago, Los Angeles: America's Global Cities* (Minneapolis, MN: University of Minnesota Press, 1999).

22 Beauregard; Dominic A. Pacyga, *Chicago: A Biography* (Chicago, IL: University of Chicago Press, 2009).

23 Beauregard.

24 Abu-Lughod, 221.

25 The Chicago City Council is made up of 50 aldermen, each of which oversees their own area of the city or "ward." Aldermen have extensive power over development decisions in their wards.

26 Beauregard.

27 Mitch Kahn, "Book Review: Paradise Lost," *Shelterforce Online*, no. 138 (2004).

28 Jean Barman, *The West Beyond the West: A History of British Columbia, Third Edition* (Toronto: University of Toronto Press, 2007); T.R. Oke, M. North, and O. Slaymaker, "Primordial to Prim Order: A Century of Environmental Change," in *Vancouver and Its Region*, ed. Graeme Wynn and Timothy Oke (Vancouver, BC: UBC Press, 1992).

29 Barman.

30 Trevor J. Barnes et al., "Vancouver, the Province, and the Pacific Rim," in *Vancouver and Its Region*, ed. Graeme Wynn and Timothy Oke (Vancouver,

BC: UBC Press, 1992); David Ley, Daniel Hiebert, and Geraldine Pratt, "Time to Grow Up? From Urban Village to World City, 1966–91," in *Vancouver and Its Region*, ed. Graeme Wynn and Timothy Oke (Vancouver, BC: UBC Press, 1992).

31 Adam Rome, *The Genius of Earth Day: How a 1970 Teach-in Unexpectedly Made the First Green Generation* (New York: Hill & Wang, 2013).

32 Rachel Carson, *Silent Spring* (Greenwich, CT: Fawcett Publications, 1962); Paul R. Ehrlich, *The Population Bomb* (San Francisco, CA: Sierra Club, 1969); Donella H. Meadows and Dennis L. Meadows, *The Limits to Growth. A Report for the Club of Rome's "Project on the Predicament of Mankinds"* (New York, NY: Universe Books, 1972).

33 Rome.

34 Daniel A. Mazmanian and Michael E. Kraft, "The Three Epochs of the Environmental Movement," in *Toward Sustainable Communities*, ed. Daniel A. Mazmanian and Michael E. Kraft (Cambridge, MA: MIT Press, 1999), 10.

35 Kent E. Portney, *Taking Sustainable Cities Seriously: Economic Development, the Environment, and Quality of Life in American Cities, 2nd Edition* (Cambridge, MA: MIT Press, 2013).

36 Samuel P. Hays, *A History of Environmental Politics since 1945* (Pittsburgh, PA: University of Pittsburgh Press, 2000).

37 Philip Lowe and Stephen Ward, "Britain in Europe: Themes and Issues in National Environmental Policy," in *British Environmental Policy and Europe: Politics and Policy in Transition*, ed. Philip Lowe and Stephen Ward (London: Routledge, 1998).

38 David Vogel, *National Styles of Business Regulation: A Case Study of Environmental Protection* (Washington, DC: Beard Books, 2003 [1986]).

39 Ibid., 70.

40 Duncan Watts, *The Environment and British Politics* (London: Hodder & Stoughton Educational, 1999).

41 Robert Paehlke, "The Environmental Movement in Canada," in *Canadian Environmental Policy and Politics: Prospects for Leadership and Innovation*, ed. Debora L. VanNijnatten and Robert Boardman (Ontario: Oxford University Press, 2009).

42 Kathryn Harrison, *Passing the Buck: Federalism and Canadian Environmental Policy* (Vancouver, BC: UBC Press, 1996).

43 James W. Harbell, "Canada Tackles Environmental Problems: There Are Some Differences up North," *Business Law Today* 12, no. 2 (2002).

44 Harrison.

45 Ibid.

46 Ibid., 69.

47 Ibid., 84.

48 Brenner; David Harvey, *A Brief History of Neoliberalism* (New York, NY: Oxford University Press, 2005).

49 Jonathon Porritt, *Capitalism as If the World Matters* (Sterling, VA: Earthscan, 2005).

50 Quoted in ibid., 60.

51 Abu-Lughod; Wim Wiewel, "The State of the Economy and Economic Development in the Chicago Metropolitan Region" (Chicago, IL: Center for Urban Economic Developmet, University of IL at Chicago, 1986).

52 City of Chicago, "Building the Basics: The Final Report of the Mayor's Task Force on Steel and Southeast Chicago" (Chicago, IL: City of Chicago, 1986).

53 Abu-Lughod; Robert G. Spinney, *City of Big Shoulders: A History of Chicago* (DeKalb, IL: Northern Illinois University Press, 2000).

54   Abu-Lughod.
55   Wiewel.
56   Spinney.
57   Abu-Lughod.
58   Jane Jacobs, *The Economy of Cities* (New York: Random House, 1969), 89.
59   Spencer et al.
60   Mike Beazley, Patrick Loftman, and Brendan Nevin, "Downtown Redevelopment and Community Resistance: An International Perspective," in *Transforming Cities: Contested Governance and New Spatial Divisions*, ed. Nick Jewson and Susanne MacGregor (New York: Routledge, 1997).
61   Spencer et al., 52.
62   Ibid.
63   Upton.
64   Ley, Hiebert, and Pratt, 260.
65   John Punter, *The Vancouver Achievement: Urban Planning and Design* (Vancouver, BC: UBC Press, 2003), xxiii; see also David Ley, *The New Middle Class and the Remaking of the Central City* (Oxford, UK: Oxford University Press, 1996).
66   Ley, Hiebert, and Pratt; Punter.
67   Barman.
68   Ann Dale and Lenore L. Newman, "Sustainable Development for Some: Green Urban Development and Affordability," *Local Environment* 14, no. 7 (2009).
69   Barnes et al.
70   Harvey, *A Brief History of Neoliberalism*; Jonathan Swarts, *Constructing Neoliberalism: Economic Transformation in Anglo-American Democracies* (Toronto: University of Toronto Press, 2013).
71   Harvey, *A Brief History of Neoliberalism*, 2.
72   See Milton Friedman, *Capitalism and Freedom* (Chicago, IL: University of Chicago Press, 2002 [1962]).
73   Jamie Peck and Adam Tickell, "Neoliberalizing Space," *Antipode* 34, no. 3 (2002): 389; see also Steven K. Vogel, *Freer Markets, More Rules: Regulatory Reform in Advanced Industrial Countries* (Ithaca, NY: Cornell University Press, 1996).
74   Parkinson.
75   Peck and Tickell, "Local Modes of Social Regulation? Regulation Theory, Thatcherism, and Uneven Development," 354.
76   Gaffkin and Warf.
77   Peck and Tickell, "Local Modes of Social Regulation? Regulation Theory, Thatcherism, and Uneven Development," 355.
78   Gaffkin and Warf, 71.
79   Spencer et al., 47.
80   Parkinson.
81   Ibid., 434.
82   Jonathan Barnett, *Redesigning Cities: Principles, Practice, Implementation* (Chicago, IL: Planners Press, 2003).
83   George E. Peterson, "Urban Policy and the Cyclical Behavior of Cities," in *Reagan and the Cities*, ed. George E. Peterson and Carol W. Lewis (Washington, DC: Urban Institute Press, 1986).
84   Gerry Riposa, "From Enterprize Zones to Empowerment Zones: The Community Context of Urban Economic Development," *American Behavioral Scientist* 39, no. 5 (1996).
85   Larry Sawers and William K. Tabb, *Sunbelt/Snowbelt: Urban Development and Regional Restructuring* (New York, NY: Oxford University Press, 1984).

86 Quoted in George E. Peterson and Carol W. Lewis, "Introduction," in *Reagan and the Cities*, ed. George E. Peterson and Carol W. Lewis (Washington, DC: Urban Institute Press, 1986), 7.
87 Swarts, 81.
88 Carroll and Little, 38.
89 Leone and Carroll.
90 Carroll and Little, 38–9.
91 Barman; William K. Carroll and R.S. Ratner, "Social Democracy, Neo-Conservatism and Hegemonic Crisis in British Columbia," *Critical Sociology* 16, no. 1 (1989).
92 Barman.
93 Mazmanian and Kraft.
94 Kirkpatrick Sale, *The Green Revolution: The American Environmental Movement 1962–1992* (New York, NY: Hill and Wang, 1993), 49.
95 Michael E. Kraft, *Environmental Policy and Politics*, 4th edn. (New York: Pearson/Longman, 2007).
96 Christopher J. Bosso, *Environment, Inc.: From Grassroots to Beltway* (Lawrence, KS: University Press of Kansas, 2005).
97 John S. Dryzek et al., "Environmental Transformation of the State: The USA, Norway, Germany and the UK," *Political Studies* 50 (2002).
98 Lowe and Ward, "Domestic Winners and Losers," 88.
99 Quoted in Watts, 85.
100 Lowe and Ward, "Britain in Europe: Themes and Issues in National Environmental Policy," 7.
101 Ibid., 19–20, citation omitted.
102 Watts.
103 Peck and Tickell, "Neoliberalizing Space."
104 Ibid.
105 Harvey, *A Brief History of Neoliberalism*; Vogel.
106 World Commission on Environment and Development, *Our Common Future* (Oxford, UK: Oxford University Press, 1987).
107 For example, J.A.A. Castro, "Environment and Development: The Case of the Developing Countries," in *World Eco-Crisis: International Organizations in Response*, ed. D.A. Kay and E.B. Skolnikoff (Madison, WI: University of Wisconsin Press, 1972).
108 See United Nations, "Agenda 21: The United Nations Programme of Action from Rio" (New York: United Nations, 1992).
109 Steven Bernstein, *The Compromise of Liberal Environmentalism* (New York, NY: Columbia University Press, 2001).
110 Andrew Jordan, "Impact on UK Environmental Administration," in *British Environmental Policy and Europe: Politics and Policy in Transition*, ed. Philip Lowe and Stephen Ward (London: Routledge, 1998).
111 Watts, 85.
112 Quoted in ibid.
113 Peter Rawcliffe, "Making Inroads: Transport Policy and the British Environmental Movement," *Environment* 37, no. 3 (1995).
114 Quoted in Kraft, 106.
115 Peck and Tickell, "Neoliberalizing Space," 384.
116 Quoted in Watts, 90.
117 Quoted in Gill Seyfang, "Consuming Values and Contested Cultures: A Critical Analysis of the UK Strategy for Sustainable Consumption and Production," *Review of Social Economy* LXII, no. 3 (2004): 329.
118 Quoted in John Barry and Peter Doran, "Refining Green Political Economy: From Ecological Modernisation to Economic Security and Sufficiency," *Analyse & Kritik* 28 (2006): 256.

119 Kraft.
120 Quoted in Sale, 77.
121 Hays; Mazmanian and Kraft.
122 Richard N. L. Andrews, *Managing the Environment, Managing Ourselves: A History of American Environmental Policy*, 2nd edn. (New Haven, CT: Yale University Press, 2006), ix.
123 Mazmanian and Kraft, 15.
124 Hays.
125 Judith A. Layzer, *Open for Business: Conservatives' Opposition to Environmental Regulation* (Cambridge, MA: MIT Press, 2014).
126 Paehlke.
127 Mark Winfield, "Policy Instruments in Canadian Environmental Policy;" Paehlke.
128 Michael Howlett, "Beyond Legalism? Policy Ideas, Implementation Styles and Emulation-Based Convergence in Canadian and U.S. Environmental Policy," *Journal of Public Policy* 20, no. 3 (2000).
129 Debora L. VanNijnatten and Robert Boardman, "Introduction," in *Canadian Environmental Policy and Politics: Prospects for Leadership and Innovation*, ed. Debora L. VanNijnatten and Robert Boardman (Ontario: Oxford University Press, 2009).
130 Harrison; Winfield.
131 Winfield, 50.
132 Ibid.
133 Barry G. Rabe, "The Politics of Sustainable Development: Impediments to Pollution Prevention and Policy Integration in Canada," *Canadian Public Administration / Administration Publique Du Canada* 40, no. 3 (1997): 429.
134 Ibid.
135 Harrison.
136 Paehlke, 8.
137 Ibid.
138 Irene Henriques and Perry Sadorsky, "Voluntary Environmental Programs: A Canadian Perspective," *The Policy Studies Journal* 36, no. 1 (2008).
139 VanNijnatten and Boardman, x.

3   Greening the Post-Industrial City

Green urban entrepreneurialism is the use of physical greening and environmental amenities to attract capital investment, skilled labor, and tourists to a city. This phenomenon defined the type of greening efforts that emerged in Birmingham, Chicago, and Vancouver in the 1990s. Green urban entrepreneurialism was enabled by the confluence of the two broader political changes discussed in the previous chapter – the need for cities to find new ways to generate revenue under neoliberal urbanism and the growing belief that environmental protection and economic development could be mutually beneficial.

As will be seen in this chapter, the perceived ability of greening to spur growth and post-industrial branding while benefiting all residents helped to soften and legitimize neoliberal urbanism. However, although largely successful at revitalizing city centers and key post-industrial spaces, the promised synthesis of growth, environmental protection, and social equity was never realized in the green entrepreneurial city. Rather, the prioritization of the economy shaped and limited city environmental initiatives, concentrating them on the provision of amenities for the well-to-do and deprioritizing both equity and environmental effectiveness. Examining green urban entrepreneurialism in Chicago, Vancouver, and Birmingham is vital for understanding city greening today, for even as these cities have taken steps beyond green urban entrepreneurialism in recent years, its priorities of growth and branding continue to impact their environmental efforts.

Green Urban Entrepreneurialism

Facing recession, concentrated poverty, deindustrialization, and the increasing mobility of globalized capital, by the 1980s city leaders were striving to find new ways to attract investment and skilled labor.[1] In what David Harvey called a move "from managerialism to urban entrepreneurialism," cities began adopting policies "in which traditional local boosterism [was] integrated with the use of local governmental powers to try to attract external sources of funding, new direct investments or new employment sources."[2] This was consistent with the tenets of neo-liberalism more broadly, wherein the role of the state was principally to create conditions conducive to the market and to capital accumulation. Urban entrepreneurialism therefore represented a shift from the Keynesian decades in which the local state served as a conduit for the national provision of social services and the infrastructure support for mass production and consumption toward a local state increasingly focused on competitiveness.[3]

One important strategy of the entrepreneurial city was direct financial incentives such as tax breaks or subsidies aimed at attracting corporate headquarters. A second main strategy, and one that would quickly incorporate greening, was the use of public funds to remake the built environment of the city.[4] The physical transformation of underutilized city centers and former industrial spaces was necessary for fulfilling urban entrepreneurialism's ultimate goal of creating a high-end service economy by appealing to tourists, particularly business tourists, and attracting new residents skilled in the advanced trades of the service economy such as computer programming, legal services, business, marketing, and design.[5] Doing so required creating amenities and city center housing that would be desirable to such residents, entice conferences, and that would generally "enhance [a city's] position in the spatial division of consumption."[6] If successful, this post-industrial reinvention could position an urban area in the rank of the world's global cities.[7]

This transformation was by no means straightforward or self-evident, however. For cities reeling from deindustrialization and disinvestment, the goals of urban entrepreneurialism often "flew directly in the face of deeply entrenched negative perceptions of older industrial cities amongst would be tourists, entrepreneurs or investors," and residents.[8] Substantial work was therefore needed to overcome the commonly held perception that cities such as Chicago and Birmingham were dirty, rough, fading industrial centers and to create – and market – a new post-industrial image.[9] Even cities like Vancouver without such a negative industrial reputation to overcome still needed to find ways to compete for new investment and skilled labor by creating an international brand that would enable them to be active players in the new global economy.[10]

Thus began the massive investment in large-scale urban prestige and redevelopment projects aimed at creating cities that were "clean and attractive" places for the flourishing of the financial and creative industries.[11] Though there certainly were differences between cities, overall the formula for entrepreneurial transformation was strikingly similar.[12] A city needed a new or refurbished stadium and upscale convention center. The convention center was complemented by nice restaurants and opportunities for sightseeing. New or renovated theaters, symphony halls, and museums further enhanced central areas of the city. Ports, harbors, or other waterways were turned into boardwalks, usually with cafes, boutiques, and entertainment opportunities. Large, mixed-use developments that included extensive high-end housing and condominium development along with boutique shopping and dining were created out of centrally located spaces that had once been used by industry.[13] When successful, the result was the physical transformation of deindustrialized city centers, a boost in tourism, and a growing number of well-to-do residents. As downtowns were transformed, local officials pointed to entrepreneurial prestige projects and mega-developments "as evidence of their own effectiveness and skill when attempting to secure re-election and career advancement" and as proof of the benefits and legitimacy of neoliberal urbanism.[14]

The prestige projects of traditional urban entrepreneurialism – convention centers, high-end shopping malls, etc. – almost inevitably would require major public subsidies, even as social welfare budgets were cut and unemployment continued to ravage many formerly industrial cities.[15] These persistent social ills were often exacerbated by gentrification and exclusion as centrally located low-income communities were displaced by rising property values and more profitable land uses.[16] That inequality was growing alongside the renaissance of city centers presented a challenge to city leaders' proclamations of the success of their redevelopment efforts, and many cities saw public push-back against the most brazenly regressive aspects of neoliberal urbanism.[17] As this occurred, local authorities became "trapped in a triangular tension between [neoliberal economic policy], an ambiguous legitimization discourse in an attempt to forge a more harmonious coexistence of inherently conflicting development logics, and increasingly louder calls from populations in depressed neighbourhoods for new initiatives in the social economy and in fostering community social services."[18] Greening soon emerged as a tool to address this tension.

From the early days of urban entrepreneurialism, the physical greening and beautification of key parts of the city contributed to the creation of "lifestyle opportunities, cultural amenities, recreational opportunities, and other 'non-economic' components to place distinction that attract managerial elites and technical workers."[19] Green urban entrepreneurialism took physical beautification a step further. Consistent with liberal environmentalism's growing discursive power at other political scales, city leaders promoting green urban entrepreneurialism explicitly insisted that enhancing the urban environment would do more than spur economic growth, though this was undoubtedly a vital goal. It was also offered as illustrative of city officials' concern for the greater good and their responsiveness to local citizens' desires that they do something to address environmental problems. Even more importantly, green urban entrepreneurialism promised to overcome the exclusionary edges of urban redevelopment through the provision of parks, green spaces, jobs, and a more attractive city and improved quality of life that were, city leaders insisted, available to all. City greening initiatives could therefore be heralded as demonstrating that urban redevelopment was truly benefiting all residents of the city, not just the new and growing middle-class or moneyed visitors.

The effectiveness of this strategy was mixed, both in terms of achieving synergy between growth, equity, and environmental protection and in terms of effectively enhancing local-state legitimacy. As will be seen in the following discussions of Chicago, Birmingham, and Vancouver, green urban entrepreneurialism did facilitate a shift away from the long-held idea that cities were antithetical to nature, and some important steps toward more ecologically sound urban development were taken. For the most part, however, because green urban entrepreneurialism continued to prioritize economic growth over environmental protection, it led to a selective incorporation of environmental concerns into neoliberal urbanism, with a focus on greening initiatives whose visibility could most contribute to broader strategies of entrepreneurial rebranding. Likewise, even as some aspects of the urban quality of life were improved, the supposedly universal benefits of a greener city often were not realized, and in some instances greening may have further exacerbated inequality and displacement. Sometimes these inequities were hidden by the spectacle of the greener city that successfully served to build cross-class support for the city's development agenda.[20] At other times resistance to green urban entrepreneurialism emerged, either from those who saw it as a source of displacement or from those who did not see it as doing enough to address environmental problems. Green urban entrepreneurialism was therefore full of contradictions. But it also opened up new understandings of cities' relationships to environmental and social sustainability and to the possibility of cities contributing to effective environmental governance.

The "Green Star" of Urban Entrepreneurialism

Chicago offers a clear example of the entrepreneurial re-creation of a formerly industrial city and the successful incorporation of greening into this transformation. By the late 1980s, Chicago seemed to be following other Rust Belt cities into continuing decline, political strife, and disinvestment. Twenty years later it was being heralded as a post-industrial success story, "buzzing with life, humming with prosperity, sparkling with new buildings, new sculptures, new parks, and generally exuding vitality."[21] In 2004 Saskia Sassen asserted that Chicago had become a member of the "new hierarchy of global cities."[22] Though this turnaround was certainly multifaceted,[23] greening and environmental amenities played no small part in Chicago's rebirth. The physical beautification of the city is often acknowledged in analyses of the Chicago's post-industrial transformation, but environmental amenities are generally mentioned alongside art installations and new buildings rather than examined in their own right.[24] A more in-depth investigation of the role of nature and the environment in Chicago's entrepreneurial endeavors illustrates the extent to which liberal environmentalism played an important part in Chicago's redevelopment. It also offers insight into how the contradictions that emerged from green urban entrepreneurialism continue to shape Chicago's sustainability efforts.

Flowers, Parks, and the Rebuilding of Chicago

Attempts to revitalize downtown Chicago began before the era of urban entrepreneurialism. In a preview of the trend that would emerge across the country in the following decades, Richard J. Daley, the mayor of the city for 23 years until his death in office in 1976, worked to attract new investment to the downtown Loop, which was suffering from remarkably high vacancy rates. The 1973 development plan Chicago 21: A Plan for Central Area Communities called for extensive infill housing and mixed-use development, more leisure opportunities and environmental amenities in the central area, as well as an expansion of direct public support for downtown businesses.[25] Though the plan was not realized, and many aspects of it were put on hold by Mayor Harold Washington (1983–1987) who strove to better balance downtown and community development,[26] the vision of Chicago 21 is strikingly in line with the entrepreneurial accomplishments of Mayor Richard M. Daley, the elder Daley's son.

Under the second Mayor Daley, elected in 1989, the City aggressively pursued the large-scale prestige projects typical of the entrepreneurial city, attracting capital and creating new opportunities for consumption and entertainment. Navy Pier was redeveloped in 1995 at a cost of upwards of $150 million and included theaters, meeting and convention space, amusement rides, restaurants, and shops. The development was soon boasting of being "the Midwest's #1 tourist and leisure destination," attracting 8.6 million tourists a year.[27] Other prestige projects included the expansion of McCormick Place to be the largest convention center in North America, the rerouting of Lake Shore Drive to create space for a walkable museum campus, the renovation of the Chicago Symphony's concert hall, and the construction of a lighted walkway along the Chicago River.[28] Each of these projects contributed to Chicago's success as a major tourist destination, and the city saw sales tax revenue increase almost threefold from 1989 to 1999.[29]

Early in his administration Daley declared his intention of planting a half a million new trees in the city by 1992.[30] It was not until the preparations for the 1996 Democratic National Convention, however, that the physical greening of the city was begun in earnest and became an important aspect of Chicago's entrepreneurial brand. Richard J. Daley had been mayor during the notorious 1968 Democratic convention at which Chicago's reputation as a rough and troubled city was exacerbated by the use of heavy police force against anti-war protesters. Richard M. Daley saw the public spotlight of the 1996 convention as an opportunity to enhance the new public image of the city he was working to build. Environmental amenities contributed to this, and in the months before the convention Daley ordered the planting of thousands of trees and countless beds of flowers, built pocket parks, and had abandoned lots and blighted areas near the convention grounds cleaned up.[31]

As media attention was poured onto the city's preparations for the convention, most coverage spoke favorably of the physical changes Chicago was undergoing.[32] A few raised concerns about the cost of the initiatives and who they were benefiting. Some estimates put the cost to city taxpayers of the preparations at upwards of $180 million,[33] though the City claimed the actual costs were much lower and that many of the beautification projects had been in the works before the convention.[34] Other commentators pointed out that the trees and flower boxes, ubiquitous around the convention grounds, stopped one block before reaching Rockwell Gardens, a low-income, predominantly African American housing project.[35] Highlighting the contrast between the lack of investment in maintaining (let alone beautifying) public housing and the millions of dollars spent by the City on trees, flowers, and parks before the convention, one protester wore a tree costume with a sign on his trunk that read "If I dress like a tree will you care about me?"[36]

Around the same time that the Democratic National Convention inspired increased attention to enhancing Chicago's physical appearance, discussions began about the potential for tree planting and other greening initiatives to contribute to the economic revitalization of the city more broadly. In 1998 the City, in partnership with the Park District and the Cook County Forest Preserve District, released a long-term plan for the expansion of parks and green space called CitySpace.[37] One of the important claims of CitySpace was that greening was a necessary precondition for attracting business and skilled labor and thereby reinvigorating the city's economy. The report noted that 63 percent of Chicago residents lived in neighborhoods where parks were either too far away or too crowded. Though potentially an issue of environmental equity, inadequate park space was seen as problematic because of its impact on future economic growth and competitiveness. The report states, "while many factors influence the decision of a company or an individual to move into or out of a city, a major consideration is quality of life. Parks, trails, and aesthetics are critical variables in the quality of life equation... To be competitive with other cities in attracting business, Chicago cannot afford to ignore any of the components that influence location decisions."[38]

CitySpace was one of the earliest articulations of green urban entrepreneurialism in Chicago, emphasizing the connection between greening, quality of life, and economic vitality in the city. Within ten years many of the particular projects CitySpace recommended, including the development of inland waterways (particularly the Chicago River) for recreation, the improvement of underutilized land along the lakefront in the area that would become Millennium Park (see Figure 3.1), and the reclamation of vacant lots for community parks, had come to pass. Between 1988 and 2000 annual expenditures on city beautification grew nearly eightfold to over $3.1 million, while forestry expenditures increased almost 70 percent, to $12.7 million.[39] The physical changes to Chicago were

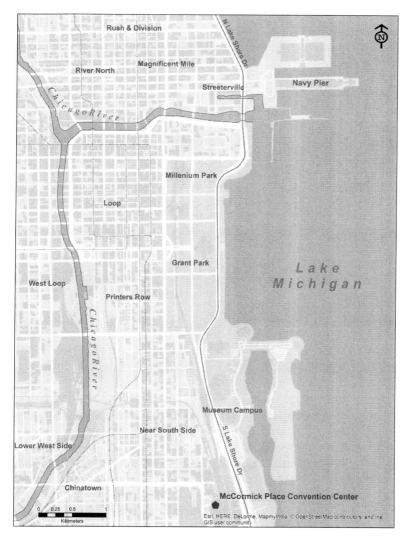

Figure 3.1 The area surrounding the downtown Loop was the focus of Daley's greening and entrepreneurial prestige projects.

Source: Map by Matt Cooney. Map data from https://data.cityofchicago.org/.

myriad, and today city officials involved in this transformation insist that CitySpace illustrated a genuine commitment to a greening agenda that benefited all parts of the city.[40] Yet it was Millennium Park that was to become the city's flagship green urban entrepreneurial development project, transforming Chicago's downtown waterfront and putting Chicago on the map as one of the country's leading green cities.

Millennium Park: The Private Benefits of Public Space

For most of Chicago's history the piece of land that is now the 24.5-acre Millennium Park was an Illinois Central Railroad yard and a dusty parking lot. Railroads were instrumental in the early economic success of Chicago. In the 1800s city leaders' willingness to provide railroads with subsidies, costly bridges, and access to prime land enabled Chicago to surpass early contenders such as St. Louis to become the Midwest's dominant city.[41] Whereas early leaders such as A. Montgomery Ward (the inventor of the mail order catalogue) worked to keep most of the Lake Michigan shoreline "open, clear and free" as early designations of the land required, Illinois Central's right of way was a notable exception. The company's rail lines, depots, and industrial debris separated downtown Chicago from Lake Michigan until 1997.[42] When the right of way was turned over to the City and the park was built, it was built over the below-grade parking lot, commuter rails, and what remained of the rail yard (see Figure 3.2). Though in the design of the park the head of the project "did everything he could to hide the fact that the park is really a roof,"[43] its design made Millennium Park the largest green roof in the world. It also served to hide the unsightly remnants of Chicago's industrial past from the downtown viewscape.

Original plans for Millennium Park were fairly modest, but they became increasingly grandiose as the potential for the park to become a cornerstone of downtown revitalization was recognized. When Millennium Park was first proposed in 1998 it had a budget of $150 million. A year later the cost had increased to $230 million. By the time the park opened in 2004 it had cost $450 million, with $270 million coming from taxpayers and the rest from wealthy private donors, corporations, and foundations.[44] As the park was being built, the cost and time overrun of its construction was criticized by many, and the park was seen as an example of Daley's excess, inefficiency, and corruption.[45] Other criticisms came from local parks advocates who argued that the resources being dedicated to this one showcase park could be better spent on improving and expanding community parks throughout the city, as Chicago continued to rank last among large, high-density U.S. cities in acres of park per capita.[46]

Within a few years of Millennium Park's opening, this criticism had all but vanished.[47] The park included sculptures, fountains, a concert

Figure 3.2 Millennium Park, which was built over a railroad line and parking lot, is the largest green roof in the world.

Source: Photo by author, 2012.

pavilion, an ice skating rink, gardens full of native plants, indoor bike lockers (complete with showers) to encourage bike commuting to downtown, and solar-powered pavilions that provide access to the parking garage beneath the park. It was seen as setting new standards for landscape architecture and became a showcase for green technologies, particularly green roofs.[48] Millennium Park was widely celebrated as one of the most distinctive, ambitious, and successful new urban parks in the country and quickly became a model for other cities striving to create outstanding public green space.[49]

Instead of raising concerns regarding its cost, commentators soon began pointing to the economic benefits of the park. Within five years Millennium Park was attracting three to four million visitors annually

and had increased tourist spending in downtown Chicago by 50 percent.[50] One early estimate predicted that in its first ten years Millennium
Park would generate up to $5 billion in increased business and residential
property values in surrounding neighborhoods and in increased revenue
to nearby retailers and hotels.[51] The park also facilitated growth of condominium development in the area, with newly built condo sales in the
city disproportionately concentrated in the Loop and the New East Side
neighborhoods, the two areas closest to Millennium Park.[52] Millennium
Park was hailed by many as one of the cornerstones of the Daley administration's revitalization of the economy of downtown Chicago.[53]

Undoubtedly successful in its own right, Millennium Park also offers
an example of how the entrepreneurial local state transfers money away
from communities toward large-scale prestige projects. Originally, when
the plans for Millennium Park were modest and the projected cost was
still $150 million, city planners claimed that parking fees from the park's
garage would fully cover the building and maintenance costs. As the cost
of the park tripled, the construction bonds levied on the parking garage
quickly became insufficient. To fill the gap, $95 million in tax increment
financing (TIF) money, intended for development of depressed neighborhoods, was diverted to the project.[54] TIFs are an urban development tool
that were used extensively by the Daley administration.[55] TIF districts
freeze property values for the purposes of all standard taxes such as
those for the Park District and Board of Education for up to 24 years.
Any additional taxes from increased property value in the district (the
"increment") is supposedly dedicated to economic development in the
area covered by the TIF. This can include infrastructure improvements,
funds to attract businesses to the area, subsidies to developers, etc. The
justification is that if the TIF successfully helps spur economic growth
in a depressed neighborhood, when the TIF ends those parts of the local
government that saw their taxes frozen for years will reap the benefits
from the improved condition of the area.[56]

The use of TIF money for Millennium Park rather than for community development was justified by the supposedly universal benefits of
the park to the residents of Chicago.[57] There was probably some truth to
this, and the park is certainly enjoyed by Chicago residents from various
walks of life. The direct economic benefits of Millennium Park, however,
accrue quite specifically to downtown property owners and businesses.
Yet an early effort to require these beneficiaries to help pay for the park
failed. Still facing difficulty in coming up with money to cover the park's
$7 million annual operating and maintenance costs, in 2005 planners
proposed the creation of a special tax in the Loop to cover these costs
and a handful of other downtown amenities. Despite the direct benefits
they received from Millennium Park as a major tourist attraction, resistance from local businesses and hotel owners to the proposal was swift
and indignant, and they argued that such a tax would unfairly burden

them for something that "everyone" benefited from. The vice-president of the Building Owners and Managers Association of Chicago summarized this sentiment well, saying that the proposal "really shifts a disproportionate burden onto the central business district businesses and residents. ... It's an issue of fairness."[58] This concern was echoed in city council meetings and, in the face of vocal business opposition, the proposal was shelved. As such, the cost of paying for the maintenance of the park fell to Chicago taxpayers as a whole while downtown businesses and property owners continued to enjoy the increased property values and sales revenue it generated.

In light of the fantastic public space Millennium Park created, there was little objection to either the use of TIF funds for the park or to the rejection of the special amenity tax in the Loop. As such the park shows the ability of green urban entrepreneurialism to create a level of legitimacy for urban transformation that obscures the distribution of the costs and benefits of these endeavors.[59] A blog on an online local magazine illustrated what seemed to be a widely shared public feeling about Millennium Park. After describing an idyllic July day spent in the park, the blogger wrote, "Maybe ... the mayor really did shake me upside down by my ankles to get all the money he could from me to fund the park. But when I look with wonder at ... Millennium Park and see others around me sharing my amazement, I begin to think maybe it was even worth it. All I can really say is: Thank you Mayor Daley."[60]

Quality of Life and Corporate Subsidies

Greening Chicago was a successful entrepreneurial strategy in that it revitalized downtown and generated tourism in a way that appeared to provide benefits to all residents. It also served to further another important goal of urban entrepreneurialism, attracting corporate headquarters. Under Daley some of Chicago's most notable new business headquarters included Boeing, United Airlines, MillerCoors, and German wind power manufacturer Nordex. The reasons for any business to relocate are of course multifold.[61] Yet Daley frequently pointed to the greening of Chicago, the improvements in the quality of life in the city under his watch, and the city's commitment to the environment, as important reasons why industries chose to relocate there.[62] Highlighting the ability of the greener city to attract corporate headquarters helped legitimize the large public expenditure on greening projects. But it also served a more nefarious purpose. It allowed officials to downplay massive taxpayer subsidies to multibillion dollar industries. An example of this can be seen in the relocation decision of Boeing.

In 2001 Boeing, one of the world's largest airline manufacturers and defense contractors, moved its headquarters to Chicago from Seattle. After the relocation decision was made, Daley and others insisted that quality of life and environmental amenities were a main reason why Boeing chose Chicago.[63] While the relocation was being considered, however, local and state governments clearly did not feel that the city could compete on its amenities alone. Though "insisting that incentives were not the major factor [in its decision], Boeing sought favorable relocation deals from each city" it was considering, and Chicago was by far the most generous in its offering.[64] In contrast to Denver, which offered very minimal subsidies, and Dallas, which promised less than $20 million, between the City of Chicago and the State of Illinois, Boeing received approximately $54 million in subsidies and tax breaks.[65] The governor of Illinois asserted that the move would bring a 100 to 1 return on the public money spent attracting the company, though it was never made clear exactly how the relocation would generate such a remarkable return.[66] Probably more accurate was an Illinois Senator's assertion that Chicago's ability to attract Boeing and (he did not say) the millions of public dollars given to the corporation "sends a signal to other companies that we're open to do business."[67] And willing to pay handsomely for it.

Despite this rather brazen form of post-industrial smokestack chasing in the form of taxpayer subsidies to one of the world's largest companies, the claims made by Daley that the quality of life in Chicago and its commitment to the environment is what made it so successful at attracting global corporate headquarters seemed to have broad resonance with much of the Chicago public.[68] As with Millennium Park, middle-class residents appeared to relate to the emphasis on the city's enhanced environment and quality of life as defining factors in the attractiveness of the city. Connecting this explicitly to economic growth and the new jobs brought by corporate headquarters further legitimized both urban greening and Chicago's broader entrepreneurial endeavors.

Celebrating Green Chicago

Several years into the twenty-first century, the list of Daley's environmental accomplishments had grown quite long. It included the creation of 200 acres of new and revitalized parks and 1300 acres of open space, the planting of upwards of 600,000 trees, policies that led to more green roofs than any other city in the nation (including a much-promoted 20,300 square foot green roof on City Hall), more LEED certified buildings than any other city in the U.S., the expansion of bike lanes, and a model brownfield remediation program.[69] For those who saw the potential for a more sustainable society as residing in cities, Chicago seemed to offer proof that even the roughest industrial city could be transformed into an environmental leader.[70]

If Chicago's physical environment had been successfully transformed through green urban entrepreneurialism, its image had been even more so. The national press lavished praise on Chicago's greening and on the economic benefits that had accompanied it.[71] The *Economist* put Daley's greening efforts at the heart of the "remarkable transformation" that the city had undergone.[72] In 2006 the *New York Times* called Chicago "one of the most beautiful cities in America,"[73] shortly followed by *MSN City Guides* asserting that Chicago had become "the green star by which aspiring cities sail."[74] In 2008 Chicago was rated the fourth most sustainable city in the United States,[75] and in 2010 the U.S. Green Building Council (the organization that sponsors LEED certification) created the Mayor Richard M. Daley Legacy Award for Global Leadership in Creating Sustainable Cities. The first winner of the award was Richard M. Daley.[76] The days of Chicago's disinvestment and decline were, by these accounts, clearly a thing of the past. Chicago had emerged as a green, economically vibrant, and global city, even if questions lurked in the shadows as to who was most benefiting from the greener Chicago.

Greening a Concrete Jungle

Birmingham, like Chicago, was remarkably transformed in the late twentieth century, with environmental amenities an important part of its revitalization. Although they faced similar economic conditions of recession and deindustrialization, in some ways Birmingham's entrepreneurial transformation was even less likely than Chicago's. Unlike Chicago, Birmingham lacked any natural waterways, a common focus of entrepreneurial prestige projects. Its city center was well-known for its modernist brutalism, devotion to the automobile, and disregard for pedestrians. That Birmingham leaders had the audacity to attempt to turn the city into a destination for tourists and a home for skilled post-industrial labor was surprising to many, and their success at doing so even more astonishing.

In the 1980s, as it became clear that manufacturing would never be the economic driver of the region it once had been, Birmingham officials decided that the city, which only decades before had been rebuilt with such gusto, would have to be transformed yet again. The 1985 Economic Strategy for Birmingham outlined two main tactics for job creation and economic growth. These were to promote business tourism through becoming a major conference and exhibition center and to attract knowledge workers and investment through "the creation of a new, international, city image."[77] As discussed above, these strategies are two of the pillars of urban entrepreneurialism. Such endeavors, though already beginning in the U.S., had not yet become common across the Atlantic. As Birmingham began to realize these goals it therefore became one of Europe's first entrepreneurial cities.[78]

Birmingham's plans faced two major and related obstacles: the concrete jungle of the city center and, what proved to be the more difficult challenge, the city's reputation as a terribly unpleasant place, "reviled for its concrete brutalism and its disdain for the pedestrian."[79] Descriptions from sources such as the *Raw Guide to Birmingham and the Black Country* did not help the situation. The *Raw Guide* colorfully described the experience of visiting the city by asserting that "the great God Motor Car ruled the minds of Birmingham's developers, leaving the befuddled pedestrian to scuttle and delve through [urine-soaked] subways and underpasses, popping up for air and daylight like a startled mole."[80] Even the Prince of Wales criticized Birmingham, calling it "a vast concrete maze where only cars felt at home."[81] To the extent that image is vital to the success of a post-industrial city, Birmingham had a lot that needed to change.

Birmingham's Gamble on International Tourism

Birmingham's ability "to offer an inviting and attractive climate to 'knowledge workers' in the service industries, tourists (preferably 'business tourists') and pedestrians with money to spend … was doubted on all sides."[82] Yet the city council was steadfast in its belief that an attractive city center could be created and that it would successfully revitalize the city's economy.[83] A few years after the Economic Strategy for Birmingham outlined the council's commitment to urban entrepreneurialism, the City Centre Strategy introduced the environment into this agenda, asserting that "the quality of the environment and the economic health of the city have a direct effect upon each other."[84] The environment in this context was not, however, a concern with the broader ecological impacts of the city and its development. Rather, it referred to the quality of the experience of residents, visitors, and consumers in the city center.[85]

The first stage of the transformation of Birmingham's city center focused on construction of a massive international convention center, the country's first. The colossal project included eleven conference halls and was accompanied by an indoor arena, symphony hall and Hyatt hotel. The International Convention Center (ICC) was a risky entrepreneurial venture on the part of the council, a multimillion-pound gamble that a collapsing industrial city could become a destination for international business and tourism.[86] The City bet heavily. Between 1986 and 1992, the ICC and the National Indoor Arena (NIA) consumed 18 percent of the Birmingham City Council's total capital spending.[87] Meanwhile, capital spending on education fell 60 percent, and Birmingham spent less on average on housing than other English local authorities, even while facing a large backlog in needed improvements to council homes. Severe cuts were also made to educational operating budgets, with funds diverted to the operating budgets of the ICC and the NIA as well as to major art events and an unsuccessful bid for the 1992 Olympics.[88] By the late 1990s the council had spent over £300 billion redeveloping its central business district.[89]

All of this was consistent with the premises of neoliberalism and urban entrepreneurialism. The idea behind this transfer of funds away from social welfare and public goods was that supporting tourist-focused endeavors would serve as a catalyst to private development. This private investment would then create new jobs, thereby eventually benefiting the city as a whole. As Birmingham's renewal unfolded, it appeared that the council's high-risk investment had paid off, at least on its own terms. The opening of the ICC by the Queen in the summer of 1991 was hailed as the beginning of the rebirth of the derelict city and indicative of its transformation into a vibrant, cosmopolitan center.[90] The ICC was soon hosting around five hundred conferences a year, including NATO meetings, the G8 summit, and annual conferences of all major political parties. As was its goal, the ICC put Birmingham on the map as a destination for business tourism in Europe.

The construction of the ICC was accompanied by broader changes in the physical appearance of the central city, creating the pleasant "environment" that, as the City Centre Strategy predicted, helped attract tourists and new residents. There were two primary ways this was done. The first was extensive pedestrianization of city streets and public squares.[91] The second was the transformation of abandoned industrial canals into environmental amenities. Together these changes, by all accounts, made Birmingham a much more beautiful, people-friendly city than it had been, at least in the tourist-oriented city center (Figure 3.3).

One of the first priorities for making the city more accessible to pedestrians was the destruction of the inner ring road that had been built with such unity of purpose only a few decades before. The road that "was intended to liberate, to create movement in and through the city [had instead come to be seen as] the 'concrete collar' that had to be broken if the city was to breathe again" and if the economy of Birmingham was to be reborn.[92] Completed in 1971, parts of the road began to be dismantled in 1988, after barely fifteen years. As the ring road was taken down, pedestrian subways were converted to crosswalks and busy freeways became city streets. A few roads were closed to vehicle traffic altogether. Accompanying this was the enhancement of the city's public spaces.[93] Numerous public plazas around the city center were constructed or improved and filled with trees, fountains, public art, and green space. These plazas both connected the main tourist and shopping attractions of the city center and made the area an enjoyable "place in which people are happy to walk and explore."[94] This would have been unthinkable in the car-dominated city center of thirty years earlier, and it is a far cry from the picture painted by the *Raw Guide* quoted above in which pedestrians were compared to moles scuttling through the city's subways. The greening of Britain's auto city was underway.

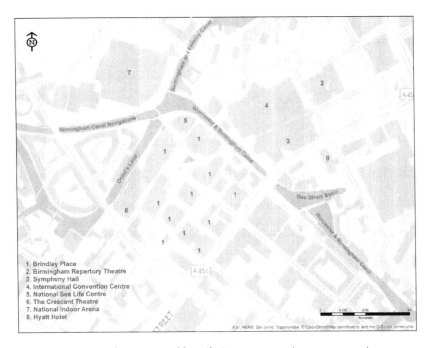

Figure 3.3 Birmingham invested heavily in numerous city center prestige projects in hopes of becoming a destination for international tourism.

Source: Map by Matt Cooney. Map data from mapcruzin.com/free-england-arcgis-maps-shapefiles.htm.

Canals, Consumption, and the Re-Creation of Urban Nature

Traffic calming and the provision of plazas and pedestrian-friendly public space were further enhanced by the creation of Birmingham's most striking environmental amenity – the transformation of its abandoned industrial canals into sites of consumption, leisure, and nature. The Birmingham Canal Navigations system was built between the 1780s and the 1850s and connects the city with much of the rest of England. It contains over 100 miles of canals, 35 of which are within the city limits, and "is one of the most intricate canal networks in the world."[95] During the city's early industrial heyday, canals allowed heavy goods to be shipped in and out of the landlocked city. The canals were especially important for lowering the cost of importing the large quantities of coal demanded by local industry after the steam engine made this commodity crucial to the booming manufacturing sector.[96] Invaluable to Birmingham's industrial development, the construction of railroads and then the modern highway system led the canals to fall into disuse. In the 1960s Cadbury, the last local company still using the canals, finally abandoned them. Birmingham's canals, "polluted and bordered by unused and vandalized factories and warehouses," became dumping grounds for burned cars and other rubbish.[97] Dirty and dangerous, the canals were seen as a liability and a hindrance to development.

The turning point for Birmingham's canals came with the construction of the ICC along the city's major central canal and, right next to the ICC, the massive Brindleyplace mixed-use development. Developers had long avoided the city center, and before Brindleyplace no new private-sector housing had been built in the central area for decades.[98] The council's lavish spending on the ICC and accompanying environmental improvements changed this. As proponents of urban entrepreneurialism predicted, the public investment "spawned significant spin-off private investment including the growth of a significant city centre housing market [that attracted] a young professional residential base into the heart of the city."[99] Construction of Brindleyplace began in 1993 and included offices, shops, restaurants and bars, an aquarium, hotels, and a fitness center, as well as private housing. Notably, the ICC and Brindleyplace successfully utilized the canals as environmental amenities, turning them from a liability to "key factors in attracting new business to 'water-side locations.'"[100] Buildings were built facing toward the canals and numerous waterside cafes and restaurants were included as part of the projects. The canals themselves were cleaned up and beautified with trees, hanging flowers, and pedestrian-friendly tow paths (Figure 3.4).

A 1999 government report examining the possible benefits of greater investment in the country's inland waterways hailed Brindleyplace as a model "project which is already realising the potential of the canals in the transformation of a derelict backwater in Birmingham into an internationally acclaimed example of waterside regeneration, attracting over five million visits a year [and making it] Birmingham's premier entertainment and leisure venue."[101] The commercial success of Brindleyplace inspired additional investment in high-end apartments and shopping centers in the area.[102] By 2007 approximately 9000 new city center homes had been constructed, 85 percent of which were for private sale and many of which were expensive luxury condominiums with price tags upwards of £1 million.[103] The canals, once liabilities, now added the water and natural amenities that Birmingham otherwise lacked but that had become a highly prized attribute of the entrepreneurial, post-industrial city.

Birmingham's physical greening and beautification – the pedestrianization, the canals, and the increase in public art and plazas – are widely seen as essential components in the success of the city's conversion to a tourist destination. Birmingham soon became the destination for more day visitors than any other UK city, with visitors highlighting the canals as their favorite feature of the city center, followed by the shopping.[104]

Figure 3.4 The restored canal through the ICC and Brindleyplace. Note the Hyatt in the background, linked to Brindleyplace by a well-landscaped pedestrian bridge. The canal-side entrance to the ICC is on the left.

Source: Photo by author, 2008.

Upon visiting Birmingham for a meeting of the G8 held at the ICC in 1998, U.S. President Bill Clinton said of the city, "I was astonished when I saw how beautiful Birmingham was. The buildings, the art, the use of water: it is an extraordinary jewel of a city."[105] By 2009 tourism was contributing £4.4 billion a year to the local economy and supporting some 60,000 jobs.[106]

Inequality and Legitimacy in the Entrepreneurial City

Employment in the coveted creative industries increased steadily alongside tourism, representing 41 percent of the job growth in Birmingham between 1998 and 2005. This significantly outpaced the British average of 28.4 percent, though the sector still represented slightly less of Birmingham's overall economy than in the rest of the country.[107] Between 1991 and 2008 employment in the banking, finance, and insurance sector also grew, increasing from 16 to 23 percent of total employment.[108] In 2009 Birmingham was ranked as one of the top three best places to locate a business in the UK and one of the top thirty business locations in Europe.[109] As was the goal of city center revitalization, over half of the job growth in the city was focused in the central business district.[110]

Unsurprisingly, as with the move to the service economy everywhere, there were serious limitations to this change. The development of new high-end housing notwithstanding, many of the best paying jobs in the new economy were held by people who commuted in from the more affluent suburbs.[111] In addition to the environmental impact of commuting, this raised questions about whether the spending by the council to revitalize the city center actually benefited the residents of Birmingham. Furthermore, most of the jobs that were being created to cater to the steadily increasing convention and tourist industry were insecure and low paying.[112] This was accompanied by persistently high levels of unemployment and poverty in many of Birmingham's central wards. Indeed, unemployment remained highest in the areas closest to the newly revitalized city center, with unemployment in Aston, Nechells, and Ladywood, the three wards in which the downtown area sits, having unemployment in May 2010 of 28 percent, 25.1 percent, and 22.7 percent respectively.[113] This was substantially higher than the city-wide rate of just over 11 percent. Poverty and unemployment were closely connected to race and ethnicity, with 76.5 percent of Aston's population, 56.5 percent of the population of Nechells, and 40 percent of Ladywood's residents black and ethnic minority, compared with 29.6 percent of Birmingham as a whole.[114] Though the causes of the poverty and unemployment in these communities were multifaceted, clearly Birmingham's new post-industrial economy had left many behind.

Despite this, Birmingham's physical and economic transformation had broad public support, providing legitimacy to the City's entrepreneurial endeavors. Even as the council spent extravagantly, and riskily, with the construction of the ICC and other developments, "local opposition to the increasingly speculative activities of the city council [was] conspicuous by its absence."[115] The reasons given for this vary. Some have attributed it to a lack of opportunity for resistance in the face of "a political consensus within the city (both within the City Council and between the public and private sectors), a supportive local media, and because there was no requirement to have a public referendum on the bond issue which part-financed the developments."[116] Others, however, have argued that the projects were widely accepted not because of the institutional suppression of dissent but because of the severity of the economic crisis facing Birmingham and the hope for economic growth that the developments promised.

According to this perspective, throughout the 1980s there was a "deep sense of foreboding" in Birmingham as social unrest swelled and people increasingly felt that the local economy, having rapidly plummeted from one of the most prosperous in the nation to one of the most deprived, was unlikely to recover.[117] This collective hopelessness regarding the future of Birmingham built support across the political and socioeconomic spectrum for the city's entrepreneurialism and the public expenditure it entailed. The design of the developments themselves helped this, alluding to and successfully repackaging the strength of the city's industrial past in a way that "legitimat[ed] the transition from an industrialized to a de-industrialized landscape, a landscape of production to a landscape of consumption [in order to] create a sense of social solidarity, civic pride and loyalty to place."[118] According to some analyses, Birmingham's physical transformation was seen by residents as "the visible manifestations of the essence of [economic] recovery" and indicative of the potential for a bright post-industrial future.[119] This weakened potential objections to the distributional inequities of this transformation.[120]

Furthermore, although the pedestrianization of the city center and the restoration of industrial canals do not offer quite the same level of spectacular affect as Chicago's Millennium Park, the environmental amenities that accompanied Birmingham's post-industrial renaissance have indeed provided some benefits to a wide variety of residents. Today the water of the canals bustle with narrowboats, and the tow paths that were once used by horses to pull heavy barges of coal are filled with joggers, walkers, picnickers and, as will be discussed at greater length in Chapter 7, cyclists from various walks of life. Though swimming is not allowed in the canals (their industrial legacy leaves the concern of lingering contaminants), animals have returned including otters (which until recently were nearly extinct in English waterways) and fish, and they provide important habitat for birds, butterflies, and other insects.[121] As in Chicago, the real, if limited, benefits of green urban entrepreneurialism to nature and to city residents helped secure public support for broader policies of urban transformation.

Greening Birmingham for All

By the early years of the twenty-first century Birmingham had successfully used a combination of traditional urban entrepreneurial prestige projects and green urban entrepreneurialism to reinvent the economy and the built environment of the city. Even so, problems of poverty and social exclusion remained, even if this did not translate into protest against the city's endeavors. Interestingly, as will be discussed in the following chapters, Birmingham soon began undertaking efforts to spread the benefits of its green transformation through a prioritization of social equity within its environmental initiatives. City officials also began thinking more holistically about Birmingham's role in broader issues of environmental governance, particularly climate change. Yet even as they did so, the fundamental goal of rebranding the city and revitalizing its economy remained paramount, limiting the city's ultimate ability to move beyond green urban entrepreneurialism.

Livability and Global City Ambitions

The story of green urban entrepreneurialism in Vancouver offers an interesting comparison to Birmingham and Chicago. As discussed in Chapter 2, Vancouver did not experience the same level of industrial greatness and decline as did the other two cities, though the industrial land surrounding False Creek was to play a vital part of the city's post-industrial transformation. Indeed, environmental protection and amenities have played a part in Vancouver's development agenda since the 1970s. Because greening had a more predominant place in Vancouver politics for longer than in either Chicago or Birmingham, when green urban entrepreneurialism emerged in Vancouver it did not illustrate a new discursive commitment to city environmentalism. Rather, green urban entrepreneurialism represented a shift from the green, livable city as a challenge to unbridled development to greening becoming a key aspect of the city's pro-development brand.

The Birth of Global Vancouver

The beginning of urban entrepreneurialism in Vancouver was the BC Place stadium, built on land purchased by the province from the railway company that was one of the city's major landowners.[122] Led by BC premier Bill Bennett, efforts to build the 55,000-seat waterfront stadium started in the late 1970s with the explicit goal that it would "help anchor a major redevelopment in the surrounding False Creek industrial district," raise Vancouver's global profile, and serve as "a symbolic gesture expressing great optimism about the future outlook" of the city and provincial economies.[123] Though plagued with financial troubles and suffering from conspicuously poor design,[124] BC Place did host a "quite remarkable" number of events and was the centerpiece of Vancouver's first global megaevent, Expo '86.[125]

Megaevents are an important element of urban entrepreneurialism and place promotion, often leaving long-term legacies in the cities who host them.[126] The 1986 World Exposition on Transportation and Communication (generally referred to as Expo '86), as well as the 2010 Olympic and Paralympic Games discussed in Chapter 4, were no exceptions. These events and the politics that surrounded them had major impacts on development and sustainability in Vancouver. Expo '86 in particular "is widely hailed as the start of the young city's transformation from a sleepy little town into the international metropolis it is today."[127] The six-month world's fair was undoubtedly undertaken with this very goal in mind, as part of a larger plan to diversify the regional and city economy by appealing to global capital, elites, and tourists. "Internationalization was the explicit intent of the fair, with marketing slogans such as: 'An invitation to the world' and 'What your world is coming to in 1986.'"[128] Through Expo '86, the beauty and economic potential of Vancouver would be shown to the world.

As with the ICC in Birmingham, the money dedicated to Expo '86 illustrated the entrepreneurial state's willingness to use public funds to spur investment and private profit, even as the public sector struggled. Indeed, "Expo '86 was propelled into existence as a loss leader. ... Construction went ahead during an economic recession while there were severe cutbacks on social programs."[129] In a highly unionized region, non-union companies were awarded building contracts and, despite substantial community organizing, over a thousand low-income residents of the nearby Downtown Eastside were evicted as hotels prepared for an influx of tourists.[130] Expo '86 ended with a $311 million public deficit, eventually paid off through provincial lottery sales.[131]

Despite its social and financial costs, from the perspective of city promotion Expo '86 was a huge success. It recorded 22 million visits from around the world and put British Columbia in general, and Vancouver in particular, on the global tourist map. A number of key pieces of tourist infrastructure remained after the event including the stadium, a convention center, a cruise-ship terminal, and the SkyTrain rapid transit line.[132] Tourism continued to increase in Vancouver after the fair, and it was estimated that Expo '86 "generated an extra 20,000 visitors per month to the city for seven years after the event."[133] As tourism flourished the natural beauty of the region was put front and center. For example, "the lead column in a 1992 *Maclean's* issue on British Columbia [asserted]: 'British Columbia's most visible asset is not its coal, timber or mineral potential. Its riches are mostly rooted in the fact that it is postcard pretty.'"[134] Vancouver's new global image had arrived.

Megadevelopments and Quality Urban Design

After Expo '86 the provincial government, as part of its broader privatization program, sold 204 acres of land that had been used for the event to a major Hong Kong developer for what many saw as a paltry price of $320 million.[135] The site, which included much of the north shore of False Creek, became the anchor of the transformation of Vancouver's deindustrialized shoreline. Throughout the 1980s Vancouver's economy had become increasingly connected with global capital, particularly investment from Hong Kong as the wealthy sought safe places to put their money in preparation for the territory being turned over to Chinese rule in 1997. This was aided by federal policies that encouraged the immigration of wealthy foreigners to Canada, creating increased personal and professional links between Vancouver and Hong Kong.[136] Though ties between Vancouver and East Asia were longstanding and had been building for years, "the purchase [of the Expo '86 site] was a dramatic expression of the globalization of Vancouver's economy and of Asian inroads into the city's commercial and residential property markets."[137] The important role of Asian investment in Vancouver real estate, though intentionally encouraged by the province and probably one of the reasons Concord Pacific (the name for the shell company set up by the Hong Kong developer) won the bid for the property,[138] continues to be a source of contention in Vancouver politics.

The master plan for the Concord Pacific Place megadevelopment was ambitious, and it was created with marked cooperation between Concord Pacific and city planners (Figure 3.5). Yaletown, the first part of the Concord Pacific development, along with Coal Harbour, another megadevelopment undertaken on the north side of the downtown peninsula around the same time, transformed Vancouver (Figure 3.6). At the core of both megadevelopments were the now-iconic glass high-rises that create density while maintaining residents' light and their views of the ocean and mountains. The shift from the low-rise housing along the parts of False Creek developed in the 1970s was stark, and with these new

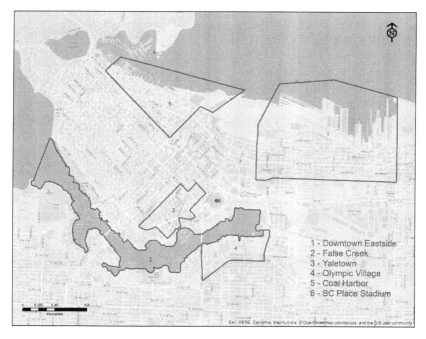

Figure 3.5 Megadevelopments such as Yaletown and Coal Harbour transformed central Vancouver.

Source: Map by Matt Cooney and Noah Villamarin-Cutter.

developments the skyline of Vancouver was dramatically changed and the population of the city center skyrocketed.

Even as many celebrated Vancouver's emerging position as an international city, the rapid growth and unfamiliarly high-density development that was occurring raised concerns about maintaining Vancouver's livability.[139] In 1990 one of the region's major newspapers ran a series called "Future Growth. Future Shock." In it an optimism for the city's global future was tempered by worries about regional growth management, increased traffic congestion, and a fear that dealing with projected population growth would lead the region to "end up like every other unattractive place on earth," thereby hurting both livability and future growth prospects.[140] The generally pro-development newspaper argued that the answer to these challenges was "sustainable development: growth that maintains the quality of life Vancouverites cherish. ... Protected and healthy, the region's spectacular environment [would] be its 'greatest business opportunity' attracting 'some of the best brains in the world' to the area."[141] Unlike calls for livability in the 1970s that strove to temper the development imperative, sustainable development would maintain Vancouver's livability by encouraging growth.

The City articulated this call for sustainable development with the principle of "Living First," championed in the 1991 Central Area Plan.[142] Living First is illustrative of Vancouver's particular type of green urban entrepreneurialism. Growth and development were undoubtedly its goal. But Living First also offered a relatively holistic approach to urban development. It "sought to create a more compact, integrated, mixed-use community in downtown Vancouver. This strategy included the encouragement of housing intensification and diversity; the development of coherent neighbourhood structure plans, a focus on transportation alternatives such as public transit, walking and cycling; and the fostering of a more domestic urban design and public realm to mitigate the effects of high-density residential living," particularly through environmental and social amenities and high-quality public spaces.[143]

Attempts to implement the ideas of Living First can be seen in the generous public amenities of Concord Pacific Place and Coal Harbour. As part of the design process, city planners required developers to include streets full of trees, parks, art, a publicly accessible pedestrian walkway and bikeway along the shore (the "seawall"), and other environmental amenities. The goal of these requirements was to maintain the quality of the living experience in the high-density developments. The combination of political commitment to quality design and the unique form of discretionary zoning in Vancouver that led to the inclusion of these amenities in the new megadevelopments set a long-term precedent for new development in the city.[144] The goal was to "create an urban living experience that [was] better than people's ideas of the suburbs. That [was] more fun. More safe. More efficient."[145] This would then attract skilled labor to the city center. The efforts were successful, and through beauty, quality design, and environmental amenities the new developments drew tens of thousands of new residents to downtown, particularly the growing "'new class' of often young, highly educated, and affluent workers" in the expanding managerial and professional jobs that were accompanying Vancouver's emergence as a global financial center.[146] As downtown was transformed from rail yards and industrial land to condominiums, the population of the city center swelled from well under 50,000 people in the early 1990s to around 85,000 by 2006, with more new developments underway and demand for new housing strong.[147]

Green urban entrepreneurialism always prioritizes enhancing the experience of the city. In this way Living First and the amenities of the new megadevelopments were not exceptional. They were, perhaps, green urban entrepreneurialism at its best. What makes these developments unique is that even in the midst of the aggressive pro-development agenda of the 1990s, Vancouver leaders were willing to require substantial public amenities from developers. Though increasing the attractiveness of the properties, this also created real costs for developers. That

Figure 3.6 Yaletown, part of the Concord Pacific Place megadevelopment, as viewed from False Creek. Trees in the foreground mark the public seawall, and BC Place Stadium is on the right.

Source: Photo by author, 2014.

city planners had developers pay for the amenities rather than passing the cost on to taxpayers is a notable contrast to Birmingham and Chicago, and is indicative of Vancouver's more ambivalent embrace of neoliberalism.

Other challenges by Vancouver officials to neoliberal urbanism's growth-first orientation can also be seen during this time period. One example is the continuation of the trend away from freeways that the city had begun several decades before, even when doing so inconvenienced downtown businesses and residents. Indeed, a major principle of Living First "was to limit any increase in vehicle access to downtown by a policy of not building additional bridges or traffic lanes, so as to let congestion become an ally in creating more amenable urban living."[148] A second divergence from neoliberal urbanism was the requirement that developers of megadevelopments provide space for schools, libraries, community centers and daycares and that the projects include 25 percent family housing and 20 percent affordable housing, integrated throughout the developments.[149] As such, Vancouver's green urban entrepreneurialism gave greater emphasis to social inclusion and environmental effectiveness than the early years of neoliberal environmentalism in Chicago and Birmingham.

Vancouver's approach to development and to post-industrial branding was wildly successful. By the end of the decade Concord Pacific Place and Coal Harbour were widely held to be "among the most successful large-scale redevelopment projects anywhere in North America."[150] In 2005 the *Economist* rated Vancouver the most livable city in the world, a distinction it would be given many times in the years to follow. Beginning in 2004, the high-end travel magazine *Conde Nast* began frequently highlighting Vancouver as one of the best cities to visit in the Americas.[151]

The Challenge of Livability

For many, Vancouver's transformation was a clear success. For others, there was a notable downside. The high-quality urban environment, increased foreign investment, and the global accolades of the city's development achievements increased demand for Vancouver property, and housing prices began to rise. The average price of a detached home in 1985 was under $125,000. By the turn of the century this had more than tripled, and by January 2016 the average price of a detached single family home in Vancouver was over $1.8 million.[152] The price of attached homes and condominiums, though not seeing quite as dramatic an increase, and tempered somewhat by the expansion in supply as the areas around False Creek were developed, roughly doubled during this same time period.[153] By the early twenty-first century only 20 percent of renters could afford a starter home, and an estimated 42 percent of young singles and 60 percent of older residents of single-room occupancy hotels (SROs) spent more than 50 percent of their income on rent; 10,000 people were on the waiting list for low-income housing in the Downtown Eastside and the same number were estimated to be looking for low-income market units.[154] The greener, more livable city was increasingly out of reach.

In addition to being a financial burden for many residents, increasing housing costs also raised concerns about gentrification. A particular focus of concern, but also resistance, was the DTES. Though many very low-income residents of the neighborhood had been evicted as their single room occupancy apartments were converted to hotels for visitors to Expo '86, the DTES remained Vancouver's poorest district. As the neighboring Coal Harbour and Concord Pacific areas were developed and became some of the most deeply gentrified in the city,[155] development pressure increased on the DTES. For a time, gentrification was slowed by three aspects of the area. The first was a combination of drugs, prostitution, HIV and other diseases, "noxious industrial plants, a local left-wing political culture that [was] tolerant of unpredictable public behaviour," and extensive social services aimed at the area's poor, all of which made the area less appealing to the middle class.[156]

The second limit to gentrification, equally if not more important than the first, was the organizing and political strength of the Downtown Eastside Residents Association (DERA). As plans for the new downtown megadevelopments unfolded nearby in the late 1980s and early 1990s, DERA successfully secured housing assistance from various levels of government. By 1992 it had over 600 new and renovated social housing units in its portfolio. Aware that this "new social housing might upgrade a landscape of run-down residential hotels and encourage private reinvestment, a raw, non-aesthetic building style was preferred for housing projects."[157] DERA also achieved other important improvements for DTES residents including a park, a community center, the blockage of a proposed casino, and the closure of a problematic liquor store.[158] The third reason that the DTES resisted gentrification through the rapid development of the 1990s was that much of this new development was on abandoned or underutilized land. Extensive tracts of land facilitated the large-scale projects favored by developers and city planners.[159] Smaller, heavily developed and populated areas such as DTES were more difficult to work with and therefore less desirable.

Eventually the city's growth pressure would reach the DTES. In 2003, the City bought an abandoned Woodward's department store building in the area that it turned into 200 units of social housing and 546 market-rate condos. The social housing was certainly a victory for affordable housing advocates. However, indicative of the growing demand for housing in the city, the market-rate condos "sold out in 12 hours, mostly to first-time homeowners in their mid-20s to mid-30s unable to afford Yaletown's and Coal Harbour's high prices and willing to wait a couple of years for occupancy. Critics feared the consequence would be to push the poor" out of the neighborhood.[160] As will be seen in the following chapters, these conflicts around development, displacement, and livability continue to be central to Vancouver politics.

Ambivalent Embrace of Neoliberal Environmentalism

As Vancouver emerged as a global, post-industrial city in the late twentieth century, greening and natural beauty contributed mightily to its appeal. A vibrant urban center with generous natural amenities drew investors, tourists, and residents to downtown, and the city gained global recognition for the quality of its urban planning. Although environmental amenities were clearly promoted as essential to growth, neoliberal environmentalism was somewhat more tempered in Vancouver than in Birmingham or Chicago. From early on the city wrestled explicitly with the social and environmental impact of new development, and more visible challenges to the exclusionary aspects of green urban entrepreneurialism emerged in Vancouver than in either other city. This undoubtedly led to more concrete environmental and social equity goals being incorporated into the city's development. However, as will be seen in the next chapter, even as Vancouver pushed to make development more sustainable, social equity in particular sat uneasily with the green branding that increasingly defined Vancouver's international reputation.

Conclusion

As evidenced in all three cities discussed in this chapter, green urban entrepreneurialism was fundamentally focused on growth. But the nods to sustainable development it incorporated meant that green urban entrepreneurialism also contained within it alternative discourses of environmental effectiveness and social well-being. Though these goals were often in tension with the prioritization of growth and development, they also offered challenges to neoliberal urbanism. This opened up spaces for alternative varieties of liberal environmentalism to emerge. As such, green urban entrepreneurialism set the groundwork for more ambitious environmental commitments as city leaders began justifying energy efficiency, enhanced transit, compact urban development, and other initiatives as economically as well as environmentally beneficial. Likewise, the promises of universal benefits from the greener city, though unrealized, created political openings for work toward a more just distribution of the benefits of urban environmentalism and a more inclusive understanding of the sustainable city. Yet even as cities have moved beyond green urban entrepreneurialism in recent years, its premises continue to shape city environmentalism. The way that calls for a more environmentally effective and equitable green city began to push Vancouver, Birmingham, and

Chicago beyond green urban entrepreneurialism, and the limits of this move, is the focus of the next chapter.

Notes

1 Jason R. Hackworth, *The Neoliberal City: Governance, Ideology, and Development in American Urbanism* (Ithaca, NY: Cornell University Press, 2007); Dennis R. Judd and Randy L. Ready, "Entrepreneurial Cities and the New Politics of Economic Development," in *Reagan and the Cities*, ed. George E. Peterson and Carol W. Lewis (Washington, DC: Urban Institute Press, 1986).
2 David Harvey, "From Managerialism to Entrepreneurialism: The Transformation in Urban Governance in Late Capitalism," *Geografiska Annaler, Series B, Human Geography* 71, no. 1 (1989): 7.
3 Susan E. Clarke and Gary L. Gaile, *The Work of Cities*, Globalization and Community (Minneapolis, MN: University of Minnesota Press, 1998); Bob Jessop, "The Entrepreneurial City: Re-Imagining Localities, Redesigning Economic Governance, or Restructuring Capital?," in *Transforming Cities: Contested Governance and New Spatial Divisions*, ed. Nick Jewson and Susanne MacGregor (New York, NY: Routledge, 1997); Arantxa Rodríguez, Erik Swyngedouw, and Frank Moulaert, "Urban Restructuring, Social-Political Polarization, and New Urban Politics," in *The Globalized City: Economic Restructuring and Social Polarization in European Cities*, ed. Frank Moulaert, Arantxa Rodríguez, and Erik Swyngedouw (Oxford, UK: Oxford University Press, 2003).
4 Phil Hubbard, "Urban Design and Local Economic Development: A Case Study in Birmingham," *Cities* 12, no. 4 (1995); Rachel Weber, "Extracting Value from the City," in *Spaces of Neoliberalism: Urban Restructuring in North America and Western Europe*, ed. Neil Brenner and Nikolas Theodore (Malden, MA: Blackwell, 2002).
5 See Richard L. Florida, *The Rise of the Creative Class: And How It's Transforming Work, Leisure, Community and Everyday Life* (New York, NY: Basic Books, 2004).
6 Hackworth, 67.
7 See Saskia Sassen, *The Global City*, 2nd edn. (Princeton, NJ: Princeton University Press, 2001).
8 Stephen V. Ward, *Selling Places: The Marketing and Promotion of Towns and Cities, 1850–2000* (London: E & FN Spon, 1998), 186.
9 Briavel Holcomb, "Revisioning Place: De- and Re-Constructing the Image of the Post-Industrial City," in *Selling Places: The City as Cultural Capital, Past and Present*, ed. Gerard Kearns and Chris Philo (Oxford, UK: Pergamon Press, 1993); Dennis R. Judd, "Promoting Tourism in US Cities," in *Readings in Urban Theory*, ed. Susan S. Fainstein and Scott Campbell (Malden, MA: Blackwell Publishers, 2002 [1995]).
10 Lance Berelowitz, *Dream City: Vancouver and the Global Imagination* (Vancouver, BC: Douglas & McIntyre, 2005).
11 Aidan While, Andrew EG Jonas, and David Gibbs, "The Environment and the Entrepreneurial City: Searching for the Urban 'Sustainability Fix' in Manchester and Leeds," *International Journal of Urban and Regional Research* 28, no. 3 (2004): 550.
12 Jamie Peck and Adam Tickell, "Searching for a New Institutional Fix: The After-Fordist Crisis and the Global-Local Disorder," in *Post-Fordism: A Reader*, ed. Ash Amin (Oxford, UK: Blackwell, 1994).

13 Mike Beazley, Patrick Loftman, and Brendan Nevin, "Downtown Redevelopment and Community Resistance: An International Perspective," in *Transforming Cities: Contested Governance and New Spatial Divisions*, ed. Nick Jewson and Susanne MacGregor (New York: Routledge, 1997); Stephen V. Ward, *Planning the Twentieth-Century City: The Advanced Capitalist World* (Chichester, UK: Wiley, 2002).

14 Helga Leitner, "Cities in Pursuit of Economic Growth: The Local State as Entrepreneur," *Political Geography Quarterly* 9, no. 2 (1990): 159.

15 Beazley, Loftman, and Nevin.

16 Hackworth.

17 See Helga Leitner, Jamie Peck, and Eric S. Sheppard, eds., *Contesting Neoliberalism: Urban Frontiers* (New York, NY: Guilford Press, 2007).

18 Rodríguez, Swyngedouw, and Moulaert, 36.

19 Leonard Nevarez, *New Money, Nice Town: How Capital Works in the New Urban Economy* (New York, NY: Routledge, 2003), 11; see also Terry Nichols Clark et al., "Amenities Drive Urban Growth," *Journal of Urban Affairs* 24, no. 5 (2002).

20 Anne M. Cronin and Kevin Hetherington, "Introduction," in *Consuming the Entrepreneurial City: Image, Memory, Spectacle*, ed. Kevin Hetherington and Anne M. Cronin (New York, NY: Routledge, 2008).

21 Economist, "Chicago: A Success Story," *Economist* 2006.

22 Saskia Sassen, "A Global City," in *Global Chicago*, ed. Charles Madigan (Urbana, IL: University of Illinois Press, 2004), 16.

23 See John P. Koval et al., eds., *The New Chicago: A Social and Cultural Analysis* (Philadelphia, PA: Temple University Press, 2006).

24 E.g. Economist; Clark et al; Eleanora Pasotti, *Political Branding in Cities: The Decline of Machine Politics in Bogotá, Naples, and Chicago* (Cambridge, UK: Cambridge University Press, 2009).

25 Chicago Department of Development and Planning, "Chicago 21: A Plan for the Central Area Communities" (Chicago, IL, 1973).

26 Fassil Demissie, "Globalization and the Remaking of Chicago," in *The New Chicago: A Social and Cultural Analysis*, ed. John P. Koval, et al. (Philadelphia, PA: Temple University Press, 2006).

27 Navy Pier, "About Navy Pier," https://navypier.com/about-us/ (accessed May 23, 2017).

28 Elmer W. Johnson, *Chicago Metropolis 2020: The Chicago Plan for the Twenty-First Century* (Chicago, IL: University of Chicago Press, 2001).

29 Demissie.

30 James Jr. Krohe, "Green Streets: Mayor Daley Has a Thing for Trees. He Wants Half a Million of Them Planted Here by 1992," *Chicago Reader*, January 18, 1990.

31 G. Robert Hillman, "Return to the National Stage," *Dallas Morning News*, August 25, 1996; Edward Walsh, "In Chicago, No Daley Double," *Washington Post*, August 24, 1996.

32 For example, Walsh.

33 Greg Hinz, "'96 Convention Countdown; the $180-Million Party; City's Primping for Democrats Adds Up," *Crain's Chicago Business*, August 19, 1996.

34 Hillman.

35 Carol Goar, "Asphalt Gardens," *Toronto Star*, August 18, 1996.

36 Quoted in Hillman, 1A.

37 City of Chicago, Chicago Park District, and Forest Preserve District of Cook County, "CitySpace: On Open Space Plan for Chicago" (Chicago, IL, 1998).

38 Ibid., ii.

39 Pasotti.

40 Chicago parks planner, personal communication, April 2015.

41 William Cronon, *Nature's Metropolis: Chicago and the Great West*, 1st edn. (New York, NY: W. W. Norton, 1991).

42 Timothy J. Gilfoyle, *Millennium Park: Creating a Chicago Landmark*, Historical Studies of Urban America (Chicago, IL: University of Chicago Press, 2006).

43 Fred A. Bernstein, "Big Shoulders, Big Donors, Big Art," *New York Times*, July 18, 2004, 24.

44 Blair Kamin, "Will Chicago's Long-Awaited Millennium Park Be Fine Art or Spectacle? Perhaps a Little of Both," *Architectural Record* 192, no. 5 (2004).

45 Stephen Kinzer, "A Prized Project, a Mayor and Persistent Criticism," *New York Times*, July 13, 2004.

46 Debbie Howlett, "Donors' Cash Turns City Green," *USA Today*, July 15, 2004; Andrew Stern, "Metal Petals Chicago Reclaims Its Architectural Crown," *Guardian*, July 5, 2004.

47 Keith Schneider, "To Revitalize a City, Try Spreading Some Mulch," *New York Times*, May 17, 2006.

48 Ibid.

49 Howlett.

50 David Usborne, "For First Time in Decades, Chicago Faces Life without a Daley in Charge," *UK Independent*, September 9, 2010.

51 Goodman Williams Group and URS Corporation, *Millennium Park Economic Impact Study* (Chicago, IL: Prepared for City of Chicago Department of Planning and Development, 2005).

52 Irish Times, "Civic Regeneration Brings Property Boom to Chicago," *Irish Times*, September 23, 2004.

53 E.g. New York Times, "After Mayor Daley," *New York Times*, September 9, 2010; Andres Viglucci, "In Chicago's Revival, a Model for Miami?," *Miami Herald*, December 30, 2007.

54 Edward K. Uhlir, "The Millennium Park Effect," *Economic Development Journal* 4, no. 2 (2005).

55 See Ben Joravsky, "Go on, Smash It," *Chicago Reader*, August 19, 2010.

56 Viglucci.

57 Howlett.

58 Quoted in Ably Gallun and Greg Hinz, "City Floats Tax Hike for Loop," *Crain's Chicago Business*, August 29, 2005, 1.

59 See Phil Hubbard and Tim Hall, "The Entrepreneurial City and the 'New Urban Politics,'" in *The Entrepreneurial City: Geographies of Politics, Regime, and Representation*, ed. Tim Hall and Phil Hubbard (Chichester, UK: Wiley, 1998).

60 Brian C. Thomas, "Millennium Park: Thank Mayor Daley for a Chicago Treasure," *Chicago Now*, July 5, 2010, www.chicagonow.com/blogs/your-doubting-thomas/2010/07/millennium-park-thank-mayor-daley-for-a-chicago-treasure.html#ixzz18xql9CLA (accessed December 23, 2010).

61 Vanessa Strauss-Kahn and Xavier Vives, "Why and Where Do Headquarters Move?," *Regional Science and Urban Economics* 39 (2009).

62 City of Chicago, "Press Release: Mayor Daley Welcomes Nordex, USA, to Chicago" (2009); Teresa Garcia-Mila and Therese J. McGuire, "Tax Incentives and the City," *Brookings-Wharton Papers on Urban Affairs* (2002).

63 Uhlir; Economist, "Green Machine," *Economist*, August 15, 2002.

64 Garcia-Mila and McGuire, 18.

65 Ibid., 112, fn35.
66 David Barboza, "Chicago, Offering Big Incentives, Will Be Boeing's New Home," *New York Times*, May 11, 2001.
67 Quoted in Garcia-Mila and McGuire, 113.
68 For example, Schneider; Adele Simmons, "Introduction," in *Global Chicago*, ed. Charles Madigan (Urbana, IL: University of Illinois Press, 2004).
69 Center for Park Excellence, "Chicago's Green Mayor: The Legacy of Richard Daley," http://cityparksblog.org/2010/10/27/chicagos-green-mayor-the-legacy-of-richard-daley/ (accessed December 16, 2010); City of Chicago, "Environment Programs and Initiatives," www.cityofchicago.org/city/en/progs/env.html (accessed November 9, 2010).
70 Warren Karlenzig, *How Green Is Your City?* (Gabriola Island, B.C.: New Society Publishers, 2007).
71 See Steve Allen, "The Greening of Chicago," *Time*, May 12, 2006; Economist, "Chicago: A Success Story."
72 "Green Machine."
73 Schneider, G6.
74 J Gordon, "Is Your City Green?," *MSN City Guides* (2007), http://cityguides.msn.com/citylife/greenarticle.aspx?cp-documentid=4848590 (accessed October 3, 2007).
75 Sustainlane, "2008 U.S. City Rankings," www.sustainlane.com/us-city-rankings/overall-rankings (accessed December 16, 2010; please note: this URL is now inaccessible).
76 Center for Park Excellence.
77 Hubbard, 246.
78 Kevin Ward, "The Limits to Contemporary Urban Redevelopment: 'Doing' Entrepreneurial Urbanism in Birmingham, Leeds and Manchester," *City* 7, no. 2 (2003).
79 Liam Kennedy, "The Creative Destruction of Birmingham," in *Remaking Birmingham: The Visual Culture of Urban Regeneration*, ed. Liam Kennedy (New York: Routledge, 2004), 1.
80 Quoted in Frank Hendriks, *Public Policy and Political Institutions: The Role of Culture in Traffic Policy*, New Horizons in Public Policy (Cheltenham, UK: Edward Elgar, 1999), 97.
81 Quoted in Hubbard, 249.
82 Hendriks, 111.
83 Hubbard.
84 Birmingham City Council 1987, quoted in Peter Brand and Michael J. Thomas, *Urban Environmentalism: Global Change and the Mediation of Local Conflict* (New York, NY: Routledge, 2005), 117.
85 Ibid.
86 Christopher Upton, *A History of Birmingham* (Chichester, Sussex, UK: Phillimore, 1993).
87 Patrick Loftman and Brendan Nevin, "Pro-Growth Local Economic Development Strategies: Civic Promotion and Local Needs in Britain's Second City, 1981–1996," in *The Entrepreneurial City: Geographies of Politics, Regime, and Representation*, ed. Tim Hall and Phil Hubbard (Chichester, UK: Wiley, 1998).
88 Ibid.
89 Beazley, Loftman, and Nevin.
90 Tim Hall, "Public Art, Civic Identity and the New Birmingham," in *Remaking Birmingham: The Visual Culture of Urban Regeneration*, ed. Liam Kennedy (New York, NY: Routledge, 2004); Ward, *Selling Places: The Marketing and Promotion of Towns and Cities, 1850–2000*.

91 Frank Webster, "Reinventing Birmingham, England, in a Globalized Information Economy," in *Globalization and Society: Processes of Differentiation Examined*, ed. Raymond Breton and Jeffrey G. Reitz (Westport, CT: Praeger, 2003).
92 Kennedy, 2.
93 Upton.
94 Ben Flatman, *Birmingham: Shaping the City* (Birmingham, UK: RIBA Publishing, 2008), 38.
95 Waterscape, "BCN," www.waterscape.com/canals-and-rivers/bcn (accessed February 10, 2011).
96 Gordon Emanuel Cherry, *Birmingham: A Study in Geography, History, and Planning* (Chichester, West Sussex, England; New York: J. Wiley, 1994).
97 Webster, 191.
98 Andrew Coulson and Geoff Wright, "Brindleyplace, Birmingham: Creating an Inner City Mixed-Used Development in Times of Recession," *Planning Practice & Research* 28: 256–74 (2013).
99 Veronica Crossa, Montserrat Pareja-Eastaway, and Austin Barber, "Reinventing the City: Barcelona, Birmingham and Dublin," in *Making Competitive Cities*, ed. Sako Musterd and Alan Murie (Chichester, UK: John Wiley & Sons Ltd, 2010), 80.
100 Upton, 214.
101 Quoted in Birmingham Post, "Waterway to Unlock Potential of Our Canals," April 26, 1999, 3.
102 Austin Barber and Stephen Hall, "Birmingham: Whose Urban Renaissance? Regeneration as a Response to Economic Restructuring," *Urban Studies* 29, no. 3 (2008); Ian Latham and Mark Swenarton, eds., *Brindleyplace: A Model for Urban Regeneration* (London, UK: Right Angle Publishing Ltd., 1999).
103 Barber and Hall; Ward.
104 Steve Martin and Graham Pearce, "Policy Review: The Internationalization of Local Authority Economic Development Strategies: Birmingham in the 1980s," *Regional Studies* 26, no. 5 (1992); Card Group, "Birmingham Visitor Survey: A Review of Visitors to the City" (Birmingham, UK 2007).
105 Quoted in University of Birmingham, "Birmingham's Global Profile," www.birmingham.ac.uk/university/about/global.aspx, 2017 (accessed May 23, 2017).
106 Marketing Birmingham, "Birmingham Visitor Economy Overview" (Birmingham, UK 2009).
107 Crossa, Pareja-Eastaway, and Barber.
108 Birmingham Economy, "Employment by Sector in Birmingham 1984–2009," www.birminghameconomy.org.uk (accessed January 5, 2011).
109 Marketing Birmingham, "Annual Review 2008–2009" (Birmingham, UK 2009).
110 Barber and Hall.
111 Crossa, Pareja-Eastaway, and Barber.
112 Hubbard.
113 Birmingham Economy, "Unemployment by Ward," www.birminghameconomy.org.uk (accessed January 5, 2011).
114 Demographic data is as of the 2001 census; "Ethnic Origin by Ward," www.birminghameconomy.org.uk (accessed January 5, 2011).
115 Hubbard, 250.
116 Beazley, Loftman, and Nevin, 190.
117 Webster, 190.
118 Hubbard, 250.

119 Ibid.
120 Hall; Hubbard; Deborah Parsons, "Shopping for the Future: The Re-Enchantment of Birmingham's Urban Space."
121 Birmingham Evening Mail, "Canals Clean – but Don't Go for a Swim," October 9, 2004; Wildlife Trust for Birmingham and the Black Country, "Biodiversity Action," www.wild-net.org/wildbbc/index.aspx?id=528 (accessed February 10, 2011; please note: this URL is now inaccessible).
122 John Punter, *The Vancouver Achievement: Urban Planning and Design* (Vancouver, BC: UBC Press, 2003).
123 Phillip Lee, "The Economic and Social Justification for Publicly Financed Stadia: The Case of Vancouver's BC Place Stadium," *European Planning Studies* 10, no. 7 (2002): 864.
124 Punter.
125 Lee, 869.
126 C. Michael Hall, "Urban Entrepreneurship, Corporate Interests and Sports Mega-Events: The Thin Policies of Competitiveness within the Hard Outcomes of Neoliberalism," *The Sociological Review* 54, no. Supplement s2 (2006).
127 Cheryl Chan, "Expo 86: When Vancouver Wooed the World – 30 Photos, 30 Years Later," *Vancouver Sun*, May 14, 2016, http://vancouversun.com/news/local-news/expo-86-when-vancouver-wooed-the-world-30-photos-30-years-later (accessed January 3, 2017).
128 David Ley, Daniel Hiebert, and Geraldine Pratt, "Time to Grow Up? From Urban Village to World City, 1966–91," in *Vancouver and Its Region*, ed. Graeme Wynn and Timothy Oke (Vancouver, BC: UBC Press, 1992), 239.
129 Ibid., 238.
130 Punter.
131 Chan.
132 Punter.
133 Cited in Andrew Smith, *Events and Urban Regeneration: The Strategic Use of Events to Revitalise Cities* (London, UK: Routledge, 2012), 195.
134 Quoted in Jean Barman, *The West Beyond the West: A History of British Columbia, Third Edition* (Toronto: University of Toronto Press, 2007), 539.
135 Kris Olds, "Globalization and Urban Change: Tales from Vancouver Via Hong Kong," *Urban Geography* 19, no. 4 (1998).
136 See Katharyne Mitchell, "Transnationalism, Neo-Liberalism, and the Rise of the Shadow State," *Economy and Society* 30, no. 2 (2001).
137 Punter, 193.
138 Ibid.
139 Ley, Hiebert, and Pratt.
140 City planner, cited in Graeme Wynn, "Introduction," in Ley, Hiebert, and Pratt, xiii.
141 Ibid., xii.
142 Berelowitz.
143 Ibid., 219.
144 Punter.
145 City planner, quoted in Barman, 395.
146 Trevor J. Barnes et al., "Vancouver, the Province, and the Pacific Rim," in *Vancouver and Its Region*, ed. Graeme Wynn and Timothy Oke (Vancouver, BC: UBC Press, 1992), 187.
147 Barman, 395.
148 Berelowitz, 219.
149 Punter.

150 Ibid., 232.
151 Barman.
152 Justin McElroy, "One Chart Shows How Unprecedented Vancouver's Real Estate Situation Is," *Global News*, February 21, 2016.
153 Ibid.
154 Punter.
155 See David Ley and Cory Dobson, "Are There Limits to Gentrification? The Contexts of Impeded Gentrification in Vancouver," *Urban Studies* 45, no. 12 (2008).
156 Ibid., 2482.
157 Ibid., 2484–5.
158 Ibid.
159 Former city planner, personal communication, August 2014.
160 Barman, 397.

4   Beyond Green Urban Entrepreneurialism

City greening has served as an effective entrepreneurial strategy, as evidenced in the previous chapter. Yet even as green urban entrepreneurialism re-shaped cities, challenges to neoliberal environmentalism emerged. Intersecting with neoliberal environmentalism but also marking an important shift, the early twenty-first century saw a maturation of cities' commitments to the environment and the adoption of wider ranging urban sustainability initiatives.

By the early 2000s, environmentalism had become incorporated into more facets of the municipal governments of Chicago, Birmingham, and Vancouver. Concrete sustainability goals had been put in place and benchmarks created, and there were emerging (if still inchoate) efforts to think more comprehensively about creating socially, economically, and environmentally sustainable urban development. Proclaimed commitments to climate mitigation and to city leadership in furthering global environmental protection marked this shift. City leaders began promoting their greening efforts as contributing to wider "regulatory processes, mechanisms and organizations" of global environmental governance.[1] The creativity and ambitiousness of many of the goals and initiatives adopted by city leaders during this time period led many commentators to celebrate urban areas as key to addressing global environmental problems, particularly climate change.

As commitments to environmental governance were made, city leaders moved away from green urban entrepreneurialism toward other varieties of liberal environmentalism. The concept of varieties of liberal environmentalism is discussed in detail in Chapter 1. To reiterate briefly, this idea posits that rather than representing only one kind of market-oriented environmentalism, liberal environmentalism contains a spectrum of relationships between the state, the environment, and the market. On one end of the spectrum is neoliberal environmentalism. Neoliberal environmentalism, of which green urban entrepreneurialism is a part, makes nods to protecting the environment but does so in a way that overwhelming prioritizes economic growth, branding, and market-based tools to reduce environmental impact. On the other end is progressive liberal environmentalism in which, though still maintaining the importance of growth and development, the state is more willing to intervene in the decisions of private actors to achieve environmental effectiveness and social equity. Between these lay ecoliberalism, where state interventions prioritize effectiveness but downplay equity, and social liberalism, in which social equity is prioritized over environmental effectiveness.

This chapter investigates the moves in Vancouver, Birmingham, and Chicago beyond green urban entrepreneurialism toward these other varieties of liberal environmentalism. Though differing in political impetus and in how far city leaders were willing to go to achieve equity and effectiveness, in each case the changes that occurred began to address the limitations of neoliberal environmentalism. While incomplete, these moves beyond green urban entrepreneurialism represented an important transition in these cities' contributions to solving global environmental problems in a socially just way.

Importantly, these efforts were still based on the assumption that taking a stand to protect the environment would ultimately create competitive advantages for the city. Because of this, even as cities moved toward other varieties of liberal environmentalism, the idea that they would sacrifice economic growth for environmental effectiveness or equity remained outside the parameters of even the most ambitious greening agenda. This is not necessarily surprising, as liberal environmentalism in all its varieties is still, at the end of the day, *liberal* environmentalism. As such, the tensions between economic imperatives and the necessity of local state regulation to complement growth with equity and environmental effectiveness that this chapter highlights begin to illuminate both the possibilities and the difficulties of cities contributing to just, effective environmental governance in the current political economic context.

Legitimacy and Effectiveness in Neoliberal Environmentalism

A few years into the twenty-first century, the physical greening of Chicago that Daley had undertaken since the start of his mayoral career turned into a broader ambition of contributing to national and global environmental governance by making Chicago, in Mayor Daley's oft-stated goal, the greenest city in America. As with the green urban entrepreneurialism discussed in the previous chapter, Daley's desire to make Chicago the greenest city in the country was quite explicitly an economic development strategy, and neoliberal environmentalism's assumptions that further greening would spur growth saturated the promotion of the city's initiatives.[2] But Daley's environmental leadership also strove to be more than that, to establish Chicago's global leadership and to help inspire environmental action by other cities and at other political scales.[3] Chicago's successes in becoming a leading green city show that despite its limitations, green urban entrepreneurialism does have potential to further effective environmental governance.

Federal Failings and Chicago's Climate Leadership

In notable contrast to Birmingham discussed below, where a growing national commitment to liberal environmentalism by the Blair government mandated the incorporation of sustainability into city development plans, in the United States the election of George W. Bush in 2000 brought even the market-based forms of environmental regulation that had been emerging over the previous decade under fire. Largely following Reagan's playbook but with a lower political profile, Bush included no environmentalists in his policy appointments to the EPA and other key regulatory positions. He took a consistent anti-environmental stand whenever "water quality standards, clean air rules, energy efficiency standards, protection of national forests and parks, and mining regulations" were seen as interfering "with industry and economic development."[4] President Bush's rejection of liberal environmentalism could also be seen in his assertion upon pulling out of the Kyoto Protocol in 2001 that achieving the goals of the international agreement would have hurt the U.S. economy.[5] As Congress had long refused to ratify the treaty, Bush's actions were largely symbolic. But many environmentalists were still appalled by his rejection of the promises of "green growth" and rather despondent as to the possibility of any real climate action being taken in the United States, at the time the world's largest emitter of greenhouse gases.

As disheartening as Bush's anti-environmentalism was for many, it is in the policy void created by Bush's hostility toward action on climate change that American cities such as Chicago became increasingly vocal about their role in furthering effective climate governance. And they did so very explicitly using the win–win discourse and assumptions of liberal environmentalism that Bush was actively rejecting. For example, the U.S. Mayors Climate Protection Agreement, a widely adopted municipal climate pledge, was established directly as a response to the Bush administration's inaction on climate change.[6] Although the Agreement was voluntary and contained no enforcement mechanism, its adoption by over 1000 mayors, both Republican and Democrat and in all 50 states and Puerto Rico, showed the extent to which city governments were willing to stand up to the federal government on the issue of climate change, clearly seeing it as having local political resonance and support.

Daley was an early signatory to the U.S. Mayor's Climate Protection Agreement, and in 2008 Chicago's greening efforts expanded to include leadership in mitigating climate change. That year Chicago unveiled the Chicago Climate Action Plan (CCAP) with the goal of reducing GHG emissions to 25 percent below 1990 levels by 2020 and 80 percent below 1990 levels by 2050.[7] As buildings were estimated to be responsible for

70 percent of total GHG emissions in Chicago, energy efficiency was a focus of the CCAP, though it also called for furthering clean energy sources, improving transportation options, and reducing waste and pollution. In addition to promoting the environmental and economic benefits of carbon reduction, the CCAP noted that much had already been done to reduce emissions from municipal operations, particularly through retrofitting city buildings, constructing green roofs, and replacing traffic lights with high-efficiency LEDs. The CCAP also highlighted the contributions local businesses and organizations had made to date in voluntarily reducing their carbon emissions.

As with Chicago's green urban entrepreneurialism, the CCAP emphasized the economic benefits of climate action and how addressing climate change would improve the quality of life for all. In announcing the plan the mayor's office asserted that the CCAP's benefits go "beyond improving the environment, which is a critical goal in and of itself. The actions that have the greatest impact will save companies and residents money, enhance our quality of life and position the city and its residents for future prosperity."[8] Likewise, Daley's preface to the CCAP stated, "Since I have been mayor, my goal has been to make Chicago a shining example of how a large city can live in harmony with its environment and as a result, *be a better place for all its residents.*"[9] The CCAP's goals were certainly ambitious. But upon the release of the CCAP some noted that exactly how the city's proposed carbon reductions would be achieved was "still a little fuzzy," and even city officials admitted that they had not exactly figured out how to make the reduction happen.[10]

Though Bush's hostility to climate change may have encouraged cities such as Chicago to make pledges to reduce emissions, the fulfillment of these pledges was greatly facilitated by the election of Barack Obama in 2008. An outspoken proponent of an ambitious kind of liberal environmentalism, Obama ran for president calling for a massive investment in "green jobs" as a way to spur economic recovery, enhance global competitiveness, and protect the nation's environment. The American Recovery and Reinvestment Act of 2009, President Obama's signature stimulus bill, included $80 billion for investment in clean energy and efficiency making it, according to some analyses, the "most important energy bill in American history."[11] Chicago benefited heartily from the Recovery Act, and by 2010 it had received $62.5 million to implement the CCAP.[12]

The CCAP Progress Report released in 2010 enumerated the city's accomplishments. It asserted that 13,341 housing units and 393 commercial and industrial buildings had been retrofitted to be more energy efficient, 30,542 appliances had been traded in for more efficient models, 1.8 million square feet of green roofs had been installed or were under construction, 120 green alleys had been installed, and 208 hybrid buses had been added to Chicago Transit Authority fleet.[13] The document also pointed to city mandates that all new municipal buildings be designed and constructed to the LEED Silver standard, and to voluntary initiatives such as the Green Bungalow program that helps residents retrofit old homes for energy efficiency. Most of the voluntary programs were undertaken through partnerships with non-profit organizations and foundations, utilizing these partnerships to leverage private and federal funds. Interestingly, the Progress Report does not state the overall emission reduction that had accrued from these accomplishments, nor if the city was on track to meet its goals. Despite this, Chicago's climate leadership was widely celebrated, and the city won the U.S. Conference of Mayors' award for the best large city climate effort, among other accolades.[14]

Voluntarism and Legitimacy in Environmental Governance

Daley's approach to climate governance emphasized reducing emissions from municipal operations and creating voluntary programs to encourage residents and businesses to become more climate friendly. This cooperative, non-regulatory approach is consistent with neoliberalism environmentalism's hesitation to impose requirements on the private sector. As discussed in Chapter 2, often such voluntarism is not sufficient to achieve environmental goals. However, Daley's strong political will and leadership was able to facilitate some important reductions in GHG emissions, even without mandates. It also undoubtedly helped to get political buy-in from business for the mayor's vision of becoming a leading green city.[15]

Despite this, not everyone in the city government was happy with Daley's voluntary approach. For example, the chief of staff of one city alderman who had mandated that all new developments in his ward meet high green building standards expressed frustration with the City's unwillingness to move beyond neoliberal environmentalism. "They're doing a good effort," he said when asked about the mayor's goal of making Chicago the greenest city in the country, "but they could do more. ... It's a good start to be talking green, but there are so many things that could be done. ... We need to make [green building] a citywide requirement. ... Now we're promoting it, we need to require it."[16] Legal mandates, however, ran the risk of creating conflict with business and developers over environmental programs, something the mayor made clear he was not willing to do.[17]

In addition to maintaining business support, Daley also successfully secured the legitimacy of his greening efforts by getting environmental groups on board with his agenda. He did this through partnerships between the City and environmental organizations and by providing funding for groups to carry out parts of his greening program. This dampened potential objections to his approach to city greening, as doing so could run the risk of losing access to the local government and its funds. This tactic of working closely with local organizations, which some considered an indication of Mayor Daley's support of environmentalism and others considered cooptation, was not unique to environmental issues. Neighborhood groups too were seen by critics as being captured by Daley, the protest that marked earlier administrations replaced by efforts to achieve insider access. "If Daley I ignored protest," a former alderman was quoted as stating, "Daley II coopts it."[18]

Bringing activist groups into the fold of city government may have given them political power, and it certainly provided access to more resources. However, it also led to a disconnect between local environmental leaders' public declarations of support for Daley's approach to greening and privately expressed skepticism as to its effectiveness. An interview with the director of one local conservation and environmental justice group offered an interesting example of this. When asked directly about the organization's relationship with the City, the director said that their relationship was quite good, noting that the City had given important financial and political support to this group. But further conversation revealed a level of frustration with the administration's efforts. After talking for some time about the persistent problem of air pollution in the neighborhood where the organization was based and the unwillingness of the City to regulate the local industries responsible for it, the director expressed skepticism about the supposed benefits of Daley's tree-planting efforts. "Daley wants a million trees in every nook and cranny, but do they really make a difference? Look [pointing out the window at streetside trees], they're scrawny."[19] Planting trees, one of Daley's hallmark initiatives, was not seen as sufficient for dealing with the environmental problems the community was facing. Similarly, another leader of a nonprofit that worked closely with the Daley administration in a number of capacities and was publicly very supportive of Chicago's environmental initiatives pointed to the "embarrassing" state of public transportation in the city, and, even more problematically, Daley's lack of strategic thinking about how improve it.[20] Despite these concerns, showing support for the mayor's environmental efforts, a reliance on resources and funding from the city government, and involvement in public–private projects was the norm for Chicago environmental groups under Daley. Inversely, mobilizing the labor and resources of nonprofits appeared to be a major strategy of the mayor to help realize his environmental goals and further Chicago's claim that it was becoming the greenest city in the U.S. while keeping costs of such efforts (grand prestige projects excluded) to a minimum.

Electoral Politics and the Push Toward Sustainability

Even as contributing to broader climate governance emerged as an important part of Chicago's environmental agenda, equity continued to be deemphasized in Mayor Daley's effort to make Chicago the greenest in the country. It was not until Daley left the mayor's office that equity in the distribution of parks, transit, and other environmental amenities gained a more visible place on the local political agenda. When Daley declared in 2010 that he would not run for re-election, Chicago faced its first truly contested mayoral race in over twenty years.[21] The election of Rahm Emanuel created a political opening that led to both continuity and some important changes in Chicago's environmental initiatives. In many ways Emanuel expanded his predecessor's entrepreneurial emphasis on enhancing environmental amenities in order to attract businesses and young professionals. He also built on many of the programs started by Daley that strove to integrate more in-depth environmental considerations into city operations and development.

Despite these similarities, greening under the Emanuel administration began to take a number of new steps beyond neoliberal environmentalism. Emanuel did not have the political invincibility of Daley and was therefore less able to coopt nor to ignore potential opposition. More susceptible to public pressure and needing to establish the legitimacy of his administration, Mayor Emanuel was persuaded, often by public denouncement and protest, to expand environmental initiatives into neighborhoods that had not been prioritized by Daley's greening agenda. He also undertook more explicit considerations, again often in response to public protest, of how sustainability intersected with social and environmental inequality in the city. Though in many ways an outspoken proponent of neoliberal urbanism,[22] as will be seen below and in the chapters to follow, to gain political legitimacy Emanuel needed both the economic benefits of green urban entrepreneurialism and to demonstrate a responsiveness to concerns of environmental inequity in Chicago. As he did so, he began shifting Chicago slowly in the direction of progressive liberal environmentalism.

Emanuel's attempt to illustrate his commitment to an equitable, sustainable city could be seen in the transition plan he released as mayor-elect.[23] Though covering a wide variety of issues from the budget to transparency in government, the transition plan was notable for the extent to which it emphasized environmental sustainability. This included calls for increasing access to open space, eliminating food deserts, promoting energy efficiency, improving public transportation, and creating world-class bicycle infrastructure, among other priorities. These goals were justified for their economic development benefits but were also recognized as helping address inequalities in the city. For example, in calling for more green space, the plan (echoing CitySpace nearly two decades earlier) noted that many neighborhoods were underserved by parks and that this inequity needed to be remedied. Similarly, the goal of improving public transportation focused on extending the Red Line of the "L," Chicago's rapid transit system, to the far South Side, a part of the city that was hit hard by deindustrialization and that is woefully underserved by public transit. As such, the transition plan offered more of a recognition of environmental inequities than had previously been seen in predominant city documents. Yet economic growth remained paramount. Emanuel clearly wanted to build on the success and publicity Daley had garnered through his greening efforts, in order "to secure Chicago's global competitiveness"[24] and make Chicago "the greenest city in the world."[25]

Released a year later, Sustainable Chicago 2015 built closely on Emanuel's transition plan.[26] However, it offered less recognition of the myriad social challenges that Chicago faced, focusing, like Daley and the CCAP, more on the ability of environmental protection and a livable city to further economic growth. It asserted that "the Sustainable Chicago action plan offers concrete initiatives, metrics, and strategies aimed at advancing Chicago's goal of becoming the most sustainable city in the country. ... To secure Chicago's global competitiveness we must invest in our future in a manner that creates economic and job opportunities now."[27] Though some of the equity issues raised in the transition plan, such as a recognition of a lack of equal access to healthy food and green space across Chicago, remained in the new document, Sustainable Chicago 2015 included less of an emphasis on how greening intersected with the city's persistent inequalities.

Despite this disconnect between Emanuel's transition plan and Sustainable Chicago 2015, as will be explored in more detail in Chapters 5–7, local environmental and social justice organizations have worked hard to hold Mayor Emanuel accountable for the effectiveness and equity impacts of his sustainability agenda. In a number of cases these groups have won, leading to a more equitable distribution of the benefits of the greener city. Yet as will also be seen, the prestige projects and green entrepreneurialism of the Daley administration have by no means subsided. The questions of how far Chicago will be able and willing to go toward progressive liberal environmentalism, and the compatibility of this move with an ongoing emphasis on city center vibrancy, remain contested and unresolved.

Ecoliberalism and Equity in the "World's Greenest City"

Vancouver, its relationship with green urban entrepreneurialism somewhat ambivalent from the start, took more concrete steps toward other varieties of liberal environmentalism than Chicago. Indeed, a commitment to climate governance in Vancouver began in 1990, coterminous with the emergence of megadevelopments and the entrepreneurial transformation of many of its post-industrial spaces. The same year that the *Vancouver Sun* published the series "Future Growth. Future Shock," which offered sustainable development as a solution to the challenges of rapid urban growth in the region (see Chapter 3), the city council adopted a report on climate change, Clouds of Change.[28] Years ahead of most cities' forays into climate policies, Clouds of Change extended Vancouver's emphasis on livability into a focus on the role the city could play in addressing the climate challenge. The report called for a 20 percent reduction in Vancouver's 1988 GHG emissions by 2005, along with the elimination of chlorofluorocarbons. "Subject to further reports on costs and trade-offs involved in achieving the objectives and targets," proposed strategies to reach this goal included the collection of methane gas from landfills, better traffic control and incentives for high-occupancy vehicles, enhanced bike infrastructure, and increased residential density, infill, and restrictions on sprawl.[29] Though the report was advisory, Clouds of Change was pivotal in establishing environmental concerns as a priority for city planners, expanding on their already-existing "philosophy of a livable city and a sustainable urban form supported by intensification, mixed land uses, and transit policies."[30]

Global Leadership and Local Community

Even as Clouds of Change highlighted the importance of densification and quality planning to ensuring environmentally sustainable growth, many communities were not so sanguine about the possibility of finding synthesis between growth and sustainability. The city saw expanding citizen disquiet about rising housing prices and increasing density, particularly as densification initiatives began to extend beyond industrial land to established residential neighborhoods. In response to pressure for more community control over planning decisions, and, more cynically, in hopes of controlling what some city officials saw as the "'tyranny of a few,' who look after their own interests at the expense of the wider community" by protesting new developments,[31] the City undertook an ambitious program of neighborhood dialogue to establish a shared vision of Vancouver's future.[32]

The culmination of this multi-year process of extensive public input and discussion was CityPlan.[33] CityPlan called for concentrating growth and density in neighborhood centers in a way that would provide a greater variety of affordable housing options and that would minimize development's impact on low-density residential neighborhoods. Echoing the ideas of Living First and Clouds of Change, an emphasis on walking, transit, and biking was included in the plan, and environmental amenities from public parks and green space to clean air and water were prioritized.[34] At the heart of CityPlan was the assertion that every neighborhood should be able to decide how it wanted to develop in order to meet the needs of the growing city while also enhancing local sustainability, livability, and identity. To do so, each neighborhood would engage in an extended community planning process. These neighborhood plans would be as democratic as possible. They were to include extensive, broad-based participation from all types of residents of the neighborhood leading to a widely accepted plan that reflected the vision and priorities of the community.[35] Through these community plans, it was asserted, growth, environmental protection, and community well-being would be harmonized.

By the early years of the twenty-first century, Vancouver seemed to be a model of the rich possibilities of progressive liberal environmental ism. Policies to incorporate affordable housing and amenities into new developments were ambitious (see Chapter 3). Neighborhoods were poised to have an important say over creating socially sustainable local communities. Vancouver's forays into climate mitigation were proving effective, with a 24 percent growth in population and 14 percent growth in jobs between 1990 and 2007 leading to only a 5 percent increase in GHG emissions. This represented a 15 percent reduction in per capita emissions, a level of reduction achieved by very few North American cities.[36] Vancouver was gaining global recognition for its commitment to environmental protection and, as mentioned in the previous chapter, was winning international awards for the quality of its urban planning and design. The synthesis of a vibrant, livable urban environment and beautiful natural surroundings were attracting tourists and new residents alike. Vancouver was seen, not without justification, as North America's model sustainable city and illustrative of the potential for urban sustainability to go hand in hand with economic vitality.

Failed Promises of Social Sustainability

Articulating its commitment to sustainability, in 2002 the city council adopted a set of wide-ranging sustainability principles to serve as a basis for city actions and operations.[37] Drawing clearly on Brundtland's definition of sustainable development, the goal of these principles was "to ensure that Vancouver becomes a community that meets the needs of the present without compromising the ability of future generations to meet their own needs."[38] Though heavy on environmental issues, true to the "three pillars" conception of sustainability that had by this time become ubiquitous, the document defined a sustainable city as "one that protects and enhances the immediate and long-term well being of a city and its citizens, while providing the highest quality of life possible. Sustainability requires integrated decision-making that takes into account economic, ecological, and social impacts as a whole."[39] As with its early forays into climate change, Vancouver was a leader in efforts to move beyond green urban entrepreneurialism toward thinking about social aspects of a sustainable city. Achieving the integration of the three pillars of sustainable development, however, would be a challenge.

This difficulty is well illustrated by the extended conflicts around the development of Southeast False Creek and the Olympic Village. Clouds of Change recommended developing the former industrial land of Southeast False Creek as a holistic (if not clearly defined) sustainable community.

However, the initial development proposal for Southeast False Creek was similar to other megadevelopments such as Yaletown and Coal Harbour, with high-density mixed use buildings intermingled with green space and "all the standard public amenities expected of a megaproject."[40] The proposal, which had been drawn up with little public consultation, was met with widespread opposition. Opponents demanded more public input into the plan and a development that reflected a more robust understanding of sustainability that prioritized social inclusion and well-being as well as more ambitious contributions to environmental protection.[41] Facing significant public pressure, the city council shelved the proposal and undertook a broad public planning process.

The vision of a sustainable community that emerged for Southeast False Creek from the public planning processes was far different from the original proposal. The plan included fewer skyscrapers; increased affordable housing to a remarkable one-third low-income, one-third middle income, and one-third market; expanded the number of child care centers; and added concrete environmental indicators.[42] For a moment it appeared that social as well as environmental sustainability would be notably enhanced by the development, and that the goals of equity and environmental effectiveness were indeed shaping Vancouver's development agenda.

Meanwhile, efforts were underway to attract the 2010 Olympic and Paralympic Winter Games to Vancouver, a megaevent that was to rival Expo '86 in its importance in enhancing the city's global visibility. Interestingly, the sustainability promises of the new plans for Southeast False Creek, where the Olympic Village would be located, helped secure Vancouver's bid. In 1999 the International Olympic Committee had released its own version of Agenda 21 that called for "the Olympic movement to work towards the sustainability of the planet."[43] When the Vancouver Organizing Committee (VANOC) first began work on its proposal for hosting the Games, a coalition of academics, social activists, and environmentalists came together to demand that the committee explicitly incorporate social and environmental sustainability into the bid process.[44] With memories of displacement of Expo '86 still fresh, particular emphasis was given to the need to protect what remained of the SRO dwellings in the Downtown Eastside. As the momentum of this coalition grew, VANOC offered reassurances that environmental and social protections would be core to the Games. The Inner City Inclusive Commitment Statement (ICI) produced to illustrate this commitment promised that low-income, inner-city residents would have access to public spaces before, during, and after the Games; that job training and a continuum of short- and long-term employment opportunities would be available for these residents; protection against homelessness as a result of the Games; and assurance that the Games would provide an affordable housing legacy.[45] With promises of its social and environmental benefits highlighted, and the popular left-leaning mayor and city council in support of the Games, in early 2003 a city-wide referendum on hosting the Games passed by 64 percent. Vancouver won the bid later that year, its ability to illustrate the sustainability criteria desired by the International Olympic Committee and the referendum's demonstration of public support for the Games vital to its successful bid.[46]

However, problems soon emerged that illustrated the difficulty of furthering social equity in a green city that was still very much driven by entrepreneurial ambitions. The first problem was with the sustainability plan for Southeast False Creek which, if fully implemented, would mean that the City would not make money on the development. There was disagreement as to whether or not this mattered. Critics asserted that the City had a responsibility to act in the market like the private sector would, maximizing the return on its property assets. Others disagreed, arguing that the City should be using its power over development to further other vital community goals, even if it meant just breaking even on the development project itself.[47] This led to a political battle in the 2005 municipal election around the proper role of the city's Property Endowment Fund, with the conservative NPA, at the time the opposition party, claiming that the Fund had been taken over as a tool to promote a radical social agenda. The NPA argued the Southeast False Creek development would ruin the City's credit rating and set a precedent that was "unsustainable."

The NPA won the election. One of the new mayor Sam Sullivan's first initiatives was to return "'economic sustainability'" to the Southeast False Creek development.[48] This meant reducing the number of child care centers from five to two and cutting over $20 million from affordable housing. The middle-income housing was eliminated and low-income housing was cut from 33 to 25 percent of the units.[49]

The second major problem facing the incorporation of social equity into Vancouver's development agenda was that it quickly became clear that VANOC's promise of a socially inclusive Olympics was not to be realized. The new city leadership's obvious disinterest in trying "to accommodate and follow-through on the commitments made to the inner city during the bid phase" was a key aspect of this.[50] Rather than protecting the poor from displacement during the Games, the NPA said the Olympics would be an opportunity to further "civility" and law and order in Vancouver, with a focus on curbing "offenses including aggressive panhandling, theft from home/business, sleeping on public property, open drug abuse, etc."[51] To achieve this, policing of the Downtown Eastside grew substantially, leading to an increase in tickets issued for minor infractions like jaywalking and sleeping in abandoned doorways. Instead of investing in homes and jobs for the city's poor, over a billion dollars was dedicated to Olympic security, much of which targeted residents of the DTES.[52] Furthermore, "no amendments to the notoriously weak Residential

Tenancy Act [were] made to prevent mass low-income tenant evictions by landlords with dollar signs in their eyes. No new Olympic-related social housing units [would] be opened before the Games."[53] As there were no enforcement mechanisms in the ICI, activists and community groups had little legal recourse.[54] The provincial government did purchase nearly two dozen single-room occupancy hotels and lodging houses, preventing the displacement of their residents, but there were insufficient funds to bring the buildings up to basic safety standards.[55]

Even as the social elements of the preparations for the Olympics were abandoned, the environmental elements flourished. Tens of millions of dollars were spent in the DTES on new awnings and murals, the renovation of two nearby city parks, and the construction of a "'greenway' ... through the centre of the neighbourhood, designed to provide safe transport for tourists from the historic Gastown district to the historic Chinatown district without exposing them, more than [was] absolutely necessary, to ... the DTES which lies, quite awkwardly, between them."[56] In the development of the Olympic Village in Southeast False Creek, though affordable housing and child care centers were cut in order to make it more profitable, expensive environmental elements remained. These included green roofs, solar heating, and an innovative high-efficiency energy system. The development qualified for LEED status, and "the US Green Building Council indicated that the Olympic Village was not only the greenest in Olympic history, but 'the most energy efficiency and sustainable neighbourhood in the world.'"[57]

City officials were confident that this high-visibility green develop would benefit Vancouver's reputation. A former planning director asserted that through the Olympic Village Vancouver could "model a kind of development which is different than what we've been able to see elsewhere. We want to test new things. We want to be the first to set the pace."[58] Yet for many, the prioritization of greening and security over poverty and homelessness in the preparation for the Games indicated that city leaders saw environmental considerations as significantly more compatible with Vancouver's emerging position as a global city than issues of social equity. Indeed, at this point Vancouver's move beyond green urban entrepreneurialism was very much toward ecoliberalism, environmental effectiveness closely connected to ongoing place promotion and branding.

Stumbling Toward Progressive Liberal Environmentalism

The NPA's deprioritization of social issues was challenged in the 2008 municipal election. Focusing on homelessness, the cost of the Olympics, and the city's $100-million loan to the developer of the Olympic Village, the young municipal political party Vision Vancouver (henceforth Vision) won control of the mayor's office and the city council.[59] Promoting an agenda of progressive liberal environmental governance, Vision and the new mayor Gregor Robertson's two main electoral promises were to end street homelessness and to make Vancouver the "world's greenest city" by 2020. According to Vision city councilors, homelessness and housing affordability were as important as greening. However, becoming the world's greenest city quickly became the most widely recognized aspect of Vision's agenda and the area where they have been most successful.[60]

Repeating the process of extensive public input that had created CityPlan, it took two years of public meetings and discussion before the council produced and adopted the Greenest City 2020 Action Plan (GCAP).[61] The GCAP is ambitious in its goals and illustrates a shift, even within this city with a long-standing commitment to environmental protection, toward a deeper integration of environmentalism into a wide breadth of city operations and initiatives. The plan begins by laying out a number of initiatives to encourage the growth of green businesses and the greening of existing enterprises as an economic development strategy for the city. Reiterating liberal environmentalism's promise of the compatibility of environmental protection and economic vibrancy, the GCAP asserts that "by embracing green economic development, Vancouver businesses can be more competitive, gain market share, and prepare for carbon regulation, all by improving their environmental performance."[62] Other foci of the GCAP include GHG reduction; green building design and construction; improved walking, cycling and public transit; waste reduction; access to green space; one-planet ecological footprint; water quality and conservation; clean air; and (in the one explicit nod to social equity) the creation of a just, sustainable food system.[63] Measurable indicators of success accompany each goal, environmental effectiveness being a clear priority.

As environmental initiatives became increasingly ambitious under Vision, and became an even more pronounced part of Vancouver's brand, social sustainability also regained emphasis. After the GCAP was adopted, city officials began working on the document A Healthy City for All, intended to accompany the GCAP with a plan to promote social well-being, health, education, inclusion, and more.[64] As such, the aim of the healthy city strategy is to achieve the social pillar of the sustainable city goals adopted over a decade earlier. However, the healthy city strategy was, according to a key participant, much harder to get off the ground than the GCAP, the political will for its adoption not as strong as for the city's greening blueprint.[65] Despite this, A Healthy City for All was passed by the council in late 2014 and began to be implemented alongside the GCAP.[66]

Vancouver has clearly become a proponent of ecoliberalism, offering up a strong commitment to environmental protection alongside economic growth. Incorporating equity into its ambitious brand of liberal environmentalism has been more difficult, and since the turn of the twenty-first century the city has had an "on-again, off-again relationship with social sustainability."[67] Partly this reflects changing political will and leadership, with the current city leadership giving a greater prioritization to social sustainability than its predecessor. As will be seen, however, the city continues to wrestle with severe problems of housing affordability, contested local ideas of how community development should proceed, and challenges to initiatives to enhance green infrastructure. As Vancouver leaders work to find solutions to these problems, some of which are deeply entrenched and complex, the long-standing progressiveness of the city and active engagement by civil society have been pushing leaders to find new ways to enhance equity in the green city. Vancouver therefore finds itself somewhere between ecoliberalism and progressive liberal environmentalism, its ambitious goals limited by inconsistent political commitment but also, and perhaps even more importantly, by the city's limited legal powers and by its place in the global real estate market. How city leaders are negotiating these challenges will be examined in the following chapters.

Branding and Growth in the "Low Carbon Revolution"

Birmingham was the most focused of the three cities on keeping green branding front and center as it expanded from a narrow emphasis on downtown beautification to a campaign to establish the city's climate leadership. Birmingham also struggled more than either Vancouver or Chicago at translating proclamations of its commitment to environmental governance into effective action. Part of this reflects the narrow focus of the city's green urban entrepreneurialism. Unlike the two other cities, in which some effective environmental policies were incorporated into their early entrepreneurial endeavors, until the late 1990s, environmental sustainability was not an important part of Birmingham's postindustrial transformation. Spurred on by national mandates, European funding opportunities, and the growing importance of climate leadership to global city status, this eventually changed. By the turn of the century, Birmingham officials began asserting that environmental sustainability, not just the provision of environmental amenities, was a defining feature of the city's redevelopment.[68]

Making this claim involved some reframing of the entrepreneurial transformation Birmingham had been undertaking. The preface of the city's 2002 Local Agenda 21 progress report illustrates this well. In it the chair of the council's Environment Committee asserts that although some may "doubt the City's commitment to the idea of sustainability ... for the last 20 years the council has been involved in a massive sustainability project, that of re-cycling a whole city. ... In order to create the conditions for growth and investment in the alternative service and business tourist industries we had to transform the environment of the city, particularly the city centre."[69] To the extent that enhancing walkability, increasing pedestrian access to jobs and services, and re-purposing under-utilized and abandoned industrial spaces have environmental as well as economic benefits, they do fulfill the win–win promises of liberal environmentalism. Yet it is hard to find evidence that these initiatives were originally undertaken for any purpose of broader environmental effectiveness. As illustrated in the previous chapter, the greening of the city center was part and parcel of Birmingham's entrepreneurial agenda of becoming a global tourist destination. It was only later, as liberal environmentalism become the dominant environmental discourse and as illustrating a commitment to environmentalism because a requisite part of good urban governance,[70] that urban renewal and green urban entrepreneurialism were reframed as the "re-cycling of the city."

National Mandates for Local Sustainability

Birmingham was further pushed toward sustainable development by new national mandates. As discussed in Chapter 2, the Blair government, elected in 1997, made liberal environmentalism foundational to its political platform, creating incentives and market-based mechanisms to encourage reduced GHG emissions and incorporating environmental considerations into a wider array of government operations. Labour's commitment to liberal environmentalism and sustainable development also influenced its urban policies. Working to illustrate a break from the Conservative policies of the previous eighteen years, "the Labour government came to power ... with a commitment to regenerate Britain's cities by recourse to social inclusion, neighbourhood renewal and community involvement."[71] This included a shift "toward a more inclusive approach to urban regeneration, moving beyond a narrow preoccupation with economic development toward an agenda shared with social and environmental issues."[72] Nevertheless, the Blair government was not to return to the post-war goals of redistribution and equalization. Though returning some power to local governments and calling for more inclusive urban policies, Labour continued the Conservatives' promotion of inter-city competition and the market ethos as the best way to deal with the pressures of the global economy.[73] Instead of promoting equality as such, Labour's urban policies emphasized "equality of opportunity" and community self-help.

One way that the government's promotion of community self-help and liberal environmentalism intersected was through the creation of Local Strategic Partnerships in most English local authorities. These quasi-public bodies included representatives from local government, business, and the voluntary sector. They were charged with creating tri-annual Local Area Agreements that laid out goals and plans for improving the area based on national development priorities. In exchange for agreeing to deliver on the Local Area Agreement, the local government received "simplified funding and accountability arrangements, and potentially new freedoms and flexibilities."[74] Birmingham's Local Strategic Partnership was to become quite important in developing the city's climate goals and in designing those goals to maximize their effectiveness as an entrepreneurial tool.

Around the same time that Local Strategic Partnerships were established, sustainability became a part of the national government's community development agenda. Initially only a guiding principle, in 2004 the government's local and regional planning guidelines made the incorporation of sustainability a legal requirement of planning decisions.[75] This was further codified in the 2004 Planning and Compulsory Purchase Act, which required "planning authorities to directly contribute to sustainable development through their planning functions."[76] The national sustainable development document Securing our Future followed. It required each Local Strategic Partnership, in consultation with the community of which it was a part, to draw up a sustainable community strategy and delivery plan.[77] These initiatives by the national government that required cities to work toward sustainable development enhanced the political legitimacy of such efforts. They also opened up new sources of national funding, particularly competitive grants, to city development proposals that furthered sustainability and GHG reduction. Birmingham quickly worked to maximize its access to these resources.

Industry in Birmingham initially resisted some of the Blair government's environmental efforts, particularly a proposed energy levy aimed at achieving the country's GHG reduction commitments under the Kyoto Protocol. Though the levy was reduced in response to business lobbying, the Birmingham Chamber of Commerce and Industry insisted that the "climate levy should be scrapped" entirely as it would hurt the competitiveness of the region's remaining heavy industry and, they claimed, cost tens of thousands of jobs in the region.[78] Anger at the levy remained even as the government published a list of energy efficiency technologies that would qualify for full tax relief and found other ways to offset the cost of the levy for those industries investing in green technology.[79]

Within a few years, Birmingham business began to change its tune, positioning itself as a committed and crucial player in creating a greener, low carbon economy.[80] In part this reflected a move by the national government toward voluntary GHG reduction initiatives that industry found more palatable than levies.[81] The change in the Chamber's position was also affected by Labour losing control of Birmingham City Council in 2004, control it had held for twenty years. Unlike the Labour council, which had critiqued the Chamber's anti-levy position,[82] the new Conservative–Liberal Democrat coalition council showed no interest in criticizing business resistance to GHG reduction mandates. Instead, it strove to incorporate the issue of climate change into Birmingham's broader marketing and rebranding efforts in a way that would benefit local industry.

Birmingham as the Birthplace of the "Low Carbon Revolution"

Birmingham's pro-business approach to climate governance was codified in 2006 when the Local Strategic Partnership developed the local sustainability plan mandated by the national government. In a closed-door workshop, the group of consultants, business leaders, environmentalists, city councilors, and other local leaders met to discuss the sustainability priorities and programs Birmingham would commit to. What emerged was a plan to promote Birmingham as the "birthplace of the low carbon revolution" in order to draw upon and polish the city's industrial heritage while benefiting its post-industrial reinvention and existing industries. According to one participant, "[At the workshop we decided that] yes, we want to be known, we want to be ambitious, we want to be a leader. And it was the Chamber who were the most vocal in saying it is good for business. Birmingham is where the carbon revolution began. ... The first steam engines were built here in Birmingham. We have a special role to play, so how do we use climate change as a way to innovate our economy and become a leading low carbon producer? ... It was seen as a strong economic driver."[83] The draft of the climate change action strategy that came out of this meeting set the ambitious goals of reducing Birmingham's greenhouse gas emissions by 60 percent by the year 2050, establishing sustainable procurement strategies, getting 30 percent of Birmingham's energy from renewable sources by 2020 and reducing the council's energy use by 30 percent by 2010, all while encouraging the development of low carbon industry.[84]

In the years that followed, councilors often referenced these goals to claim that Birmingham was the pioneer of the "low carbon revolution." Reiterating that the city was where James Watt and colleagues invented the modern steam engine and that it once was one of the grandest manufacturing cities in the world represented an effort to re-establish Birmingham's global city credentials. It also strove to gloss over the more recent industrial past marked by a lack of competitiveness, industrial decline, and the perceived unruliness of the city's organized labor.[85] For example, a statement released by a number of councilors in support of committing Birmingham to becoming a carbon-neutral city strove to put Birmingham in league with other global cities, stating "at a time when cities such as London, Melbourne and San Francisco are responding to climate change, we too in the West Midlands, *here the cradle of the Industrial Revolution*, can and must make the right sort of history again, and become a global leader in meeting the challenges of climate change."[86] This is just one example, but the extent to which this idea could be found in virtually every council and Strategic Partnership environmental document and sustainability plan during these years is striking.[87] Indeed, by the end of the decade selling itself as the birthplace of the low carbon revolution clearly had become Birmingham's own particular green brand. In interviews city leaders were quick to confirm that the principal purpose of making Birmingham a forerunner in climate governance was to improve Birmingham's global city image in order to attract inward investment.

Birmingham's final climate action strategy, announced a year after the draft plan, was even more ambitious than originally proposed, calling for a 60 percent reduction in emissions as early as 2026 rather than 2050. The Strategic Partnership claimed that in adopting this goal the city was taking "its rightful place among exemplar cities including London, Vienna and Munich in leading the sustainability agenda," and putting it "ahead of Berlin, Cape Town, Chicago, Toronto and New York."[88] Deputy Leader of the City Council Paul Tilsley, a major proponent of the city's low carbon brand, asserted that the "announcement [of the GHG reduction goal] demonstrates Birmingham's global leadership in tackling climate change. ... By demonstrating leadership Birmingham will use its position as a global city to ... provide a beacon for other cities to follow."[89] The rhetoric surrounding Birmingham's climate goals once again highlighted greening as a key to city leaders' entrepreneurial agenda and global city ambitions.

Meanwhile, local political support for action to address climate change was growing. A 2007 survey found that 83 percent of Birmingham residents felt that climate change was the most important global issue compared with 15 percent saying that terrorism was the most important. The vast majority expressed support for tougher building standards and greater investment in renewable energy by the council.[90] Yet many were skeptical as to the council's commitment to actually achieving its climate agenda. Critics were particularly concerned that the climate plan was not clear on how such a striking reduction in emissions could be achieved by the UK's second largest and most car dependent city in such a short period of time.[91] A report conducted by the council's own Climate Change & Sustainability Scrutiny Committee found a lack of clear leadership on the part of the council and, despite its bold rhetoric, excessive hesitation about taking the steps necessary to achieve their climate goals. The report was particularly critical of the City's unwillingness to mandate zero carbon developments or to adopt other policies that were perceived as negatively impacting industry or economic development.[92]

In response to public skepticism, there was "a flurry of action from council leaders, who proceeded to sign any petition, bang any drum and jump on any populist bandwagon in an attempt to show that they were taking the most serious issue of the 21st century seriously."[93] The result was climate festivals, programs to encourage residents to take personal actions to reduce their carbon emissions, and, eventually, some genuine changes in city policies. The most important of these new policies, discussed at length in the next chapter, addressed energy production. These policies did have some real carbon benefits, but, as will be seen, Birmingham's efforts continued to focus on green technologies and efficiencies that benefited city center businesses through reduced costs.

Importantly, however, more so than either Vancouver or Chicago, Birmingham's climate agenda also included focused attempts to use GHG reduction initiatives to address the social justice challenge of fuel poverty. Even as green branding remained paramount throughout the first decade of the twentieth century, equity became an important part of how Birmingham approached city environmentalism. Though ultimately unsuccessful, its early forays into fuel poverty elimination were touted as setting new standards for just climate mitigation. This issue is investigated in detail in Chapter 5.

Equitable Greening in Rhetoric and Practice

In 2012 Labour retook control of the city council. Striving to put its own mark on city environmental efforts, the new council leadership dropped the discourse of the "birthplace of the low carbon revolution" and replaced it with the goal of making Birmingham a "leading green city."[94] To determine how to achieve this, Labour leaders created a Green Commission made up of councilors, business representatives, community members, and others. The purpose of the Commission was to analyze the city's environmental accomplishments and to come up with new sustainability and carbon mitigation plans. The resulting proposals maintained a predominant emphasis on growth but also highlighted the importance of equity and effectiveness in city environmental efforts. This is clearly articulated in the Green Commission's vision statement that calls for Birmingham leaders "to create a leading green city for a better life and make Birmingham more prosperous, healthier, fairer, resource-efficient and better for business. In doing this we will enhance the quality of life and well-being for all of our citizens."[95] The Green Commission paints a picture of a city that is just, green, and prosperous. It is to be a city that fulfills the multiple goals of progressive liberal environmentalism.

However, as will be seen, Birmingham's increasingly clear calls for just, effective environmental governance have not been realized. These failures can partly be attributed to changing national regulations and budget cuts that have severely constrained city efforts. But a lack of local political will is also a culprit, with Birmingham officials unwilling to match their ambitious goals with bold actions. In a city that remains quite poor, any policy that could possibly put a burden on business or development, even if the environmental and social benefits are clear, is resisted. This disconnect between rhetoric and action has been the defining feature of Birmingham's vacillation between different varieties of liberal environmentalism.

Conclusion

This chapter has illustrated that although the first decade of the twentieth century saw Chicago, Vancouver, and Birmingham moving beyond neoliberal environmentalism toward other varieties of liberal environmentalism, these moves remained partial and contested. Undoubtedly there was growing recognition of the importance of incorporating effectiveness and equity into the greening of each city, and all three cities increasingly framed their efforts as contributing to broader environmental governance. Yet in practice the entrepreneurial goal of enhancing the city's place in the global economy and the perceived imperative of supporting businesses and economic growth over other goals continued to shape city environmental efforts.

More detailed consideration of the politics of these incomplete moves beyond green urban entrepreneurialism will be the focus of the rest of the book. The next three chapters shift away from the broad discussion of the cities' greening agendas presenting in this chapter and in Chapter 3 toward a more in-depth examination of how the tensions between growth, equity, and effectiveness have played out in particular issue areas. Looking at energy, development, and green amenities, these chapters will illustrate that the economic benefits of city environmentalism clearly remain paramount and continue to shape and justify urban greening. But diving into each issue will also show how the increasing emphasis on social equity and cities' contributions to addressing global environmental problems seen in this chapter have become even more significant. What is clear from the following investigation is that in the face of growing fiscal pressures, changing national regulatory environments, pressing environmental problems, and ongoing poverty and inequality, city leaders are both "rolling with"[96] and challenging the logics of neoliberal urbanism. In so doing they are also showing the potential – and the difficulties – of moving toward the increased justice and sustainability of progressive liberal environmentalism.

Notes

1   Maria Carmen Lemos and Arun Agrewal, "Environmental Governance," *Annual Review of Environment and Resources* 31 (2006): 298.
2   For example, City of Chicago, "Press Release: City Shifting to Blue Cart Recycling Program by End of 2011" (2008); "Press Release: Daley Repeats Call for Federal, State Action to Rebuild Infrastructure" (2009); "Press Release: Chicago Celebrates Arbor Day with Mayoral Visit to SW Side School" (2010).
3   See "Chicago Climate Action Plan: Our City, Our Future" (Chicago, IL, 2008).
4   Michael E. Kraft, *Environmental Policy and Politics*, 4th edn. (New York, NY: Pearson/Longman, 2007), 107.
5   See Associated Press, "Bush: Kyoto Treaty Would Have Hurt Economy," *NBCNews.com*, June 30, 2005 (accessed May 20, 2016).
6   Anne Underwood, "Mayors Take the Lead," *Newsweek*, April 16, 2007.

7   City of Chicago, "Chicago Climate Action Plan: Our City, Our Future."
8   City of Chicago, "Press Release: Daley, Business, Foundation Leaders Announce Climate Action Plan" (2008), www.cityofchicago.org (accessed October 20, 2010)
9   "Chicago Climate Action Plan: Our City, Our Future," 3, emphasis added.
10 Mick Dumke, "The Political Climate," *Chicago Reader*, September 19, 2008, www.chicagoreader.com/TheBlog/archives/2008/09/19/political-climate (accessed July 1, 2010).
11 Jorge Madrid and Bracken Hendricks, "The Recovery Act: The Most Important Energy Bill in American History," Grist, http://grist.org/green-jobs/2011-02-16-the-most-important-energy-bill-in-american-history/ (accessed July 5, 2016).
12 City of Chicago, "Climate Action Plan: Progress Report, First Two Years" (Chicago, IL, 2010).
13 Ibid.
14 Mayors Climate Protection Center, "Taking Local Action: Mayors and Climate Protection Best Practices" (The United States Conference of Mayors, 2010), ARUP, "Climate Action in Megacities: C40 Cities Baseline and Opportunities" (2011).
15 Local manufacturing sector CEO, personal communication, July 2008.
16 Personal communication, May 2010.
17 Mick Dumke, "Green and Long Green: Daley's Environmental Commissioner on Making Business as Usual Eco-Friendly," *Chicago Reader*, June 5, 2008.
18 Quoted in Richard C. Longworth, "The Political City," in *Global Chicago*, ed. Charles Madigan (Urbana, IL: University of Illinois Press, 2004), 82.
19 Personal communication, May 2010.
20 Personal communication, May 2010.
21 Susan Saulny, "Chicago's 'Mayor for Life' Decides Not to Run," *New York Times*, September 7, 2010.
22 See Kari Lydersen, *Mayor 1%: Rahm Emanuel and the Rise of Chicago's 99%* (Chicago, IL: Haymarket Books, 2013).
23 Rahm Emanuel, "Chicago 2011 Transition Plan" (Chicago, IL, 2011).
24 City of Chicago, "Sustainable Chicago 2015" (Chicago, IL, 2012), 2.
25 "Environment and Sustainability," City of Chicago, www.cityofchicago.org/city/en/progs/env.html (accessed February 15, 2016).
26 "Sustainable Chicago 2015."
27 Ibid., 2.
28 City of Vancouver, "Clouds of Change: Final Report of the City of Vancouver Task Force on Atmospheric Change" (Vancouver, BC, 1990).
29 Sean Pander, "City of Vancouver Climate Protection Progress Report" (Vancouver, BC: City of Vancouver, 2007), 2.
30 John Punter, *The Vancouver Achievement: Urban Planning and Design* (Vancouver, BC: UBC Press, 2003), 154.
31 Artibise and Seelig, 1990, cited in Mark Kear, "Spaces of Transition Spaces of Tomorrow: Making a Sustainable Future in Southeast False Creek, Vancouver," *Cities* 24, no. 4 (2007): 329.
32 Punter.
33 City of Vancouver, "Cityplan: Directions for Vancouver" (Vancouver, BC, 1995).
34 Ibid.
35 "Community Planning 101 – Backgrounder" (Vancouver, BC, n.d.); Lance Berelowitz, *Dream City: Vancouver and the Global Imagination* (Vancouver, BC: Douglas & McIntyre, 2005).

36 Pander.
37 City of Vancouver, "Appendix B: Definition of a Sustainable Vancouver Adopted by Council April 2002" (Vancouver, BC: City of Vancouver, 2002).
38 Merrill Cooper, "Social Sustainability in Vancouver" (Ottawa, Ontario: Canadian Policy Research Networks, 2006), 1.
39 City of Vancouver, "Appendix B: Definition of a Sustainable Vancouver Adopted by Council April 2002," 1.
40 Punter, 229.
41 Kear.
42 Noah Quastel, "Political Ecologies of Gentrification," *Urban Geography* 30, no. 7 (2009).
43 Rob VanWynsberghe, Bjorn Surborg, and Elvin Wyly, "When the Games Come to Town: Neoliberalism, Mega-Events and Social Inclusion in the Vancouver 2010 Winter Olympic Games," *International Journal of Urban and Regional Research* 37, no. 6 (2013): 2078.
44 David Eby, "Still Waiting at the Altar: Vancouver 2010's on-Again, Off-Again, Relationship with Social Sustainability" (Geneva, Switzerland: COHRE Expert Workshop on Protecting and Promoting Housing Rights in the Context of Mega Events, 2007).
45 Ibid.
46 VanWynsberghe, Surborg, and Wyly.
47 Kear.
48 Kear, 333.
49 Eby.
50 Ibid., 10.
51 Quoted in ibid., 11.
52 Libby Porter et al., "Planning Displacement: The Real Legacy of Major Sporting Events 'Just a Person in a Wee Flat': Being Displaced by the Commonwealth Games in Glasgow's East End; Olympian Masterplanning in London Closing Ceremonies: How Law, Policy and the Winter Olympics Are Displacing an Inconveniently Located Low-Income Community in Vancouver; Commentary: Recovering Public Ethos: Critical Analysis for Policy and Planning," *Planning Theory & Practice* 10, no. 3 (2009).
53 Ibid., 411.
54 Eby., VanWynsberghe, Surborg, and Wyly.
55 Porter et al.
56 Ibid., 413, citations omitted.
57 Andrew Smith, *Events and Urban Regeneration: The Strategic Use of Events to Revitalise Cities* (London, UK: Routledge, 2012), 172, citation omitted.
58 Former co-director of planning, quoted in Kear, 327.
59 Justine Hunter, "Vision Prevails in Landslide Victory," *Globe and Mail*, November 17, 2008.
60 City council member, personal communication, August 2014.
61 City of Vancouver, "Greenest City 2020 Action Plan" (Vancouver, BC: City of Vancouver, 2011).
62 Ibid., 11.
63 Ibid.
64 "A Healthy City for All: Vancouver's Healthy City Strategy, 2014–2025" (2014).
65 Personal communication, August 2014.
66 City of Vancouver, "Healthy City Strategy Success Stories," City of Vancouver, http://vancouver.ca/people-programs/healthy-city-strategy-success-stories.aspx (accessed March 1, 2017).

67 Eby.
68 For example, Birmingham City Council, "Towards a Sustainable City: Birmingham City Council Achievements, Local Agenda 21, 1992–2002" (Birmingham, UK: Birmingham City Council, 2002).
69 Ibid., 3.
70 See David Gibbs, Andy Jonas, and Aidan While, "Changing Governance Structures and the Environment: Economy–Environment Relations at the Local and Regional Scales," *Journal of Environmental Policy & Planning* 4 (2002).
71 Robert Imrie and Mike Raco, "Community and the Changing Nature of Urban Policy," in *Urban Renaissance? New Labour, Community and Urban Policy*, ed. Robert Imrie and Mike Raco (Bristol, UK: Policy Press, 2003), 4.
72 Graham Haughton and Aidan While, "From Corporate City to Citizens City? Urban Leadership after Local Entrepreneurialism in the United Kingdom," *Urban Affairs Review* 35, no. 1 (1999): 4.
73 Craig Johnstone and Mark Whitehead, "Horizons and Barriers in British Urban Policy," in *New Horizons in British Urban Policy: Perspectives on New Labour's Urban Renaissance*, ed. Craig Johnstone and Mark Whitehead (Burlington, VT: Ashgate, 2004).
74 Birmingham City Council, "Birmingham Local Area Agreement" (Birmingham, UK, 2006).
75 Andrew E.G. Jonas and Aidan While, "Greening the Entrepreneurial City? Looking for Spaces of Sustainability Politics in the Competitive City," in *The Sustainable Development Paradox: Urban Political Economy in the United States and Europe*, ed. Rob Krueger and David Gibbs (New York, NY: Guilford Press, 2007); Mike Raco, "Spatial Policy, Sustainability, and State Restructuring: A Reassessment of Sustainable Community Building in England," in *The Sustainable Development Paradox: Urban Political Economy in the United States and Europe*, ed. Rob Krueger and David Gibbs (New York, NY: Guilford Press, 2007).
76 Libby Porter and Dexter Hunt, "Birmingham's Eastside Story: Making Steps Towards Sustainability?," *Local Environment* 10, no. 5 (2005): 532.
77 Food UK Secretary of State for Environment, and Rural Affairs, "Securing the Future: Delivering UK Sustainable Development Strategy" (Colegate, UK, 2005).
78 O'Brien, J., "Autumn Statement: Lobbying Pays off with Curb on Energy Levy," *Birmingham Post,* November 10, 1999.
79 Birmingham Post, "Budget: Job Fears Grow over Climate Charges," March 8, 2001.
80 Local environmental activist, personal communication, July 2008.
81 Joanna Geary, "Carbon Trading a Weapon in Battle for the Environment," *Birmingham Post*, July 27, 2005.
82 Birmingham Post, "Fast-Buck, Slow-Death Warning," March 21, 2001.
83 Sustainability official, personal communication, July 2008.
84 Paul Dale, "Council Pledge to Slash CO2 in Brum by Two Thirds," *Birmingham Post*, September 8, 2007.
85 Tim Hall, "Public Art, Civic Identity and the New Birmingham," in *Remaking Birmingham: The Visual Culture of Urban Regeneration*, ed. Liam Kennedy (New York, NY: Routledge, 2004).
86 Quoted in Neil Connor, "Miliband Backs Brum Campaign," *Birmingham Post*, October 26, 2006, emphasis added.
87 Be Birmingham, "Birmingham 2026 – Our Vision for the Future, Sustainable Community Strategy" (Birmingham, UK, 2008); "Birmingham Environmental

Partnership: 08/09 Annual Report" (Birmingham, UK, 2009); "Birmingham Environmental Partnership: 09/10 Annual Report" (Birmingham, UK, 2010); Birmingham City Council, "Birmingham Local Area Agreement"; "Making Birmingham Green: Birmingham Climate Change Action Plan 2010+" (2010); Paul Tilsley, "Agenda: Why We Need to Lead a New Industrial Revolution," *Birmingham Post*, January 9, 2008; "Agenda: Time for Change," *Birmingham Post*, January 7, 2009.

88 Quoted in Paul Dale, "Council Pledge to Slash CO2 in Brum by Two Thirds," *Birmingham Post*, September 8, 2007.

89 Quoted in ibid.

90 "Global Warming 'Now Bigger Threat Than Terrorism,'" *Birmingham Post*, January 23, 2007.

91 Birmingham Post, "Greening of City: Good Start, Now Let's Have Action," December 26, 2006; Peter Beck, "Letter: Fiddling While Our World Burns," *Birmingham Post*, September 25, 2006.

92 Overview and Scrutiny Committee, "Report of the Sustainability and Climate Change Overview and Scrutiny Committee" (Birmingham, UK: Birmingham City Council, 2007).

93 Birmingham Post, "City Council Climate Change Strategy Is Based on Hot Air" March 16, 2009.

94 Birmingham's Green Commission, "Building a Green City" (Birmingham, UK: Birmingham City Council, 2013).

95 Ibid., 3.

96 Roger Keil, "The Urban Politics of Roll-with-It Neoliberalism," *City* 13, no. 2–3 (2009).

5   Energy and Climate Justice

Energy production and efficiency is the first area that will be examined to help illuminate the contested moves in Vancouver, Birmingham, and Chicago between different varieties of liberal environmentalism. The issue of energy is important for a number of reasons. First of all, energy use is a major source of carbon emissions in most cities, so this sector is often a focus of cities' delves into climate governance. Second, energy efficiency is one of the easiest ways to achieve liberal environmentalism's win–win promise of saving money while protecting the environment. Third, energy use and production are interwoven with issues of pollution and climate justice, and the importance of reducing emissions in a socially just way can be seen in each of these cases.

Liberal Environmentalism and the Challenge of Multiscalar Climate Justice

Energy efficiency sits comfortably across all varieties of liberal environmentalism. It is not energy per se that businesses and households want, it is the services that energy provides (turning on the lights, running machinery, cooling buildings, etc.). Therefore, using less energy to achieve the same services is a clear win–win, saving money and reducing energy production's accompanying greenhouse gases. The payback time for many efficiency technologies is fairly short, and they are often seen as the low-hanging fruit of urban carbon reductions. LED lights, building weatherization, and high-efficiency appliances have all become standard ways for municipalities, households, and business to save money and emissions by reducing energy consumption.

As important as it is, efficiency quickly runs into limitations. Even efficiency technologies with fairly short payback periods still require an up-front investment that not everyone is willing or able to make. This is exacerbated when the payback is longer or when upfront investments are substantial. In these instances, relying on voluntary adoption of efficiency measures is unlikely to be sufficient. Achieving substantial reductions in energy use will therefore require either mandates or subsidies, and cities vary in their willingness to take these steps. Similar limitations emerge around switching to low carbon energy sources, particularly when oil and gas prices are low.

In addition to potentially furthering the economic benefits promised by all varieties of liberal environmentalism, energy efficiency and greener energy production can also contribute to environmental and climate justice. These benefits may accrue at both the local and global scales. On a local scale, switching away from fossil fuels can reduce the environmental justice burdens of energy production, particularly exposure to air pollution in neighborhoods near power plants. Efficiency measures and access to renewables can also further well-being by saving low-income households money on their energy bills.

Globally, carbon emissions are a justice issue in that there is a "geographic mismatch" between the rich countries that have done the most to cause climate change and benefited from the consumption of fossil fuels and those countries, particularly in the global South, who will suffer most from it through sea-level rise, food insecurity, and the increasing intensity of extreme weather events.[1] To many, this chasm between those who have caused climate change and those who will be most impacted by it is deeply unjust. Addressing this injustice will require rapid and significant cuts in GHG emissions from rich countries combined with efforts to reduce communities' vulnerability to the climate disruption that has already been locked in by past emissions.[2] By undertaking programs to reduce their GHG emissions, the energy policies of cities in the global North can therefore contribute to global climate justice.

As important as the above claim is that climate justice is a multiscalar issue, examining climate mitigation at the level of the city illustrates that achieving climate justice on the local and global scale simultaneously is more difficult than it may appear.[3] Accomplishing multiscalar climate justice is challenging because of the differences between people's carbon emissions within rich states themselves, differences that are connected to domestic income distribution, region, and urban design.[4] The thorniness comes that, on the one hand, global climate justice requires that any and all efforts be taken by rich, high-emitting countries to reduce emissions dramatically in order to limit the impacts of climate change as much as possible. On the other hand, doing so may raise the cost of fuel, transportation, housing, and goods in the global North. If one recognizes that there is variation in carbon emissions and climate vulnerability within rich countries, climate mitigation efforts by cities in the global North that disproportionately impact low-income residents can be understood as furthering injustices on a local level.

A number of factors determine whether or not climate mitigation policies exacerbate existing inequalities. Some approaches to carbon reduction undoubtedly have regressive effects by making daily necessities more expensive. These effects can be counteracted with appropriate pro-poor policy design,[5] but achieving energy efficiency and greener energy production in an effective, just way is by no means straightforward.[6] Even for the most committed city, attaining the money and carbon savings of energy efficiency and clean energy production – and doing so in a way that furthers local as well as global climate justice – is challenging. It requires a difficult combination of local political will, enabling national policies, and successful navigation of changing global energy markets.

Green Energy and Fuel Poverty

The potential and the difficulties of moving toward green, just energy production and efficiency can be seen in the impressive success and abysmal failures of Birmingham's climate initiatives. As discussed in Chapter 4, in the early 2000s Birmingham promoted its contribution to climate governance with enthusiasm and not a little bravado, claiming it was becoming the "birthplace of the low carbon revolution." Two of the major energy policies it adopted to achieve its carbon reduction goals will be examined here. One, combined heat and power generation (CHP) in the city center, has been very successful. It has reduced carbon emissions, saved the city and downtown property owners money on energy bills, and given Birmingham national recognition as a leader in this green technology. The other major policy, Birmingham Energy Savers (BES), illustrates city leaders' recognition of the importance of combining GHG reductions and social justice, particularly by reducing fuel poverty. Indeed, more than the other two cities examined here, Birmingham city leaders have focused explicitly on the equity impacts of reducing carbon emissions. However, this move toward progressive liberal environmentalism was not successful. A combination of local implementation failures and changing national energy policies meant that Birmingham came nowhere near to achieving the goals of BES and is struggling to find other ways to further efficiency, reduce carbon emissions, and eliminate the scourge of fuel poverty.

Combined Heat and Power – Building Birmingham's Win–Win

Combined heat and power, also known as cogeneration, is a form of power generation that utilizes the heat that is usually a waste product of energy production. Instead of being released, the heat is captured and redirected to provide heating, air conditioning, and hot water for buildings. The efficiency of these schemes can be up to 75 or 80 percent, much higher than the 30 to 40 percent efficiency of typical power generation, thereby reducing energy use and GHG emissions.[7] CHP also reduces energy costs over the long term and so provides both financial and environmental benefits.

Birmingham's first major CHP plant was on Broad Street, in the city center. Conceptualized in 2003, it began operating in 2007 and provides power for all the major downtown prestige projects including the ICC, the Repertory Theater, the National Indoor Arena (renamed the Barclaycard Arena after major renovations in 2004), and the Hyatt hotel. It also provides power for a number of municipal buildings and smaller adjacent businesses. The Broad Street CHP scheme was a joint project between the Birmingham City Council and a private energy firm, the latter of which invested nearly £4 million in the project in exchange for twenty-five year energy contracts from the businesses connected to the district energy system.[8] Illustrative of Birmingham's ability to successfully compete for the grants that were key to the Blair government's urban sustainable development agenda, the scheme also received substantial funding from the national government. In 2004, the government's Community Energy Program gave the council £700,000 for the early stages of the initiative, followed the next year by an additional £1.3 million to connect a CHP scheme in the children's hospital to Aston University's new Eastside campus.[9] Some adjacent low-income council housing blocks were also connected to the system (Figure 5.1).[10]

Birmingham's CHP schemes were greatly facilitated by government grants, but the ambitious uptake and expansion of the city's district energy system is generally attributed to strong leadership from powerful members of the city council.[11] Deputy Leader Tilsley, a major proponent of Birmingham's "low carbon revolution," was particularly instrumental. According to an informant close to the project, Tilsely saw the Birmingham district energy scheme as a key component of this "revolution" and as his opportunity "to be like Joseph Chamberlain" in making a long-lasting mark on the city by re-shaping it around clean energy and low carbon development.[12] CHP was also seen by the Local Strategic Partnership as a way to attract companies to the city center with guaranteed low-cost energy, thereby creating jobs and "putting [Birmingham] at the center of the low carbon" economy.[13]

From city councilors to the voluntary sector to local businesses, district energy is consistently highlighted as Birmingham's most important success in its efforts to reduce emissions and promote environmental sustainability. Even in the face of the severe austerity measures of Prime Minister David Cameron, elected in 2010, the expansion of CHP moved ahead. The new Birmingham Library that opened in 2013 was connected to the Broad Street district energy scheme, cutting energy use and GHG emissions in the building by an estimated 70 percent from conventional systems.[14] In 2015 the city's two major CHP systems, the Broad Street scheme and the Eastside scheme, were connected via the refurbished New Street train station, a redevelopment that both greatly improved the user experience of the station and was offered as an exemplar of green development.[15]

Figure 5.1 A sign on the Children's Hospital tracks and publicizes the carbon savings from the hospital's connection to the Birmingham District Energy scheme.

Source: Photo by author, 2016.

District energy represents the best of the promises of liberal environmentalism's technological fixes to the problem of climate change, and Birmingham is one of the leading cities in the country at providing this form of highly efficient heat and power generation. Even if becoming the "birthplace of the low carbon revolution" has been an elusive goal, the city's commitment helped put Birmingham on the map as a leader in low carbon technologies, winning an award from the Queen in 2008. CHP has provided lower cost energy to city center businesses, municipal operations, and some low-income residents of the city. Birmingham's district energy schemes are also estimated to reduce the city's carbon emissions by 20,000 tonnes per year over more traditional forms of electricity generation and heating.[16] As such, district energy continues to be a major part of Birmingham's efforts to reduce carbon emissions while spurring city center development.[17]

Fuel Poverty and the Weight of National Energy Policies

In contrast to the success of district energy, Birmingham's equally ambitious initiative to reduce carbon emissions in a way that also eliminated fuel poverty in the city was much less successful. This program, which came to be known as Birmingham Energy Savers (BES),[18] is worth extensive examination in that it clearly and explicitly focused on the intersection of environmental sustainability and social justice. Its failure offers a sobering reflection on the difficulties of moving toward progressive liberal environmentalism.

Fuel poverty has long been a major concern in Great Britain. The official definition of fuel poverty has changed somewhat over the years, but it basically means being in a situation where one spends too much of one's income on heating the home, with those in the most severe fuel poverty often having to choose between heating and food. Birmingham, reflecting both the poor condition of much of its housing stock and its high levels of poverty, has an estimated 20.1 percent of its population living in fuel poverty, nearly double the estimated rate of fuel poverty across England as a whole.[19] Addressing fuel poverty is therefore a priority for Birmingham leaders.

Fuel poverty is clearly a social justice concern, contributing to discomfort, disease, and extra winter deaths, particularly among the elderly.[20] Some have argued that fuel poverty is also a climate justice issue, as it fundamentally means insufficient access to the services provided by fossil fuels, specifically heating the home. However, from the perspective of multiscalar climate justice, increasing fuel consumption, which has been the main emphasis of UK fuel poverty relief efforts, is deeply problematic in that it increases overall carbon emissions, thereby exacerbating climate injustice on a global scale.[21] Therefore, a locally *and* globally just response to fuel poverty is to increase people's ability to have a sufficiently warm home without increasing fuel consumption and its accompanying emissions. This can be achieved by enhancing the efficiency of homes and switching to less polluting energy sources.[22] Indeed, the "low-hanging fruit" of insulation and efficient appliances should offer fairly easy technological fixes to the injustice of fuel poverty. But the failure of BES shows that this is not always so straightforward.

As the Local Strategic Partnership was discussing how to rebrand Birmingham as a leading low carbon city (see Chapter 4), there was also a growing recognition that the successful regeneration of the city center had not solved Birmingham's persistent challenges of poverty and unemployment.[23] The city center had been reinvigorated and the economy of the city had become increasingly post-industrial, but issues of social inequality remained pronounced. Some members of the Strategic Partnership therefore saw the city's carbon reduction goals as a way to also further social equity, particularly by providing low carbon energy technologies to council houses and the city's poor.[24]

Consistent with Birmingham's tendency to establish quite ambitious sustainability goals, when the pilot programs were launched in late 2010, BES had the goal of upgrading 10,000 council houses with energy efficiency retrofits and solar panels, then using the proceeds from the national solar feed-in tariff[25] to refinance the program to retrofit an additional 200,000 homes.[26] The even more ambitious long-term goal of BES was to retrofit all 450,000 homes in the city, including those that were privately owned.[27] This would have been an incredible accomplishment, and as it was being rolled out BES was celebrated as creating green jobs, reducing carbon emissions, helping solve fuel poverty, and "setting a green standard beyond that of any city in the world."[28] Shorter term, it was expected that BES would help 26,000 households out of fuel poverty.[29]

Though a city program, BES, as well as Birmingham's plans to achieve overall emissions reductions of 60 percent by 2026 (see Chapter 4), relied heavily on national energy policies.[30] In 2008, the UK passed two important pieces of legislation, the Energy Act and the Climate Change Act, the latter of which set a legally binding goal for the country of reducing emissions by 80 percent over 1990 levels by 2050. Three major programs to emerge from the government's new commitment to climate mitigation were feed-in tariffs, the Green Deal, and the Energy Company Obligation (ECO). The feed-in tariff was vital for justifying the upfront costs of BES's plan to install renewable energy on council housing. Because of the generosity of the tariffs, the council was confident it would be able to quickly recoup the costs of the installations, and then generate revenue from them that could be invested in further retrofits.[31] Whereas the feed-in tariff encouraged the installation of renewable energy, the idea of the Green Deal and ECO was that they would work together to increase home energy efficiency across the country, helping the nation reach its GHG reduction goal. The Green Deal offered loans to individual households to fund efficiency measures. ECO required large energy companies to pay for improvements in the energy efficiency of their customers' buildings, especially those most vulnerable to fuel poverty.

Despite the promise of BES, and the national policies supporting Birmingham's investment in a low carbon plan to reduce fuel poverty, BES failed to come anywhere close to achieving its goals. Though there were a few isolated successes,[32] after several years of effort BES had provided some form of efficiency measures to only 3400 homes,[33] a far cry from eliminating fuel poverty in 26,000 households and eventually enhancing efficiency for all dwellings in the city. In the spring of 2016

BES was officially cancelled, admitting to a failure that had been obvious for some time.

The reasons for the failure of BES are myriad and sit awkwardly in the intersection of local and national energy politics. Locally, there were many problems with the design and implementation of the program. One major problem was the failure of the City to recognize that even basic technological changes such as improving insulation and increasing the efficiency of homes can be political. Officials acted as if simply providing people the opportunity to receive help with efficiency and weatherization would inspire them to do so. But the way BES marketed its programs through blanket advertising and cold calling "allow[ed] for little targeting of specific housing types or demographics. Such an approach [was] seen to be offputting to consumers and … fail[ed] to effectively address individual household complexities."[34] This failure to address individual household needs was especially problematic for fuel-poor households, many of whom distrusted the local government because of past failed responses to their concerns.[35]

BES suffered from other local implementation failures as well.[36] One was the complexity of the process of acquiring a BES installation. The city officials originally involved in setting up the program insisted it should be cheap and simple, but as it was implemented BES ended up being expensive and complicated.[37] This negated the potential energy cost savings for many households. Another problem was that the large energy company contracted to implement BES was given insufficient oversight by the council.[38] The company was interested in using BES to fulfill its obligations under ECO rather than maximizing energy efficiency in the city. This meant that the company wanted to do the easiest projects possible, rather than take on large projects with a bigger impact such as retrofitting a whole neighborhood to achieve economies of scale.[39] The council could have mandated such an approach when it contracted with the company for BES, but it was unwilling to do so, nor was it willing to hold the company accountable for its failure to achieve the goals of BES.[40]

In addition to local design and implementation problems, changing national policies also had an important role to play in the failure of BES, particularly the retrenchment of the Green Deal and ECO. The national Green Deal and its goal of inspiring households across the country to invest in energy retrofits was widely recognized to be a failure, with fewer than two thousand homes nationally taking out Green Deal loans by late 2014.[41] In July 2015, the Green Deal was cancelled altogether. Although few bemoaned the loss of this program, with no alternative taking its place the government's financial commitment to funding home efficiency improvements was for all practical purposes eliminated.[42]

ECO was more successful, leading to the installation nationally of 819,000 efficiency measures by 2014.[43] Even while touting its success, in mid-2014 the Department of Energy & Climate Change (DECC) announced cuts of 33 percent to the emissions reduction obligation energy companies had to meet under ECO. Unsurprisingly, this led to an immediate decrease in the installation of efficiency measures, with DECC estimating the change would lead to 553,000 fewer efficiency improvements being installed at a loss of almost three million metric tons of carbon savings per year. The government did negotiate a reduction in consumer energy bills in exchange for the cuts to ECO. Even with these rate cuts, some estimates expected the energy companies to see an extra £245 million in profits annually because of the forgone investments in efficiency.[44]

The Cameron government's justification for weakening the ECO requirements was to ease consumers' utility costs, as the average energy bill increased 75 percent between 2004 and 2014.[45] This is an interesting justification, as the potential for carbon reduction measures to hurt the poor through higher energy bills is a main social justice concern of such efforts. But in this case justifying cuts to ECO as a way to benefit the poor through reduced energy bills was a spurious argument. According to the government's own analysis, energy and climate policies only accounted for one-fifth of the decade's increase in utility bills, with much of the increase due to higher international energy prices.[46] This meant that without the energy efficiency measures implemented over that same time period, utility bills would have increased even further, particularly for the fuel-poor households that ECO targeted.[47] Therefore, though cuts in ECO requirements may have provided some short-term relief for rate-payers, these cuts are likely to increase costs in the long-run as energy efficiency improvements are forgone.

With ECO cut, the Green Deal cancelled, and BES formally ended, Birmingham was left without clear tools for reducing fuel poverty or for achieving the efficiency improvements that BES promised. Even as it succeeds in providing green energy to its businesses through CHP, fuel poverty remains a daunting problem, and the city struggles to realize its ambitions of "mak[ing] Birmingham more prosperous, fairer and a better place to be" for all.[48] A combination of overly ambitious upfront goals without a clear understanding of the investment and political effort it would take to achieve them and a deteriorating national regulatory environment are moving the city's climate justice goals increasingly out of reach.

Retrofits and Climate Justice

Chicago's retrofit program, like Birmingham's CHP, shows the potential of liberal environmentalism to further more environmentally sound energy practices. Even with a focus on voluntarism and weak local government mandates, strong political will can facilitate moderately effective approaches to reducing carbon emissions and achieving the financial benefits of energy efficiency. Chicago also shows the vital role that grass-roots groups can play in spurring action by city officials, in this case action to address the environmental justice impacts of energy production. Yet, as with the failures of Birmingham Energy Savers, Chicago's major climate justice victory was facilitated by changing national regulations and energy markets, illustrating again the embeddedness of city greening in larger political-economic processes.

The Limits of Voluntarism

Whereas Birmingham's greatest success in climate mitigation has been in the efficiency and cost savings of district energy schemes, Chicago has been most successful at promoting energy efficiency in existing buildings. The efficiency efforts that have been undertaken in Chicago illustrate the potential, but also the limitations, of liberal environmentalism in practice. As proponents of liberal environmentalism assert, reducing energy use from building operations is a win–win because it saves money as well as reduces carbon emissions. Furthermore, consistent with the neoliberal end of the spectrum of varieties of liberal environmentalism, financial incentives and voluntary initiatives can, if done correctly, encourage such changes. As seen in Chapter 4, Chicago's move beyond green urban entre-preneurialism has largely remained committed to this more neoliberal approach to environmentalism, and there has been limited political inter-est in mandates or regulation. This commitment to voluntarism, along with public–private partnerships, has largely defined Chicago's energy efficiency programs.

With significant fanfare, in 2012 Mayor Emanuel announced a $7.3 billion plan called "Building a New Chicago" that was to repair and rebuild the city's aging infrastructure. The Chicago Infrastructure Trust was at the core of this plan. The idea of the Trust was that it would "transform Chicago with mega-projects so sexy they could be bankrolled entirely by private investors in exchange for a chunk of the profits. ... [It was heralded] as a 'breakout strategy' for modernizing buildings, bridges and broadband without waiting for Washington handouts."[49] The Trust, it was promised, would attract investors with an interest in stability and return on investment who would cover the upfront costs of infrastructure improvements. In exchange, they would receive long-term returns from the revenue generated from the new infrastructure.

The premise of the Infrastructure Trust is based on a number of assumptions. First, it assumes that investing in infrastructure improve-ments will indeed generate a measurable payback. Second, it assumes that there are investors willing to make this long-term investment in the city. A few years into the program, very few investors had been willing to do so, and the Trust took off much more slowly than anticipated.[50] Retrofitting municipal buildings offered a partial exception, as the cost savings from energy efficiency improvements were fairly easy to predict and, crucially, the City had direct control over the buildings. Retrofitting Chicago municipal buildings was therefore the first project of the Trust, with 60 municipal buildings undergoing retrofits by 2014, for an energy savings of 18 percent and a payback to the investor, Bank of America, of nearly 5 percent over 15 years.[51] The clear win–win of the municipal retrofit plan led it to be well-received locally, even as community groups raised larger concerns about the lack of transparency and public accountability within the Trust as a whole.[52]

Further illustrating the potential benefits of this public–private partnership approach to municipal efficiency, in late 2016 the City announced a project coordinated by the Trust to retrofit more than 270,000 city streetlights to high-efficiency LEDs. These retrofits will reduce energy use from streetlights by 50–75 percent, generating both energy and cost savings. The lights will be owned and operated by the City, with the electricity cost savings generated by the LED lights going to the private company that paid for the modernization.[53]

From the perspective of equity and climate justice, the money saved by such endeavors would ideally go to funding retrofits in lower income households, green energy production, or other ways to reduce fossil fuel use that may not have clear financial paybacks but are necessary for achieving equity and GHG emission reductions. The Trust, wherein the cost savings go to a private investor rather than being reinvested in the city, therefore represents a missed opportunity to lower emissions further and to mitigate local climate injustices. However, as the up-front costs of energy efficiency improvements are one of the major barriers to their implementation, and as sufficient government funds for such improvements do not appear to be forthcoming, the approach taken by the Trust does enable efficiency improvements that the City would be hard-pressed to fund on its own.

Chicago's other major efficiency program, Retrofit Chicago, has also been committed to neoliberal approaches to environmentalism, in this case voluntary measures. But it has been complemented by a tentative foray into local government mandates, specifically the Energy Benchmarking Ordinance, passed in 2013. This law requires all "existing commercial, institutional, and residential buildings larger than 50,000 square feet to track whole-building energy use, report to the City annually, and verify data accuracy every three years. The law covers less than 1% of Chicago's buildings, which account for ~20% of total energy used by all buildings."[54] On one hand, this initiative is fairly bold, and when it passed few other cities in the country had any similar reporting requirements.[55] Even as they took this step toward regulation, however, the City made the decision not to mandate anything other than reporting. The explanation for this was the mayor's belief that "information is the key to action…. [The City] wanted to be sure that every decision-maker had access to the best information about energy efficiency [and the] big environmental and economic opportunity" reducing energy consumption offered them.[56]

Ideally, once the Energy Benchmarking Ordinance ensures that information on energy use is available, building owners will then enter into a voluntary commitment called the Chicago Energy Challenge to reduce building energy use by 20 percent. The City's related program, Retrofit Chicago, helps facilitate this by providing information on state, federal, and private resources available to building owners that invest in efficiency. By 2015, 50 commercial buildings had committed to the Chicago Energy Challenge and together had reduced energy use by nearly 12 percent, preventing about 70,000 tonnes of carbon emissions. By mid-2016 the program had expanded to 62 buildings covering about 43 million square feet of office space. This made it, according to the City, "one of the largest voluntary efficiency programs in the country."[57] Reiterating the themes that have defined Chicago's greening for decades, in a press release Emanuel asserted, "the Energy Challenge moves the City of Chicago and its residents forward by reducing costs for building owners, cutting carbon pollution, and putting people to work in 21st-century jobs. ... [This] is a true win–win that makes our environment safer and our economy stronger for every Chicagoan."[58] Though it is not clear how "every Chicagoan" benefits from efficiency improvements in large commercial and institutional buildings, the energy savings from the program are real and growing. The Chicago Energy Challenge has been celebrated by the National Resource Defense Council as well as the Midwest Energy Efficiency Alliance as best practice for encouraging efficiency in large commercial, residential and institutional buildings.[59]

While the program remains promising, 62 buildings committing to the Chicago Energy Challenge's voluntary goal is barely 3 percent of the more than 1800 buildings that are required to report their energy use through the Energy Benchmarking Ordinance.[60] This begs the question as to the effectiveness of information gathering and the promise of cost savings alone as impetuses for energy efficiency. Making large buildings more efficient is complicated, and for many building owners the difficulty of doing so is apparently not worth the benefits of energy savings. Balancing what Chicago officials see as politically viable with the substantial environmental potential of more aggressive initiatives to reduce emissions from buildings will continue to be the challenge for Chicago's efforts to achieve highly effective contributions to climate change mitigation through energy efficiency.

Coal and Climate Justice in Chicago

Efficiency is one way that cities can reduce GHG emissions. As efficiency can only go so far, cleaning up energy production is also vital to reducing urban carbon emissions. One of the most important changes that has occurred in Chicago has been the move away from coal, an especially carbon-intensive energy source.[61] One aspect of this was the Emanuel administration's decision to contract for coal-free energy for all municipal operations.[62] Even more noteworthy was the closure in 2012 of the city's two coal-fired power plants.

The environmental justice battle to close the Fisk and Crawford coal-fired power plants, both of which were located in the predominantly Latino neighborhoods of Little Village and Pilsen, had been underway for nearly a decade when Emanuel became mayor. Credit for the closure can therefore only partly be attributed to him, though city officials insist that there was a "huge amount of ... mayoral engagement on [the] topic" of closing the plants.[63] Indeed, this vital contribution to GHG reductions and environmental justice in the city occurred in the confluence of Chicago's ongoing green branding, the contested mayoral election, and a changing global market and national regulatory environment that made coal decreasingly competitive. The victory therefore illustrates the complexity of cities' abilities to further socially just, environmentally effective climate and energy initiatives.[64]

The Fisk and Crawford power plants, built before World War I, were the two largest point sources of air pollution in Chicago, contributing to elevated instances of asthma and other respiratory diseases in the areas surrounding the plants.[65] Since the early 2000s community members, led by the Little Village Environmental Justice Organization (LVEJO) and the Pilsen Environmental Rights and Reform Organization (PERRO), had been working to have the plants switch to natural gas or to be shut down.[66] As the campaign progressed, a broader coalition formed, including these local environmental justice groups as well as large environmental organizations and public health groups. Though not without tensions, the Chicago Clean Power Coalition was celebrated by many as "one of the most determined, diverse and successful clean energy campaigns in the nation"[67] (Figure 5.2). When the plants were finally shut down in 2012, the closure not only eliminated the source of a local environmental injustice but also reduced global carbon emissions by about five million metric tons a year.[68]

A number of factors led to the shuttering of Fisk and Crawford after years of community effort. The broad-based Clean Power Coalition gave the issue visibility beyond the two neighborhoods most actively involved. The 2011 local election created an opening that activists used to get the power plants onto the city's wider political agenda. The local alderman, who had long resisted calls to close the plants, was in a tight election and activists targeted him, highlighting the campaign contributions he had received from the plants' owner, Midwest Generation. Facing a runoff, the alderman agreed to support the ordinance to clean up the plants, his changed position necessary to get other aldermen on board. Even more important

Figure 5.2 This anti-Fisk and Crawford campaign advertisement in an L station
         reads, "The coal-fired power plants in Pilsen and Little Village have
         a new filter. His name is Peter." The Clean Power Coalition was able
         to build visibility and support across the city for the campaign to
         shutter the plants.
Source: Photo by author, 2012.

was the mayoral election, the first after Daley's resignation. Extensive community organizing and pressure led candidate Emanuel to promise that if
elected he would address the plants, a promise that was key to getting support from environmental groups.[69] Emanuel was elected and in February
2012 his office announced that the new mayor had negotiated an agreement by which both plants would soon be closed.[70]

  This victory for local and global climate justice was undoubtedly the
result of years of dedicated and effective community organizing targeting a
political opportunity created by the municipal election. Yet it was not just a
local phenomenon. It was also enabled by the changing economics of coal
and federal regulations that made running the plants increasingly unvi-
able financially. According to the U.S. Energy Information Administration
(EIA), 60 gigawatts of coal-fired energy production capacity are set to
retire by 2020. The EIA cites "the need to comply with the Environmental
Protection Agency's (EPA) Mercury and Air Toxics Standards (MATS)
regulations together with weak electricity demand growth and continued
competition from generators fueled by natural gas" as being the driving

forces behind these closures.[71] Indeed, only months after closing Fisk and Crawford, Midwest Generation declared bankruptcy, citing decreased electricity demand and the low cost of natural gas.[72]

This is not to say that activist pressure did not speed up the closures of Fisk and Crawford, perhaps significantly. As already mentioned, the campaign had been going on for nearly ten years, with Mayor Daley notably silent on community concerns about the health impacts of the power plants. There was nothing inevitable about Mayor Emanuel's response to the Clean Power Coalition's organizing and, indeed, many "thought [closing the plants] to be impossible."[73] But activists were able to capitalize on the confluence of an opening in the local political context, careful coalition building and effective organizing, and changing regulatory and economic conditions on the national scale to achieve this victory.[74]

A victory for climate justice and for the environment, it is less clear that the coal plants' closure was able to enhance the mayor's political legitimacy beyond his initial election. Attempting to illustrate his environmental credentials and responsiveness to community concerns, Emanuel's re-election campaign in 2014–15 highlighted the closure of the plants in one of his campaign ads. This garnered swift push-back from many of the community groups who had been involved in the long effort to shut down Fisk and Crawford, and protesters slammed Emanuel for "exploiting [their] success to bolster his campaign."[75] In a contentious election in which Mayor Emanuel was forced into an unprecedented run-off, largely because of his handling of school closures and other issues that deeply impacted low-income communities and communities of color,[76] activists were not going to let him get away with taking credit for a community victory. This tension, as will be discussed in the next two chapters, can be seen in many of Chicago's ongoing environmental initiatives. Even as some of the City's efforts are making important contributions to environmental sustainability and are beginning to expand Chicago's greening in more just and equitable directions, there is still much frustration with and distrust of Mayor Emanuel's proclaimed goal of making the city more sustainable for all.

High Ambition and City Limits

Like Birmingham and Chicago, Vancouver's efforts to green the energy sector show the necessity of local political will in enhancing efficiency as well as the extent to which changing policies beyond the scale of the city may impact these efforts. Overall, Vancouver has been quite successful at increasing energy efficiency and lowering the carbon emissions of its new and existing buildings. Yet Vancouver's attempt to intervene in national policy debates in order to further its broader contribution to climate mitigation and enhance its green brand have been less successful. Vancouver therefore illustrates both the potential effectiveness of city leadership and the limits of even the most ambitious cities in making broader contributions to global climate governance.

Greening New Development

As discussed in the previous chapter, even as Mayor Sullivan deprioritized social sustainability in the Southeast False Creek/Olympic Village development,[77] his administration continued to promote Vancouver's leadership on environmentally sustainable urban development. In addition to making the Olympic Village an exemplar green community, in 2005 Vancouver adopted the requirement that all applications for rezoning in the city include plans for a LEED Silver building, with rezonings on sites larger than two acres having to meet additional sustainability measures. Like the environmental amenities that by this point had become an expected part of megadevelopments, these requirements began to "institutionalize sustainability and gear the city towards a development pathway that consumes and wastes less energy."[78] In 2007, "Council passed a motion directing staff to begin planning for significant, long-range GHG reductions with the eventual goal of becoming a carbon-neutral city." This included the goal of having all new construction be carbon neutral by 2030 and an 80 percent reduction in community emissions by 2050.[79]

The Greenest City 2020 Action Plan, introduced in Chapter 4, built on these goals, rebranding them for the new Vision Vancouver mayor and council and striving to further institutionalize environmentally effective building practices. The GCAP included two main energy and climate goals for buildings. The first was to require that by 2020 all new buildings be net zero carbon. The second was to reduce energy use and GHG emissions in existing buildings by 20 percent from 2007 levels.[80] This goal was further strengthened in 2015 with the council supporting a commitment to make the city fossil-fuel free by 2050, with 100 percent of the energy used in Vancouver coming from renewable sources.[81]

As efficiency is the cheapest way to reduce fossil fuel use, and has the co-benefits of saving money, building efficiency has been a main focus of moving toward this goal of a fossil-fuel-free city.[82] Interestingly, and perhaps offering a challenge to the city's ability to achieve its goal, buildings in Vancouver represent a smaller part of overall carbon emissions than in many cities (e.g. 55 percent in Vancouver vs. Chicago's 70 percent). Vancouver's temperate climate is part of the reason for this. Even more important is that the city's electricity comes from the provincial energy provider, BC Hydro. BC Hydro was created by the BC government to provide cheap electricity to industry during the post-World War II boom in the province's extractive sector. Because of the bountiful water resources in the province, the utility generates the vast majority of its power from GHG-free hydroelectricity.[83] The electricity used in buildings in Vancouver therefore has little climate impact. Rather, natural gas is the main source of carbon emissions from buildings. Although 58 percent of the energy used in a typical building in Vancouver comes from natural gas, it is responsible for 96 percent of an average building's GHG emissions.[84]

This means that changing global energy markets have had a quite different impact on Vancouver than Chicago. As discussed above, the falling cost of natural gas facilitated the closing of the Fisk and Crawford coal-fired power plants in Chicago, benefiting local environmental justice and reducing the city's carbon emissions. In Vancouver, inexpensive natural gas is making the City's efficiency and climate goals more difficult to achieve. The relatively high cost of electricity compared to natural gas has led to a shift in the market toward electricity conservation. Conversely, the falling cost of natural gas has meant a "more challenging business case for natural gas efficiency measures and retrofits to existing buildings."[85] Since Vancouver is fundamentally concerned with overall carbon emissions, rather than energy use per se, this offers another illustration of the limits of relying on cost savings as an incentive to reducing emissions. Despite this challenge, Vancouver has adopted a number of methods to increase the efficiency of the city's buildings in order to reduce overall energy use, including the use of natural gas, and accompanying GHG emissions. The main strategies have been voluntary efforts to encourage benchmarking and efficiency enhancements, the construction of low carbon district heating schemes, and strict efficiency requirements for new buildings and remodels.

Energy benchmarking in Vancouver offers an interesting comparison to Chicago. Both cities assert that energy benchmarking will lead to adoption of voluntary energy efficiency measures. But unlike Chicago, Vancouver does not have the legal ability to mandate that building owners report their energy use. It is therefore in the difficult place of having both benchmarking *and* proceeding efficiency improvements be voluntary. In contrast to Chicago, however, the reliance on voluntarism is out of legal necessity, not political calculations. Indeed, Vancouver officials clearly recognize the limitations of voluntary benchmarking and are working with the provincial government and other local governments in the region to create a policy to mandate benchmarking and annual energy reporting in large buildings in the province.[86]

In the meantime, the City has been striving to advance voluntary building efficiency improvements. In early 2016, the City created a $1 million-dollar Building Energy Retrofit Fund to help facilitate efficiency upgrades in existing building stock. The Fund focuses on providing money for heritage home retrofits, supporting landlords in making their properties greener, and developing a shared reporting system for voluntary energy benchmarking. Like Retrofit Chicago's role as a clearinghouse for existing efficiency programs and funds, Vancouver's Building Energy Retrofit Fund aims to leverage $8 million from the province, utilities, and private investors. The City claims that the benefits of this million-dollar public investment will be broadly shared and that the Fund will "help create green jobs, preserve affordable housing stock by investing in older rental buildings, preserve character homes, and maximize uptake of utility incentives for energy retrofits."[87] Even as they call for greater regulatory powers, Vancouver officials see such voluntary efforts as an important part of their strategy, and claim that the City's active promotion of federal and provincial efficiency incentives has significantly increased their uptake by Vancouver property owners.[88]

The City uses voluntary initiatives and incentives when it must, but Vancouver officials are willing to mandate changes when they are legally able to do so. Consistent with Vancouver's move toward strong eco-liberalism that pushes the market in greener directions, Vancouver has adopted ambitious green building standards to further its goal of making the city fossil fuel free. In 2014, the Vancouver Building By-Law was changed to require that by 2020 all new homes use 50 percent less energy than homes did in 2007. In an effort to improve existing building stock as well as make new buildings greener, the by-law also required that all home remodels over $5000 undertake sustainability audits, with efficiency upgrades required for larger remodels.[89] In 2016, the requirement for new buildings was strengthened with the Zero Emissions Building Plan that set out a strategy for all new buildings to have zero carbon emissions by 2030.[90]

These efforts seem to be effective. As of 2015, "prescribed improvements for energy efficiency in single family homes (such as increased insulation, better air sealing, improved windows and more efficient heating systems) have reduced GHG emissions from new houses by over 50% as compared to those built to the 2007 requirements. Comprehensive incentives for home energy retrofits coupled with active City promotion of opportunities resulted in significant improvements to efficiency of over 10% of existing owner-occupied houses in Vancouver."[91] Furthermore, "the majority of large new office and condominium towers are being built to achieve LEED Gold certification and many are starting to connect to low carbon neighbourhood energy systems."[92] The city certainly still has a long way to go before becoming fossil-fuel free, though officials believe that reaching the goal by 2050 is "ambitious but achievable."[93] They also seem to believe that there is political support for their aggressive mandates for green buildings and other carbon-free technologies, including among developers who, publicly at least, assert that achieving the goal of zero carbon developments will be challenging but within their capabilities.[94]

Vancouver's greening efforts continue to earn widespread recognition. Between 2011 and 2015 the city received nearly forty awards for everything from recycling to walkability to resilience to "green city perception ranking."[95] Its green building standards have been highlighted in many of its accolades. In 2013 Vancouver won the World Green Building Council Government Leadership Award for the best green building policy of any municipality in the world.[96] At the global climate meeting in Paris in 2015, Vancouver's GCAP won an award from C40 Cities Climate Leadership Group for its demonstration of "world-leading policies and programmes that reduce emissions and improve sustainability."[97] These awards and the global publicity they garner continue to ensure that greening remains a predominant part of Vancouver's brand. As Mayor Robertson is quoted saying in the introduction to Part 2 of the Greenest City 2020 Action Plan, "Cities around the world must show continued leadership to meet the urgent challenge of climate change.... The future of Vancouver's economy and livability will depend on our ability to confront and adapt to climate change. Moving toward 100% renewable energy is another way that Vancouver is working to become the greenest city in the world."[98] Economic prosperity and global leadership remain high priorities for the city's ambitious green agenda.

The only major concern that has been publically raised about Vancouver's green building agenda is that the expense of constructing to aggressive zero carbon building standards will exacerbate the city's already high housing costs. Officials dismiss this concern, however, asserting that the problems of the Vancouver housing market are much bigger than the moderate cost increase of building to greener standards. Particularly when considering the long-term savings in the cost of operating a carbon neutral building, plus the imperative of addressing climate change, officials insist that any additional upfront building costs are more than worth it.[99]

Indeed, if complemented by affordable rents, green buildings with lower operating costs can offer important benefits to low-income residents, as well as reduce a city's exacerbation of global climate injustice. Yet this synergy between green buildings and affordability is by no means inevitable. It relies not just on reducing household energy bills but also on a holistic approach to housing provision and building design that prioritizes social equity as well as efficiency. The challenges Vancouver is facing in synthesizing green development and affordability will be discussed at length in Chapter 6.

Securing Vancouver's Green Brand

Locally, Vancouver's successful push for green buildings is making a contribution to global climate change mitigation. Yet like both Birmingham and Chicago, Vancouver's ability to fully achieve its energy and climate goals is connected to policies on other political scales. The GCAP recognizes this dependence, asserting that "the success of this plan ... depends on continued action from the provincial and federal governments to decrease the carbon content of vehicle fuels and electricity, and to support

Canadian cities with new regulatory authority that enables each municipality to build a low-carbon future."[100] The GCAP notes that 39 percent
of Vancouver's GHG reduction goal is projected to come from changes
in provincial regulations, making the city's success contingent on action
by BC.[101]

Fortunately, British Columbia has made some progress in this direction. In the early 2000s the provincial government formally recognized
the need to address climate change. In 2008, BC adopted legally binding
emissions reduction targets and North America's first carbon tax, covering three-quarters of the province's GHG emissions. Five years into the
tax, which ramped up over its first several years, fuel consumption in
BC had decreased by 17.4 percent, 19 percent more than the rest of the
country's reduction over the same time period, measured on a per capita
basis. Meanwhile, BC's economic growth was in line with the rest of the
country, implying that the tax did not have a conspicuous impact on
growth in the province.[102]

Carbon taxes are seen by many environmental economists as the most
practical and efficient way to reduce emissions, but they do raise equity
concerns. When a carbon tax leads to basic necessities such as food,
heating, and transportation becoming more expensive, this disproportionately hurts lower and moderate income people who spend a greater
proportion of their income on these necessities. BC's carbon tax was
originally designed to avoid this outcome, with one-third of the revenue
from the tax going back to low and moderate income provincial residents
in a way that was estimated to be progressively redistributive. As the tax
was raised, however, some argued that the credits were not keeping up
with the increase in the tax, making it increasingly regressive.[103] Others
disagreed, arguing that the cuts in other tax rates that have accompanied the revenue-neutral carbon tax have compensated for the costs of
the carbon tax.[104] Not sufficient on its own to reduce British Columbia's
overall carbon emissions, and with equity concerns not fully resolved, the
carbon tax is important in that it has contributed to Vancouver's GHG
reductions by encouraging alternative transportation and fewer trips by
automobile.[105] The carbon tax also partly softened the impact of low
natural gas prices on the uptake of efficiency measures.[106]

The BC carbon tax has helped facilitate movement toward Vancouver's
climate goals, but federal policies have presented a challenge to the city.
Like the United States, the Canadian government has a poor record on
climate change. Though Canada did not pull out of the Kyoto Protocol
until 2011, it had been clear for some time that the country would come
nowhere close to achieving the cuts it had committed to under the agreement.[107] Since provinces have control over many of the major sources
of GHG emissions, as seen with BC's carbon tax, much could still be
done provincially. But the federal government's broader energy policies,
particularly its push to expand oil exports, has had a direct impact on

Vancouver. Most striking has been the debate over the expansion of an oil pipeline to Vancouver's English Bay and the threat the City sees this pipeline posing to regional well-being and to its green brand.

Canada is the world's fifth largest oil producer, though oil represents just a small percentage of the country's overall economy.[108] When oil company Kinder Morgan proposed nearly tripling the capacity of its major pipeline from Alberta oilfields through BC, Vancouver quickly raised objections.[109] The reasons for the City's opposition were multi-faceted. One concern was the carbon impact. Officials saw an increase in oil exports through the region as incompatible with the local and provincial goals of dramatically reducing emissions and adapting to climate change. Another concern focused on the economic impact of the pipeline. This concern was two-fold. First, a major oil spill in English Bay would clearly hurt Vancouver's lucrative tourist industry, and the pipeline's increased capacity and accompanying seven-fold increase in oil tanker traffic was seen as raising the likelihood of such an event. Yet this was not all. Officials argued that even without a spill the increased tanker traffic could hurt the city's economy by "diluting or damaging the City's green brand, which is a draw for business and one reason Vancouver is consistently ranked one of the most livable cities in the world."[110] This brand, the City asserts, "is valued at $31 billion due to [Vancouver's] reputation as a 'green, clean and sustainable' city" (Figure 5.3).[111]

Despite Vancouver's involvement in legal battles to stop the pipeline expansion, the federal government responded only minimally to the concerns raised by the City. The economic benefits of greening have been clearly established in the minds of Vancouver leaders, but they have not become institutionalized in Canadian politics more broadly, at least not in comparison to the more concrete value of oil exports. In November 2016, Liberal Prime Minister Justin Trudeau, though receiving applause a year earlier at the UN Paris Climate conference for his strong proclaimed commitment to climate change mitigation, approved the pipeline expansion. In a twist of the ideas of liberal environmentalism, Trudeau justified his decision by claiming that it was the best for the Canadian economy and, incredibly, for the environment.[112] In response, Mayor Robertson, along with a number of First Nations representatives and environmental groups, pledged to continue their fight to stop the pipeline.[113]

Vancouver is distinguished for its commitment to matching its ambitious goals and green bravado with action. In no small part because of the strict green building standards discussed above, as well as its district heating systems, hydroelectric power, and dense urban form, Vancouver has the lowest per capita carbon emissions relative to both population and economic activity of any major city in North America.[114] The city undoubtedly faces a number of challenges, including inconsistent federal leadership and the problem of housing affordability that will be discussed in the following chapter. Overall, however, Vancouver's energy

Figure 5.3   Vancouver fears that the seven-fold increase in tanker traffic on
         English Bay that will accompany the expanded Kinder Morgan oil
         pipeline will damage the city's green brand.
Source: Photo by author (2014).

and efficiency initiatives illustrate the ability of strong political leadership
to move a city toward significant, effective contributions to addressing
global environmental problems.

Conclusion

This chapter has examined ways that Birmingham, Chicago, and
Vancouver have worked to increase energy efficiency and green energy
production. In each city, the financial benefits of reducing energy consumption have been paramount, and efficiency clearly fits within the
win–win priorities of liberal environmentalism. Yet the effectiveness of
each city's efficiency efforts has varied. Political will, legal structures, and
changing energy markets have all impacted these cities, sometimes furthering the effectiveness of their energy efforts and sometimes thwart-
ing them. Likewise, each city's ability to further equity locally, even as
reduced emissions advance global climate justice, is also connected to
both local political will and policies beyond the scale of the city. The complexity of this relationship between local, national, and global politics in

cities' abilities to move toward progressive liberal environmentalism will become even clearer in an examination of housing and development, an issue area with an especially large impact on local social equity and well-being. It is to this issue that we now turn.

Notes

1 Morey Burnham et al., "Extending a Geographic Lens Towards Climate Justice, Part 1: Climate Change Characterization and Impacts," *Geography Compass* 7, no. 3 (2013): 239; see also A. Agarwal, S. Narain, and A. Sharma, "The Global Commons and Environmental Justice – Climate Change," in *Environmental Justice: Discourses in International Political Economy*, ed. John Byrne, Leigh Glover, and Cecilia Martinez (New Brunswick, NJ: Transaction Pub., 2002); African Development Bank et al., "Poverty and Climate Change: Reducing the Vulnerability of the Poor through Adaptation" (2003); IPCC, "Climate Change 2014: Synthesis Report Summary for Policy Makers" (2014); John S. Dryzek, Richard B. Norgaard, and David Schlosberg, *Climate-Challenged Society* (New York, NY: Oxford University Press, 2013).
2 African Development Bank et al; Siri Eriksen et al., "When Not Every Response to Climate Change Is a Good One: Identifying Principles for Sustainable Adaptation," *Climate and Development* 3, no. 1 (2011).
3 Gordon Walker, *Environmental Justice: Concepts, Evidence and Politics* (New York, NY: Routledge, 2012).
4 David Sattherwaite, "How Urban Societies Can Adapt to Resource Shortage and Climate Change," *Philosophical Transactions of the Royal Society* 369 (2011).
5 Milena Buchs, Nicholas Bardsley, and Sebastian Duwe, "Who Bears the Brunt? Distributional Effects of Climate Change Mitigation Policies," *Critical Social Policy* 31, no. 2 (2011).
6 See Vanesa Castan Broto and Harriet Bulkeley. "A Survey of Urban Climate Change Experiments in 100 Cities," *Global Environmental Change* 23 (2013); Corina McKendry, "Cities and the Challenge of Multiscalar Climate Justice: Climate Governance and Social Equity in Chicago, Birmingham, and Vancouver," *Local Environment* 21, no. 11 (2016).
7 Federal Energy Management Program, "Energy Efficiency Improvements through the Use of Combined Heat and Power (CHP) in Buildings" (Washington, DC: U.S. Department of Environment, 2000).
8 Birmingham District Energy Company, "Birmingham District Energy Scheme" (Birmingham, UK: Birmingham District Energy Company, 2015).
9 Food Department for the Environment, and Rural Affairs, "Press Release: £15.5 Million Heating Boost for Thousands of Homes, September 16, 2004" (Hermes Database, 2004); Food Department for the Environment, and Rural Affairs, "Press Release: £10.6 Million for Energy Efficient Community Heating" (Hermes Database, 2005).
10 Graeme Brown, "Manton House and Reynolds House in Birmingham to Be Connected to Biomass Combined Heat and Power System," *Birmingham Post*, August 26, 2009.
11 Birmingham Evening Mail, "How Brum's Fuelling a Greener Future," May 20, 2008; Terry Slavin, "Street Smarts: Cities Rise to Climate Challenge," *Guardian*, December 5, 2007.
12 Anonymous, personal communication, June 2016.
13 City sustainability officer, personal communication, July 2008.

14 Birmingham City Council, "Delivery of New Combined Heat and Power Engine," www.birmingham.gov.uk/cs/Satellite?c=Page&childpagename=Lib-Library-of-Birmingham%2FPageLayout&cid=1223386258774&pagenam e=BCC%2FCommon%2FWrapper%2FWrapper (accessed May 18, 2016; please note: this URL is now inaccessible).
15 Birmingham's Green Commission, "Carbon Roadmap Update – Autumn 2015" (Birmingham, UK: Birmingham Green Commission, 2015).
16 Birmingham Post, "Hospital Plan to Save 20,000 Carbon Tonnes," February 19, 2009.
17 Birmingham City Council, "Making Birmingham Green: Birmingham Climate Change Action Plan 2010+" (2010); Birmingham's Green Commission, "Birmingham's Green Commission Autumn 2016 (sic) Update – Factsheet" (Birmingham, UK: Birmingham's Green Commission, 2015).
18 BES was originally called the Green New Deal.
19 DECC, "Annual Fuel Poverty Statistics Report, 2014" (Department of Energy & Climate Change, 2014); "2012 Sub-Regional Fuel Poverty Data: Low Income High Costs Indicator" (UK Department of Energy & Climate Change, 2014). The devolved authorities measure fuel poverty slightly differently than England.
20 Guardian, "The Scandal of Britain's Fuel Poverty Deaths," *Guardian*, September 11, 2014.
21 Corina McKendry, "Participation, Power, and the Politics of Multiscalar Climate Justice," in *The Social Ecology of the Anthropocene*, ed. Richard Matthew, et al. (World Scientific Publishers, 2016); Gordon Walker and Rosie Day, "Fuel Poverty as Injustice: Integrating Distribution, Recognition and Procedure in the Struggle for Affordable Warmth," *Energy Policy* 49 (2012).
22 Emily Gosden, "Government Fuel Poverty Strategy 'Meaningless' and 'Inadequate', Campaigners Warn," *Telegraph*, July 22, 2014; Richard Howard, "Warmer Homes: Improving Fuel Poverty and Energy Efficiency Policy in the UK" (Policy Exchange, 2015).
23 City councilor, personal communication, June 2016.
24 City sustainability officer, personal communication, July 2008.
25 A solar feed-in tariff is a program in which individuals are paid by the utility for electricity generated by a personal solar array beyond that which is used by the household.
26 Larry Elliot, "10,000 Birmingham Council Homes to Get Solar Panels," *UK Guardian*, October 3, 2010.
27 Ibid.
28 Councilor Tilsely, quoted in ibid.
29 Birmingham Energy Savers, "BES Gets Official Launch" (2013).
30 Anon, "Birmingham Carbon Plan Analysis" (Birmingham, UK: Presented to Birmingham's Green Commision, 2012).
31 ENDS Report 430, "Councils Invest in Renewables for Housing," 30 November 2010.
32 E.g. Birmingham's Green Commission, "Ecopods Cut Energy Bills" (2014).
33 "Birmingham's Green Commission Autumn 2016 (sic) Update – Factsheet."
34 Anna Watson, "To What Extent Has Green Deal Policy Facilitated Energy Efficiency Retrofit Supply Chain Development: A Case Study of Birmingham" (University of Sussex, 2014), 31.
35 Green Commission member, personal communication, March 2015.
36 Ibid.; city councilor, personal communication, June 2016; Watson, 2014.
37 Former sustainability official, personal communication, June 2016.
38 Green Commission member, personal communication, March 2015.
39 Former sustainability officer, personal communication, June 2016.
40 Green Commission member, personal communication, March 2015.

41 Paul Hatchwell, "Green Deal Uptake Too Slow," *ENDS Report*, February 25, 2014.

42 BBC News, "Green Deal Funding to End, Government Announces," *BBC News*, July 23, 2015.

43 DECC, "Foundations in Place: The Green Deal and ECO Annual Report" (Department of Energy & Climate Change, 2014).

44 Conor McGlone, "DECC Admits Energy Firms Benefit from ECO Cuts," *ENDS Report*, July 28, 2014.

45 Paul Hatchwell, "Climate Policies Add Little to Energy Bills, Says CCC," *ENDS Report*, December 11.

46 Ibid.

47 Ibid.

48 Birmingham's Green Commission, "Carbon Roadmap Update – Autumn 2015," 1.

49 Crain's Chicago Business, "Why Emanuel's Chicago Infrastructure Trust Is Off to Such a Slow Start," May 16, 2014.

50 Ibid.

51 Chicago Infrastructure Trust, "Municipal Buildings Retrofit," Chicago Infrastructure Trust, http://chicagoinfrastructure.org/initiatives/construction-underway-municipal-buildings-retrofit/ (accessed July 6, 2016).

52 Kari Lydersen, *Mayor 1%: Rahm Emanuel and the Rise of Chicago's 99%* (Chicago, IL: Haymarket Books, 2013).

53 Chicago Infrastructure Trust, "Press Release: Mayor Emanuel Announces New Street Lights; Requests Public Feedback before Installation," December 13, 2016, http://chicagoinfrastructure.org/2016/12/13/mayor-emanuel-announces-new-street-lights-requests-public-feedback-before-installation/ (accessed January 16, 2017).

54 City of Chicago, "Energy Benchmarking," City of Chicago, www.cityofchicago.org/city/en/progs/env/building-energy-benchmarking–transparency.html (accessed July 6, 2016).

55 City sustainability official, personal communication, April 2015.

56 Ibid.

57 City of Chicago, "Press Release: Mayor Emanuel Announced Third Expansion of the Retrofit Chicago Energy Challenge," July 28, 2016, https://www.cityofchicago.org/city/en/depts/mayor/press_room/press_releases/2016/july/Retrofit-Chicago-Energy-Challenge.html (accessed January 16, 2017).

58 Ibid.

59 MEEA, "Retrofit Chicago Celebrated for Helping Residents, Businesses and City Buildings Save Money, Increase Energy Efficiency," Midwest Energy Efficiency Alliance, http://mwalliance.org/conference/inspiring-efficiency-awards/2015-impact-retrofit-chicago (accessed January 16, 2017); NRDC, "Retrofit Chicago Commercial Building Iniative: Best Practices Report" (National Resources Defense Council, 2014).

60 City of Chicago, "Sustainable Chicago 2015: Action Agenda, 2012–2015 Highlights and Look Ahead" (Chicago, IL: City of Chicago, 2015).

61 U.S. Energy Information Administration, "FAQs: How Much Carbon Dioxide Is Produced When Different Fuels Are Burned?," U.S. Department of Energy, https://www.eia.gov/tools/faqs/faq.cfm?id=73&t=11 (accessed March 5, 2017).

62 City of Chicago, "Press Release: Mayor Emanuel Reduces Costs and Acquires Cleaner Energy with New Electricity Supply Agreement for City Facilities," November 12, 2012, www.cityofchicago.org/city/en/depts/mayor/press_room/press_releases/2013/november_2013/mayor-emanuel-reduces-costs-and-acquires-cleaner-energy-with-new.html (accessed July 6, 2016).

63 Sustainability official, personal communication, April 2015.
64 See McKendry, "Cities and the Challenge of Multiscalar Climate Justice: Climate Governance and Social Equity in Chicago, Birmingham, and Vancouver."
65 Respiratory Health Association, "Power Plants: Victory for Clean Air and Healthy Lungs!," www.lungchicago.org/air-quality-power-plants/ (accessed January 28, 2015).
66 See Kari Lydersen, *Closing the Cloud Factories: Lessons from the Fight to Shut Down Chicago's Coal Plants* (Chicago, IL: Midwest Energy News, 2014).
67 Jeff Biggers, "Historic Victory: Coal Free Chicago Will Electrify Clean Energy Movement " *Huff Post Chicago*, February 29, 2012.
68 Julie Wernau, "Fisk, Crawford Coal Plants Had Long History, as Did Battle to Close Them," *Chicago Tribune*, September 2, 2012.
69 Ibid.
70 Lydersen, *Closing the Cloud Factories: Lessons from the Fight to Shut Down Chicago's Coal Plants*.
71 U.S. Energy Information Administration, "Today in Energy," www.eia.gov/todayinenergy/detail.cfm?id=15491 (accessed January 26, 2015).
72 Steve Daniels, "Midwest Generation Files Chapter 11," *Crain's Chicago Business*, December 17, 2012.
73 Sustainability official, personal communication, April 2015.
74 Environmental justice activist, personal communication, April 2015.
75 Quoted in John Byrne, "Activists: Emanuel Taking Too Much Credit for Power Plant Closings," *Chicago Tribune*, November 26, 2014.
76 See Lydersen, *Mayor 1%: Rahm Emanuel and the Rise of Chicago's 99%*.
77 The Olympic Village development was renamed "The Village of False Creek" in 2011.
78 Sarah Burch, "Transforming Barriers into Enablers of Action on Climate Change: Insights from Three Municipal Case Studies in British Columbia, Canada," *Global Environmental Change* 20 (2010): 294.
79 Sean Pander, "City of Vancouver Climate Protection Progress Report" (Vancouver, BC: City of Vancouver, 2007), 3.
80 City of Vancouver, "Greenest City 2020 Action Plan" (Vancouver, BC: City of Vancouver, 2011).
81 "Greenest City 2020 Action Plan Part Two: 2015–2020" (Vancouver, BC: City of Vancouver, 2015).
82 Ibid.
83 Jean Barman, *The West Beyond the West: A History of British Columbia, Third Edition* (Toronto: University of Toronto Press, 2007).
84 City of Vancouver, "Clarification of Our Position on Natural Gas," City of Vancouver, http://vancouver.ca/news-calendar/clarification-of-citys-position-on-natural-gas.aspx (accessed January 17, 2017).
85 "Greenest City 2020 Action Plan Part Two: 2015–2020," 16.
86 Ibid.
87 City of Vancouver, "Press Release: New Fund to Spur Energy Efficiency Upgrades for Buildings," February 4, 2016, www.electricenergyonline.com/detail_news.php?ID=563223&cat=;16;89&niveauAQ=0 (accessed January 17, 2017).
88 "Energy Retrofit Strategy for Existing Buildings" (2014).
89 "Energy-Efficiency Requirements and Resources for New Homes," City of Vancouver, http://vancouver.ca/home-property-development/energy-efficiency-requirements-and-resources-for-new-homes.aspx (accessed July 7, 2016).

90 "Vancouver Takes Next Step to Advance Renewable City Strategy," City of Vancouver, http://vancouver.ca/news-calendar/vancouver-takes-next-step-to-advance-renewable-city-strategy.aspx (accessed January 17, 2017).

91 "Greenest City 2020 Action Plan Part Two: 2015–2020," 16.

92 Ibid., 18.

93 Mark Hume, "Vancouver's Green Shift to Renewable Energy by 2050 Is a 'Realistic Target,'" *Globe and Mail*, November 2, 2015.

94 Barbara Carss, "Vancouver Developers to Pursue Zero Emissions," Canadian Apartments, https://www.reminetwork.com/articles/vancouver-developers-to-pursue-zero-emissions/ (accessed January 18, 2017).

95 City of Vancouver, "Greenest City 2020 Action Plan Part Two: 2015–2020," 75.

96 World Green Building Council, "Rick Fedrizzi, City of Vancouver & Saint-Gobain CEO honoured in WorldGBC Awards," World Green Building Council, www.worldgbc.org/news-media/rick-fedrizzi-city-vancouver-saint-gobain-ceo-honoured-worldgbc-awards (accessed June 4, 2017).

97 City of Vancouver, "Vancouver Wins C40 Cities Award for Greenest City Action Plan at COP21 in Paris," City of Vancouver, http://vancouver.ca/news-calendar/vancouver-wins-c40-cities-award-for-greenest-city-action-plan.aspx (access January 18, 2017).

98 "Greenest City 2020 Action Plan Part Two: 2015–2020," unpaginated first page.

99 Personal communications, August 2014.

100 City of Vancouver, "Greenest City 2020 Action Plan," 19.

101 Ibid.

102 Stewart Elgie and Jessica McClay, "BC's Carbon Tax Shift Is Working Well after Four Years (Attention Ottowa)," *Canadian Public Policy / Analyse de Politiques* 39, no. Supplement (2013).

103 Marc Lee, "Fair and Effective Carbon Pricing: Lessons from BC" (Vancouver, BC: Canadian Centre for Policy Alternatives & Sierra Club BC, 2011).

104 Eduardo Porter, "Does a Carbon Tax Work? Ask British Columbia," *New York Times*, March 1, 2016.

105 John D. Sutter, "There's a Cheap, Proven Fix to the World's Biggest Problem," *CNN*, April 19, 2016.

106 City of Vancouver, "Greenest City 2020 Action Plan Part Two: 2015–2020."

107 Guardian, "Canada Pulls out of Kyoto," *The Guardian*, December 12, 2011.

108 Economist, "Beyond Petroleum," *Economist*, January 31, 2015.

109 David P. Ball, "'No Rational Given,' Say Rejected Kinder Morgan Intervenors," *The Tyee*, April 4, 2014.

110 City of Vancouver, "Greenest City 2020 Action Plan 2014–2015 Implementation Update" (Vancouver, BC: City of Vancouver, 2015), 14.

111 Ibid., 13.

112 Ian Austen, "Justin Trudeau Approves Oil Pipeline Expansion in Canada," *New York Times*, November 29, 2016.

113 The Canadian Press, "Vancouver Mayor 'Profoundly Dissappointed' by Kinder Morgan Approval," *Huffpost British Columbia*, November 29, 2016.

114 Economist Intelligence Unit, "US and Canada Green City Index: Assessing the Environmental Performance of 27 Major US and Canadian Cities" (Munich, Germany: Siemens, 2011).

6 Green Urban Development

In well-designed urban development, efficiencies enabled by greater density can curb sprawl, reduce pollution, and limit GHG emissions. These potential benefits are at the heart of the argument that cities can make an important contribution to environmental sustainability.[1] Ideally, compact urban form allows for population growth without destroying additional farmland and open space on the urban fringe. It enables public transit and walking, therefore reducing automobile use and associated pollution and carbon emissions. Homes in dense urban areas tend to be smaller and closer together. This, along with the prevalence of multi-family units, reduces overall energy use and makes it easier to provide high-efficiency district energy systems.[2] For these reasons, people living in dense urban areas tend to have lower per capita carbon emissions than people with the same income who live in suburbs with larger, less efficient homes and sparse to non-existent public transportation.[3]

The environmental benefits of density are complemented by potential social benefits. Residents in dense urban areas can avoid car ownership, thereby reducing their overall cost of living.[4] Public transit and walkability can increase access to services and employment, particularly for people with lower incomes or those with a disability for whom driving is difficult or impossible.[5] In the face of high housing costs in many urban areas, increasing the supply of housing through densification can benefit lower-income residents by stabilizing or even driving down overall prices. This process of "filtering" is said to occur as wealthier residents move into newer homes, leaving a larger supply of older houses and apartments available at a lower price.[6]

Despite its potential, there is nothing inevitable about density leading to these environmental or social benefits.[7] Density without investments in transit and efficiency may increase congestion and energy use, worsening the environmental impact of a city rather than improving it.[8] Likewise, densification that is exclusively high-end condominiums may do little to increase affordability.[9] Instead it may drive lower-income people into the suburbs, increasing their commutes and therefore the financial and environmental burden of transportation. Relatedly, filtering alone, particularly in the tightest housing markets, is not nearly as effective at addressing housing affordability as explicit investment in creating housing for low and moderate-income residents.[10] Even more problematically, some argue that green urban development itself may exacerbate displacement by making city center living more attractive to the middle class, thereby driving up demand and housing costs, spurring gentrification.[11] Much depends on the particulars of how dense urban development is done and if social and environmental goals are explicitly incorporated into the creation of a compact urban area.[12]

Vancouver, Chicago, and Birmingham, for different reasons, exemplify some of the myriad difficulties in achieving the promised benefits of compact urban development. These difficulties range from NIMBYism to gentrification to city officials' desire to appease developers. Each of these issues are multifaceted, and this chapter only begins to illuminate the complex debates surrounding each of them. Yet looked at together, the challenges that have emerged in these three cities around efforts to incorporate environmental and social goals into their development agendas show that more is occurring to further these goals than the most critical accounts of neoliberal greening would suggest. They also show how much more needs to be done to ensure that the environmental and social potential of green urban development is achieved.

Green Building in Whose Backyard?

The environmental and social benefits of density have been at the center of Vancouver's development agenda for decades.[13] Though moderately high-density in-fill development had begun a few decades earlier, the 1990 climate policy report Clouds of Change specifically highlighted densification as a way to reduce the city's GHG emissions.[14] CityPlan, the 1995 community planning document discussed in Chapter 4, asserted that density was necessary to discourage regional sprawl.[15] The skyscraper developments on the industrial land around False Creek, as discussed in previous chapters, began Vancouver's forays into a new form of particularly high-density development. Density hit the peak of its discursive reign in 2006. Mayor Sullivan, in the midst of the controversies around his cuts to affordable housing in Southeast False Creek (see Chapter 4), released a plan called EcoDensity. EcoDensity, the City asserted, was "an unprecedented planning effort to use density, design, and land use as catalysts for an environmentally sustainable, affordable and livable Vancouver" and to reduce the city's carbon emissions.[16]

None of this has been uncontroversial. Since at least the 1980s, conflicts have arisen between city officials' prioritization of housing construction, the desires of communities to retain the existing look and feel of their neighborhoods, and political push-back against the power of developers in city politics. In the late 1980s, as Vancouver began rapid development along False Creek and development pressures began creeping into established neighborhoods, political pressure from property owners led NPA Mayor Gordon Campbell to give local control over zoning and design guidelines to some affluent neighborhoods.[17] Similarly, CityPlan was a city-wide response to the fear that planners were pushing unwanted densification onto communities, and it strove to balance community control over development with the housing needs of a growing city.

EcoDensity was much more controversial, becoming a lightning rod for the tension between community control and the proclaimed social and environmental benefits of densification. The concept of EcoDensity, complete with shiny brochures, emerged whole-cloth from Mayor Sullivan at a press conference during the World Urban Forum held in Vancouver in 2006. Not only had the proposal included no public input, but hardly anyone outside the mayor's office had even heard of EcoDensity before the press conference.[18] In a city that had become accustomed to extensive public participation in the planning process, this presentation of EcoDensity as a done deal raised significant public ire. Two years of polarized debate and revision followed before EcoDensity was adopted by the city council.[19]

In the years of debate around EcoDensity, both critics and proponents cited CityPlan in support of their positions. Opponents argued that EcoDensity was a top-down imposition of unwanted densification contrary to the neighborhood planning process of CityPlan. They asserted that rather than communities deciding where and how they would grow, EcoDensity would be a giveaway to developers, allowing profitable, highrise development in areas that had not previously been open to them. Proponents, on the other hand, claimed EcoDensity was merely a rearticulation of the goal of CityPlan to achieve sustainability through density, walkability, and mixed-use development.[20]

Whether or not EcoDensity represented any real shift in Vancouver's approach to development, the controversy it engendered re-shaped how densification is promoted by city officials. According to one Vision council member, Mayor Sullivan "freaked people out. He terrified people by saying, 'We are going to densify every neighborhood!' Which we are! But ... EcoDensity kind of made [density] an even dirtier word than it might have been if we'd let people come to the conclusion that densifying has to happen" in order to reduce carbon emissions and meet the city's housing needs.[21] With the election of Mayor Robertson and the Vision Vancouver council in 2008, the phrase EcoDensity fell out of favor. Densification is still certainly a priority of the local government, but it has been given a lower profile, with the affordability and the carbon benefits of new development emphasized over density itself.[22]

Amenities and the Power of Developers in Vancouver Politics

Affordable housing is an especially important part of the local political debate. The roots of Vancouver's affordability crisis are complicated. Its position as one of the least affordable cities in the world is influenced by high demand, limited land availability, large flows of foreign capital into the property market, and the retrenchment of federal and provincial funding for housing, as well as city planning policies. Because of the complexity of its causes, although there is wide agreement in Vancouver that housing affordability is a major problem, there is much less consensus as to what should be done about it.[23] For city officials facing the political limits of what the municipal government can control and the financial constraints of minimal government funding for social housing, increasing housing supply through densification is seen the main solution to making housing more affordable in the medium term.[24] As density also contributes to achieving many of the environmental goals of the GCAP, the issues of affordability, dense urban development, and environmental sustainability are closely interwoven in Vancouver.

Enthusiastic embrace of new development is not new in Vancouver. It was one of the defining features of the city's green urban entrepreneurialism. As seen in earlier discussion of the Concord Pacific development and Southeast False Creek (Chapters 3 and 4), even in the midst of rapid development, Vancouver was more willing than most cities to require developers to include environmental elements in new housing. Yet local government enthusiasm for securing affordable housing has been much less consistent. Though deprioritized by Mayor Sullivan, recently the local government has begun to re-emphasize the creation of affordable housing. The challenge is that the City's ability to incentivize the construction of affordable housing and the rental units needed to take pressure off the housing market are limited. The tool most readily available is the sway the City has over developers seeking to upzone land for higher density.

As seen in early chapters, it embarked on the post-industrial redevelopment of False Creek and elsewhere, the City used its power over land use and zoning decisions to extract funding from developers for a variety of community and environmental amenities. This process of negotiating Community Amenity Contributions (CACs) from developers has since become an institutionalized part of Vancouver's planning process. Planners claim that through the negotiation of CACs they are able to "claw back about 70 to 75 percent" of the increase in land value that a developer receives when land is rezoned.[25] In a city with a limited budget, virtually no taxing power, and in which residents have high expectations for quality public amenities, planners see CACs as crucial.

CACs are controversial, however. One critique focuses on their potentially corrupting effects. Because each proposed upzoning leads to negotiation of a different CAC, decision makers that are too cozy with developers may not negotiate the best possible deal for the city.[26] Others argue that even if planners are not subtlety corrupted by their relationships with developers, planners' poor negotiating skills often lead to fewer contributions than developers could be providing.[27] A third critique is that because CACs can only be negotiated in exchange for rezoning, not for proposed developments that fit within existing city zoning designations, they incentivize the approval of excessively dense developments in order to enable the negotiation of more CACs. Despite these controversies, whether fixed fees from developers would solve the problems with CACs while maintaining the same level of amenity provision is a subject of local debate.[28]

City officials and planners acknowledge that CACs incentivize allowing greater building heights. They argue that because the most profitable units for developers are those that are several stories up with the clearest views of the mountains and ocean, height is needed to generate the revenue that can then be "clawed back" for CACs. Neither planners nor councilors interviewed see this as a problem, however, reiterating the environmental and housing supply benefits of greater density as well as the importance of the amenities the city receives from the new developments.[29]

For planners, the key is to develop in such a way as to balance the benefits of dense green growth, city finances, and community well-being. This means encouraging market-rate, high-end condominium development that can fund amenities and affordable housing. It also means using cost levy waivers, density and height bonuses, and a relaxation of parking requirements to encourage the construction of purpose-built rentals.[30] Finally, it means pushing hard on developers for the inclusion of affordable housing along with the high green building standards that will lead the new buildings to have the smallest environmental footprint possible.

None of this is easy, and planners readily admit that "the three pillars of sustainability don't always go with lockstep. But," one senior planner insisted, "when we pull back a layer, we often see they are actually all advancing simultaneously. ... Not every decision has to entirely advance all three pillars. But if you are not pulling back and taking a perspective of 5,000 feet and saying, 'ok, have we got [progress] generally across the three pillars of sustainability?' Then you're probably not doing it right."[31] Encouraging development and using the revenue it generates to advance social and environmental goals will, city officials insist, create a sustainable city for all.

Many in Vancouver reject the City's claim that it is using the land-use tools available to it to maximize the social and environmental benefits of development for the city as a whole. Rather, some see the council's focus on new development as evidence that Vision is in the pockets of developers. This critique, along with calls to bring back the community planning process and vision of CityPlan that many say has been abandoned, can be heard from across Vancouver's political spectrum.[32] The feeling that the city council is pushing development regardless of community preference has led to numerous conflicts within the community planning process about the relationship between development, sustainability, and community well-being. These conflicts have challenged the legitimacy of Vancouver's densification initiatives and, in doing so, have led to efforts to find better ways to balance local preferences and needs of the city as whole (Figure 6.1).

Figure 6.1 Efforts to increase density in established residential neighborhoods, such as this new apartment complex in Kitsilano, have often engendered community resistance.

Source: Photo by author, 2014.

The Search for a "Sustainable" Community

A brief discussion of three contentious community planning processes will illustrate the push-back against densification in Vancouver and the City's response to it. Without claiming that the final community plans discussed below maximize either social or environmental sustainability, what these planning conflicts show is the difficulty of even a city that is committed to progressive liberal environmentalism enacting policies that will make it greener and more inclusive while responding both to the growth imperative and community priorities. Two of the contentious community planning processes examined here, in the neighborhoods of Grandview-Woodland and Marpole, show one of the notable difficulties in using new development to achieve affordability and environmental goals. The challenge is that in the already dense city, high-end condominiums and new affordable apartments alike have to go somewhere. The change in the feeling of the neighborhood that often accompanies such developments is not always welcome. Furthermore, in the heated public debates around development is hard to distinguish legitimate community concerns about insufficient input in the planning process from NIMBYism that hurts less politically powerful residents of the city.

Grandview-Woodland is a diverse, centrally located neighborhood that contains a sizable immigrant population, a substantial stock of low-rise affordable apartments built in the 1950s, and a vibrant small business area along Commercial Drive. In 2013 city planners and residents undertook a community planning process to develop Grandview-Woodland's local area plan. The process itself, many participants assert, was a good one. There was space for genuine community input and a wide variety of voices contributed. Community members anticipated a plan that kept the diversity and small-scale feel of the neighborhood while gently increasing density in a few areas in order to enable additional affordable housing.[33] Many were therefore incensed when the draft plan presented by the City included a 36-story development near the neighborhood's busy Broadway Skytrain transit stop, accompanied by several more 22- and 26-story towers. Though there were many aspects of the plan that did reflect the community planning process, including preserving much of the low-income rental properties and the feel of Commercial Drive, the introduction of a 36-story tower was way beyond anything that had been discussed by the community.[34]

When pushed on why the plan included such developments, planners claimed the towers were "a collective decision of the planning department."[35] Illustrative of the distrust many have about Vision's relationship with developers, however, local activists placed the blame for the towers squarely with the mayor who, they claimed, wanted "a 36-story tower development at the corner of the neighborhood, no matter what."[36] Protest was intense, and the City withdrew the draft plan for further input and consideration. Shortly thereafter, Mayor Robertson acknowledged that they had been mistaken in trying to move "too fast" on the densification of this area. But this mistake, he insisted, would not stop progress on Vision's broad social and environmental agenda, of which increasing density was an important aspect.[37]

The community plan in Marpole was also controversial. Located at the far south edge of the city, Marpole has a larger number of renters, a lower median income, and a higher number of recent immigrants than the city average.[38] It also has substantial areas of single-family homes, the value of which have skyrocketed along with Vancouver's soaring real estate market. In Marpole, opposition to the proposed community plan was led by "the Marpole Residents Coalition, which was formed after homeowners realized the city was proposing to upzone vast areas of single-family homes to allow for townhouses, duplexes and other higher-density housing. 'We feel like we got dropped on our heads,' [the Coalition's spokesman] said. ... 'People are feeling like they're under siege.'"[39] Again following community protests, the City backed off on the proposed upzoning in the particular area of Marpole that was of most concern to the protesters, though the final community plan does include densification along most of the area's major arteries.[40]

As in Grandview-Woodland, vocal Marpole residents felt that the proposed plan, particularly specific high-density projects, were inconsistent with the shared vision the community had for the neighborhood. These developments were therefore seen as reflecting the inadequacy of public participation in the face of city officials determined to increase density regardless of local preference. That in both cases the City backed off from the initial proposal in response to community protest confirmed for protesters not that the council was concerned with their input, but that officials were afraid of the electoral consequences of pushing densification too far.[41]

Unsurprisingly, city officials saw the community responses to the proposed densification quite differently. For example, the idea that the Marpole plan was "dropped on the heads" of unsuspecting residents was strongly questioned by a city council member who participated in the two-year community planning process that led to the creation of the plan. Indeed, she considers the opposition that emerged after the plan was completed to be a deeply problematic reflection of the excessive power of privileged homeowners and their ability to fight changes needed by the broader community. Of particular concern to this councilor was that the main spokesperson of the Marpole Residents Coalition told her in a meeting aimed at getting at their worries about the plan that the Coalition included no renters because no one in the neighborhood rents. According to the councilor, when she told him that over half of Marpole residents are renters, he accused her of falsifying the numbers. "In fact," she noted, "the majority of Vancouver rents, and most City Hall meetings are *not* dominated by renters."[42]

In Grandview-Woodland this concern about the representativeness of those who attend planning meetings or who protest proposed developments led to the creation of a Citizens Assembly to draft a new community plan. The Assembly consisted of 48 people randomly selected from willing volunteers and reflecting the age breakdown of the community, the proportion of renters and homeowners in the neighborhood, a gender balance, and First Nations people.[43] The City promoted the Citizens Assembly as a way to ensure that the plan truly represented the neighborhood. Opponents saw it as an attempt to silence and exclude the long-time community activists with the most knowledge about the planning process. The city planners' slick and compelling presentations, activists asserted, would be used to get the inexperienced Assembly members to go along with the City's desire for towers in the neighborhood.[44]

The final report that emerged from the Citizens' Assembly calls for densification but it does not include anything close to the towers that had garnered so much protest.[45] It instead supports development that "gently increase[s] density, encouraging coach houses, row houses, townhouses and low and medium highrises."[46] It remains to be seen how the implementation of the plan will unfold, though evidence suggests that new development will remain controversial in the neighborhood.[47]

What both Grandview-Woodland and Marpole illustrate is that the City's vision of densifying the entire city in order to increasing housing supply, affordability, and to lower carbon emissions has not been fully embraced by the public. If these goals are to be achieved, more will have to be done to ensure that the concerns of various groups are addressed, that the planning process is transparent, and that participation is genuine and representative. Without this, the push-back against new development may challenge the broader legitimacy of Vancouver's greening agenda.

The third contested community plan, that of the Downtown Eastside, also shows the difficulty of balancing neighborhood needs and the 5000 feet up perspective that planners insist they are trying to take. As discussed in earlier chapters, the DTES has long been home to many of Vancouver's poorest residents. Its central location has been putting gentrification pressure on the area for decades, though the severity of its social problems and effective community organizing limited gentrification in the neighborhood for some time (see Chapter 3). With rising housing costs putting ever-greater pressure on the area, the City decided it was time for a development plan. Unsurprisingly, this was not an easy task. One of the many challenges was that the plan covers not just the DTES but also historic Chinatown, tourism-focused Gastown, and a few other nearby neighborhoods. This diversity meant that those coming to the table to create the plan brought with them "a lot of disagreement on the future [of the] neighborhood," making finding a shared vision challenging.[48]

After four years of work, a community plan was finally created.[49] Planners saw the result as an exemplar of balancing differing community needs and finding creative ways to fund them. They assert that the parts of the DTES where most of the services for low-income residents are concentrated will be protected, with new development in that area required to be 60 percent social housing and 40 percent market rentals. Gastown, by contrast, continues to be nearly all market-rate housing, with developer fees helping to fund affordable units elsewhere. In Chinatown, some large developments on the southern edge of the neighborhood will be used to pay for heritage revitalization, a priority for residents of that community. Looking at the plan as a whole, a key city planner argued, "not everyone gets everything they want, but everyone gets something. And in the end, hopefully the balance comes out of the mix and results in a sustainable neighborhood. ... I think it's incredibly aggressive, but it's doable. But it's barely doable. It relies on playing in the market in ways we've never had in the past, ... throw[ing] everything we have at [developers].... We have some pretty huge larger objectives. Affordability, urban sustainability, energy, climate change, rising sea level. And all of those we have to try to bring down to the local level and make them make sense."[50]

The number of new affordable housing units and the protections for existing low-income housing included in the plan are seen by some as very ambitious, while others see them as woefully insufficient to prevent displacement. Some affordable housing advocates in the DTES publicly supported the plan. They noted that considering the intensity of real estate speculation in the area and the dearth of funding for social housing from higher levels of government, the plan is a good one. They recognize that protecting existing low-income housing and ensuring that more can be developed "may mean higher densities than would likely be desirable under other circumstances .... This is why the local Plan envisions the creation of 4,400 social housing units, but also plans for 3,000 market rental housing over the same 30-year period in the DTES [to help pay for the social housing]. ... [W]e feel considerable effort has gone into developing this plan [and] that it strives to achieve important community priorities."[51] In other words, it may not be perfect, but it is as good as could be hoped for in Vancouver's current political and financial climate.

Others disagreed, seeing the plan as furthering gentrification of the area. One commentator asserted that the plan "contains familiar themes: incentives to developers for condo development, supports to entrepreneurs for boutique storefronts, subsidies for heritage building renovation and no controls to stop the rent increases and reno-evictions that will result from these government interventions on behalf of the rich. ...[Y]ou can read the shrug between the lines about the gentrification, evictions, and low-income store closures that are inevitably part of revitalizing higher-end retail and market housing in the DTES."[52] Other critics rejected the clause committing development to 60 percent social housing and 40 percent market rate housing, saying that it offers too broad a definition of social housing and allows too many market rentals, thereby making it virtually meaningless for securing housing for those in very high need.[53] Furthermore, this critique continues, facing an influx of middle class residents, the poor residents of the DTES are unlikely to feel comfortable or welcome in their own, transformed, neighborhood. What city planners see as an important balance between competing interests in the wider neighborhood, others see as an attack on the social sustainability of the DTES.

Elusive Affordability

In each of the three community planning processes discussed above, city officials and planners saw themselves as striving to achieve a balance between developer needs for profit, the City's ability to negotiate community amenities from developers, affordability, and the environmental benefits of density, all within pronounced fiscal and legal constraints. Public resistance to new development, whether against new rental apartments or high-end condos, is seen by many planners and city councilors as a threat to long-term affordability and environmental sustainability in Vancouver. Yet even while dismissing many of the community protests as either unrealistic in the face of budget constraints or as a veiled protection of homeowner interests at the expense of renters, the community resistance that has emerged has forced decision-makers to better ground their development ambitions in the sense of place and community held by neighborhoods. As Vancouver continues toward greater density and greener buildings, as communities demand a continued voice in the planning process, and as there is a move to prioritize purpose-built rentals and new social housing instead of just constructing condos, it is possible that social sustainability in urban development will begin to match Vancouver's long-standing commitment to environmental sustainability.

Recent policy changes on the provincial and federal levels may also benefit housing affordability in Vancouver. In the summer of 2016, BC passed a 15 percent tax on home purchases by non-Canadians, waiving it a few months later for non-citizens with work visas.[54] This was a response to the widespread belief in the region that home purchases by wealthy international investors, particularly from China, have played a large role in driving up home prices while leaving large numbers of much-needed housing vacant.[55] The same year the federal government also made changes to rules impacting the house market. These included stricter requirements for mortgage insurance and enhanced efforts by the Canada Revenue Agency to ensure that people who claim a tax exemption for a primary residence actually live there.[56]

Not everyone has been happy with these changes, with the real estate industry particularly displeased with the property transfer tax.[57] But the changing federal and provincial policies did seem to achieve their desired impact of cooling off the housing market, at least in the short-term. Home sales to foreign citizens fell from over 13 percent of the region's sales in the weeks before the new tax to 3 percent a few months after it went into effect.[58] In a shift that one newspaper called "returning to earth," by late 2016 home sales in the Vancouver region had dipped, along with a small decline in home prices.[59] Though much more clearly needs to be done, to the extent that the City of Vancouver has faced difficulties in addressing its affordability crisis alone, even as it has worked to increase the housing supply, the engagement of other levels of government may make achieving more equitable access to housing possible.

Environmental Gentrification and Resistance

Vancouver shows the difficulty of achieving progressive liberal environmentalism even with city leadership that is striving for more inclusive development. In Chicago, this commitment has been much less evident, and in some communities the environmental gentrification that is a major critique of urban greening can clearly be seen. An examination of the importance of environmental amenities to the transformation of the area around the Cabrini-Green public housing complex to mixed income and high-end developments, and the new trend of Transit-Oriented Development (TOD) in Chicago illustrate this process. Chicago demonstrates the egregiousness of green neoliberal urbanism's ability to exacerbate displacement. But the growing community challenges to environmental gentrification may also be leading, if haltingly, to more environmentally and socially sustainable development in some areas.

Greening and the Transformation of Central Chicago

The story of the rise and fall of public housing in Chicago is one that has been examined in-depth by many. As neither the tearing down of public housing in Chicago nor the growth of market rate city center housing were done with an eye to greening or environmental effectiveness, this section touches only the surface of this long and complicated story. The destruction of public housing in Chicago, particularly Cabrini-Green, is important to examine at least briefly here, however, because it illuminates the synergy between green urban entrepreneurialism and the replacement of low-income neighborhoods with mixed- and high-income housing.

One of the clearest indicators of the success of Chicago's entrepreneurialism is the demographic transformation that the city center has undergone since the 1990s. Between 1990 and 2010, the city's central area boomed. The population of the area increased 114 percent, with census

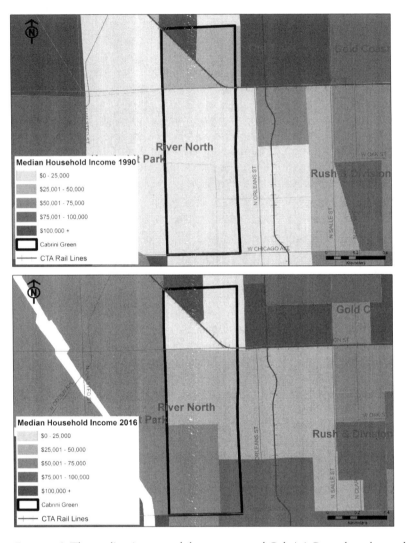

Figure 6.2 The median income of the area around Cabrini-Green has changed dramatically as public housing projects have been demolished and market-rate housing has expanded.

Source: Map by Matt Cooney.

data showing Chicago's greater Loop "adding residents faster than any other urban core in America."[60] This growth was largely constituted of people between the ages of 25 and 34 and wealthier families and individuals with annual household incomes of more than $200,000, the target populations of urban entrepreneurialism.[61] Clearly, Chicago's efforts to transform the city center and make it attractive to young professionals and the well-to-do has been achieved (Figure 6.2).

Unlike Vancouver, the transformation of Chicago's downtown to a major population center was not explicitly promoted as part of a larger commitment to effective environmental governance. For example, the 2003 Chicago Central Area Plan mentions the benefits of density, but the benefits it highlights   from walkability and access to transit -- are that they help create an interesting and vibrant downtown, not any potential contribution to climate goals or lowering residents' environmental impacts.[62] This therefore offers a counter example to those who have highlighted the marketing of environmentally friendly city center living as an elite form of consumption that is created specifically to appeal to middle-class consumers' environmental ethics and aesthetic preferences.[63] Though some new residents certainly may have had these preferences, they were not actively cultivated in Chicago as part of the effort to attract new well-off residents. This does not mean, however, that environmental amenities did not facilitate the process of city center growth.

Even as new condominiums and transformed industrial buildings led to a doubling of the number of central area residents, between 2000 and 2010 Chicago's overall population declined by nearly 7 percent. Much of this decline was because of the destruction of high-rise public housing buildings. Because African Americans were disproportionately represented in these housing projects, and therefore disproportionately displaced by their demolition, more than three-quarters of Chicago's population loss during this time was a decline in its number of black residents.[64]

Promoted as solutions to urban poverty and housing shortages after World War II (see Chapter 2), not long after being constructed many of Chicago's public housing projects began to fall into disrepair, and the city became the poster child for the problems with public housing.[65] Cabrini-Green, a housing development with 3,600 homes across eight high-rise towers and nearly 600 row houses, was one of the most notorious. Facing gang-related violence and the highly publicized death of a seven-year-old boy struck by a stray bullet on his way to school, Cabrini-Green became "a symbol – and a scapegoat – for all that [was] wrong with public housing."[66]

Though it did have many serious problems, some have argued that Cabrini-Green's notoriety did not emerge because it was the most troubled of Chicago's public housing projects. Indeed, by many indicators it was one of the more successful. Rather, it was put front and center in the arguments about the failure of public housing partly because its central location in the Near North Side close to wealthy neighborhoods and downtown meant that Cabrini-Green received the most attention from the media and from Chicago's white and middle-class residents.[67] This is important, for in addition to garnering heightened public attention, Cabrini-Green's prime location also made it particularly ripe for gentrification.[68]

In 1993, the Chicago Housing Authority (CHA), which manages the city's public housing, received a $50 million federal grant to demolish three of Cabrini-Green's high rises and replace them with the same number of low-rise units.[69] Around the same time, the ambitious CHA director, Vincent Lane, began calling for transforming Cabrini-Green into a mixed-income neighborhood. Lane asserted, "We need socioeconomic diversity or we will never solve the problems of the inner city ... if we can do this ... I predict you will see people moving from the suburbs back downtown, more commercial space being used and our schools upgraded."[70] Lane's vision for completely transforming Cabrini-Green was resisted by residents as well as some local officials because of the displacement it would entail. Yet it was in line with Congress's move toward the promotion of housing vouchers, mixed-income neighborhoods, and public–private partnerships in the low-income housing sector.[71] When the federal government eliminated the requirement that demolished public housing units be replaced one-to-one with new public housing or housing voucher units, the destruction of Chicago's public housing rapidly escalated.[72] In 2011 the last of Cabrini-Green's towers was demolished.

Replacing low-income public housing with mixed-income neighborhoods was presented as a way to improve the lives of public housing residents, a promise that, at best, has only very partially been achieved.[73] Though improving the well-being of residents may have been a genuine goal of many city officials, the move to create mixed-income neighborhoods was also, as Lane clearly articulated, a part of the entrepreneurial transformation of Chicago's urban core. Plans for tearing down housing projects began before greening became an important part of Mayor Daley's agenda, and simply reducing the amount of public housing available obviously had the most direct role in displacing low-income residents. But the transformation of Cabrini-Green and the surrounding area to a mixed-income neighborhood and high-end condominiums could not have succeeded without well-off people being willing to buy homes in neighborhoods that had long been perceived as off limits to the middle class. Indeed, in 1990, with Daley only recently elected mayor, many saw it as unimaginable that there would be a demand for "upscale dwellings in the very shadow of ... public-housing communities" in the city center.[74]

The combination of the destruction of public housing buildings and significant public investment in downtown beautification and high-quality urban amenities gave developers confidence in the potential profitability of the city center. As Cabrini-Green and other public housing buildings came down, there was a shift from the construction of apartments and public housing that had dominated central area development for decades to privately financed condominium construction in central Chicago.[75] Shortly thereafter, green urban entrepreneurialism further enhanced the physical environmental of the city center (see Chapter 2). By the early 2000s, as the well-to-do began moving into the city from the suburbs,

Figure 6.3 The non-profit City Farm was wedged between Cabrini-Green and
 new condominiums from 2003 until late 2016. The farm provided
 living wages but also beautified the site of a former gas station,
 making the area more appealing to new residents.

Source: Photo by author, 2008.

they cited amenities as one of the main reasons for doing so.[76] Therefore,
though less directly displacing people than the dismantling of public housing, green urban entrepreneurialism's beautification of Chicago's central
area increased the appeal of city center living for middle class residents,
thereby facilitating the area's transformation (Figure 6.3).

In the midst of this, public housing residents fought to protect affordable housing in the central area. Between 1996 and 2015 a series of lawsuits against the CHA by a Cabrini-Green residents' group slowed down
the destruction and redevelopment of Cabrini-Green. Over the years, the
lawsuits led to increased participation of residents in the redevelopment
plans and a substantial increase in the number of public housing units
included in the redevelopment.[77] A final legal agreement in 2015 won
guarantees of at least 33 percent affordable units in all new buildings
falling under the agreement.[78] The plan for the 65 acres of Cabrini-Green
land calls for 2340 residential units, and the CHA agreed to create a total
of 1,800 low-income residences in the area.[79] Residents did not get everything they had demanded, and 1,800 low-income homes is decidedly

fewer than the 3,600 that once were on the site. Yet the alderman for the area called the agreement "a 'great compromise,' saying the residents got more public housing than they otherwise would have."[80] The settling of the lawsuits also opened up acres of prime land to development. In Chicago's hot downtown property market, developers have been willing to meet the agreement's affordable housing requirements in order to build the high-end rentals and condominiums that continue to be in high demand.[81]

Transit-Oriented Development

Though city-center development in Chicago has not historically been promoted for its environmental benefits, this began to change with the increasing emphasis on transit-oriented development (TOD) in a number of Chicago's increasingly popular neighborhoods. The idea of TOD is that it places new housing very near public transportation, thereby reducing the necessity of residents owning a personal car. Requirements for the construction of parking spaces in the new developments are either reduced or eliminated to lower construction costs, discourage car ownership, and to increase the environmental benefits of high-density living.

Though TOD has been gaining popularity around the country, Chicago was slower than comparable cities in actively encouraging TOD near its fixed transit hubs.[82] Until 2013, when Chicago adopted its first major TOD ordinance, all new developments were required to include at least one parking space per housing unit. The TOD ordinance softened this requirement, allowing up to half of the parking units to be forgone if the development was within 600 feet of an L or Metra rail station or 1,200 feet from a station if the street had been certified as pedestrian-friendly.[83] The stringent 600/1,200 feet requirement meant that only about 1.2 percent of the city's land was eligible for the reduced parking requirements, but TOD advocates saw it as an important step in the right direction.[84] The ordinance was strengthened in 2015, doubling the area eligible for TOD designation, eliminating all parking requirements under certain conditions, and increasing allowable building size if the development included more affordable units.[85]

In terms of Chicago realizing the environmental benefits of urban density, these new efforts to encourage development that reduces personal vehicle use are crucial. Yet TOD is controversial and has become a focal point for concern about gentrification and affordable housing in some of Chicago's rapidly changing communities.[86] Because it is explicitly promoted for its environmental benefits, TOD illustrates the intersection of green development and equity in Chicago even more clearly than the city center development discussed above.

As with its progress on its TOD ordinance, Chicago has been slowly strengthening its requirements for affordable housing in new development.

The 2007 Chicago Affordable Requirements Ordinance mandated that all new developments over ten units that required a zoning change or that were a planned development in the downtown area include at least ten percent affordable units. It also had a buy-out option whereby developers could contribute money to an affordable housing fund in lieu of building affordable units themselves.[87] Many affordable housing advocates saw this buy-out option as unacceptable, and noted that it was counter to the City's stated goal of creating genuinely mixed-income communities.

In response to growing concerns about displacement and housing affordability, in 2015 affordable housing requirements were strengthened. While only applying "to developers who seek a zoning change, city financial assistance or city-owned land," the new ordinance requires that a quarter of required affordable units be built by developers either on-site or within two miles of the new development and increases the cost of buying out the additional units.[88] Though initial proposals to strengthen the law went even farther than this, "downtown apartment and condominium developers warned the city that the current hot streak of development would grind to a halt if onerous fees were imposed."[89] In response, proposed fees were lowered and some neighborhoods received an extensive phase-in period for the new requirements. As with green building standards discussed in Chapter 5, Chicago leaders appear wary of demanding too much from developers, even in the midst of high demand.

The challenges of the intersection between the goal of using new TOD to reduce automobile dependence and the need for affordable housing can be seen in the controversies surrounding TOD in Logan Square. Demand for housing in Logan Square has been rising over the past several years, though prices are still below the city's most popular neighborhoods. This led the U.S. News & World Report in 2016 to identify Logan Square as one of Chicago's five "up-and-coming neighborhoods to buy a home."[90] But the growing popularity of the neighborhood, and the changing demographics that have accompanied this, have led to concerns about gentrification. Long a Latino neighborhood, between 2000 and 2014 Logan Square lost over 35 percent of its Latino population while the white population increased nearly 50 percent. This brought the overall Latino population down from 65 percent of the neighborhood's total to under half[91] (Figure 6.4). Many see TOD (along with the linear park The 606 discussed in the next chapter) as exacerbating this gentrification. Others, however, see TOD as a potential salve to rapidly rising prices and displacement.

The alderman for the ward that includes most of Logan Square, Joe Moreno, has long required high green building standards in his ward. He has also been one of the most outspoken proponents of TOD and has facilitated the construction of over a thousand new housing units in his ward over the past several years. In justifying this rapid proliferation of

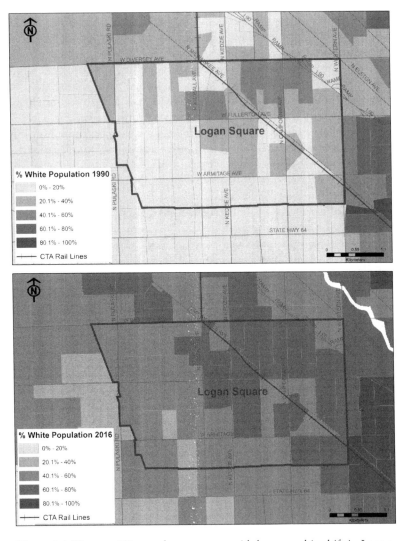

Figure 6.4 The past 25 years have seen a rapid demographic shift in Logan
Square as the neighborhood, once largely Latino, becomes
increasingly white.

Source: Map by Matt Cooney.

new development, Moreno highlights both the environmental and social
benefits of TOD, asserting that in the face of escalating housing costs,
the 10 percent affordability requirement under the Chicago Affordable
Requirements Ordinance means that more development will lead to the
construction of new affordable housing in the neighborhood.[92] Sharing

Vancouver officials' confidence in filtering, Moreno also argues that increasing the supply of market rate housing will itself help affordability in the area by taking "pressure off the local rental market," thereby softening rent increases.[93] In response to questions about displacement, a representative of Moreno's office noted that before the surge in new development, Logan Square had been losing population. Much of this loss, he asserted, was caused by affordable multi-family flats being converted to large, single-family homes. This hurt both lower-income families and local businesses, problems that the alderman's representative is confident the new boom in development will help remedy.[94]

Opponents of TOD strongly doubt the assertion that new developments will help existing Logan Square residents. Rather, they see TOD and the high-end condominiums and apartments that it mostly entails as exacerbating gentrification. Even if the area's proximity to the city center has been attracting more well-to-do and whiter residents for some time, protesters argue that new TODs are exacerbating this transformation under the guise of green development. Rather than benefiting existing residents and reducing the environmental impact of commuting by car as proponents claim, "the concept [of TOD] is being perverted and used as justification to allow developers to run rampant with huge luxury buildings [that]... will ultimately push the families that most rely on public transportation further and further away from the transit hubs."[95] Indeed, this is one of the potential ironies of successfully attracting middle-class and well-to-do residents to transit-friendly city center developments. If increased demand for such development leads to higher rents and home prices, unless transit equity is enhanced for lower-income neighborhoods, those who rely most heavily on transit will not have access to it. This issue, addressed again in Chapter 7, raises a serious concern for both social and environmental equity.[96]

Community activists have been working to convince city leaders that merely increasing the supply of homes, with developers achieving the minimum affordability requirements demanded by law, is not enough (Figure 6.5). Rather, affordability must be maximized in new developments. Especially in neighborhoods like Logan Square where the strong housing market puts the City in a good bargaining position, many argue that more can be done to make developers of TODs reinvest the hundreds of thousands of dollars they save by not building parking spaces into constructing more affordable units.[97]

Despite ongoing protests, anti-gentrification and affordable housing activists have not been able to stop the rapid proliferation of new developments in Logan Square. There have been some new commitments to expanding affordable housing,[98] but for the most part construction continues to focus on higher end market units.[99] In Chicago, even in neighborhoods where housing demand is strongest, so far it appears unlikely that local leaders will be willing to maximize the equity potential benefits

Figure 6.5 Protest signs on the site of a forthcoming Logan Square
          development. The sign on the far left reads "10% is not enough,
          real affordability now." Another sign at the site, not pictured, says
          "Transit Oriented Displacement."
Source: Photo by author, 2015.

of green development through requiring more affordable units from
developers. Chicago's forays into progressive liberal environmentalism
remain partial and tentative.

The Development Imperative and the Sidelining of Effectiveness

The story of green housing and development in Birmingham is quite different than either Vancouver or Chicago, with concerns about environmental gentrification not having anywhere near the political importance
as in the other two cities. Rather than green urban development being
prioritized over equity and affordability, Birmingham is quick to drop
its calls for environmentally effective development in order to maximize
new construction. As such, despite city leaders' ongoing proclamations of
becoming a leading green city, Birmingham illustrates the important limitation of liberal environmentalism that when there are real or perceived
trade-offs between growth and environmental protection, the latter may
very well be sacrificed.

There are some partial exceptions to this in the city, but for the most part environmental effectiveness has not been incorporated into the core of Birmingham's development agenda. For planners, the need for new investment and the pressure to deliver tens of thousands of new homes over the next few decades are the clear priorities, and pushing too hard on environmental sustainability is seen as a hindrance to this pressing goal. The result of this is missed opportunities to maximize the environmental effectiveness and long-term social benefits of Birmingham's new development.

Birmingham's Failed "Sustainability Quarter"

Birmingham leaders' prioritization of development over environmental benefits, even while proclaiming a commitment to the latter, is not new. It first came to the fore around the turn of the twenty-first century with the development plan for a 420-acre former industrial area adjacent to the city center that came to be called Eastside (not to be confused with Vancouver's Downtown Eastside). This area was abandoned by most manufacturers when industry relocated to larger and more up-to-date factories outside the city center in the middle of the twentieth century. As part of the city's post-war road building frenzy (see Chapter 2), a huge elevated interchange known as Masshouse Circus cut Eastside off both physically and visually from the city center only a few blocks away, further damaging what remained of the economy of the neighborhood.[100]

Other than a call for more "environmentally friendly transportation modes than the car, particularly buses and bicycles," the original mid-1990s development plan for Eastside mentioned nothing about sustainability as a guiding principle.[101] Yet a few years later the city council claimed that Eastside was to become Birmingham's "Sustainability Quarter" and would "herald an exemplar for sustainable urban living in the UK."[102] Part of the broader effort to rebrand Birmingham as a leading sustainable city discussed in Chapter 4, the reframing was also done to attract money from the European Regional Development Fund (ERDF) whose 2000 guidelines made environmental sustainability one of its criteria for determining whether development projects would be funded. The new proposal for Eastside included "land remediation; promotion of energy and water efficient design; energy consumption strategy; measures to promote sustainability in business and building such as local sourcing and recruitment, carbon free development, use of waste materials etc.; measures to promote the natural environment and encourage wildlife in the new city park; waste reduction and recycling schemes."[103] Importantly in terms of both creating and illustrating the public legitimacy of the project, the city council committed to establish a sustainability advisory team for the Eastside that would "link to the private sector by providing seminars, events and documents to developers interested in the area ... so that new sustainable ideas can be considered" in the design and development of the project.[104] The proposal was successful, enabling Birmingham to leverage over £50 million of ERDF and private funds toward what would come to be a £6 billion project. Much of the ERDF money was used for removing Masshouse Circus, seen as a crucial first step to the revitalization of the Eastside by making it accessible to the newly redeveloped and pedestrianized city center[105] (Figure 6.6).

The incorporation of environmental sustainability into the Eastside redevelopment plans and the proclaimed goal of making it the city's Sustainability Quarter garnered enthusiasm among local environmental organizations, with many feeling that the project offered an important opportunity for building a more sustainable Birmingham.[106] In 2002, fulfilling its promise to the ERDF, the council formed the Eastside Sustainability Advisory Group (ESAG). ESAG was made up of close to twenty organizations, including a number of local environmental and sustainable development groups.[107] A major task of ESAG was writing the report Sustainable Eastside – A Vision for the Future. Offering a holistic

Figure 6.6 Part of the 420-acre Eastside. The large buildings in the background, including the notable curves of the Selfridges department store built in 2003, highlight how close Eastside is to the city center.

Source: Photo by author, 2008.

understanding of sustainability, this hundred-page document laid out a vision of a vibrant economy based around local businesses, affordable housing, environmentally sound building that maximized the reuse of existing historic structures in the area, bountiful public green space, and a prioritization of people over cars.[108]

The report was widely hailed by councilors and others as "full of practical ideas to [help make developments in Eastside] at the forefront of innovation in terms of energy, water management and other aspects of sustainability."[109] Sustainability advisors were appointed to work closely with the council and to provide developers with information and support "on issues as wide ranging as transport, waste reduction, biodiversity, social diversity and community participation."[110] The council touted these efforts as indicative of its commitment to making "Eastside a national and international model for best practice" of urban sustainable development.[111]

Despite the frequency with which councilors pointed to Eastside as proof of their commitment to sustainable development, and the significant public and voluntary sector resources that were invested in the sustainability vision for the area, Birmingham's effort to build local legitimacy through its sustainable development plans were soon limited by serious shortcomings of the project's implementation. Many argued that although the emphasis on sustainability led to the incorporation of some environmentally beneficial elements, when sustainability conflicted with the short-term financial imperatives of developers it was quickly deprioritized.[112] Of particular concern was that developers were cutting corners in order to construct the buildings at the lowest possible cost, and the corners they cut were the environmental elements, particularly those whose payback was long.[113]

Underlying the lost opportunity for making Eastside an exemplar sustainability quarter was the council's unwillingness to push developers to incorporate environmental elements into building designs. Though developers were provided resources and suggestions for how to make their projects more environmentally friendly, there was nothing to guarantee that these elements were included in the final construction nor to reprimand developers for cutting these elements in order to save money once their project was approved.[114] Furthermore, though ESAG could have been a powerful mechanism for communicating the public's sustainability priorities to the city council, the group was not regularly consulted. A "review of advice given to Council's planning office ... indicates that this advice (even where concrete practical changes were suggested) had no impact on any single planning decision."[115] Within a few years ESAG disbanded, leaving its participants disillusioned and frustrated.[116]

Shortly thereafter, the global financial crash led to virtually all new construction across the city, including in Eastside, grinding to a halt. As development slowly reemerged several years later, the vision of making

Eastside Birmingham's Sustainability Quarter had evaporated. According to one senior planner, "All the proposals that were around at that time which contributed towards [making Eastside the Sustainability Quarter] all fell away with the recession. ... It is more about growth, economic growth, how can we get the value kick started again, how can we get the homes people need and the jobs to support that and particularly the infrastructure to support that. ... Everybody shifted more towards trying to get things to happen and the sustainable side of things has just taken a back seat."[117] Though this planner claims that there are some efforts "to pick [sustainability] up again as the economy improves and development is coming forward," these efforts remain at best secondary to the primary goal of maximizing new development.

Leadership and Limitations in Council Housing

The approach to sustainable development that was seen in Eastside – impressive rhetoric accompanied by voluntary efforts and a hesitance to require inclusions of concrete sustainability measures – can also be seen in other aspects of planning and development in Birmingham. This includes initiatives to secure more affordable housing in the city. As in Eastside, there is a tension between the City's proclaimed environmental sustainability goals and how new housing developments are facilitated in practice. On one hand, Birmingham is quite ambitious and creative in its initiatives to enhance well-being and equity through constructing new market rate and council housing. On the other hand, the power of developers in this process can clearly be seen, and the prioritization of growth and development is weakening long-term environmental benefits.

The Birmingham City Council, like most British local authorities, was a major provider of public housing for much of the twentieth century through its construction and management of municipally owned council housing. As mentioned in Chapter 2, this stopped for many years when city councils lost the legal ability to build new public housing, with the responsibility given to non-profit Housing Authorities. Municipal stock was further limited by the Thatcher government's "Right to Buy" legislation that enabled home ownership for better-off council housing residents but also contracted the stock of council houses. This contraction was exacerbated by local authorities being prohibited from putting the money from the sales back into new housing construction. As with the story of public housing in Chicago, the extensive history of British council housing and the of impact of Right to Buy is beyond the scope of this book. What is crucial for current purposes is that by 2009 a severe crisis of affordable housing across the country had become undeniable, and municipalities were once again given the right to construct social housing. Birmingham, needing an additional 80,000 new homes by 2031 and having to deal with a large portfolio of decrepit council housing stock, quickly started looking for ways to get new homes built in the city.[118]

To facilitate rapid new housing development, in 2009 the council created the Birmingham Municipal Housing Trust (BMHT). The work of the BMHT includes building council housing for rent as well as working through public–private partnerships to build homes for sale at both affordable and market prices.[119] Unlike development on private land, where affordability goals are frequently waived by the national government in order to encourage more development,[120] the council and the BMHT have control over how construction proceeds on council-owned land. They therefore "can dictate what the percentage [of affordable housing] should be" in a new development. Usually this is around 35 percent, and some developments on council-owned land are as high as 50–50 council housing and homes for private sale.[121]

This is significant because the council is a major landowner throughout the city and much of this land is already cleared or derelict, ready for new development. The council also owns a large portfolio of existing homes that it is striving to bring up to higher quality standards. However, although the council owns land, it does not have the upfront capital to construct new housing on its own. This is where the BMHT comes in. The BMHT set up a program that encourages developers to construct new homes on council-owned land by taking away some of the risk and the up-front cost of development. The crux of this program is that when developers work with the BMHT on a new development, the developer gets to build private homes but does not have to pay the council for the land until the unit sells. Any higher than expected profits on the sale of the private homes is split with the council. In exchange, the developer also builds council homes on the land. These mixed-tenure developments are seen as win–wins by housing planners as they generate revenue for the city from the private sales as well as facilitate the construction of more council houses than Birmingham would otherwise be able to achieve.[122]

According to planners, the other benefit of these mixed-tenure developments, with virtually indistinguishable council houses and market homes side by side, is to make the areas more marketable. For decades council housing served a wide swath of society, but as more well-off council house residents bought their homes through Right to Buy, what was left were poorer developments. Increasingly, poverty and social stigma accompanied council housing.[123] Not unlike the construction of mixed-income neighborhoods in Chicago, Birmingham is trying to change this perception of council housing through higher quality design and mixed tenures. "If you have a mix of tenures," a housing planner asserted in an echo of the CHA's Vincent Lane, "it builds a much more coherent and sustainable community."[124] Interestingly, gentrification does not appear to be a major concern in Birmingham. Neighborhoods are certainly changing through BMHT initiatives, and new market-rate condominiums continue to be built in the city center. Unlike Chicago's destruction of its public housing projects, however, Birmingham is increasing its overall stock of affordable and council-owned homes, thereby expanding access rather than restricting it.[125]

In addition to facilitating the construction of affordable housing, building on city-owned land also means the council can require that builders meet whatever environmental standards the council desires. In contrast to its ambitious push for affordable housing, however, the council is not willing to go as far as it could in securing green buildings. Rather, it has been backing away from some of its environmental requirements. When the BMHT was first formed, environmental sustainability was pushed hard in the new housing, with high-level green ratings and the frequent inclusion of solar panels on new council housing. This is no longer the case. Some green features like high-efficiency boilers and insulation are still being included, but planners are concerned about any environmental elements that cannot be justified by a fairly short-term payback. Solar panels in particular are no longer being included in new developments.[126]

Solar panels are not the epitome of a green building, of course. Yet the abandonment of renewable energy sources for these new homes is indicative of the broader shortcomings of green development in Birmingham. One reason the City is no longer including solar panels goes back to the end of the national feed-in tariff. As discussed in the context of Birmingham Energy Savers in Chapter 5, the elimination of the tariff increased the payback time of the cost of installing solar panels, decreasing their appeal. The other reason given by planners as to why solar panels have been dropped from new council houses is that the panels hurt the legitimacy of the council's housing efforts by creating excessively high expectations from tenants. When residents saw solar panels on their homes, many thought they would not have to pay any energy bills. "Then when they find it hasn't work out like that" some become frustrated with the council and think the City misled them.[127] The new homes certainly offer significant efficiency improvement over the old council homes and the aging stock of private rentals in the city. Overall, however, "sustainability has been seen as an add-on"[128] in housing development. If the payback is long or environmental initiatives raise political challenges, they are dropped. This failure to maximize the environmental effectiveness of the new homes rapidly being constructed in Birmingham is a missed opportunity to create new housing stock that lowers carbon emissions and fuel poverty as far as possible.

Lack of political will to push harder on environmentally effective new development is exacerbated by changing national policies. The end of the feed-in tariff was one such change. Another was Prime Minister Cameron's elimination of national green building standards. In 2006, at the height of Britain's commitment to liberal environmentalism, then-chancellor Gordon Brown put national requirements in place that by 2016 all new homes would be zero net carbon.[129] Similar regulations for new commercial buildings soon followed. If these requirements had remained in place, they would have negated the pressure Birmingham planners feel to not push too hard on green building requirements in new developments, as the standards would have applied nationally to all new construction. However, after nearly a decade of work by councils and the building industry to be ready to achieve the goal of carbon neutral development, in 2015 the Cameron government canceled the requirement entirely.[130]

The reason for eliminating the green building requirement was to take away a burden on house-builders that was claimed to be limiting new home starts. Though some builders apparently lobbied heavily for the change, others were frustrated, calling the move "short-sighted, unnecessary, retrograde and damaging to the house-building industry, which has invested heavily in delivering energy-efficient homes."[131] In Birmingham, some Labour councilors saw the change as part of Cameron's wider rejection of the partisan consensus around sustainability and climate change mitigation that had been built up in the UK over decades.[132] Like the elimination of the Green Deal, the end of the feed-in tariff, and cuts to ECO (see Chapter 5), this national change has made it harder for Birmingham to reduce the environmental impact of its development imperative.

Slowly Shifting the Development Paradigm

Birmingham continues to make gestures toward more environmentally sustainable development. The city Development Plan adopted by the council in early 2017 has as one of its priorities the creation of "sustainable neighbourhoods." Among other features, this means walkability and transit access, "environmental sustainability and climate proofing through measures that save energy, water and non-renewable resources and the use of green and blue infrastructure," abundant green space, and a strong sense of place for neighborhood residents.[133] Throughout the Development Plan "sustainable growth" and becoming a leading green city are highlighted as city priorities.

Reflecting on this, some city officials think that there has been a shift toward a recognition that "growth in itself is not acceptable, that the growth has to be inclusive [and sustainable]. And actually the market will not do that. … [T]he local authority [has] to push for that."[134] But even if some planners and officials feel it is important to put more substantive policies into place to achieve the city's environmental and social goals, others' "eyes glaze over" when such issues are raised.[135] It therefore remains to be seen if Birmingham's new Development Plan and its proclaimed commitments to greening and inclusion will shift development in the city or if new developments will continue to go the way of the

Eastside Sustainability Quarter – high ambitions that are not matched by the political will and resources to achieve them.

Conclusion

Justified by growing demand, the need for economic revitalization, or the environmental benefits of city center housing, Vancouver, Chicago, and Birmingham are all working to increase new development. Even as city leaders prioritize development, efforts have been made to extract some social and environmental concessions from developers. Whether this is public amenities and affordable housing in Vancouver, Chicago's expansion of affordable housing mandates and TOD, or Birmingham's creative approach to facilitating the construction of new council housing, city leaders are slowly increasing the social and environmental benefits of urban development. Yet their efforts are also tempered by other concerns, particularly the fear that if too much is demanded of developers they will simply not build. This is particularly pronounced in Birmingham, though Chicago officials have expressed this concern as well. Even in Vancouver's lucrative housing market, critics assert that city officials have not gone far enough in securing amenities and affordable housing from developers.

The debates around development, sustainability, neighborhood change, and displacement discussed above are complicated and are by no means unique to these cities. While certainly not resolving these debates, this chapter has strived to illustrate a more complicated picture of the relationship between green urban development and social sustainability than some discussions of environmental gentrification suggest. Environmental amenities and the appeal of low carbon urban living may indeed be bolstering property values and driving displacement, as critics assert. But new urban developments may also be providing cash-strapped cities with the ability to build new affordable housing, a responsibility that national governments have largely abdicated. Furthermore, the environmental benefits of urban development that minimizes automobile use, energy consumption, and the destruction of greenfields cannot be dismissed, particularly when examined from the perspective of cities' contributions to global environmental governance. Finally, though community voice in determining neighborhood development is vital for pushing city leaders to make new developments more inclusive and sustainable, it can also raise the specter of elite resistance to any but the most modest new developments. Gentrification is but one potential outcome of the relationship in cities between development and greening.

In the midst of all of this, what becomes clear from these cases is the vital role of local state legitimacy and political will in achieving development that maximizes social and environmental benefits. It is difficult to know if leaders in these cities are truly demanding as much as possible from developers on environmental standards and affordability; in each city critics insist that they are not. In each city there are also key players – planners, advocates, and city officials – who are rejecting the lingering fears that there must be a trade-off between greening, inclusive communities, and development, and are striving to find ways to achieve all three goals. How far they will be willing and able to push this shift is unclear. Each case offers evidence that social and environmental goals may be abandoned if the housing market weakens, national policies make city goals more difficult to achieve, or if city leadership loses interest in those priorities. Vancouver, Chicago, and Birmingham could move the boundaries of sustainable urban development toward progressive liberal environmentalism. But the difficulties they face in doing so are substantial.

Notes

1 Alan Durning, *Unlocking Home: Three Keys to Affordable Communities* (Seattle, WA: Sightline Institute, 2013); David Owen, *Green Metropolis: Why Living Smaller, Living Closer, and Driving Less Are the Keys to Sustainability* (New York, NY: Riverhead Books, 2009).
2 City of Vancouver, "Greenest City 2020 Action Plan" (Vancouver, BC, 2011).
3 Harriet Bulkeley, *Cities and Climate Change* (London, UK: Routledge, 2013); David Sattherwaite, "How Urban Societies Can Adapt to Resource Shortage and Climate Change," *Philosophical Transactions of the Royal Society* 369 (2011).
4 Elizabeth C. Delmelle, Eva Haslauer, and Thomas Prinz, "Social Satisfaction, Commuting and Neighborhoods," *Journal of Transport Geography* 30 (2013).
5 Todd Litman, "Evaluation Public Transit Benefits and Costs" (Victoria, BC: Victoria Transport Policy Institute, 2015).
6 Durning; Stuart S. Rosenthal, "Are Private Markets and Filtering a Viable Source of Low-Income Housing? Estimates from a 'Repeat Income' Model," *The American Economic Review* 104, no. 2 (2014).
7 Sigit D. Arifwidodo, "Exploring the Effect of Compact Development Policy to Urban Quality of Life in Bandung, Indonesia," *City, Culture and Society* 3 (2012); Mike Jenks, Elizabeth Burton, and Katie Williams, eds., *The Compact City: A Sustainable Urban Form?* (London, UK: E & FN Spon, 1996).
8 Marcial H. Echenique et al., "Growing Cities Sustainably," *Journal of the American Planning Association* 78, no. 2 (2012).
9 Calista Cheung, "Deconstructing Canada's Housing Markets: Finance, Affordability and Urban Sprawl," in *OECD Economics Department Working Papers* (OECD Publishing, 2014).
10 Miriam Zuk and Karen Chapple, "Housing Production, Filtering and Displacement: Untangling the Relationships," in *Berkeley IGS Research Brief* (Berkeley, CA: Institute of Government Studies, 2016).
11 For example, Noah Quastel, "Political Ecologies of Gentrification," *Urban Geography* 30, no. 7 (2009); see also chapter one.
12 Robert D. Bullard, ed. *Growing Smarter: Achieving Livable Commities, Environmental Justice, and Regional Equity* (Cambridge, MA: MIT Press, 2007); Elizabeth Burton, "The Compact City: Just or Just Compact? A Preliminary Analysis," *Urban Studies* 37, no. 11 (2000); Katie Williams,

Elizabeth Burton, and Mike Jenks, eds., *Achieving Sustainable Urban Form* (London New York: E & FN Spon, 2000).

13 See John Punter, *The Vancouver Achievement: Urban Planning and Design* (Vancouver, BC: UBC Press, 2003).

14 City of Vancouver, "Clouds of Change: Final Report of the City of Vancouver Task Force on Atmospheric Change" (Vancouver, BC, 1990).

15 "CityPlan: Directions for Vancouver" (Vancouver, BC, 1995).

16 "EcoDensity: How Density, Design, and Land Use Will Contribute to Environmental Sustainability, Affordability, and Livability" (Vanvoucer, BC 2008), 1.

17 Punter.

18 City councilor, personal communication, August 2014.

19 Marit Rosol, "Vancouver's 'EcoDensity' Planning Initiative: A Struggle over Hegemony?," *Urban Studies* (2013).

20 Ibid.

21 Personal communication, August 2014.

22 See City of Vancouver, "Greenest City 2020 Action Plan."; "Greenest City 2020 Action Plan Part Two: 2015–2020" (Vancouver, BC: City of Vancouver, 2015).

23 Lori Culbert and Chad Skelton, "Housing Affordability a Hot Topic," *Vancouver Sun*, 18 October 2014; Barbara Yaffe, "Barbara Yaffe: Vancouver Must Explore Options to Ease Housing Affordability Crisis," *Vancouver Sun*, November 4.

24 City councilor, personal communication, August 2014.

25 City planner, personal communication, August 2014.

26 Patrick M. Condon, "Vancouver's 'Spot Zoning' Is Corrupting Its Soul," *The Tyee*, July 14, 2014.

27 Former city planner, personal communication, August 2014.

28 Gordon Price and Patrick Condon, "Debate: Should Vancouver Change How It Zones Big Projets?," *The Tyee*, August 13, 2014.

29 Personal communications, August 2014.

30 See CBC News, "Vancouver Rentals Quadruple, but Residents Question Affordability," *CBC News British Columbia*, November 20, 2015; City of Vancouver, "Creating and Preserving Market Rental Housing," http://vancouver.ca/people-programs/creating-new-market-rental-housing.aspx (accessed February 3, 2015).

31 City planner, personal communication, August 2014.

32 Opposition city council candidates, personal communications, August 2014.

33 Grandview-Woodland community activists, personal communications, August 2014.

34 Charles Campbell, "At Ground Zero for Vancouver's Towering Debate," *The Tyee*, June 25, 2013.

35 Quoted in ibid.

36 Grandview-Woodland community activist, personal communication, August 2014.

37 Quoted in Jeff Lee, "Party Moved 'Too Fast' on East Van Towers Bid," *Vancouver Sun*, May 5, 2014.

38 City of Vancouver, "Marpole Community Plan" (Vancouver, BC, 2015).

39 Jeff Lee, "Citizens' Assembly Releases Grandview-Woodland Report," *Vancouver Sun*, June 19, 2015.

40 City of Vancouver, "Marpole Community Plan."

41 Grandview-Woodland community activist, personal communication, August 2014.

42 Personal communication, August 2014.

43 See www.grandview-woodland.ca/ for a detailed discussion of the Citizens Assembly and notes from their meetings and workshops (accessed March 10, 2015).
44 See https://ourcommunityourplan.wordpress.com/ for numerous blog posts from the organization Our Community, Our Plan!, an outspoken critic of the original plan for towers and initially of the Citizens Assembly (accessed March 10, 2015).
45 Citizens' Assembly on the Grandview-Woodland Community Plan, "Final Report" (City Vancouver: Vancouver, BC, 2015).
46 Lee, "Citizens' Assembly Releases Grandview-Woodland Report."
47 For example, John Mackie, "Tower Proposal Splits Commercial Drive," *Vancouver Sun*, August 6.
48 City planner, personal communication, August 2014.
49 City of Vancouver, "Downtown Eastside Plan" (Vancouver, BC: City of Vancouver, 2014).
50 Personal communication, August 2014.
51 Nathan Edelson and Karen O'Shannacery, "Revitalizing the Heart of the City," *The Tyee*, March 13, 2014.
52 Ivan Drury, "Vancouver Rightists Rising against the Downtown Eastside," *The Mainlander*, March 10, 2014.
53 Maria Wallstam and Nathan Crompton, "Social Housing without Guarantees: The Myth of the 60/40 Ration in the DTES Oppenheimer District," *The Mainlander*, March 12, 2014.
54 Canadian Press, "B.C. Lifts Foreign Buyers Tax for People with Work Permits as Housing Market Cools," *Financial Post*, January 30, 2017; Mike Hager, "Real Estate Developers Slammed B.C. Over Surprise Foreign-Buyer Tax," *Globe and Mail*, December 13, 2016.
55 Iain Marlow and Brent Jang, "Vancouver's Real Estate Boom: The Rising Price of 'Heaven,'" *Globe and Mail*, October 10, 2014; Kazi Stastna, "Real Estate Rules Don't Discriminate against Foreigners," *CBC News*, March 19, 2012.
56 Barbara Shecter, "Government Intervention on Housing Causes Vancouver to 'Temporarily Freeze in Its Tracks,'" *Financial Post*, January 4, 2017.
57 See Hager.
58 Ibid.
59 Shecter.
60 Greg Hinz, "The Hottest Urban Center in the U.S. – Chicago's Mega-Loop," *Crain's Chicago Business*, March 2, 2013.
61 Ibid.
62 City of Chicago, "Chicago Central Area Plan" (City of Chicago, 2003).
63 For example, Noah Quastel, Markus Moos, and Nicholas Lynch, "Sustainability-as-Density and the Return of the Social: The Case of Vancouver, British Columbia," *Urban Geography* 33, no. 7 (2012).
64 Alan Ehrenhalt, "A Neighborhood in Chicago," in *The Great Inversion and the Future of the American City* (New York: Alfred A. Knopf, 2012).
65 Mitch Kahn, "Book Review: Paradise Lost," *Shelterforce Online*, no. 138 (2004).
66 Don Terry, "The Final Farewell at Cabrini-Green," *New York Times*, December 10, 2010, A25.
67 Pam Belluck, "Gang Gunfire May Chase Chicago Children from Their School," *New York Times*, November 17, 1997; Terry.
68 Elvin K. Wyly and Daniel J Hammel, "Islands of Decay in Seas of Renewal: Housing Policy and the Resurgence of Gentrification," in *The

Gentrificaion Reader, ed. Loretta Lees, Tom Slater, and Elvin Wyly (New York, NY: Routledge, 2010 [1999]).

69 Larry Bennett, "Transforming Public Housing," in *The New Chicago: A Social and Cultural Analysis*, ed. John P. Koval, et al. (Philadelphia, PA: Temple University Press, 2006).

70 Quoted in ibid., 272.

71 Ibid; Wyly and Hammel.

72 Bennett.

73 See Diane K. Levy, Zachary J. McDade, and Kassie Dumlao Bertumen, "Effects from Living in Mixed-Income Communities for Low-Income Families: A Review of the Literature" (Washington, DC: Urban Institute, 2011).

74 Bennett, 275.

75 City of Chicago.

76 Hinz; Mark Joseph and Robert Chaskin, "Living in Mixed-Income Development: Resident Perceptions of the Benefits and Disadvantages of Two Developments in Chicago," *Urban Studies* 47, no. 11 (2010).

77 Bennett.

78 Mina Bloom, "Cabrini-Green Rowhouse Settlement: Everything You Need to Know," *DNAInfo*, September 15, 2015.

79 Dawn Rhodes, "Cabrini-Green Residents, CHA Settle Lawsuit – Adding Public Housing in Area," *Chicago Tribune*, September 13, 2015.

80 Quoted in Bloom.

81 See Curbed, "What Will the Cabrini-Green of the Future Look Like?," Curbed, http://chicago.curbed.com/2016/1/7/10848958/what-will-the-cabrinigreen-of-the-future-look-like (accessed July 28, 2016).

82 Center for Neighborhood Technology, "Transit-Oriented Development in the Chicago Region: Efficient and Resilient Communities for the 21st Century" (Chicago, IL: Center for Neighborhood Technology, 2013).

83 Blair Kamin, "Transit-Oriented Apartment Projects a Positive Development," *Chicago Tribune*, March 21, 2015.

84 Yonah Freemark, "Minneapolis Strikes Again: How Chicago Could Revamp Its Parking Requirements," Metropolitan Planning Council, www.metroplanning.org/news/blog-post/7162 (accessed July 9, 2015); TOD advocate, personal communication, June 2015.

85 Mary Wisniewski, "New Buildings near 'L' Mostly Aimed at Well-to-Do," *Chicago Tribune*, May 2, 2016.

86 John Greenfield, "Activists Worry CTA-Friendly Housing Will Accelerate Logan Square Gentrification," *Chicago Reader*, April 18, 2016.

87 City of Chicago, "Housing: Affordable Requirements Ordinance," City of Chicago, www.cityofchicago.org/city/en/depts/dcd/supp_info/affordable_housingrequirementsordinance.html (accessed August 3, 2016).

88 Mary Ellen Podmolik, "Aldermen OK Stricter Affordable Housing Law," *Chicago Tribune*, March 18, 2015.

89 Ibid.

90 Alex Mayster, "5 up-and-Coming Neighborhoods in Chicago to Buy a Home," *U.S. News & World Report*, August 9, 2016.

91 Paul Biasco, "Logan Square Hispanics Vanishing as Neighborhood Becomes More White," *DNAInfo*, May 16, 2016.

92 Ibid.

93 Greenfield.

94 Personal communication, June 2015.

95 Quoted in Greenfield.

96 Wisniewski.

97 Jacky Grimshaw, "One Development Ordinance Does Not Serve All Neighborhoods," *Crain's Chicago Business*, July 22, 2016.

98 For example, May Rice, "88-Unit Affordable Housing Complex Proposed for Logan Square," *Chicagoist,* May 19, 2016.

99 For example, A.J. Latrace, "New Logan Square Transit-Oriented Development Quietly Opens," Curbed Chicago, http://chicago.curbed.com/2017/1/23/14363678/logan-square-apartment-for-rent-mode (accessed March 6, 2017).

100 Ian Jefferson, Chris Rogers, and Dexter Hunt, "Achieving Sustainable Underground Construction in Birmingham Eastside?," *IAEG2006 Paper number 312* (2006).

101 Birmingham City Council, 1995, quoted in Libby Porter and Dexter Hunt, "Birmingham's Eastside Story: Making Steps Towards Sustainability?," *Local Environment* 10, no. 5 (2005): 528.

102 Ibid., 526; see also Carina Weingaertner and Austin Barber, "Urban Regeneration and Sustainability: Challenges for Established Small Businesses. Paper Presented at the ENHR International Conference, June 25–28" (Rotterdam, 2007).

103 Porter and Hunt, 533.

104 EU Committee of the Regions, "Eastside – Masshouse Redevelopment" (2007). http://pes.cor.europa.eu/NEWS/Documents/News/2007/01%20Example%20by%20Albert%20BORE_EN.pdf (accessed May 23, 2017).

105 David Bell, "£50m Boost for City Centre," *Birmingham Evening Mail*, June 21, 2001; EU Committee of the Regions.

106 Environmental activist, personal communication, July 2008.

107 See Birmingham Friends of the Earth, "Eastside Sustainability Advisory Group" (n.d.), www.birminghamfoe.org.uk/ESAG/ (accessed January 19, 2011).

108 Keith Budden and Karen Leach, "Sustainable Eastside – a Vision for the Future" (Birmingham, UK: Birmingham City Council, 2002).

109 Birmingham Post, "Eastside Development Report Calls for Some Enlightenment," November 2, 2002.

110 Steve Pain, "Eastside Will Get Advice on Green Issues," *Birmingham Post*, May 15, 2003.

111 Birmingham Post, "Sustainability Team for Eastside Project," November 17, 2003.

112 David Middleton, "Tomorrow's World: With Flora, Greenery and Wildlife, Revamped Birmingham Is the New Central Park," *Birmingham Post*, November 28, 2006; Libby Porter and Austin Barber, "The Meaning of Place and State-Led Gentrification in Birmingham's Eastside," *City* 10, no. 2 (2006).

113 Birmingham Post, "'We Must Not Cut Corners on Eastside,'" March 3, 2005.

114 City biodiversity officer, personal communication, July 2008; Joanna Geary, "Tomorrow's World: Eastside in the Green Spotlight," *Birmingham Post*, November 28, 2006.

115 Porter and Hunt, 538.

116 ESAG member, personal communication, July 2008.

117 Personal communication, June 2016.

118 Birmingham City Council, "Birmingham Municipal Housing Trust," www.birmingham.gov.uk/bmht (accessed June 7, 2016); city planner for housing development, personal communication, June 2016.

119 Lesley Sheldrake, "Affordable Housing DIY," *The Planner*, April 7, 2015.

120 Housing planner, personal communication, June 2016.

121 Ibid.

122 City planner, personal communication, June 2016.

123 James Meek, "Where Will We Live?," *London Review of Books*, 1–9 January 2014.

124 Personal communication, June 2016.

125 Sarah Kirby, "Press Release: Plans for More than 2,000 New Homes," ed. Birmingham City Council (Birmingham, UK: Birmingham City Council, 2014).

126 Personal communication, June 2016.

127 Personal communication, June 2016.

128 City councilor, personal communication, June 2016.

129 Matt Weaver, "Brown Pledges to Build 'Zero Carbon' Homes," *Guardian*, December 6, 2006.

130 Chancellor of the Exchequer, "Fixing the Foundations: Creating a More Prosperous Nation" (London, UK: Controller of Her Majesty's Stationery Office, 2015).

131 Chief executive of the UK Green Building Council, quoted in Philip Oldfield, "UK Scraps Zero Carbon Homes Plan," *Guardian*, July 10, 2015.

132 Personal communication, June 2016.

133 Birmingham City Council, "Birmingham Plan 2013" (Birmingham, UK: Birmingham City Council, 2017), 108.

134 City councilor, personal communication, June 2016.

135 Sustainability officer, personal communication, June 2016.

7 Environmental Amenities

By creating attractive environmental amenities, the green entrepreneurial city drew skilled labor and tourists to a revitalized, post-industrial city center. As argued in the past few chapters, this narrowly focused form of neoliberal environmentalism has expanded in recent years to a broader environmental agenda that includes cities' contributions to global environmental governance and considerations of the social equity implications of greening. This chapter revisits the issue of environmental amenities, focusing on green space and green transit, particularly cycling. These two types of amenities are useful to examine because they are illustrative of both the entrepreneurial and the more progressive possibilities of liberal environmentalism.

Undoubtedly, green space and cycling appeal to the young professionals, tourists, and other populations that the entrepreneurial city seeks to attract, and the provision of such amenities is often focused on benefiting these groups. Yet they can also contribute to environmental effectiveness. These amenities can change the environmental impact of urban areas by reducing carbon emissions, air pollution, and countering some of the externalities of development. Furthermore, these aspects of the greener built environment raise issues of equity and social well-being. These issues include, on the one hand, inequity in the distribution of amenities and their potential exacerbation of gentrification and, on the other, their ability to enhance mobility, health, and access to the city for all. As such, to the extent that environmental amenities can further social as well as environmental goals, though they are foundational to green urban entrepreneurialism, they can also contribute to cities' moves toward other varieties of liberal environmentalism.

Parks, Bikes, and a Greener City for All

Green space has numerous environmental benefits. These range from managing the urban heat island effect and absorbing carbon dioxide to storm water capture and providing habitat for urban wildlife. Social benefits include enabling exchanges among different groups of people, creating potentially democratic spaces, supporting mental and physical well-being and relaxation, and offering opportunities for recreational activities and play.[1] Access to parks and green space is often inequitable, however, and environmental justice advocates are increasingly working to ensure poor communities and communities of color have equal access to this environmental good.[2] Yet access alone is not enough. Parks and green spaces must meet the social needs of nearby communities, with care taken that they are not designed "in such a way that only one kind of person – often a tourist or middle-class visitor – feels welcomed."[3] Complicating calls for a more just distribution of culturally appropriate parks and green space, many see gentrification as accompanying this amenity. This raises difficult questions of how to increase green space in park-poor neighborhoods without displacing existing residents.[4]

Like parks and green space, enhanced green transit can also be an amenity for the well-to-do, a remedy for transportation inequities, and a way to lower the environmental impact of urban areas. Transportation is a justice issue in that it "is basic to many other quality of life indicators such as health, education, employment, economic development, access to municipal services, residential mobility, and environmental quality."[5] In most cities, vehicles are also a main source of localized air pollution and global GHG emissions. Therefore, switching to "post-carbon mobility" will be vital for maintaining economic activity and improving community health without exacerbating climate change.[6] For these reasons, moving to a greener transportation system should be a clear example of the win–win–win promises of progressive liberal environmentalism.

In practice, however, challenges to achieving these multiple goals often arise. The logistical and political difficulties of changing existing car-oriented infrastructure toward a greater prioritization of greener transportation modes is one such challenge. Another emerges from the tension cities face between the need to provide good transit infrastructure for users that can fund the system and the justice imperative of improving transit for poorer communities and people for whom driving a car is not an option. As will be seen in the cases below, funding and political will are vital to overcoming these difficulties in moving toward effective, just green transit.

Green transportation has many aspects, but this chapter focuses primarily on cycling infrastructure, a small but growing facet of urban mobility.[7] From the perspective of environmental sustainability, cycling can be one piece of a comprehensive green transportation strategy that also includes efficient, accessible public transportation, walkable streets, and people-friendly urban design, all of which encourage alternatives to the private automobile.[8] Although clearly not a mode of travel that everyone can or would want to take, improvements to cycling infrastructure can be a low-cost, convenient way to increase access to the city. As will be seen, however, efforts to turn cycling into an integrated part of a larger transportation system have at times engendered strong political resistance. Cycling infrastructure therefore offers insight into the complexities of securing local state legitimacy when undertaking initiatives to enhance effective environmental governance.

As has been the case with the other greening issues examined in this book, the ways that the debates about open space and green transit are playing out in Birmingham, Chicago, and Vancouver are quite different. These differences are illustrative of each city's trajectory beyond green urban entrepreneurialism as well as the limits of their moves toward more effective, equitable varieties of liberal environmentalism. Although the debates and policies that have emerged in the three cities are different, many of the underlying tensions are similar. Questions of how greening can contribute to economic growth, concerns about who wins and who loses from the changing built environment of the city, and the limitations of municipal governments in shifting how people live in and move about urban space emerge in each case. As each city is working to enhance green transit and green space, they are illustrating that city infrastructure can be re-shaped in ways that further environmental sustainability and create more equitable access to the green city. However, as with other moves beyond neoliberal environmentalism, how far this will progress is not at all clear, and achieving these interconnected goals remains contested, partial, and by no means guaranteed.

Health and the Value of Nature

Despite frequent pronouncements of becoming a leading green city, the trajectory of Birmingham's greening efforts places it somewhere between neoliberal environmentalism and social liberalism (see Figure 1.1), with environmental effectiveness becoming less of a priority than economic benefits, social equity, and, increasingly, than public health. Birmingham leaders have good reason to focus on using environmental amenities to improve public health, as city residents face a number of health problems. Overall Birmingham has higher rates of cancer, diabetes, and deaths from cardiovascular disease than England as a whole. Nearly a quarter of both children and adults are obese, and "life expectancy for both men and women is lower than the England average," particularly in the city's most deprived neighborhoods.[9] The recent shift in emphasis away from climate change toward health can be seen as a step back from Birmingham's commitment to effective environmental governance, even as it opens up possibilities for prioritizing social well-being within broader environmental goals. As health becomes an important justification for greening, however, the political will to achieve the health and the environmental benefits of improved green spaces and transit often remains partial.

From Climate Governance to Health in the
Greening of Birmingham Transit

The shift from a prioritization of Birmingham's contribution to climate governance to a focus on the health of local residents can be seen in the changing justifications offered for improving the city's transportation infrastructure. In 2012, when becoming the birthplace of the low carbon revolution was still an important aspect of the city's branding strategy, Birmingham published its Low Carbon Transport Strategy. The plan aimed to enhance "green growth" and reduce carbon emissions through improving transportation in the city.[10] This included providing better public transit as well as "enhanced streets, high-quality pedestrian routes and a series of accessible open spaces, parks and squares."[11] Improved transportation was presented at this time as an important environmental goal, as it was estimated that a quarter of Birmingham's carbon emissions were from this sector.[12] Yet consistent with many of Birmingham's moves beyond green urban entrepreneurialism, in practice the Low Carbon Transport Strategy marked less of a stark shift in policy than an expansion of the pedestrianization of the city that had been occurring for nearly two decades.

With the change of council leadership shortly following the release of the report, the Low Carbon Transport Strategy was replaced by Birmingham Connected and the Birmingham Mobility Action Plan (BMAP).[13] In contrast to its centrality in the Low Carbon Transport Strategy, the BMAP barely mentions climate change. GHG reduction is only one of the plan's many goals, with economic justifications for improved transit particularly foregrounded. BMAP asserts that through enhancing its transportation infrastructure, "by 2031 Birmingham will be renowned as an enterprising, innovative and green city that has delivered sustainable growth meeting the needs of its population and strengthening its global competitiveness."[14] Touting the economic benefits of enhanced transportation was also a part of the Low Carbon Transportation Strategy, and it is consistent with Birmingham's longstanding promotion of greening as a tool for growth. The striking shift between the Low Carbon Transportation Strategy and the BMAT is that health and local equity issues have replaced climate change. Social equity justifications for the BMAT include creating a more equitable transport system, connecting communities to jobs and to each other, and raising health standards through promoting walking and cycling and by reducing air pollution.[15]

Air pollution is a serious problem in Birmingham, with Public Health England estimating that poor air quality leads to an extra 520 deaths per year in the city.[16] The BMAP recognizes this problem and clearly asserts that reducing auto dependence is vital to addressing Birmingham's air pollution. The report states, "We make no secret that we want to contain the growth in the number of cars on the roads, because an over-reliance on cars means major damage to public health and road safety: it causes poor air quality, traffic collisions, congestion for all road users and dissuades people from walking and cycling due to safety concerns (which in turn affects public health)."[17] This is a bold statement against the primacy of cars in Birmingham, but actual initiatives to reduce car dependence and its accompanying congestion and air pollution have been much more modest. They have included city center prestige transit projects (particularly a new train station) and some enhancements to cycling infrastructure, with policies seen as a threat or inconvenience to personal vehicles taken off the table.

Cycling, Air Pollution, and the Persistence of Car-Centricism

Cycling shows this shift in Birmingham from an emphasis on climate governance to equity and health as well as the lack of political will for moving away from car-centricism. Though "intrinsically anti-bike" because of the overwhelmingly auto-oriented infrastructure of the 1960s and 1970s that continues to shape most of the city,[18] Birmingham has begun work on enhancing its bike networks. Birmingham Connected established the goal that "cycling will become a mainstream form of transport over the next 20 years" with 5 percent of trips taken by bike in 2023 and 10 percent by 2033.[19] To support movement toward this goal, the City received tens of millions of pounds in national government grants to fund the "Birmingham Cycle Revolution."[20] The purpose of the Cycle Revolution is to "help to make [the] city healthier, greener, safer and less congested."[21] Yet bringing about this "revolution," which even a city councilor who is a major cycling advocate in the city calls "a very loose term," is proving difficult.[22]

One limitation to cycling in Birmingham is the city's lack of bike infrastructure. The solution has been to build on the successful transformation of one of Birmingham's greatest environmental amenities, the canal towpaths, by turning them into bikeways. As discussed in Chapter 3, over the past century the canals have gone from key industrial infrastructure, to dangerous and derelict, to waterfront amenities for new city center developments. They are now becoming key aspects of the city's green transit system. Used for recreational cycling and walking for a number of years, in many ways the towpaths make excellent bike lanes. They are completely separated from vehicular traffic, thus both protecting cyclists from automobiles and avoiding the political difficulty of taking road space away from cars to create bike lanes. Mostly unpaved until recently, as part of the Birmingham Cycle Revolution, the City has enhanced most of its towpaths "with a clean, well-drained, grippy grit surface" to facilitate cycling.[23] Improved canal access points have also been established throughout the city (Figure 7.1).

In addition to enhancing bike infrastructure, another promising aspect of the Birmingham Cycle Revolution is that social equity is foundational

Figure 7.1 Canal towpaths are a key part of Birmingham's cycling
    infrastructure.
Source: Photo by author, 2016.

to the program.[24] From the outset the program has prioritized the potential financial and health benefits to low-income residents of access to bike
infrastructure, cycling skills, and to bicycles themselves. One of the bold-
est things the council did to ensure the Cycle Revolution benefited lower-
income residents was to give away three thousand bikes to people living
in deprived parts of the city. The bikes were accompanied by sixteen cycle
centers that provide free bike maintenance, bike activities, and cycling
instruction. At six of the centers bikes can also be rented for free.[25]

Councilors involved in giving away the bright orange Big Birmingham
Bikes recognized that it was a political risk in terms of the expense,
whether or not the free bikes would actually lead to more cycling, and
what to do when the bikes began to be resold. Another worry was that

the program was "big brotherish," as each bike was tagged with a GPS to track data on usage and what routes were being taken.[26] But the analysis of councilors involved in the program is that it has worked, that recipients feel the GPS tracking is reasonable in exchange for a free bike, and that the program has led to an increase in cycling, particularly among Birmingham's large population of South Asian women, many of whom do not drive.[27]

Though prioritizing creating cycling opportunities for lower-income residents, the Cycle Revolution has also tried to increase biking across the population as a whole. The program has installed bike racks around the city and has offered a plethora of bike activities, guided rides, and prizes. Together, these efforts are striving to create "the culture change [that] is the initiative's biggest challenge" in the car-loving city.[28]

The enhanced towpaths and getting bikes into the hands of people who may not otherwise have access to them are the major successes of the Birmingham Cycle Revolution. But the program also faces some deep challenges. Interestingly, the first challenge is also one of its successes – the canal towpaths. The towpaths do offer an important enhancement to the city's cycling infrastructure, but they are also in many ways inadequate. They are very narrow in places, often have no separation between the path and the water-filled canals, and some sections are quite isolated. All of these factors could make them feel unsafe to inexperienced riders and to women riding alone.[29] It is also not clear that the narrow paths could accommodate any significant volume of cyclists, particularly when they are also being used by pedestrians. Furthermore, once cyclists leave the towpaths, they still need to be able to get safely to their final destinations. With poor cycle routes on city streets, biking safely from the towpaths to other destinations is often difficult.

Cycling advocates both within and out of the local government agree that the canals alone are insufficient. However, efforts to improve the city's cycling infrastructure beyond the canals have run into the second and even more daunting challenge to the Cycle Revolution. This challenge is resistance from many city councilors to taking road space away from cars in their districts to make room for cyclists. In this regard, there is a notable disconnect between the proclamations of the BMAP and how its goal of reducing the primacy of the automobile plays out in practice. According to one pro-cycling councilor, when asked in general terms about improving bike lanes throughout the city, most city councilors will say, "'Yes, cycling is great!' But when it comes to the [question of] 'are you going to give up some road space [so] the cyclist can have it?' That's a very different question because obviously that is a politically hard thing."[30] Few councilors are willing to take the political risk of inconveniencing drivers in their districts. When concrete steps to get people out of their cars are proposed, be it congestion charges, removing parking spaces, or creating designated bike lanes "it's really easy for people to pull out the 'well, this is really anti-motorist' [argument]' and that debate, that tone of debate, has happened a lot."[31] As the creation of designated bike lanes on city streets inevitably takes some space away from cars, this concern makes it hard to get council approval for sizable improvements to cycling infrastructure.[32]

The green transit rhetoric in Birmingham has moved from carbon reduction to health and clean air. But the cultural and political importance of the personal automobile remains strong in the city, and councilors perceive there to be widespread political resistance to any efforts that might limit car use.[33] This is making it difficult for the city to shift far enough toward green transit to bring Birmingham's air pollution down to safe levels and to lower its carbon emissions from this sector.

Valuing Nature in Austerity

For a city with a lingering reputation as a concrete jungle, Birmingham has a surprising amount of green space, with 571 parks, more than 3,500 hectares of publically accessible open space, and 250 miles of urban brooks and streams.[34] The amount of green space the city has is a mixed blessing, however. National government grants are funding improvements to the canals as cycling infrastructure, but overall there is limited budget to maintain parks and open space. This situation has been worsening over the past several decades of national budget cuts[35] and became even more pronounced with the Cameron government's introduction of severe austerity measures beginning in 2010.

What has emerged in Birmingham in response to a small and diminishing budget for maintenance of green space is consistent with neoliberalism's ideal of voluntarism complementing a limited state. To maintain the city's green space, a barebones park staff is augmented by hundreds of volunteers that do much of the park maintenance work. This is vital to maintaining Birmingham's green space. Yet it has also led to inequalities in park quality as residents of some neighborhoods have more time, ability, and resources to maintain their community open space than others.[36]

One effort to change how parks are valued, and thereby secure more resources for their funding and maintenance, has been an attempt to calculate the monetary value of the ecosystem services provided by green space. This goal was articulated in the Green Living Spaces Plan adopted by the council as an advisory planning document in September 2013.[37] By calculating the impact on the city budget of benefits from green space such as flood mitigation, health savings, and facilitation of climate change adaptation, Green Living Spaces strives "to change the political profile of urban green space" and create greater recognition of its financial value to the city.[38] Green Living Spaces is an ambitious plan that boosted the city's reputation for environmental sustainability. The national government cited Green Living Spaces as a best practice for other local authorities, and the plan led to an invitation for Birmingham to join the Biophilic Cities Network, a selective global network of cities committed to enhancing urban green space.[39]

If taken seriously, the Green Living Spaces plan could impact city development and budget decisions in a number of ways. One hope of its proponents is that in giving quantifiable value to green spaces and nature in the city, this value will be incorporated into land use decisions. For example, the cost of managing additional flooding caused by paving over green space could be incorporated into the price at which the council sells a plot of land for development.[40] Valuing nature in such a way could change the cost calculation of destroying green space, giving incentive for incorporating ecosystem services into new developments and enhancing existing parks and open spaces.

This ecosystem services model also has the potential to enable the same kind of analysis for public health. As poor health and poverty are strongly correlated in Birmingham, the plan prioritizes "enhancing nature particularly in the city's most deprived areas as a way to improve health and well-being."[41] As with flood prevention, advocates hope that if the health benefits of parks can be quantified in terms of their savings to the city's pinched health budget, this money could then be reinvested in further improvements to parks and open space.[42] The approach of Green Living Spaces still prioritizes the economic benefits of green space. Rather than merely seeing green space as having value as amenity that can spur tourism and raise property values, however, Green Living Spaces strives to also give quantifiable value to the health and environmental benefits of greening.

The ecosystem services method of valuing nature has the potential to inspire the conservation of green space in a context of austerity. Yet so far, it is not clear that Green Living Spaces is having a substantive impact on city development and budget decisions, and the parks budget remains on the cutting board. Already having endured cuts along with most other city services as the Birmingham City Council budget has been reduced by hundreds of thousands of pounds since 2010,[43] the proposed 2017–2018 city budget called for a further £1.8 million cut to park maintenance. This represents a cut of about 20 percent of its total budget, and the proposal called for addition cuts of £2.4 million each of the following three years.[44]

In response, 30 parks, recreation, and conservation organizations in Birmingham sent a letter to the council in protest. In it they highlighted the economic, environmental, and social benefits of the city's green spaces. The letter asserted that the cuts "to the parks and nature conservation budget for Birmingham City Council will damage our communities, increase the need for future spending on health and reduce investment in our city in addition to the inevitable decline in the quality of our green spaces for people and reduced habitat for wildlife."[45] Though consistent with the idea behind Green Living Spaces, the argument that budget cuts today will create additional financial burdens in the future is difficult for a council striving to provide basic services to its residents to embrace. It seems even less likely that the council would worry about reduced habitat for wildlife, the benefit of which is even harder to measure than health and flood mitigation.

Barriers to Green Amenities

In Birmingham, the importance of including equity and social well-being within policies to enhance green space and low carbon mobility is recognized. Yet as in the failure of Birmingham Energy Savers to reduce fuel poverty (see Chapter 5) and in its prioritization of housing development over green building (see Chapter 6), fiscal and political barriers stand in the way of Birmingham achieving its goal of economically, socially, and environmentally beneficial transit and green space. The growing focus on the health and financial benefits of greening may eventually overcome some of the political barriers to creating a more sustainable city. Yet so far proponents struggle to move considerations of health and long-term well-being into the core of transportation and budget decisions.

Re-shaping Mobility for the High-Density City

As has been made clear throughout this book, increasing density has been a principle way that Vancouver has strived to meet many of its social and environmental goals. A variety of controversies have arisen around densification, from push-back against apartments in neighborhoods of single-family homes to fears of displacement of the city's poor. Another important challenge to consider with increasing density is the pressure that additional people put on the city's infrastructure. Vancouver's overburdened public transportation system is a particular concern, and continuing to secure public green space also remains a priority. As environmental amenities are core to Vancouver's green brand and its livability, not adequately addressing these limitations could become a threat to the city's entrepreneurial and environmental goals.

Vancouver leaders are well aware of the need to mitigate the impacts of density on transit and green space. As discussed in Chapter 4, the latter issue has been addressed through requiring new developments to include abundant public parks and green space, and over 92 percent of residents are within a five-minute walk of public green space (Figure 7.2).[46] The City has also long been working to reduce car trips by enhancing public transit and by improving walking and cycling infrastructure. This has been done both as an aspect of the city's livability agenda and in order to maximize the mobility benefits of density while reducing the negative outcome of more people leading to more car trips to and within the city. Though public transit in Vancouver is seen by many as inadequate, the city has seen measurable increases in walking and cycling, as well as an overall reduction in trips in the city by personal vehicle.

Figure 7.2 Amenity requirements from new developments have helped ensure that almost all Vancouver residents are within a five-minute walk of public green space.

Source: Photo by author, 2014.

The successful expansion of Vancouver's bike infrastructure has been particularly notable, and has done much to overcome the potential downsides of densification though ambitious re-envisioning of how people move about the city. However, the expansion of dedicated cycle lanes has also been a source of political conflict, threatening the legitimacy of the council's greening agenda. Furthermore, Vancouver has faced numerous difficulties trying to expand its public transportation infrastructure, even in the face of overcapacity. The challenges of green transit in Vancouver illustrate the potential dangers of cities embracing the environmental benefits of densification without the accompanying power to make sure such benefits are fully achieved. As with many of its efforts, Vancouver shows both the promise and limitations of municipal leadership in creating a more sustainable city.

Transit Capacity and the Limits of Densification

The Greenest City 2020 Action Plan states that "Vancouver is rising to meet the green transportation challenge by creating compact neighbourhoods with higher density to provide easy access to work, shopping and recreation. The City has shifted investment to walking, cycling and transit infrastructure instead of building new roads."[47] Indeed, the ability of high-density development to facilitate non-motorized and public transportation is one of the major environmental and social benefits attributed to it. Vancouver has illustrated this benefit through its successful decoupling of population growth from personal vehicle use. Between 1996 and 2011, even as the population of downtown increased by 75 percent and the number of jobs increased 26 percent, the number of vehicles entering downtown decreased by 20 percent.[48] Between 2008 and 2015 green transit went from 40 percent of all trips taken in the city to 50 percent, and overall per capita vehicle miles travelled decreased by 21 percent.[49] Seeking to build on this success, Transportation 2040, the regional transportation plan adopted by the city council in 2012, sets the even more ambitious goal of two-thirds of all trips in Vancouver being taken by foot, bike, or public transportation by 2040.[50]

Despite the successful track record of decreasing personal vehicle use in the city, critics saw the calls by the GCAP and Transportation 2040 to use densification "to support shorter trips and sustainable transportation choices"[51] as unrealistic. With public transit in Vancouver already at capacity,[52] greater densification, critics asserted, would not enhance sustainable transportation choices. Rather, it would just lower the quality of life for existing residents by making transit infrastructure more crowded.[53] Furthermore, the city has faced difficulty in securing the regional and provincial transit funding necessary to adequately serve existing development, let alone new density. The claim that greater density will facilitate transit use is therefore seen by many as yet another justification for rampant development.

This concern is by no means unfounded. The challenge of securing transit funding can be seen in the conflict over the Broadway corridor that runs through Vancouver to the University of British Columbia, one of the most heavily used transit routes in North America.[54] Decisions about regional transit are made by TransLink, the statutory authority that oversees public transportation, regional cycling, major roads, and bridges across the metropolitan Vancouver region.[55] TransLink is advised by a Mayor's Council consisting of representatives of all 21 municipalities in the region, the Tsawwassen First Nation, and the unincorporated metro area. Vancouver staff and councilors feel that TransLink often fails to recognize the severity of the Vancouver's transit needs. This leads to "epic, epic disagreements" between city officials and TransLink on everything from where to locate train stations to how much capacity new stations should have.[56] According to city planners, TransLink has consistently underestimated the city's transit demand, thereby undersupplying the system and leading to the current problems of over-capacity. Disagreements between urban and suburban mayors about how limited transit funds should be invested exacerbates the problem.[57] Transportation 2040 was therefore something of a breakthrough, as the "Mayors Council ground this thing out, and actually came to agreement among themselves," incorporating the priorities of both the city and the more suburban parts of the region.[58]

Despite the important agreement it represented, the provincial government refused to fund Transportation 2040, and proposals to use BC carbon tax revenue to fund expanded public transportation were rejected. Questions of how to find necessary funds for the plan led to an unprecedented regional plebiscite vote in 2015 to determine support for a 0.05 percent sales tax for infrastructure improvements, including a new subway along the busy Broadway corridor. Despite being "supported by most of the region's mayors, police and fire chiefs, and a coalition including business, unions, and environmental groups," the plebiscite lost by nearly 62 percent, "making it uncertain how improvements to transit and transportation [would] be funded over the next decade."[59] The vote was seen as a particular blow to the legitimacy of Mayor Robertson's development agenda, and it left Vancouver at a loss as to how to meet its transit needs as there was, as the mayor put it, "no Plan B."[60]

However, only months after the loss of the plebiscite, the election of Prime Minister Trudeau changed the transportation funding environment significantly, with increasing federal money for transportation a major part of Trudeau's platform. In June 2016, British Columbia was the first province to receive money under the newly formed federal Public Transit Infrastructure Fund, with almost a billion dollars dedicated to priority transportation projects in Metro Vancouver, including the first stages of the Broadway subway.[61] Although this will help Vancouver move toward its green transit goals, it also illustrates the limits of the local government's powers. Vancouver has control over zoning and housing development decisions, but it remains at the mercy of the provincial and the federal governments for fully achieving the low carbon transportation benefits of high-density development.

Leadership and Legitimacy in Vancouver's Bikeways

In contrast to having to negotiate with TransLink, the province, and the federal government for investment in heavy transportation infrastructure, the City of Vancouver has control over surface streets and therefore on the construction of bike lanes. Vancouver has invested heavily in cycling infrastructure, ending 2015 with a 275-kilometer bike network, up from 156 kilometers in 2009 (Figure 7.3).[62] The increase in bike lanes, many of which are protected lanes separated with a physical barrier from traffic, has led to cycling becoming "the fastest growing mode of transportation in Vancouver."[63] Permanent counters at nine locations across the city found a 100 percent increase in cycling volumes between 2008 and 2014,

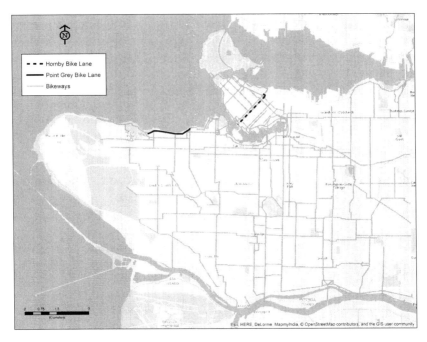

Figure 7.3 Vancouver's extensive bike lane network expanded from 156 to 275
            kilometers between 2009 and 2015. The highlighted routes are two
            that were the source of significant local controversy.

Source: Map by Matt Cooney.

with annual bicycle trips up from about 50,000 to 100,000 over that six-
year period.[64] By 2015 about 10 percent of trips to work by Vancouver
residents were done by bike.[65]

Despite the city's success at providing an amenity that many residents
clearly value and utilize, as well as cycling's ability to reduce carbon emissions and congestion, the creation and expansion of some of the most significant cycle routes in the city have been quite controversial. Resistance
to the new bike lanes has focused on inconvenience to motorists, the
lanes' impacts on businesses, and whether or not there is equity in how
the City is using its limited financial resources to build new dedicated
bike lanes. Some have seen the Vision council's rapid roll-out of new
lanes as beyond their mandate and therefore illegitimate. Officials counter that the controversies around bike lanes do not represent a threat to
the legitimacy of the council's investment in green mobility. Rather, they
see the controversies as short-term overreactions to changes that people
will come to accept as the new infrastructure becomes the status quo.

Two controversies over new dedicated bike lanes illustrate this conflict
and the City's response to it. The first was resistance from business to a

separated bike lane along Hornby Street, a major downtown corridor and a link between two other main bike routes. The second was a bike lane through the wealthy Point Grey neighborhood. The plan for the $3.2 million two-way separated bike lane along Hornby Street was approved by the council in 2010, "after a marathon public hearing."[66] Though many spoke out in favor of the bike lane, and the City claimed that "opinion polls show[ed] the majority of residents support[ed] the plan," shop owners along the route feared a loss of business.[67] The Downtown Vancouver Business Improvement Association (DVBIA) and the Canadian Federation of Independent Business were particularly vocal. They "denounced the plan, saying the new lane [would] cost small business in the area anywhere from five to 25 per cent in sales, by removing 150 metered parking spots along the street."[68] Unlike Birmingham leaders, who have quickly backed away from removing parking spaces to make space for bike infrastructure, the Vancouver council rejected this argument, countering that each block of the route would still have parking, more than 150 parking spots would be added nearby, and that the bike lane would make businesses more accessible to people arriving by other modes of transportation.

A study conducted a year after the Hornby Street bike lane was constructed found that for the first several months the new bike lane did have a modest negative impact on nearby business, though not nearly as severe as the 25 percent loss in sales that opponents feared.[69] Within a few years, the negative impact of the lane seemed to have abated, however, as businesses and residents had time to adjust to the changed traffic flow.[70] In 2015, the executive director of the DVBIA, if still not overwhelmingly enthusiastic, told reporters that the organization recognized the Hornby Street bike lanes were there to stay and that the local businesses needed to adapt.[71] Furthermore, he admitted, rather than keeping people away, increasingly "the lanes seem to be bringing in an ever-growing number of people who choose two wheels."[72] Accepting the permanence of the bike lanes, local businesses turned their concerns to other issues effecting the area such as homelessness and high property taxes.[73] Evidence for small business animosity toward the city's expansion of bike lanes remains, however, with the executive director of another centrally located business improvement association asserting that despite the many problems she had with the local government, it could be worse; "at least we haven't had a bike lane hoisted upon us." Bike lanes are fine, she continued echoing the arguments of the DVBIA, but they block businesses and take away parking, so they do not belong on main roads.[74]

A quite different but even more contentious fight emerged in 2013 when the City proposed closing seven blocks of a road in a wealthy, waterfront neighborhood to through traffic in order to create a dedicated bike lane. The intensity of the conflict that emerged around the Point Grey Road bike lane was startling even to many people who had long been involved in Vancouver's bike lane controversies. One councilor described the conflict as one that "jumped the shark," noting that on multiple occasions she got spit at and yelled at by people opposed to the road closure.[75]

There were two contradictory points of opposition to this bike lane. On one hand, because it went through an extremely wealthy neighborhood, some argued that the bike lane was a favor to these rich residents, calming their neighborhood and creating a private road and bike lane exclusively for their use.[76] On the other hand, many of these same wealthy home owners were some of the most outspoken opponents of the road closure because of its inconvenience to them, forcing them to drive a few blocks out of their way to get to their destinations.[77]

The City's response to the complaints of elitism and of inconvenience was the same – a reminder that over the past few decades dozens of road sections all over the city had been calmed by blocking them to through traffic. Sometimes the restrictions were trying to limit cruising for prostitutes; other times they were redirecting traffic away from a residential street that had become heavily used by commuters. Closing roads to excessive and inappropriate vehicle traffic, city officials insisted and other analyses have confirmed, is not attached to any particular income bracket.[78] Rather, proponents continued, on Point Grey Road as elsewhere, the changes were part of Vancouver's broader goal of keeping cars in their appropriate places on major arterial streets and making roads and neighborhoods safer and more comfortable for cyclists and pedestrians.

After a number of contentious public meetings, the Point Grey Road bike lane was approved, largely along political party lines. In August 2014, about a year after opening, the new bike lane saw 2,700 bike trips, making it one of Vancouver's busiest bike routes.[79] After some months of adjustment, the calming effect on the residential road was also achieved, with 15,000 vehicles being diverted off Point Grey Road to the main arterial.[80]

Numerous ideas have been put forth as to why, despite Vancouver having a robust cycling culture and a large and growing number of people taking trips by bike, dedicated bike lanes continue to generate a reaction that to many observers seems "far out of proportion to any actual inconvenience."[81] One argument is that people who do not cycle see the lanes as encouraging cyclists to behave badly, ignoring traffic laws and inconveniencing pedestrians and drivers. A commentator for the BBC used game theory and psychology to argue that drivers see cyclists as free riders, getting more road space and being able to avoid certain rules of the road, such as weaving in and out of traffic and passing lines of cars, thereby "offend[ing] the moral order" of the road.[82] Vancouver urban planner and former NPA city councilor Gordon Price sees two underlying causes of the extreme responses. First, bike lanes are not a very complex issue and therefore they are easy to have a strong opinion about.

Second, non-cyclists see cyclists and efforts to promote cycling as a moral judgement on them, telling them they should be doing more to keep fit, pollute less, and save money.[83]

The city council member mentioned above who was spat at and yelled at during the Point Grey Road bike lane controversy offers a different analysis, and one that has resonance for much of the City's greening agenda. Her analysis is that the controversy was not really about "seven blocks of residential road no longer being used as a commuter road.... It became about something else entirely. ... I think it's just fear of change. ... We've been a change-agent council. The mayor, [another Vision councilor], myself, we are all people who are not here to make sure the potholes are filled. ... We are here because we want to change the growth of the city."[84] Vision Vancouver leaders do not see the legitimacy of their greening efforts challenged by vocal opposition to pieces of their agenda. Rather, they consider themselves to be enacting a wider vision that has been legitimized by their electoral victories.[85] They are therefore willing to implement their sustainability plans even when parts of them are controversial.

Yet the tensions between pushing the City's ambitious greening goals, vocal resistance to change from groups that may or may not represent broader public opinion, and how changes can occur at a rate that is not overly disruptive to the social fabric of the community[86] are all raised in Vancouver's sustainability efforts. There is no indication that the City is going to stop expanding cycling infrastructure. What remains to be seen is if this can be done in a way that better mitigates the concerns of opponents or if, alternatively, the growing number of cyclists in the city will overshadow objections and controversies will fade as the changed traffic patterns become the new status quo. City officials are betting the political legitimacy of their green transit efforts on the latter.

Rethinking Use of Public Space

Vancouver has been successful at increasing access to the city for those who cannot or choose not to drive. The potential social and environmental benefits of its commitment to green transit are substantial, and the political will of city officials to achieve a robust green transportation network offers a stark contrast to Birmingham's tepid move away from the automobile. Yet as Vancouver continues its pursuit of rapid development and densification, it may run up against the limits of its ability to achieve the transit benefits of a denser city. This can already be seen in the difficulty Vancouver has faced in increasing public transportation infrastructure sufficiently to meet demand and in the resistance to new dedicated bike lanes. But what can also be seen is a willingness in Vancouver to rethink how urban space is used, to take public space away from private vehicles and re-dedicate it to people and to modes of transportation that are more affordable, more environmentally benign, and more accessible for all.

Amenities and Equity in the Greener City

As has been seen, Birmingham's provision of green amenities is increasingly focused on well-being and health. This raises the possibility of enhancing equity in environmental amenities, but this potential is weakened by a lack of political will and funding to achieve its goals. In contrast, Vancouver's expansion of green transit has ignored outspoken opposition in order to further the city's climate agenda and mitigate some of the impact of densification on quality of life. Chicago offers yet another picture of the complexity of green amenities' relationship with progressive varieties of liberal environmentalism. In Chicago, efforts to expand green space and cycling infrastructure wrestle more explicitly than in either Birmingham or Vancouver with the intersection of environmental effectiveness, equity, and economic growth. Particularly important in Chicago has been the ability of community organizations to challenge the legitimacy of the city's greening efforts when they are seen as not adequately addressing issues of equity and environmental justice.

Chicago has a history of inequality in the provision of both parks and public transportation. Although the legacy of this inequality remains, some of the efforts begun by Daley to green the city center, including enhancing cycling infrastructure and increasing parks and green space, are finally beginning to bear fruit in neighborhoods across the city. Community demands for environmental amenities have played no small part in this. As discussed below, public pushback against inequity in the city's bike-share program and in the provision of bike lanes have led to greater access to cycling infrastructure, and creative projects to enhance green space in park-poor neighborhoods have led to a number of important community victories. Yet the economic justification for investment in green transit and parks is still predominant, leading to a continued prioritization of city center amenities. The tensions between growth and equity that shadow all of Chicago's greening efforts therefore remain pronounced, raising the ongoing question of whom the green city is for.

Access and the Legitimacy of Chicago's Cycling Infrastructure

Chicago has one of the most extensive public transportation networks in North America. But the city's transit system has long been critiqued for underserving lower-income neighborhoods, making it difficult and time-consuming for transit-dependent people to get to jobs or services in other parts of the city.[87] Increasing transit equity has therefore been a focus of many social and environmental justice organizations, the myriad benefits to communities of more affordable, equitable access to the city seen as paramount to achieving other community goals. For city officials however, achieving transit justice is only one of many transit goals that also include reducing carbon emissions and attracting new employers to the city center. Both of these goals are furthered not by increasing the quality of transportation infrastructure in lower-income neighborhoods but by inspiring well-to-do residents to choose green transit over personal vehicles. This tension between equity, growth, and environmental goals, as well as the ways increasing equity in green transit is helping legitimize Mayor Emanuel's sustainability agenda, can be seen in Chicago's expansion of its cycling infrastructure.

The Chicago Climate Action Plan (CCAP), adopted under Mayor Daley in 2008 (see Chapter 4), noted that 21 percent of Chicago's emissions came from transportation, including cars, buses, trucks, and trains.[88] The CCAP called for a combination of expanded public transit, transit oriented development, making walking and biking easier, and promoting car share to reduce these emissions. Typical for Daley's environmental efforts, though the CCAP asserted that enhanced transportation options would benefit all Chicagoans, the improvements that occurred under his administration have been critiqued for failing to take seriously the transit injustices that plague the city.[89] Under Daley's entrepreneurialism the priority was transit "infrastructure projects that create[d] place-based advantages for capital in the global economy and generate[d] local revenues by configuring infrastructure for the tourist economy and spaces of affluent consumption" rather than enhancing the quality and accessibility of transit for those who needed it most.[90]

This could be seen in Daley's initiatives to increase cycling, a long-standing aspect of his greening agenda.[91] These efforts included investment in bike lanes, cycle access to trains and buses, and bike racks.[92] By the end of Daley's administration, the city had "200 miles of on-street bikeways, 36 miles of trails, and more bike parking … than any other city in the United States."[93] Daley gained publicity for these changes, including Chicago being rated by *Bicycling Magazine* as the most bike-friendly American city over a million people in 2001.[94] Despite these improvements, and even though bicycle commuting increased from 0.5 percent to 1.3 percent between 2000 and 2010,[95] many cycling and pedestrian advocates were not impressed by Daley's efforts. Automobile infrastructure was still prioritized, and the 200 miles of bike lanes were not always safe, including many miles of marked shared lanes ("sharrows") that are the least safe type of cycling infrastructure.[96]

Mayor Emanuel's Transition Plan (see Chapter 4) called for the creation of 100 miles of protected bike lanes by 2015. The Chicago Streets for Cycling Plan 2020, published by the Chicago Department of Transportation (CDOT) in 2012, went even further, identifying a 645-mile bike network to be constructed across the city, with the goal of increasing cycling infrastructure in high-density areas with strong bike usage while also ensuring that every Chicago resident lives within a half mile of a bike lane.[97] By early 2016 Emanuel's first goal had been achieved, with 108 miles of barrier and buffer-protected lanes added to the city's cycling network.[98] The bike lane extensions were not uncontroversial, however. Some communities resisted bike lanes as forerunners of gentrification, though this objection was largely overcome with a shift to more community control over the process by which routes were chosen and installed.[99] Others saw the investment in cycling infrastructure as yet another benefit to the middle class, as the first protected lanes installed by the Emanuel administration were in downtown, and bike enhancements were concentrated in the central areas of the city.

Mayor Emanuel dismissed this equity critique of his administration's investment in cycling infrastructure, and was unabashed about the use of bike lanes as a development strategy. He justified the City's investment in downtown bike lanes as "part of [his] effort to recruit entrepreneurs and start-up businesses because a lot of those employees like to bike to work."[100] Cycling equity groups kept the issue of cycling access for lower-income communities at the forefront of city discussions about biking, however, challenging the legitimacy of investments that did not benefit all of Chicago's residents.[101] Facing public pressure, in 2016 the Emanuel administration said that the City would begin to focus on getting extra "input on areas that still need [bike infrastructure], particularly in mid- and far-South Side areas that have not received as much attention as other neighborhoods."[102] Though remaining in many ways an entrepreneurial amenity, Emanuel's expansion of bike lanes is beginning to move beyond the city center, and there is a surprisingly equitable, though still imperfect, distribution of bike lanes across the city.[103]

Chicago's bike-share system, Divvy, offers another example of the tension between cycling infrastructure as an amenity for the well-to-do and its potential for enhancing transit equity. Bike-share, wherein bicycles are made available at numerous locations around a city for people to rent for a very short time (30 minutes in Chicago), is gaining popularity as an urban amenity and as part of cities' public transportation networks.[104] As bike-share systems are expanding across the U.S. and elsewhere, equity concerns have been raised about their distribution, with lower-income city residents and African Americans consistently less likely to live near bike-share stations than other residents of the same cities.[105] Other barriers for equitable access to bike-share infrastructure include the cost of annual memberships and that most programs require a debit or credit card, denying unbanked people access to the system. When these factors are combined with other barriers to cycling, it is not surprising that bike-share users in North America skew heavily white, well-to-do, and educated.[106]

Chicago launched Divvy in 2013 with much fanfare, and thousands of trips were taken the first weekend of the program.[107] Consistent with the

Figure 7.4 Divvy bike-share stations such as this one are particularly concentrated in the Loop.

Source: Photo by author, 2015.

national trend of bike-share systems targeting the more well-off, when Divvy was launched stations were concentrated in areas where demand was expected to be the highest, "within a couple miles of the lakefront, clustered mainly in the Loop and densely populated neighborhoods along transit lines."[108] Emanuel's transportation commissioner justified this placement as necessary to make Divvy viable, arguing that "you've got to make sure it's sustainable so you start in the densest areas with all these services and then that allows you to spread it out to everybody"[109] (Figure 7.4).

This argument is consistent with the logic of green urban entrepreneurialism that has undergirded many of Chicago's environmental efforts in that it prioritizes amenities for city center residents and tourists with claims that "everybody" will benefit. It is also worth noting that Divvy was expected to pay for itself through user fees, sponsorship, and ad money, a standard that is never applied to the much more environmentally destructive and massively expensive government investment in infrastructure for the automobile.[110] The result of this logic was significant inequity in who had access to Divvy as a piece of the city's public transit infrastructure, with many of Chicago's poorest neighborhoods excluded.[111]

As soon as Divvy was launched, equity concerns were raised. A "Bronzeville activist and bicycle enthusiast …[blasted] rollout plans for Divvy as generally 'disrespectful' to minority communities."[112] The president of the Black Metropolis Convention and Tourism Council noted that the distribution of Divvy bike docks in the city center "makes economic sense for a gentrifying inner city and sustaining the wealthy but it does not make sense if you are trying to empower other communities … It is icing on the cake for Lincoln Park but it is infrastructure for us."[113]

Acknowledging these concerns but focused on proving the system's financial sustainability, initially CDOT, which runs the program, asserted that the concentration of docks in and around the city center would only change if new grant funding became available. When additional access concerns were raised, particularly that those with lower incomes could not afford to pay the $75 annual membership fee (raised to $99 in 2016), CDOT officials insisted that "Chicago [would not] be offering either discounted memberships or the option of a monthly payment program to low-income residents."[114] As Divvy was launched it seemed that although it might make some contribution to reducing carbon emissions and traffic congestion, it would do nothing to alleviate the inequity of Chicago's transit system.

The strength of the public push-back soon changed this, and within a year several initiatives had been undertaken to make Divvy available to more of Chicago's residents. In 2014, the City announced plans for an additional 175 stations that would give Divvy the largest service area and more bike docking stations than other any bike-share system in North America.[115] This expansion meant that the number of Chicago's 55 wards served by Divvy would grow from 13 to 33 and that over half of the city's population would live in a bike share coverage area.[116] Additional stations were announced the following year, bringing up the percentage of city residents served by Divvy to over two-thirds[117] (Figure 7.5).

Impressive in its size and coverage, and an important about-face to the City's insistence that it could not expand the system to serve lower-income neighborhoods, there was a trade-off in this expansion of the reach of the system. In the areas farther from the city center, docking stations are placed about a half a mile apart.[118] Such spacing allows greater coverage, but the wide distances between stations means that use of Divvy in these areas will almost certainly be lower than if stations had been

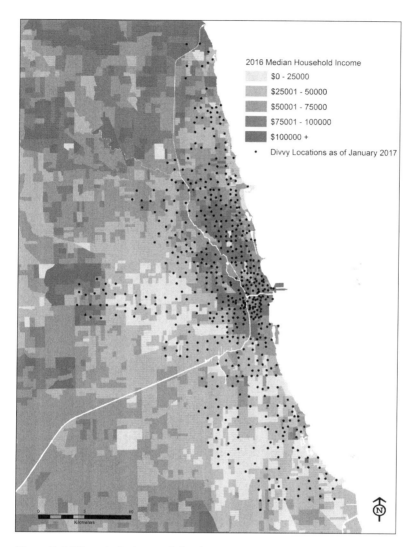

Figure 7.5 Divvy is the largest bike-share system in the United States, serving over two-thirds of Chicago residents.

Source: Map by Matt Cooney. Map data from https://member.divvybikes.com/stations.

a quarter mile apart, the optimal spacing for encouraging strong bike-share uptake.[119] This will particularly impact low- and moderate-income residents and people of color, who are about half as likely as white and middle- and high-income Chicagoans to live within a quarter mile of a Divvy station.[120] For now, however, transit equity groups see Divvy's expansion as a victory, with one bike equity organization asserting that "the addition of Divvy stations in new neighborhoods on the South and West Sides will encourage more residents of color to embrace the use of bikes as an alternative form of transportation. The forward progress on expansion ... brings the community one step closer to achieving equitable access in all Chicago neighborhoods."[121]

Another important initiative to increase access to Divvy accompanied the expansion of docking stations. Despite early insistence that there would not be a heavily discounted Divvy rate, in July 2015 Divvy for Everyone (D4E) was launched. D4E enables Chicago residents with incomes of up to three times the poverty level to join Divvy for five dollars for the first year. In partnership with local community organizations, it also enables people without credit or debit cards to become members.[122] A year into the program over a thousand people had signed up for D4E, surpassing the goal of 750.[123] This, in conjunction with more docking stations, increased bike lanes, and bike equity advocates' provision of cycling classes and other efforts to encourage lower-income Chicagoans to cycle, appear set to continue expanding cycling as a viable piece of the city's transportation infrastructure.

Community Green Space in the Shadow of Displacement

The 1998 parks planning document CitySpace was mentioned in Chapter 3 as one of Chicago's first clear articulations of green urban entrepreneurialism, justifying the expansion of parks as vital to the city's competitiveness and ability to attract new businesses and residents. Many of the plan's recommendations focused on the city center, such as improving access to the Chicago River and enhancing the area that would become Millennium Park. But CitySpace also recognized the inadequacy of parks and open space throughout Chicago.[124] Since then, city parks planners and the Park District have worked to expand green space across the city. They have created the legal framework for communities to turn vacant lots into gardens, have sold lots cheaply to residents and community groups to make neighborhood amenities and, more recently, have used federal storm water management funds to transform school grounds into public green space.[125]

The creative ways being found to reduce inequity in access to parks and green space are a victory for park-poor communities, but concerns about new green spaces exacerbating displacement have yet to be adequately addressed. This is not a new concern in Chicago. Though politically overshadowed by the success of Chicago's green urban entrepreneurialism, many low-income and working-class communities were skeptical of Mayor Daley's greening agenda and saw his expansion of environmental amenities as forerunners to gentrification.[126] As greening moved into neighborhoods outside the Loop, "community leaders and residents [became] skeptical of why the City 'all of a sudden' decide[d] to invest in street and sidewalk repairs, park improvements, and city buildings in [their] area. ... Their communities [had] always needed and desired these improvements, but [felt] the City [did] not attend to them until the area [was] on the verge of gentrification."[127] The cleaner streets, better and new parks, trees, and other amenities that marked Chicago's post-industrial transformation were therefore seen as a double-edged sword, improving the quality of life for people who were able to stay in newly greened neighborhoods but also leading to fear of displacement for many and the disintegration of existing community bonds.[128] This concern about environmental gentrification has continued under Emanuel, even as the City asserts that it is striving to bring green space to all neighborhoods, not just those on the verge of gentrification.

The complexity of this issue is well-illustrated by The 606. The 606 is a combination park, walkway, and bike trail that was built on three miles of unused elevated rail line that runs through "four ethnically and economically diverse Chicago neighborhoods: Wicker Park, Bucktown, Humboldt Park and Logan Square."[129] Before The 606 was constructed, the Logan Square community area (which includes the neighborhoods of Logan Square, Bucktown, and Palmer Square) was one of the most park-poor parts of the city and therefore a priority for development of new green space under CitySpace.[130] Work on The 606, then called the Bloomingdale Trail, began in 2002. An extensive community planning process identified the abandoned rail line as one of the main places where open space could be created in the densely built-out neighborhood. In the initial visioning process community members were clear that they wanted the park not only to provide green space for recreation but also transit benefits, particularly "bike routes and safe walking routes through the neighborhoods, [and] increased access to the Chicago River."[131]

After the community vision was established, city planners, in cooperation with the Trust for Public Land and numerous community organizations, began the long process of work on the trail, including land acquisition, examining structural issues of the 100-year-old rail line and its 37 bridges, and holding extensive community planning and design meetings. After more than a decade of work, The 606 opened in June 2015. The Trust for Public Land representative who oversaw much of the work asserted that she had never seen the level of volunteer commitment and community engagement in any park project that she saw with The 606.[132]

Even as community members worked to create the park, some also raised concerns about gentrification and rising property values along The 606, as the two working-class neighborhoods the park passed through, Logan Square (a focus of controversies around TOD discussed in Chapter 6) and Humboldt Park, were already feeling the pinch of gentrification. As this concern was raised, housing advocates and housing

Figure 7.6 The 606 linear park and trail has inspired new construction and raised property values along its 2.7 miles.

Source: Photo by author, 2015.

affordability officials were brought into conversations about the park, the goal being to connect park planning to larger discussions about displacement and affordability in the area. From the perspective of the parks organizations deeply involved in the process, the vital thing was for community members "to still consider The 606 as a victory and a major investment that these communities and organizations advocated for for ten years without fearing displacement. ... [Addressing gentrification] has to be driven by a larger conversation, and that's what's happening."[133] Yet as The 606 was opened with much fanfare and public celebration, many residents questioned whether this "larger conversation" had been adequate to protect lower income residents living near the trail from displacement (Figure 7.6).[134]

Emanuel, though also asserting that increased property values was beneficial, announced a number of initiatives that he claimed would protect affordable housing in the neighborhoods around The 606. These included housing vouchers received by residents of the neighborhoods, a number of affordable housing projects near the new park, and the recently strengthened affordable housing requirements for new construction (see Chapter 6). With the exception of the affordable housing requirements, many saw these as inadequate. Advocates pointed out that housing vouchers do not guarantee continued residency and many of the affordable housing projects Emanuel pointed to were neither newly constructed nor particularly close to The 606.[135]

Protesters and real estate developers alike agree that although the nearby neighborhoods were facing gentrification pressures before the park opened, The 606 has been responsible for raising area property values even further.[136] In response, a year after the park opened the Logan Square Neighborhood Association organized an anti-gentrification march along the trail.[137] They called for the City to think more ambitiously about how to stop displacement in the neighborhood, and offered a variety of creative proposals to keep lower-income residents in their homes.[138] However, if the controversies around the development of TOD in Logan Square are any indication, initiatives that the City adopts to limit displacement will not substantially slow the rapid transformation the area is undergoing (Figure 7.7).

Plans to build elevated parks and non-motorized transportation corridors similar to The 606 are underway in other parts of the city.[139] Park planners are confident that now that they have figured out how to undertake the complex process of turning a railway line into a park, future endeavors will be quicker to accomplish.[140] As new trails are proposed, such as the Paseo that will connect the largely Latino neighborhoods Little Village and Pilsen (the former sites of the Fisk and Crawford coal-fired power plants discussed in Chapter 5), community groups are insisting that affordability be incorporated as an integral part of the projects, not as an afterthought like it was with The 606. The Little Village Environmental Justice Organization, long a strong advocate for green space in Little Village, even threatened to oppose the Paseo unless affordability and displacement were adequately addressed in the plan.[141] Parks planners counter that issues of affordability are being incorporated into the early planning processes of new parks, but that the issue is complicated and "there's no magic bullet" to stopping displacement.[142] As with other greening cities in which environmental gentrification has become a concern, in Chicago the challenge of creating the green infrastructure that neighborhoods need and desire, while ensuring this infrastructure serves the communities it has promised to benefit, remains pronounced and unresolved.

Between Growth and Equity

Chicago is pulled between the pro-growth priorities of neoliberal environmentalism and the equity and effectiveness of progressive liberal environmentalism. Though enhancing the amenities and attractiveness of the city center remains of paramount importance, the need to maintain the legitimacy of these efforts in the face of public protest has pushed the City

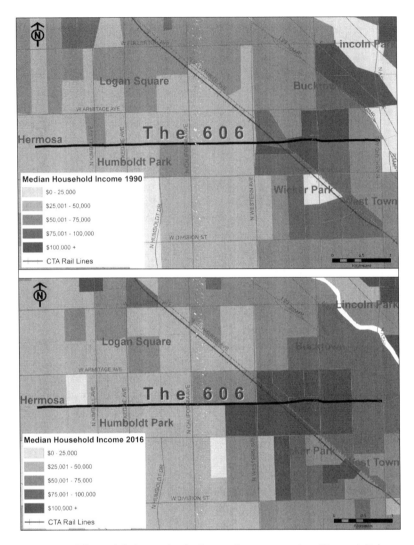

Figure 7.7 The racial change in the Logan Square area (see Figure 6.3) has
          been accompanied by a change in median income, particularly
          along The 606. Long-term residents fear being priced out of their
          neighborhood.

Source: Map by Matt Cooney.

toward a more equitable distribution of green amenities. As such, Mayor
Emanuel's efforts to make Chicago a sustainable city go farther than his
predecessor, and prestige greening has been complemented by broader
changes in the built environment of the city. What remains unclear is
if the threat of environmental gentrification will be overcome or if the

greening of more of Chicago's neighborhoods will continue to be seen by residents as a way to facilitate their displacement.

Conclusion

Green space and non-motorized transit infrastructure shape a city in a variety of ways. They effect a city's environmental impact, make the city more or less attractive to visitors and potential residents, and influence who benefits from the greener city and in what ways. As has been seen throughout this book, one important impetus for the enhancement of these amenities has long been the entrepreneurial re-creation of the post-industrial city as an economic development strategy. However, following the trajectory of urban greening more broadly, these amenities have also become about more than economic development. Non-motorized transit infrastructure and green spaces have also become about carbon reduction, about equity in access to nature and transit, and about health and well-being.

The myriad ways that green space and transit are justified shows both a weakness and a strength of city greening. The weakness is the extent to which it illustrates that for many city leaders, the commitment to creating a greener city is not deeply rooted in a broader analysis of the relationship between humans and nature. Rather, justifications for creating a greener city can be pulled from whatever priorities have political resonance in the moment, be it health, climate change, or traffic congestion. This may make it harder for political leaders to articulate a vision of a sustainable city that can build support for the short-term inconvenience of, for example, lost car parking spots or changed traffic patterns.

Then again, a strength of the myriad justifications offered for enhancing green amenities is the possibility of building a wider coalition in support of the greener city. Particularly as pressure builds to ensure that green amenities benefit as many residents as possible, these amenities offer an opportunity for reconsidering cities' prioritization of cars, of hard surfaces, and of natural beauty that particularly benefits the well-to-do. Green space and non-motorized transit infrastructure may indeed fulfill the win–win assumptions of neoliberal environmentalism's promise to enhance the environment and spur economic growth. But when provided equitably, they may also enable a rethinking of how and for whom cities are constructed as well as begin the process of mitigating the ecological impact of the build urban environment.

Notes

1 Merrill   Cooper,   "Social   Sustainability   in   Vancouver"   (Ottawa, Ontario: Canadian Policy Research Networks, 2006); Donna L. Erickson, *Metrogreen: Connecting Open Space in North American Cities* (Washington, DC: Island Press, 2006).

2 Gordon Walker, *Environmental Justice: Concepts, Evidence and Politics* (New York, NY: Routledge, 2012).
3 Setha Low, Dana Taplin, and Suzanne Scheld, *Rethinking Urban Parks: Public Space and Cultural Diversity* (Austin, TX: The University of Texas Press, 2005), 1; see also Julian Agyeman, *Introducing Just Sustainabilities: Policy, Planning, and Practice* (New York, NY: Zed Books, 2013).
4 Winifred Curran and Trina Hamilton, "Just Green Enough: Contesting Environmental Gentrification in Greenpoint, Brooklyn," *Local Environment* 17, no. 9 (2012); Jennifer R. Wolch, Jason Byrne, and Joshua P. Newell, "Urban Green Space, Public Health, and Environmental Justice: The Challenge of Making Cities 'Just Green Enough,'" *Landscape and Urban Planning* 125 (2014).
5 Robert D. Bullard and Glenn S. Johnson, "Introduction," in *Just Transportation: Dismantling Race & Class Barriers to Mobility*, ed. Robert D. Bullard and Glenn S. Johnson (Stony Creek, CT: New Society Publishers, 1997), 3.
6 Richard Gilbert and Anthony Perl, "Transportation in the Post-Carbon World," in *The Post-Carbon Reader: Managing the 21st Century's Sustainability Crisis*, ed. Richard Heinberg and Daniel Lerch (Healdsburg, CA: Watershed Media, 2010).
7 E.g. Brian McKenzie, "Modes Less Traveled – Bicycling and Walking to Work in the United States: 2008–2012," in *American Community Survey Reports* (United States: U.S. Census Bureau, 2014).
8 John Pucher and Ralph Buehler, eds., *City Cycling* (Cambridge, MA: MIT Press, 2012).
9 Public Health England, "Birmingham Unitary Authority Health Profile 2015" (England, UK: Public Health England, 2015).
10 Birmingham City Council, "Birmingham Low Carbon Transport Strategy" (Birmingham, UK: Birmingham City Council, 2012).
11 Anon, "Birmingham Carbon Plan Analysis" (Birmingham, UK: Presented to Birmingham's Green Commision, 2012), 19.
12 Birmingham City Council.
13 "Birmingham Connected: Moving Our City Forward – Birmingham Mobility Action Plan White Paper" (Birmingham, UK: Birmingham City Council, 2014).
14 Ibid., 9.
15 Ibid.
16 Cited in Jonathan Walker, "Road Charging for High-Pollution Vehicles to Be Imposed in Birmingham by 2020," *Birmingham Mail*, December 17, 2015.
17 Birmingham City Council, 10.
18 Keith Gabriel, "Cycle Revolution Long Overdue in Car-Clogged Brum," *Birmingham Post*, June 12, 2014.
19 Birmingham City Council, 31.
20 Ashley Preece, "City Cycle Routes Gear up for £2.8m Improvement Scheme," *Great Barr Observer*, December 4, 2015.
21 Birmingham City Council, "Birmingham Cycle Revolution," Birmingham City Council, www.birmingham.gov.uk/birminghamcyclerevolution (accessed August 5, 2016).
22 Personal communication, June 2016.
23 Birmingham City Council, "Birmingham Cycle Revolution."
24 Council cabinet member, personal communication, June 2016.
25 Birmingham's Green Commission, "Birmingham's Green Commission Autumn 2016 (sic) Update – Factsheet" (Birmingham, UK: Birmingham's Green Commission, 2015).

26 Personal communication, June 2016.
27 Ibid.
28 Gabriel; see also Birmingham City Council, "Birmingham Cycle Revolution Spring/Summer Programme," ed. Birmingham City Council (Birmingham, UK, 2016).
29 Jan Garrard, Susan Handy, and Jennier Dill, "Women and Cycling," in *City Cycling*, ed. John Pucher and Ralph Buehler (Cambridge, MA: MIT Press, 2012).
30 Personal communication, April 2016.
31 Ibid.
32 But see Neil Elkes, "Why Six Cycle Lanes Have Been Scrapped and 'Superhighways' Are In," *Birmingham Mail*, December 14, 2016.
33 City planner, personal communication, June 2016; council cabinet member, personal communication, June 2016.
34 Steven Morris, "Birmingham Joins San Francisco and Oslo in Global Green Cities Club," *The Guardian*, April 3, 2014.
35 Parks advocate, personal communication, June 2016.
36 Ibid.
37 Birmingham City Council, "Green Living Spaces Plan" (Birmingham, UK: Birmingham City Council, 2013).
38 Sustainability West Midlands, "Birmingham City Council – Green Living Spaces Plan," www.sustainabilitywestmidlands.org.uk/resources/birmingham-city-council-green-living-spaces-plan-2/ (accessed May 17, 2016).
39 Morris; Sustainability West Midlands.
40 City parks officer, personal communication, June 2016.
41 Timothy Beatley, "Green, British-Style," *Planning*, November 2013.
42 City parks officer, personal communication, June 2016.
43 Birmingham City Council, "Responding to the Challenge, Looking to the Future" (Birmingham, UK, 2014).
44 Neil Elkes, "How Cutting Parks Budget Will Cost Birmingham More in the Long Run," *Birmingham Mail*, January 3, 2017.
45 Quoted in ibid.
46 City of Vancouver, "Greenest City 2020 Action Plan 2012–2013 Implementation Update" (Vancouver, BC, 2013).
47 "Greenest City 2020 Action Plan" (Vancouver, BC, 2011), unpaginated first page.
48 "Transportation 2040" (City of Vancouver, 2012).
49 "Greenest City 2020 Action Plan 2014–2015 Implementation Update" (Vancouver, BC, 2015).
50 "Transportation 2040."
51 Ibid., 15.
52 Emily Jackson, "Transit Ridership Slips in Vancouver Where System Is 'at Capacity': City Report," *Metro News*, May 12, 2015; University of British Columbia, "UBC-Broadway Line," UBC, http://planning.ubc.ca/vancouver/transportation-planning/transportation-options/transit/ubc-broadway-line (accessed August 13, 2015).
53 Grandview-Woodland community activist, personal communication, August 2014.
54 University of British Columbia.
55 TransLink, "About Us," TransLink, www.translink.ca/en/About-Us.aspx (accessed August 13, 2016).
56 Sustainability planner, personal communication, August 2014.
57 City councilor, personal communication, August 2014.

58 City councilor, personal communication, August 2014.
59 Lisa Johnson and Tamara Baluja, "Transit Referendum: Voters Say No to New Metro Vancouver Tax, Transit Improvements," *CBC News*, July 2, 2015.
60 Quoted in ibid.
61 Kelly Sinoski, "B.C. First to Land Transit Project Cash as Justin Trudeau Unveils Funding Deal," *Vancouver Sun*, June 16, 2016.
62 City of Vancouver, "Greenest City 2020 Action Plan 2014–2015 Implementation Update"; Jordan Clark, "Vancouver's Built Environment Initiatives," in *Urban Sustainability Programs: Case Studies*, ed. David J. Hess (www.davidjhess.org, 2012, accessed May 23, 2017).
63 City of Vancouver, "Protected Bicycle Lanes," City of Vancouver, http://vancouver.ca/streets-transportation/protected-bicycle-lanes.aspx (accessed August 11, 2016).
64 "2014 Transportation Monitoring Report" (Vancouver, BC: City of Vancouver, 2015).
65 Matt Robinson, "Vancouver Leads the Pack for Bike Commutes," *Vancouver Sun*, May 4, 2016.
66 CBC News, "Vancouver's Hornby Bike Lane Gets Green Light," *CBC News*, October 6, 2010.
67 Ibid.
68 Ibid.
69 Stantec Consulting Ltd., "Vancouver Separated Bike Lane Business Impact Study" (Vancouver, BC: Stantec Consulting Ltd., 2011).
70 Jeff Lee, "Jury Is Still out on Impact of Downtown Vancouver Bike Lanes," *Vancouver Sun*, September 27, 2014.
71 Alison Bailey, "Downtown Vancouver Businsses' Attitudes towards Bike Lanes Have Changed in the Last 5 Years," *News 1130*, May 27, 2015.
72 Ibid.
73 Lee.
74 Personal communication, August 2014.
75 Personal communication, August 2014.
76 Pete McMartin, "Down with the Rich! And While We're at It, Bike Lanes!," *Vancouver Sun*, July 30, 2013.
77 Cheryl Chan, "Divisive Bike Route for Point Grey Road Approved by Vancouver City Council," *Vancouver Sun*, July 30; city councilor, personal communication, August 2014.
78 City councilor, personal communication, August 2014; McMartin.
79 City of Vancouver, "Greenest City 2020 Action Plan 2014–2015 Implementation Update," 21.
80 Sunny Dhillon, "Controversial Vancouver Bike Lane Seems to Be Effective," *Globe and Mail*, January 1, 2015.
81 Frances Bula, "Vancouver Bike Lanes Incite Outrage as City Supports Riders," *Globe and Mail*, September 1, 2014.
82 Tom Stafford, "The Psychology of Why Cyclists Enrage Car Drivers," *BBC*, February 12, 2013.
83 Cited in Bula.
84 Personal communication, August 2014.
85 Quoted in Frances Bula, "Vancouver's Bike Lanes: Gordon Price on When to Ignore the Opposition," *Globe and Mail*, July 30, 2013.
86 See Karl Polanyi. *The Great Transformation: The Political and Economic Origins of Our Time.* 2nd Beacon Paperback ed. (Boston, MA: Beacon Press, 2001 [1944]).
87 Nathalie P. Voorhees Center for Neighborhood and Community Improvement, "Transit Equity Matters: An Equity Index and Regional Analysis of the

Red Line and Two Other Proposed CTA Transit Extensions" (Chicago, IL: University of Illinois at Chicago, 2009).

88 City of Chicago, "Chicago Climate Action Plan: Our City, Our Future" (Chicago, IL, 2008).

89 Stephanie Farmer, "Uneven Public Transportation Development in Neoliberalizing Chicago, USA," *Environment and Planning A* 43 (2011).

90 Ibid., 1160.

91 Mayor's Bicycle Advisory Council, "The Bike 2000 Plan" (Chicago, IL: City of Chicago, 1992).

92 City of Chicago, "Bike 2015 Plan," City of Chicago, www.bike2015plan. org/intro.html# (accessed August 16, 2016).

93 CDOT, "Chicago Streets for Cycling Plan 2020" (Chicago, IL: Chicago Department of Transportation, 2012), 10.

94 TransAlt, "Making Chicago 'the City That Bikes'," *TransAlt*, Summer 2003.

95 CDOT.

96 Nicholson N Ferenchak and Wesley E Marshall, "The Relative (in) Effectiveness of Bicycle Sharrows on Ridership and Safety Outcomes," in *Transportation Research Board 95th Annual Meeting* (Washington, DC, 2016); John Greenfield, "Life Cycle: How Did Chicago's Progressive New Transportation Czar Gabe Klein Get That Way?," www.newcity.com/2011/12/07/life-cycle-how-did-chicago%E2%80%99s-progressive-new-transportation-czar-gabe-klein-get-that-way/ (accesssed August 16, 2016).

97 CDOT.

98 Greg Hinz, "City Touches the Brakes on Bike-Lane Expansion," *Crain's Chicago Business*, April 11, 2016.

99 John Greenfield to Grid Chicago, May 10, 2012, http://gridchicago.com/2012/bike-facilities-dont-have-to-be-the-white-lanes-of-gentrification/ (accessed August 16, 2016); Jose Lopez, "Jose Lopez Offers the PRCC's Perspective on the Paseo Bike Lanes." In *Grid Chicago*. Chicago, IL, http://gridchicago.com/2012/jose-lopez-offers-the-prccs-perspective-on-the-paseo-bike-lanes/ (accessed August 16, 2016); Jay Wallsjasper, "Bike Lanes in Black and White," People for Bikes, www.peopleforbikes.org/blog/entry/bike-lanes-in-black-and-white (accessed December 10, 2013).

100 Quoted in Alex Davies, "Rahm Emanuel Thinks Bike Lanes Will Attract Tech Companies to Chicago," *Business Insider*, December 5, 2012.

101 See Go Bronzeville, "About," http://gobronzeville.org/about (accessed August 16, 2016); Slow Roll Chicago, "About Slow Roll Chicago," http://slowrollchicago.tumblr.com/about (accessed August 16, 2016).

102 Hinz.

103 See Alex Levin, Matt Milkovich, and Gray Turek, "Bicycle Resource Equity in Chicago" (Chicago, IL: DePaul University, 2016).

104 Susan A. Shaheen, Stacey Guzman, and Hua Zhang, "Bikesharing across the Globe," in *City Cycling*, ed. John Pucher and Ralph Buehler (Cambridge, MA: MIT Press, 2012).

105 Julia Ursaki and Lisa Aultman-Hall, "Quantifying the Equity of Bikeshare Access in U.S. Cities," in *Transportation Research Board 95th Annual Meeting* (Washington, DC, 2016).

106 Susan A. Shaheen et al., "Public Bikesharing in North American during a Period of Rapid Expansion: Understanding Business Models, Industry Trends and User Impacts" (San Jose, CA: Mineta Transportation Institute, 2014).

107 City of Chicago, "Press Release: Chicago Welcomes Divvy Bike Sharing System," July 1, 2013, www.cityofchicago.org/city/en/depts/cdot/provdrs/bike/news/2013/jul/chicago_welcomesdivvybikesharingsystem.html (accessed August 16, 2016).

108 Chip Mitchell and Robin Amer, "Divvy Blues: Bike-Share Program Leaves Some Behind," *WBEZ News*, June 28, 2013.

109 Quoted in Bob Secter and Alex Bordens, "Divvy Opens Strong in White Neighborhoods," *Chicago Tribune*, July 10, 2013.

110 Though it lost money for the first two years, in 2015 a statement from the CDOT Commissioner asserted that, "The overall system revenue, including the Blue Cross Blue Shield sponsorship [$12.5 million over five years] and advertising on kiosks, brings in income to Divvy and the city's bike programs. Overall Divvy is not losing money. CDOT is investing the revenue from Divvy in bike infrastructure improvements such as bike lanes, bicycle safety education and other programs that benefit the entire city of Chicago, not just Divvy users." Quoted in John Greenfield, "More Deets on the Divvy Funding Situation," http://chi.streetsblog.org/2015/07/24/more-deets-on-the-divvy-funding-situation/ (accessed August 16, 2016).

111 Mitchell and Amer.

112 Secter and Bordens.

113 Quoted in ibid.

114 Mitchell and Amer.

115 City of Chicago, "Press Release: Divvy to Expand Next Spring by 175 Stations and 1,750 Bikes," August 21, 2014, www.cityofchicago.org/city/en/depts/cdot/provdrs/bike/news/2014/aug/DivvyExpansion.html (accessed August 16, 2016).

116 John Greenfield, "CDOT's Sean Wiedel Provides an Update on Divvy Installation, Equity Efforts," http://chi.streetsblog.org/2015/04/24/cdots-weidel-provides-update-on-divvy-installation-equity-efforts/#more-101485 (accessed August 16, 2016).

117 City of Chicago, "Press Release: Mayor Emanuel Announced Divvy Adding Stations to Cover New Neighborhoods on South and West Sides of Chicago," June 10, 2016, www.cityofchicago.org/city/en/depts/cdot/provdrs/bike/news/2016/june/mayor-emanuel-announces-divvy-adding-stations-to-cover-new-neigh.html (accessed August 16, 2016).

118 John Greenfield, "The Pros and Cons of Divvy's New Expansion Map," http://chi.streetsblog.org/2014/08/22/the-pros-and-cons-of-divvys-new-expansion-map/#more-96287 (accessed August 16, 2016).

119 NACTO, "Walkable Station Spacing Is Key to Successful, Equitable Bike Share," in *NACTO Bike Share Equity Practitioners' Paper #1* (National Association of City Transportation Officials, 2015).

120 Levin, Milkovich, and Turek.

121 Quoted in City of Chicago, "Press Release: Mayor Emanuel Announced Divvy Adding Stations to Cover New Neighborhoods on South and West Sides of Chicago."

122 City of Chicago, "Press Release: Mayor Emanuel Announces Divvy Expanding Access to Popular Bike Share System through Divvy for Everyone (D4E) Program," July 7, 2015, www.cityofchicago.org/city/en/depts/mayor/press_room/press_releases/2015/july/mayor-emanuel-announces-divvy-expanding-access-to-popular-bike-s.html   (accessed August 16, 2016).

123 Annie Grossinger, "Affordable Divvy for Everyone Enters Second Year," LISC Chicago, www.lisc-chicago.org/news/2679 (accessed August 16, 2016).

124 City of Chicago, Chicago Park District, and Forest Preserve District of Cook County, "CitySpace: On Open Space Plan for Chicago" (Chicago, IL, 1998).

125 Park planner, personal communication, June 2015; city sustainability official, personal communication, June 2015.

126 For example, Field Museum, "Engaging Chicago Communities in the Chicago Climate Action Plan, Community #1: South Chicago" (Chicago, IL: The Field Museum Environment, Culture, and Conservation Program, 2009); Philip Nyden, Emily Edlynn, and Julie Davis, "The Differential Impact of Gentrification on Commuities in Chicago" (Chicago, IL: Loyola University Chicago Center for Urban Research and Learning, 2006).

127 13.

128 Ibid.

129 Trust for Public Land, "The 606: Frequently Asked Questions," Trust for Public Land, www.the606.org/resources/frequently-asked-questions/ (accessed February 15, 2017)

130 City parks planner, personal communication, June 2015.

131 City of Chicago, "Logan Square Open Space Plan" (Chicago, IL: City of Chicago, 2004), 10.

132 Personal communication, June 2015.

133 Personal communication, June 2015.

134 John Byrne, "Mayor Emanuel's 606 Affordable-Housing Plan Draws Doubts," *Chicago Tribune*, August 12, 2015.

135 Ibid.

136 Leonor Vivanco, "The 606 Trail, a Study in Contrasts, Celebrates Its First Birthday," *Chicago Tribune*, June 3, 2016.

137 Logan Square Neighborhood Association, "Issues and Programs," Logan Square Neighborhood Association, 2017, www.lsna.net/Issues-and-programs/index.html (accessed May 23, 2017).

138 See Leonor Vivanco, "Marchers Take to the 606 Trail to Protest Gentrification," *Chicago Tribune*, May 17, 2016.

139 Jay Koziarz, "Abandoned Rail Tracks Will See 606-Style Trail Come to Pilsen Neighborhood," *Curbed Chicago*, March 12, 2016; Andrea V. Watson, "Residents Give Wish List for When Englewood Gets Its Own Bloomingdale Trail," *DNAInfo*, January 12, 2016.

140 Personal communication, June 2015.

141 John Greenfield, "Little Village Residents Hope Paseo Won't Be a Path to Gentrification," *Chicago Reader*, March 23, 2016.

142 Personal communication, June 2016.

8 Conclusion: Cities and the Challenge of Environmental Governance

The first chapters of this book argued that city greening became an economic development strategy in Chicago, Birmingham, and Vancouver as part of their larger post-industrial transformations. Green urban entrepreneurialism, though promising to benefit all residents, prioritized creating a city center that was appealing to tourists and young professionals, and that could help attract business headquarters and new employment in the creative and high-end service industries. Using greening to spur economic growth was a principal goal.

Even as city leaders have begun to move away from green urban entrepreneurialism toward other varieties of liberal environmentalism, economic growth remains a priority, with equity and environmental effectiveness too often downplayed. As has been seen, the needs of developers and real estate interests are often privileged by city officials and planners. Gentrification remains a strong concern of many communities in greening cities, even while a lack of equitable access to environmental goods is a major problem for other neighborhoods. Though local leaders say they have a commitment to the environment, politically difficult steps necessary to further environmental effectiveness may be avoided. The critiques made of city environmentalism, including that it is little more than a tool of capital accumulation and cover for displacement with limited environmental merit, are therefore not wholly unfounded.

This book has also raised another possibility. This possibility is that even though city greening is embedded within neoliberal urbanism, it is pushing its boundaries. The environmental and social benefits of well-planned density, green transportation, low carbon infrastructure, clean energy, and other aspects of the green city are not insignificant. And as equity and effectiveness gain a foothold in city environmental policies, a shift can be seen toward a rethinking of what and for whom the green city is for. Through this, the greening of post-industrial cities may provide an opening wedge that challenges inequalities and the environmental impact of urban areas.

Although none of the three cases examined in this book have fully achieved the potential benefits of the green city, their sustainability goals remain articulations of progressive possibility. Cities' proclamations of their intentions to create a greener city for all residents set standards of environmental effectiveness and social equity to which particular policy proposals, from condominium developments to carbon taxes, can be held. Increasingly, local activists and community groups are doing so, pushing for density with affordability, access for all to green transportation, and the elimination of long-standing sources of environmental injustices. City officials are rethinking building codes, investing in high-efficiency district heating schemes, and expanding green space and cycling infrastructure. For officials, encouraging economic growth remains paramount, but so is making a contribution to solving larger problems, be it the health impact of air pollution, transit access, or global climate change. In this regard, cities are fulfilling many of the hopes invested in them as key players in furthering just, effective environmental governance.

However, even as steps are taken toward progressive liberal environmentalism in each city, such a shift is by no means complete, nor is it inevitable. Effectiveness and equity in cities' greening remains circumscribed by local political will and the development imperative. It is also shaped by the broader political context in which cities are embedded. Budgets are cut, national environmental regulations are eliminated, and influxes of capital shape investment and housing affordability. Some of these difficulties are surmountable by local leaders, others less so. But as cities strive to become greener, more prosperous, and more just, the real and perceived barriers they face will continue to influence how city leaders understand and negotiate the relationship between growth, equity, and effectiveness.

Some city officials quite explicitly acknowledge the tensions in navigating the political-economic contexts shaping the greening options available to them. For example, during an interview, a Labour cabinet member in the Birmingham City Council paused after passionately outlining the ways that greening the city could be a boon for local industry and economic growth. This "is all very neoliberal," she said. "I'm a socialist!"[1] For her, the creation of a just, green city required working within the political and discursive constraints of the historical moment in which she found herself, even if this meant articulating a vision of effective liberal environmentalism that was not wholly consistent with her political ideals. This emerged in various ways throughout interviews in each of the cities investigated here. Whether skeptical of or embracing the primacy of markets and growth, many saw the use of market tools, the need to attract investment and new residents, and the importance of saving money through efficiency as the only way of moving toward their broader social and environmental goals.

Keil has called this "roll-with-it" neoliberalism, in which reformed elite practices further neoliberalization even as new social concerns enter the local political debate.[2] City greening reflects this, but it is also something more. Even as local civil and political leaders "roll with" neoliberalism, they are also creating space for more holistic understandings of the sustainable city to emerge. The cases examined in this book show that syntheses of equity and environmentally beneficial urban development are possible, even if they are by no means inevitable nor easy to achieve. The cases have also shown that there is no natural progression between varieties of liberal environmentalism. Therefore, city leaders must be held accountable to the environmental and equity implications of their greening agendas, pushed beyond growth and political expediency to think broadly about their contributions to effective, just environmental governance.

Varieties of Liberal Environmentalism and the Effectiveness of City Greening

One of the challenges of offering an analysis of the greening of Chicago, Vancouver, and Birmingham is that the environmental agendas of each of these cities are, not surprisingly, in flux. New programs are rolled out while others are sidelined. New evidence emerges as to the effectiveness, or lack thereof, of particular aspects of a city's greening agenda. Changing national regulations or shifts in the global economy thwart or enhance local environmental efforts. The vignettes presented in Chapters 5–7 therefore should not be taken as the definitive analysis of the programs investigated therein. Rather, they should be seen as snapshots that offer insights into the conflicts, challenges, and successes that these cities are grappling with in their efforts to become more environmentally and socially sustainable. Even if the details of any given program change, as they inevitably will, the tensions and synergies between greening, equity, and growth that have been illuminated above are likely to remain defining features of city environmentalism for the foreseeable future.

That being said, for purposes of summary it is useful to think about where within the spectrum of the varieties of liberal environmentalism Vancouver, Chicago, and Birmingham are today and what trajectory each city appears to be on. As discussed in Chapter 1 and seen in the chapters that followed, the four varieties of liberal environmentalism – neoliberal environmentalism, ecoliberalism, social liberalism, and progressive liberal environmentalism – are ideal-types. One variety of liberal environmentalism rarely fully defines the complexity of greening initiatives in a city. Cities move between the varieties over time and are in different places on the spectrum with different issues. Therefore, without reifying the varieties of liberal environmentalism as fixed or rigidly defined, the following summary of each city illustrates some of the potential outcomes that may emerge from efforts to negotiate growth, environmental effectiveness, and social equity within the confines of liberal environmentalism.

Long a leader in greening and livability, the early twenty-first century saw greening become part of Vancouver's development and branding strategy, and Vancouver emerged on the world stage with a clear commitment to ecoliberalism. Its environmental ambitions were high and it made concrete progress toward achieving them, gaining accolades as one of the greenest cities in North America. However, questions of social equity, though never fully ignored, were decidedly downplayed in comparison to environmental effectiveness. The push-back this engendered, particularly as housing prices skyrocketed, led to equity and social well-being gaining priority on the local political agenda. As such, of the three cities examined here, Vancouver has gone the farthest toward progressive liberal environmentalism, with city officials increasingly willing to intervene in the market to secure social as well as environmental progress. But even as Vancouver sets high standards for green building, affordable housing, and low carbon development, difficulties in achieving its goals in the face of limited financial resources and regulatory power remain significant. The city also struggles with the need to better balance officials' ambitious greening goals with a speed of change that maintains the legitimacy of these efforts and that enables the inclusive, community-driven development agenda that residents demand.

Chicago today is somewhere between neoliberal environmentalism and progressive liberal environmentalism. The growth and branding imperatives that were such a successful part of Daley's green urban entrepreneurialism clearly remain a priority. However, under Mayor Emanuel, local groups have been able to use his political vulnerability and ongoing promise that greening will benefit everyone to push the city toward progressive liberal environmentalism. The result has been a slow, and by no means complete, move in the direction of a more equitable distribution of the benefits of the greener city. Some of the city's most egregious environmental injustices have been remedied. Green transit is focused on attracting employers and skilled workers to the city center, but Divvy is also being spread throughout Chicago's neighborhoods. New green spaces in long underserved areas are alleviating this environmental inequity, though it remains to be seen if concerns about displacement and housing affordability will be more robustly addressed. Overall, local calls for equity and environmental justice to be at the heart of city environmental efforts are re-shaping Chicago's greening, even if city leaders remain hesitant to challenge the primacy of growth in responding to these demands. If this shift can be strengthened, Chicago may become an example of how a greener city can truly be for all residents. More likely, however, is that Chicago will remain closer to neoliberal environmentalism, with moves toward inclusion and environmental effectiveness important but tempered by inconsistent and tepid political will.

When Birmingham first began proclaiming its commitment to environmental governance, it strove to integrate green growth, reduced carbon emissions, and social justice. The city center had been reinvigorated, spurring the green economy was a priority of the local business community, and city sustainability officials were focused on how they could get the maximum social benefit from their climate mitigation efforts by reducing fuel poverty. Unfortunately, many of the city's ambitious goals have not been achieved, and the council's commitment to climate governance has been eclipsed by a focus on growth and, to a lesser extent, social well-being, which sees the environment as an add-on. Where there are clear economic benefits to greening, such as with district energy schemes, or where political resistance is minimal, such as bike lanes along the canal towpaths, Birmingham has seen movement toward environmentally beneficial development. Likewise, the growing emphasis on health has opened up new possibilities for enhancing just, green development in the city. However, this progress remains tempered by an unwillingness on the part of city leaders to complement the growth imperative with the harder political choices that will be necessary to achieve the city's ambitious environmental and social goals. On the spectrum of varieties of liberal environmentalism Birmingham therefore is between neoliberal environmentalism and social liberalism. Greening remains on the local political agenda, but concerns about growth and social welfare are prioritized over the environment, even if this means missed opportunities to use greening to further these twin goals over the long-term.

Taken together, the success with which these three cities have achieved their greening goals, and in so doing made measurable contributions to just, effective environmental governance, is mixed. But if, as argued in Chapter 1, the effectiveness of cities' efforts can be partly judged by whether they "are having a lasting impact on … the wider notion of development,"[3] more evidence for their success can be seen. This impact is clearest in that the notion that cities are antithetical to nature has been replaced by aspirations of urban development that helps protect the environment. This, as well as equity concerns gaining an increasingly predominant place in discussions of city greening, are leading to the emergence of new norms and means of legitimate conduct in city environmental governance.[4] Even as progressive liberal environmentalism remains elusive, these changing ideas of development and new norms of legitimate conduct in city environmentalism are important signs of the effectiveness of city greening.

Between Global Governance and "Thinking Locally"

Over fifteen years ago, Betsill found that city policies to reduce GHG emissions were more successful politically if they were *not* promoted as climate change policies but instead framed as solutions to problems already on the local political agenda such as improving air quality or public transportation. Often "the most effective way to get municipal governments to mitigate global climate change," she argued, "is by not talking about global climate change; the best strategy may be to 'think locally, act locally.'"[5] In the years following her study this changed in many places, with climate governance and cities' contributions to climate change mitigation being explicitly promoted as indicative of their commitment to good governance. Today, however, it may be that Betsill's suggestion should be revisited.

In some cities, like Birmingham, there has clearly been a shift in political discourse away from climate change toward other issues that are seen as more pressing and resonant for residents, particularly cost-savings and health. But even when this shift is not as dramatic, as in Chicago, or where it has not happened at all and a commitment to climate governance remains pronounced, as in Vancouver, there are reasons for proponents of city greening to think and act locally. In places where climate change and sustainability are highly partisan, a focus on the localized benefits of policies that also have global environmental benefits could enable a surmounting of some of the ideological resistance to carbon mitigation. In the face of ongoing austerity and persistent challenges of poverty and inequality, thinking and acting locally may also be valuable because it facilitates a specific recognition of the local equity impacts of environmental initiatives. This, then, calls for creative ways to further city environmental goals in a socially just way.

That being said, for cities to make an effective contribution to just, global environmental governance, acting locally must done with an eye on the importance of the global. Not doing so runs the risk of falling into what Purcell calls the "local trap." The local trap is "the tendency of researchers and activists to assume something inherent about the local scale. The local trap equates the local with 'the good'; it is preferred presumptively over non-local scales."[6] The local trap is problematic in a number of ways. Most importantly for the issue of city greening is that in its focus on the local as a discrete site of social change, the local trap serves to hide the broader context of national policies and globalization that local initiatives must negotiate. Indeed, much of the appeal of the local is that it is seen as well-defined and manageable, in contrast to the perceived uncontrollability of processes "such as globalization, the financialization of capital, the erosion of the national state, and the intensification of interspatial competition."[7] The manageability of the local is illusionary, however. Cities are deeply embedded in these global processes, and as long as city leaders feel that they are in an ongoing competition with other cities for investment, tourists, and skilled labor, their environmentalism will be shaped and limited by the needs of this competition. The local trap, in ignoring the broader political economic and policy contexts in which local decisions are made, easily underplays this constraint on city environmental initiatives.

Yet even in the face of these broader constraints, city policies matter. Many city leaders and environmentalists have been working for decades to improve the environment and lessen the ecological impact of their urban areas, and many of their efforts have borne fruit. If more cities continue to adopt such programs, their environmental impact will not be irrelevant. This is perhaps even more the case for the incorporation of social equity considerations into greening initiatives. As city greening efforts have been challenged for their distributional impacts, their local legitimacy has increasingly been connected to their ability not just to beautify city centers, or even to reduce global carbon emissions, but to ensure that the promise that all will benefit from the greener city is realized. Local political contestations, from electoral campaigns to city council meetings to protests, have made greening with equity an important part of the urban environmental agenda.

Those who would either critique or celebrate city greening efforts must wrestle with this ambivalence between the importance and the limitations of the political scale of the city. Local decision-makers must be held accountable to the environmental and social impacts of their development decisions even while the limits of what is possible on the city level is acknowledged. National and global policies to further just environmental governance must be strengthened, with an eye to how they can better facilitate cities' contributions to social and environmental sustainability. Recognizing that the win–win–win promises of progressive liberal environmentalism, though possible, cannot always be achieved, requires an examination of how such trade-offs are decided, who wins and who loses, and how local and global environmental governance can help find solutions to potential trade-offs. Analyses and policies must think and act globally, nationally, *and* locally.

Re-imagining the Future

Embedded in the stories of the greening of Chicago, Birmingham, and Vancouver is the story of environmentalism in the neoliberal era, of the desire for walking more lightly on the planet sitting uneasily alongside the desire to increase economic growth, of the need to "roll with" the moment of neoliberal capitalism in which we exist but also to challenge its most socially and environmentally destructive tendencies. As such, these three cases can help us understand both the potential and the limitations of liberal environmentalism, as well as of cities as players in furthering equitable environmental governance.

Global environmental issues, particularly climate change, pose a great danger to human well-being and to ecological integrity. They also offer an opportunity for beginning a process of re-envisioning of the kind of social, economic, and political structures we want to create in response to a rapidly changing planet.[8] The beginning of this dialogue can be seen in Chicago, Vancouver, and Birmingham. Even if their success is by no means guaranteed, and though they do not challenge existing structures and institutions of power as much as would be necessary to achieve robust progressive liberal environmentalism (let alone a more radical form of just sustainability), their work makes a more equitable, green future seem possible. To the extent that cities' climate initiatives, green housing and development efforts, and improvements to transit and green space enhance the quality of life for all, as they begin to shift the commonsense idea of what a city's relationship to nature can and should be, and if through these efforts people and communities are re-imagining their neighborhoods as places of environmental health, beauty, and inclusion, there is much potential here.

This book therefore concludes with guarded optimism about city greening. It is not a panacea. Issues of distribution and exclusion remain pronounced, and there are many ways in which city leaders are limited (by political-economic structures or by lack of political will) in what they can do to make their cities more environmentally and socially sustainable. As has been seen, much more action needs to be taken on other political scales to remedy the deep social and environmental problems that are often manifested particularly starkly in cities. But one can recognize these limitations while also seeing the real changes that are occurring because of city greening. There are not always easy solutions to the tensions between growth, equity, and environmental effectiveness. Yet in striving to achieve all three goals, green cities can be sites for envisioning the kind of future we want to create.

Notes

1 Personal communication, June 2016.
2 Roger Keil, "The Urban Politics of Roll-with-It Neoliberalism," *City* 13, no. 2–3 (2009).
3 Harriet Bulkeley et al., *Transnational Climate Change Governance* (Cambridge, UK: Cambridge University Press, 2014), 172.
4 Ibid.
5 Michele M. Betsill, "Mitigating Climate Change in US Cities: Opportunities and Obstacles," *Local Environment* 6, no. 4 (2001): 404.
6 Mark Purcell, "Urban Democracy and the Local Trap," *Urban Studies* 43, no. 11 (2006): 1923.
7 Neil Brenner and Nikolas Theodore, "Preface: From the 'New Localism' to the Spaces of Neoliberalism," *Antipode* 34, no. 3 (2002): 341.
8 Paul Wapner, *Living through the End of Nature: The Future of American Environmentalism* (Cambridge, MA: MIT Press, 2010).

Postface: Green Cities in an Uncertain Moment

Since concluding the research for this book in mid-2016, the national and global contexts in which Chicago, Birmingham, and Vancouver are operating have changed substantially. Most notably, Great Britain voted to leave the European Union and Donald Trump was elected President of the United States. As of this writing it is too soon to know exactly how these events will shape city greening efforts. In interviews shortly before the Brexit vote, numerous officials in Birmingham said that their sustainability goals would be significantly more difficult to achieve if the country left the EU. There are a number of reasons for this. Strong European environmental protections have helped push the UK and the Birmingham governments toward sustainable development. In addition, Birmingham has a history of successfully winning European development grants, many of which have supported the city's greening efforts. These funds will not be available when Britain is not an EU member. Finally, many worried that leaving the EU will hurt Birmingham's economy, making investments in achieving ambitious environmental goals even less of a priority for city officials already concerned with maximizing growth and development.

In Chicago, within days of Trump's election, Mayor Emanuel was standing up to the president-elect's proposed immigration policies. When Trump announced in June 2017 (as this book was going to press) that the United States would pull out of the Paris Climate Agreement, Chicago was one of the cities that doubled down on its commitment to reducing carbon emissions. However, to the extent that cities need federal funding and regulations to achieve many of their environmental goals, Trump's proposed roll-backs of both will make many of Chicago's goals increasingly hard to reach. The appointment of Scott Pruitt as the head of the EPA, a climate-change denier who has a history of hostility toward the agency he now runs, is particularly disheartening. Greening is unlikely to fall off Chicago's political agenda, and Emanuel's commitment to climate governance may even be strengthened, but the federal resources and regulatory support the city needs to succeed will undoubtedly recede.

National trends in Canada are somewhat more promising for Vancouver's greening initiatives. Prime Minister Trudeau's plans to enact a Canadian-wide carbon tax will certainly help Vancouver achieve its zero-emission goal over the long term. Federal investment in affordable housing and public transportation, long moribund, is once again increasing in Canada and in BC, raising hopes that Vancouver's affordable housing crisis can be contained and its green transit goals be reached. On the other hand, the ongoing insistence of the federal government on enhancing fossil fuel infrastructure such as the Kinder Morgan pipeline threatens Vancouver's environmental goals and its green brand. Furthermore, the election of President Trump may also impact trade relations and energy policies between Canada and the U.S., and how this would affect Vancouver is yet unknown.

Despite the serious challenges for sustainability they present, the upheavals of Brexit and the Trump presidency also mean that cities have a more important role than ever in furthering environmental governance. If global action on climate change, promising after the Paris Climate Agreement in 2015, begins to falter as the U.S. rescinds its Paris commitments, cities may once again offer a vital political scale for action to reduce emissions. City climate initiatives alone will not be enough to stabilize global temperature rise, but this does not mean that their contributions are insignificant. Though this book has issued a strong word of caution in terms of putting too much hope in cities and their ability to solve environmental problems in a socially just way, it has also illustrated their potential. The win–win elements of liberal environmentalism that cities have embraced cut emissions and reduce pollution while saving the city, businesses, and residents money. It is possible that the challenges of the current political moment will inspire city leaders to take a longer view of the payback of environmental initiatives and of their role in global environmental governance and that this will inspire more ambitious carbon reduction policies. If cities can do this while also focusing on achieving environmental goals in a way that benefits lower-income residents, the successes of liberal environmentalism may expand even further. In what promises to be a difficult time for proponents of sustainability, it is more important than ever that greening and equity be seen not as competing priorities but as potentially synergistic, and that creative and ambitious ways be found to imagine and construct cities that are prosperous, environmentally sustainable, and socially just. City leaders' willingness to do this will shape the future.

References

Abu-Lughod, Janet L. (1999) *New York, Chicago, Los Angeles: America's Global Cities*. Minneapolis, MN: University of Minnesota Press.

African Development Bank (2003) Asian Development Bank, UK Department for International Development, European Commission Directorate-General for Development, German Federal Ministry for Economic Cooperation and Development, Netherlands Ministry of Foreign Affairs, Organization for Economic Cooperation and Development, et al. "Poverty and Climate Change: Reducing the Vulnerability of the Poor through Adaptation."

Agarwal, A., S. Narain, and A. Sharma (2002) "The Global Commons and Environmental Justice – Climate Change." In *Environmental Justice: Discourses in International Political Economy*, ed. John Byrne, Leigh Glover and Cecilia Martinez. New Brunswick, NJ: Transaction Pub.

Agyeman, Julian (2005) *Sustainable Communities and the Challenge of Environmental Justice*. New York, NY: New York University Press.

Agyeman, Julian (2013) *Introducing Just Sustainabilities: Policy, Planning, and Practice*. New York, NY: Zed Books.

Agyeman, Julian, Robert D. Bullard, and Bob Evans, eds. (2003) *Just Sustainabilities: Development in an Unequal World*. London, UK: Earthscan.

Alberti, Marina (1996) "Measuring Urban Sustainability." *Environmental Impact Assessment Review* 16: 381–424.

Allen, Steve (2006) "The Greening of Chicago." *Time*, May 12.

Andrews, Richard N. L. (2006) *Managing the Environment, Managing Ourselves: A History of American Environmental Policy*. 2nd edn. New Haven, CT: Yale University Press.

Anon (2012) "Birmingham Carbon Plan Analysis." Birmingham, UK: Presented to Birmingham's Green Commision, 2012.

Arifwidodo, Sigit D. (2012) "Exploring the Effect of Compact Development Policy to Urban Quality of Life in Bandung, Indonesia." *City, Culture and Society* 3: 303–11.

ARUP (2011) "Climate Action in Megacities: C40 Cities Baseline and Opportunities." http://publications.arup.com/Publications/C/Climate_Action_in_Megacities.aspx (accessed August 6, 2015).

Associated Press (2005) "Bush: Kyoto Treaty Would Have Hurt Economy." *NBCNews.com*, June 30 (accessed May 20, 2016).

Austen, Ian (2016) "Justin Trudeau Approves Oil Pipeline Expansion in Canada." *New York Times*, November 29.

Bailey, Alison (2015) "Downtown Vancouver Businesses' Attitudes towards Bike Lanes Have Changed in the Last 5 Years." *News 1130*, May 27.

Ball, David P. (2014) "'No Rational Given,' Say Rejected Kinder Morgan Intervenors." *The Tyee*, April 4.

Barber, Austin, and Stephen Hall (2008) "Birmingham: Whose Urban Renaissance? Regeneration as a Response to Economic Restructuring." *Urban Studies* 29, no. 3: 281–92.

Barber, Benjamin (2013) *If Mayors Ruled the World: Dysfunctional Nations, Rising Cities*. New Haven, CT: Yale University Press.

Barboza, David (2001) "Chicago, Offering Big Incentives, Will Be Boeing's New Home." *New York Times*, May 11.

Barman, Jean (2007) *The West Beyond the West: A History of British Columbia, Third Edition*. Toronto: University of Toronto Press.

Barnes, Trevor J., David W. Edgington, Kenneth G. Denike, and Terry G. McGee (1992) "Vancouver, the Province, and the Pacific Rim." In *Vancouver and Its Region*, ed. Graeme Wynn and Timothy Oke. Vancouver, BC: UBC Press.

Barnett, Jonathan (2003) *Redesigning Cities: Principles, Practice, Implementation*. Chicago, IL: Planners Press.

Barry, John, and Peter Doran (2006) "Refining Green Political Economy: From Ecological Modernisation to Economic Security and Sufficiency." *Analyse & Kritik* 28: 250–75.

BBC News (2015) "Green Deal Funding to End, Government Announces." *BBC News*, July 23.

Be Birmingham (2008) "Birmingham 2026 – Our Vision for the Future, Sustainabile Community Strategy." Birmingham, UK.

Be Birmingham (2009) "Birmingham Environmental Partnership: 08/09 Annual Report." Birmingham, UK.

Be Birmingham (2010) "Birmingham Environmental Partnership: 09/10 Annual Report." Birmingham, UK.

Beal, Vincent (2012) "Urban Governance, Sustainability and Environmental Movements: Post-Democracy in French and British Cities." *European Urban and Regional Studies* 19, no. 4: 414–19.

Beatley, Timothy, ed. (2012) *Green Cities of Europe: Global Lessons on Green Urbanism*. Washington, DC: Island Press.

Beatley, Timothy (2013) "Green, British-Style." *Planning*, November.

Beauregard, Robert A. (2006) *When America Became Suburban*. Minneapolis, MN: University of MN Press.

Beazley, Mike, Patrick Loftman, and Brendan Nevin (1997) "Downtown Redevelopment and Community Resistance: An International Perspective." In *Transforming Cities: Contested Governance and New Spatial Divisions*, ed. Nick Jewson and Susanne MacGregor. New York, NY: Routledge.

Beck, Peter (2006) "Letter: Fiddling While Our World Burns." *Birmingham Post*, September 25.

Bell, David (2001) "£50m Boost for City Centre." *Birmingham Evening Mail*, June 21.

Belluck, Pam (1997) "Gang Gunfire May Chase Chicago Children from Their School." *New York Times*, November 17.

Bennett, Larry (2006) "Transforming Public Housing." In *The New Chicago: A Social and Cultural Analysis*, ed. John P. Koval, Larry Bennett,

Michael I. J. Bennett, Fassil Demissie, Roberta Garner, and Kiljoong Kim. Philadelphia, PA: Temple University Press.

Berelowitz, Lance (2005) *Dream City: Vancouver and the Global Imagination.* Vancouver, BC: Douglas & McIntyre.

Bernstein, Fred A. (2004) "Big Shoulders, Big Donors, Big Art." *New York Times,* July 18.

Bernstein, Steven (2001) *The Compromise of Liberal Environmentalism.* New York, NY: Columbia University Press.

Bernstein, Steven (2011) "Legitimacy in Intergovernmental and Non-State Global Governance." *Review of International Political Economy* 18, no. 1: 17–51.

Bernstein, Steven, Jennifer Clapp, and Matthew Hoffman (2009) "Reframing Global Environmental Governance: Results of a CIGI/CIS Collaboration." Center for International Governance Innovation.

Betsill, Michele M. (2001) "Mitigating Climate Change in US Cities: Opportunities and Obstacles." *Local Environment* 6, no. 4: 393–406.

Biasco, Paul (2016) "Logan Square Hispanics Vanishing as Neighborhood Becomes More White." *DNAInfo,* May 16.

Biggers, Jeff (2012) "Historic Victory: Coal Free Chicago Will Electrify Clean Energy Movement." *Huff Post Chicago,* February 29.

Birmingham City Council (2002) "Towards a Sustainable City: Birmingham City Council Achievements, Local Agenda 21, 1992–2002." Birmingham, UK: Birmingham City Council.

Birmingham City Council (2006) "Birmingham Local Area Agreement." Birmingham, UK: Birmingham City Council.

Birmingham City Council (2010) "Making Birmingham Green: Birmingham Climate Change Action Plan 2010+." Birmingham, UK: Birmingham City Council.

Birmingham City Council (2012) "Birmingham Low Carbon Transport Strategy." Birmingham, UK: Birmingham City Council.

Birmingham City Council (2013) "Green Living Spaces Plan." Birmingham, UK: Birmingham City Council.

Birmingham City Council (2014) "Birmingham Connected: Moving Our City Forward – Birmingham Mobility Action Plan White Paper." Birmingham, UK: Birmingham City Council.

Birmingham City Council (2014) "Responding to the Challenge, Looking to the Future." Birmingham, UK: Birmingham City Council.

Birmingham City Council (2016) "Birmingham Cycle Revolution." Birmingham, UK: Birmingham City Council, www.birmingham.gov.uk/birminghamcyclerevolution (accessed August 5, 2016).

Birmingham City Council (2016) "Birmingham Cycle Revolution Spring/Summer Programme." Birmingham, UK: Birmingham City Council.

Birmingham City Council (2017) "Birmingham Plan 2013." Birmingham, UK: Birmingham City Council.

Birmingham City Council (n.d.) "Birmingham Municipal Housing Trust." www.birmingham.gov.uk/bmht (accessed June 7, 2016).

Birmingham City Council (n.d.) "Delivery of New Combined Heat and Power Engine." www.birmingham.gov.uk/cs/Satellite?c=Page&childpagename=Lib-Library-of-Birmingham%2FPageLayout&cid=1223386258774&pagename=BCC%2FCommon%2FWrapper%2FWrapper (accessed May 18, 2016; please note: this URL is now inaccessible).

Birmingham District Energy Company (2015) "Birmingham District Energy Scheme." Birmingham, UK: Birmingham District Energy Company.

Birmingham Economy (n.d.) "Employment by Sector in Birmingham 1984–2009." www.birminghameconomy.org.uk/ (accessed January 5, 2011).

Birmingham Economy (n.d.) "Ethnic Origin by Ward." www.birminghameconomy.org.uk/ (accessed January 5, 2011).

Birmingham Economy (n.d.) "Unemployment by Ward." www.birminghameconomy.org.uk/ (accessed January 5, 2011).

Birmingham Energy Savers (2013) "BES Gets Official Launch." www.energysaverspartnerships.co.uk/birmingham/news/news/2013/bes-launch.aspx (accessed January 15, 2015).

Birmingham Evening Mail (2004) "Canals Clean – but Don't Go for a Swim." October 9.

Birmingham Evening Mail (2008) "How Brum's Fuelling a Greener Future." May 20.

Birmingham Friends of the Earth (n.d.) "Eastside Sustainability Advisory Group." www.birminghamfoe.org.uk/ESAG/ (accessed January 19, 2011).

Birmingham Post (1999) "Waterway to Unlock Potential of Our Canals." April 26.

Birmingham Post (2001) "Budget: Job Fears Grow over Climate Charges." March 8.

Birmingham Post (2001) "Fast-Buck, Slow-Death Warning." March 21.

Birmingham Post (2002) "Eastside Development Report Calls for Some Enlightenment." November 2.

Birmingham Post (2003) "Sustainability Team for Eastside Project." November 17.

Birmingham Post (2005) "'We Must Not Cut Corners on Eastside'." March 3.

Birmingham Post (2006) "Greening of City: Good Start, Now Let's Have Action." December 26.

Birmingham Post (2009) "Hospital Plan to Save 20,000 Carbon Tonnes." February 19.

Birmingham Post (2009) "City Council Climate Change Strategy Is Based on Hot Air." March 16.

Birmingham Post (2013) "Building a Green City." Birmingham, UK: Birmingham City Council.

Birmingham Post (2014) "Ecopods Cut Energy Bills." http://greencity.birmingham.gov.uk/news/ecopods-cut-energy-bills/ (accessed January 15, 2015).

Birmingham Post (2015) "Carbon Roadmap Update – Autumn 2015." Birmingham, UK: Birmingham Green Commission.

Birmingham's Green Commission (2015) "Birmingham's Green Commission Autumn 2016 (sic) Update – Factsheet." Birmingham, UK: Birmingham's Green Commission.

Bloom, Mina (2015) "Cabrini-Green Rowhouse Settlement: Everything You Need to Know." *DNAInfo*, September 15.

Boardman, Brenda (2010) *Fixing Fuel Poverty: Challenges and Solutions.* London, UK: Earthscan.

Bosso, Christopher J. (2005) *Environment, Inc.: From Grassroots to Beltway.* Lawrence, KS: University Press of Kansas.

Bouteligier, Sofie (2013) *Cities, Networks, and Global Environmental Governance.* New York, NY: Routledge.

Brand, Peter, and Michael J. Thomas (2005). *Urban Environmentalism: Global Change and the Mediation of Local Conflict.* New York, NY: Routledge.

Brenner, Neil (2004) "Urban Governance and the Production of New State Spaces in Western Europe, 1960–2000." *Review of International Political Economy* 11, no. 3: 447–88.

Brenner, Neil, and Nikolas Theodore (2002) "Preface: From the 'New Localism' to the Spaces of Neoliberalism." *Antipode* 34, no. 3: 341–47.

Brenner, Neil, and Nikolas Theodore, eds. (2002) *Spaces of Neoliberalism: Urban Restructuring in North America and Western Europe.* Malden, MA: Blackwell.

Brenner, Robert (2006) *The Economics of Global Turbulence.* New York, NY: Verso.

Broto, Vanesa Castan, and Harriet Bulkeley (2013) "A Survey of Urban Climate Change Experiments in 100 Cities." *Global Environmental Change* 23: 92–102.

Brown, Graeme (2009) "Manton House and Reynolds House in Birmingham to Be Connected to Biomass Combined Heat and Power System." *Birmingham Post,* August 26.

Budden, Keith, and Karen Leach (2002) "Sustainable Eastside – a Vision for the Future." Birmingham, UK: Birmingham City Council.

Buchs, Milena, Nicholas Bardsley, and Sebastian Duwe (2011) "Who Bears the Brunt? Distributional Effects of Climate Change Mitigation Policies." *Critical Social Policy* 31, no. 2: 285–307.

Bula, Frances (2013) "Vancouver's Bike Lanes: Gordon Price on When to Ignore the Opposition." *Globe and Mail,* July 30.

Bula, Frances (2014) "Vancouver Bike Lanes Incite Outrage as City Supports Riders." *Globe and Mail,* September 1.

Bulkeley, Harriet (2013) *Cities and Climate Change.* London, UK: Routledge.

Bulkeley, Harriet (2016) *Accomplishing Climate Governance.* Cambridge, UK: Cambridge University Press.

Bulkeley, Harriet, and Michele M. Betsill (2003) *Cities and Climate Change: Urban Sustainability and Global Environmental Governance.* New York, NY: Routledge.

Bulkeley, Harriet, and Michele M. Betsill (2005) "Rethinking Sustainable Cities: Multilevel Governance and the 'Urban' Politics of Climate Change." *Environmental Politics* 14, no. 1: 42–63.

Bulkeley, Harriet, and Michele M. Betsill (2013) "Revisiting the Urban Politics of Climate Change." *Environmental Politics* 22, no. 1: 136–54.

Bulkeley, Harriet, Vanesa Castan Broto, Mike Hodson, and Simon Marvin, eds. (2011) *Cities and Low Carbon Transitions.* New York, NY: Routledge.

Bulkeley, Harriet, JoAnn Carmin, Vanesa Castan Broto, Gareth A.S. Edwards, and Sara Fuller (2013) "Climate Justice and Global Cities: Mapping the Emerging Discourse." *Global Environmental Change* 23: 914–25.

Bulkeley, Harriet, Liliana B. Andonova, Michele M. Betsill, Daniel Compagnon, Thomas Hale, Matthew J. Hoffman, Peter Newell, *et al.* (2014)*Transnational Climate Change Governance.* Cambridge UK: Cambridge University Press.

Bullard, Robert D., ed. (2007) *Growing Smarter: Achieving Livable Commities, Environmental Justice, and Regional Equity.* Cambridge, MA: MIT Press.

Bullard, Robert D., and Glenn S. Johnson (1997) "Introduction." In *Just Transportation: Dismantling Race & Class Barriers to Mobility,* ed. Robert D. Bullard and Glenn S. Johnson. Stony Creek, CT: New Society Publishers.

Burch, Sarah (2010) "Transforming Barriers into Enablers of Action on Climate Change: Insights from Three Municipal Case Studies in British Columbia, Canada." *Global Environmental Change* 20: 287–97.

Burnham, Morey, Claudia Radel, Zhao Ma, and Ann Laudati (2013) "Extending a Geographic Lens towards Climate Justice, Part 1: Climate Change Characterization and Impacts." *Geography Compass* 7, no. 3: 239–48.

Burton, Elizabeth (2000) "The Compact City: Just or Just Compact? A Preliminary Analysis." *Urban Studies* 37, no. 11: 1969 2001.

Byrne, John (2014) "Activists: Emanuel Taking Too Much Credit for Power Plant Closings." *Chicago Tribune*, November 26.

Byrne, John (2015) "Mayor Emanuel's 606 Affordable-Housing Plan Draws Doubts." *Chicago Tribune*, August 12.

Campbell, Charles (2013) "At Ground Zero for Vancouver's Towering Debate." *The Tyee*, June 25.

Canadian Press (2016) "Vancouver Mayor 'Profoundly Dissappointed' by Kinder Morgan Approval." *Huffpost British Columbia*, November 29.

Canadian Press (2017) "B.C. Lifts Foreign Buyers Tax for People with Work Permits as Housing Market Cools." *Financial Post*, January 30.

Caradonna, Jeremy L. (2014) *Sustainability: A History*. Oxford, UK: Oxford University Press.

Card Group (2007) "Birmingham Visitor Survey: A Review of Visitors to the City." Birmingham, UK.

Carroll, William K., and Williams Little (2001) "Neoliberal Transformation and Antiglobalization Politics in Canada: Transition, Consolidation, Resistance." *International Journal of Political Economy* 31, no. 3: 33–66.

Carroll, William K., and R.S. Ratner (1989) "Social Democracy, Neo-Conservatism and Hegemonic Crisis in British Columbia." *Critical Sociology* 16, no. 1: 29–53.

Carson, Rachel (1962) *Silent Spring*. Greenwich, CT: Fawcett Publications.

Carss, Barbara (2016) "Vancouver Developers to Pursue Zero Emissions." Canadian Apartments, https://www.reminetwork.com/articles/vancouver-developers-to-pursue-zero-emissions/ (accessed January 18, 2017).

Castro, J.A.A. (1972) "Environment and Development: The Case of the Developing Countries." In *World Eco-Crisis: International Organizations in Response*, ed. D.A. Kay and E.B. Skolnikoff. Madison, WI: University of Wisconsin Press.

CBC News (2010) "Vancouver's Hornby Bike Lane Gets Green Light." *CBC News*, October 6.

CBC News (2015) "Vancouver Rentals Quadruple, but Residents Question Affordability." *CBC News British Columbia*, November 20.

CDOT (2012) "Chicago Streets for Cycling Plan 2020." Chicago, IL: Chicago Department of Transportation.

Center for Neighborhood Technology (2013) "Transit-Oriented Development in the Chicago Region: Efficient and Resilient Communities for the 21st Century." Chicago, IL: Center for Neighborhood Technology.

Center for Park Excellence (2010) "Chicago's Green Mayor: The Legacy of Richard Daley." http://cityparksblog.org/2010/10/27/chicagos-green-mayor-the-legacy-of-richard-daley/ (accessed December 16, 2010).

Chan, Cheryl (2013) "Divisive Bike Route for Point Grey Road Approved by Vancouver City Council." *Vancouver Sun*, July 30.

Chan, Cheryl (2016) "Expo 86: When Vancouver Wooed the World – 30 Photos, 30 Years Later." *Vancouver Sun*, May 14.

Chancellor of the Exchequer (2015) "Fixing the Foundations: Creating a More Prosperous Nation." London, UK: Controller of Her Majesty's Stationary Office.

Checker, Melissa (2011) "Wiped out by the 'Greenwave': Environmental Gentrification and the Paradoxical Politics of Urban Sustainability." *City & Society* 23, no. 2: 210–29.

Cherry, Gordon Emanuel (1994) *Birmingham: A Study in Geography, History, and Planning*. Chichester, West Sussex, England; New York: J. Wiley.

Cheung, Calista (2014) "Deconstructing Canada's Housing Markets: Finance, Affordability and Urban Sprawl." In *OECD Economics Department Working Papers*: OECD Publishing.

Chicago Department of Development and Planning (1973) "Chicago 21: A Plan for the Central Area Communities." Chicago, IL.

Chicago Infrastructure Trust (2016) "Municipal Buildings Retrofit." Chicago Infrastructure Trust, http://chicagoinfrastructure.org/initiatives/construction-underway-municipal-buildings-retrofit/ (accessed July 6, 2016).

Chicago Infrastructure Trust (2016) "Press Release: Mayor Emanuel Announces New Street Lights; Requests Public Feedback before Installation." December 13, http://chicagoinfrastructure.org/2016/12/13/mayor-emanuel-announces-new-street-lights-requests-public-feedback-before-installation/ (accessed January 16, 2017).

Citizens' Assembly on the Grandview-Woodland Community Plan (2015) "Final Report." Vancouver, BC.

City of Chicago (1986) "Building the Basics: The Final Report of the Mayor's Task Force on Steel and Southeast Chicago." Chicago, IL: City of Chicago.

City of Chicago (2003) "Chicago Central Area Plan." Chicago, IL: City of Chicago.

City of Chicago (2004) "Logan Square Open Space Plan." Chicago, IL: City of Chicago.

City of Chicago (2008) "Chicago Climate Action Plan: Our City, Our Future." Chicago, IL: City of Chicago.

City of Chicago (2008) "Daley, Business, Foundation Leaders Announce Climate Action Plan." Chicago, IL: City of Chicago.

City of Chicago (2008) "Press Release: City Shifting to Blue Cart Recycling Program by End of 2011." Chicago, IL: City of Chicago, May 6, www.cityof-chicago.org (accessed October 10, 2010).

City of Chicago (2009) "Press Release: Daley Repeats Call for Federal, State Action to Rebuild Infrastructure." Chicago, IL: City of Chicago, February 4, www.cityofchicago.org (accesssed October 10, 2010).

City of Chicago (2009) "Press Release: Mayor Daley Welcomes Nordex, USA, to Chicago." April 30, www.cityofchicago.org (accessed December 10, 2010).

City of Chicago (2010) "Climate Action Plan: Progress Report, First Two Years." Chicago, IL: City of Chicago.

City of Chicago (2010) "Press Release: Chicago Celebrates Arbor Day with Mayoral Visit to SW Side School." April 30, www.cityofchicago.org (accessed December 15, 2010).

City of Chicago (2012) "Press Release: Mayor Emanuel Reduces Costs and Acquires Cleaner Energy with New Electricity Supply Agreement for City Facilities." November 12, www.cityofchicago.org/city/en/depts/mayor/press_room/press_releases/2013/november_2013/mayor-emanuel-reduces-costs-and-acquires-cleaner-energy-with-new.html (accessed July 6, 2016).

City of Chicago (2012) "Sustainable Chicago 2015." Chicago, IL: City of Chicago.

City of Chicago (2013) "Press Release: Chicago Welcomes Divvy Bike Sharing System." July 1, www.cityofchicago.org/city/en/depts/cdot/provdrs/bike/news/2013/jul/chicago_welcomesdivvybikesharingsystem.html (accessed August 16, 2016).

City of Chicago (2014) "Press Release: Divvy to Expand Next Spring by 175 Stations and 1,750 Bikes." August 21, www.cityofchicago.org/city/en/depts/cdot/provdrs/bike/news/2014/aug/DivvyExpansion.html (accessed August 16, 2016).

City of Chicago (2015) "Bike 2015 Plan." City of Chicago, www.bike2015plan.org/intro.html (accessed August 16, 2016).

City of Chicago (2015) "Press Release: Mayor Emanuel Announces Divvy Expanding Access to Popular Bike Share System through Divvy for Everyone (D4E) Program." July 7, www.cityofchicago.org/city/en/depts/mayor/press_room/press_releases/2015/july/mayor-emanuel-announces-divvy-expanding-access-to-popular-bike-s.html (accessed August 16, 2016).

City of Chicago (2015) "Sustainable Chicago 2015: Action Agenda, 2012–2015 Highlights and Look Ahead." Chicago, IL: City of Chicago.

City of Chicago (2016) "Press Release: Mayor Emanuel Announced Divvy Adding Stations to Cover New Neighborhoods on South and West Sides of Chicago." June 10, www.cityofchicago.org/city/en/depts/cdot/provdrs/bike/news/2016/june/mayor-emanuel-announces-divvy-adding-stations-to-cover-new-neigh.html (accessed August 16, 2016).

City of Chicago (2016) "Press Release: Mayor Emanuel Announced Third Expansion of the Retrofit Chicago Energy Challenge." July 28, https://www.cityofchicago.org/city/en/depts/mayor/press_room/press_releases/2016/july/Retrofit-Chicago-Energy-Challenge.html (accessed January 16, 2016).

City of Chicago (n.d.) "Energy Benchmarking." City of Chicago, www.cityofchicago.org/city/en/progs/env/building-energy-benchmarking–transparency.html (accessed July 6, 2016).

City of Chicago (n.d.) "Environment and Sustainability." City of Chicago, www.cityofchicago.org/city/en/progs/env.html (accessed February 15, 2016).

City of Chicago (n.d.) "Environment Programs and Initiatives." City of Chicago, www.cityofchicago.org/city/en/progs/env.html (accessed November 9, 2010).

City of Chicago (n.d.) "Housing: Affordable Requirements Ordinance." City of Chicago, www.cityofchicago.org/city/en/depts/dcd/supp_info/affordable_housingrequirementsordinance.html (accessed August 3, 2016).

City of Chicago, Chicago Park District, and Forest Preserve District of Cook County. "CitySpace: On Open Space Plan for Chicago." Chicago, IL: City of Chicago, 1998.

City of Vancouver (1990) "Clouds of Change: Final Report of the City of Vancouver Task Force on Atmospheric Change." Vancouver, BC: City of Vancouver.

City of Vancouver (1995) "CityPlan: Directions for Vancouver." Vancouver, BC: City of Vancouver.

City of Vancouver (2002) "Appendix B: Definition of a Sustainable Vancouver Adopted by Council April 2002." Vancouver, BC: City of Vancouver.

City of Vancouver (2008) "EcoDensity: How Density, Design, and Land Use Will Contribute to Environmental Sustainability, Affordability, and Livability." Vancouver, BC: City of Vancouver.

City of Vancouver (2011) "Greenest City 2020 Action Plan." Vancouver, BC: City of Vancouver.

City of Vancouver (2012) "Transportation 2040." Vancouver, BC: City of Vancouver.

City of Vancouver (2013) "Greenest City 2020 Action Plan 2012–2013 Implementation Update." Vancouver, BC: City of Vancouver.

City of Vancouver (2014) "A Healthy City for All: Vancouver's Healthy City Strategy, 2014–2025." Vancouver, BC: City of Vancouver.

City of Vancouver (2014) "Downtown Eastside Plan." Vancouver, BC: City of Vancouver.

City of Vancouver (2014) "Energy Retrofit Strategy for Existing Buildings." Vancouver, BC: City of Vancouver.

City of Vancouver (2015) "2014 Transportation Monitoring Report." Vancouver, BC: City of Vancouver.

City of Vancouver (2015) "Greenest City 2020 Action Plan 2014–2015 Implementation Update." Vancouver, BC: City of Vancouver.

City of Vancouver (2015) "Greenest City 2020 Action Plan Part Two: 2015–2020." Vancouver, BC: City of Vancouver.

City of Vancouver (2015) "Marpole Community Plan." Vancouver, BC: City of Vancouver.

City of Vancouver (2016) "Press Release: New Fund to Spur Energy Efficiency Upgrades for Buildings." February 4, www.electricenergyonline.com/detail_news.php?ID=563223&cat=;16;89&niveauAQ=0 (accessed January 17, 2017).

City of Vancouver (n.d.) "Clarification of Our Position on Natural Gas." City of Vancouver, http://vancouver.ca/news-calendar/clarification-of-citys-position-on-natural-gas.aspx (accessed January 17, 2017).

City of Vancouver (n.d.) "Community Planning 101 – Backgrounder." Vancouver, BC: City of Vancouver.

City of Vancouver (n.d.) "Creating and Preserving Market Rental Housing." http://vancouver.ca/people-programs/creating-new-market-rental-housing.aspx (accessed February 3, 2015).

City of Vancouver (n.d.) "Energy-Efficiency Requirements and Resources for New Homes." City of Vancouver, http://vancouver.ca/home-property-development/energy-efficiency-requirements-and-resources-for-new-homes.aspx (accessed July 7, 2016).

City of Vancouver (n.d.) "Healthy City Strategy Success Stories." City of Vancouver, http://vancouver.ca/people-programs/healthy-city-strategy-success-stories.aspx (accessed March 1, 2017).

City of Vancouver (n.d.) "Protected Bicycle Lanes." City of Vancouver, http://vancouver.ca/streets-transportation/protected-bicycle-lanes.aspx (accessed August 11, 2016).

City of Vancouver (n.d.) "Vancouver Takes Next Step to Advance Renewable City Strategy." City of Vancouver, http://vancouver.ca/news-calendar/vancouver-takes-next-step-to-advance-renewable-city-strategy.aspx (accessed January 17, 2017).

City of Vancouver (n.d.) "Vancouver Wins C40 Cities Award for Greenest City Action Plan at COP21 in Paris." City of Vancouver, http://vancouver.ca/news-calendar/vancouver-wins-c40-cities-award-for-greenest-city-action-plan.aspx (accessed January 18, 2017).

Clark, Jordan (2012) "Vancouver's Built Environment Initiatives." In *Urban Sustainability Programs: Case Studies*, ed. David J. Hess. www.davidjhess.org/ (accessed May 23, 2017).

Clark, Terry Nichols, Richard Lloyd, Kenneth K. Wong, and Pushpam Jain (2002) "Amenities Drive Urban Growth." *Journal of Urban Affairs* 24, no. 5. 493–515.

Clarke, Susan E., and Gary L. Gaile (1998) *The Work of Cities*. Globalization and Community. Minneapolis, MN: University of Minnesota Press.

Condon, Patrick M. (2014) "Vancouver's 'Spot Zoning' Is Corrupting Its Soul." *The Tyee*, July 14.

Connor, Neil (2006) "Miliband Backs Brum Campaign." *Birmingham Post*, October 26.

Cooper, Merrill (2006) "Social Sustainability in Vancouver." Ottawa, Ontario: Canadian Policy Research Networks.

Coulson, Andrew, and Geoff Wright (2013) "Brindleyplace, Birmingham: Creating an Inner City Mixed-Used Development in Times of Recession." *Planning Practice & Research* 28: 256–74.

Coyle, Stephen (2011) *Sustainable and Resilient Communities: A Comprehensive Action Plan for Towns, Cities, and Regions*. Hoboken, NJ: John Wiley & Sons, Inc.

Crain's Chicago Business (2014) "Why Emanuel's Chicago Infrastructure Trust Is Off to Such a Slow Start." May 16.

Cronin, Anne M., and Kevin Hetherington (2008) "Introduction." In *Consuming the Entrepreneurial City: Image, Memory, Spectacle*, ed. Kevin Hetherington and Anne M. Cronin, 1–17. New York, NY: Routledge.

Cronon, William (1991) *Nature's Metropolis: Chicago and the Great West*. 1st edn. New York, NY: W. W. Norton.

Crossa, Veronica, Montserrat Pareja-Eastaway, and Austin Barber (2010) "Reinventing the City: Barcelona, Birmingham and Dublin." In *Making Competitive Cities*, ed. Sako Musterd and Alan Murie. Chichester, UK: John Wiley & Sons Ltd.

Culbert, Lori, and Chad Skelton (2014) "Housing Affordability a Hot Topic." *Vancouver Sun*, October 18.

Curbed (2016) "What Will the Cabrini-Green of the Future Look Like?" Curbed, http://chicago.curbed.com/2016/1/7/10848958/what-will-the-cabrinigreen-of-the-future-look-like (accessed July 28, 2016).

Curran, Winifred, and Trina Hamilton (2012) "Just Green Enough: Contesting Environmental Gentrification in Greenpoint, Brooklyn." *Local Environment* 17, no. 9: 1027–42.

Dale, Ann, and Lenore L. Newman (2009) "Sustainable Development for Some: Green Urban Development and Affordability." *Local Environment* 14, no. 7: 669–81.

Dale, Paul (2007) "Council Pledge to Slash CO2 in Brum by Two Thirds." *Birmingham Post*, September 8.

Dale, Paul (2007) "Global Warming 'Now Bigger Threat than Terrorism'." *Birmingham Post*, January 23.

Daniels, Steve (2012) "Midwest Generation Files Chapter 11." *Crain's Chicago Business*, December 17.

Davies, Alex (2012) "Rahm Emanuel Thinks Bike Lanes Will Attract Tech Companies to Chicago." *Business Insider*, December 5.

DECC (2014) "2012 Sub-Regional Fuel Poverty Data: Low Income High Costs Indicator." Department of Energy & Climate Change, 2014. DECC. "Annual Fuel Poverty Statistics Report, 2014." Department of Energy & Climate Change.

DECC (2014) "Foundations in Place: The Green Deal and ECO Annual Report." Department of Energy & Climate Change.

Delmelle, Elizabeth C., Eva Haslauer, and Thomas Prinz (2013) "Social Satisfaction, Commuting and Neighborhoods." *Journal of Transport Geography* 30: 110–16.

Demissie, Fassil (2006) "Globalization and the Remaking of Chicago." In *The New Chicago: A Social and Cultural Analysis*, ed. John P. Koval, Larry Bennett, Michael I. J. Bennett, Fassil Demissie, Roberta Garner, and Kiljoong Kim. Philadelphia, PA: Temple University Press.

de Moncuit, Lucas (2014) "Carbonn Cities Climate Registry: 2013 Annual Report." Bonn: Bonn Center for Local Climate Action and Reporting.

Department for the Environment, Food, and Rural Affairs (2004) "Press Release: £15.5 Million Heating Boost for Thousands of Homes, September 16, 2004." Hermes Database.

Department for the Environment, Food, and Rural Affairs (2006) "Press Release: £10.6 Million for Energy Efficient Community Heating." Hermes Database.

Desfor, Gene, and Roger Keil (2004) *Nature and the City: Making Environmental Policy in Toronto and Los Angeles*. Tucson, AZ: University of Arizona Press.

Dhillon, Sunny (2015) "Controversial Vancouver Bike Lane Seems to Be Effective." *Globe and Mail*, January 1.

Dooling, Sarah (2009) "Ecological Gentrification: A Research Agenda Exploring Justice in the City." *International Journal of Urban and Regional Research* 33, no. 3: 621–39.

Drummond, Ian, and Terry Marsden (1999) *The Condition of Sustainability*. New York, NY: Routledge.

Drury, Ivan (2014) "Vancouver Rightists Rising against the Downtown Eastside." *The Mainlander*, March 10.

Dryzek, John S., Christian Hunold, David Schlosberg, David Downes, and Hans Hernes (2002) "Environmental Transformation of the State: The USA, Norway, Germany and the UK." *Political Studies* 50: 659–82.

Dryzek, John S., Richard B. Norgaard, and David Schlosberg (2013) *Climate-Challenged Society*. New York, NY: Oxford University Press.

Dumke, Mick (2008) "Green and Long Green: Daley's Environmental Commissioner on Making Business as Usual Eco-Friendly." *Chicago Reader*, June 5.

Dumke, Mick (2008) "The Political Climate." *Chicago Reader*, September 19.

Durning, Alan (2013) *Unlocking Home: Three Keys to Affordable Communities*. Seattle, WA: Sightline Institute.

Eby, David (2007) "Still Waiting at the Altar: Vancouver 2010's on-Again, Off-Again, Relationship with Social Sustainability." Geneva, Switzerland: COHRE Expert Workshop on Protecting and Promoting Housing Rights in the Context of Mega Events.

Echenique, Marcial H., Anthony J. Hargreaves, Gordon Mitchell, and Anil Namdeo (2012) "Growing Cities Sustainably." *Journal of the American Planning Association* 78, no. 2: 121–37.

Economist (2002) "Green Machine." *Economist*, August 15.

Economist (2006) "Chicago: A Success Story." *Economist*, March 16.

Economist (2015) "Beyond Petroleum." *Economist*, January 31.

Economist Intelligence Unit (2011) "US and Canada Green City Index: Assessing the Environmental Performance of 27 Major US and Canadian Cities." Munich, Germany: Siemens.

Edelson, Nathan, and Karen O'Shannacery (2014) "Revitalizing the Heart of the City." *The Tyee*, March 13.

Ehrenhalt, Alan (2012) "A Neighborhood in Chicago." In *The Great Inversion and the Future of the American City*. New York, NY: Alfred A. Knopf.

Ehrlich, Paul R. (1969) *The Population Bomb*. San Francisco, CA: Sierra Club.

Elgie, Stewart, and Jessica McClay (2013) "BCs Carbon Tax Shift Is Working Well after Four Years (Attention Ottawa)." *Canadian Public Policy / Analyse de Politiques* 39, no. Supplement: S1–S10.

Elkes, Neil (2016) "Why Six Cycle Lanes Have Been Scrapped and 'Superhighways' Are In." *Birmingham Mail*, December 14.

Elkes, Neil (2017) "How Cutting Parks Budget Will Cost Birmingham More in the Long Run." *Birmingham Mail*, January 3.

Elliot, Larry (2010) "10,000 Birmingham Council Homes to Get Solar Panels." *UK Guardian*, October 3.

Emanuel, Rahm (2011) "Chicago 2011 Transition Plan." Chicago, IL.

ENDS Report 430 (2010) "Councils Invest in Renewables for Housing." November 30, 17–18.

Eriksen, Siri, Paulina Aldunce, Chandra Sekhar Bahinipati, Rafael D'Almeida Martins, John Isaac Molefe, Charles Nhemachena, Karen O'Brien, *et al.* (2011) "When Not Every Response to Climate Change Is a Good One: Identifying Principles for Sustainable Adaptation." *Climate and Development* 3, no. 1: 7–20.

Erickson, Donna L. (2006) *Metrogreen: Connecting Open Space in North American Cities*. Washington, DC: Island Press.

EU Committee of the Regions (2007) "Eastside – Masshouse Redevelopment." http://pes.cor.europa.eu/NEWS/Documents/News/2007/01%20Example%20 by%20Albert%20BORE_EN.pdf (accessed May 23, 2017).

Evans, J.P. (2012) *Environmental Governance*. New York, NY: Routledge.

Farmer, Stephanie (2011) "Uneven Public Transportation Development in Neoliberalizing Chicago, USA." *Environment and Planning A* 43: 1154–72.

Federal Energy Management Program (2000) "Energy Efficiency Improvements through the Use of Combined Heat and Power (CHP) in Buildings." Washington, DC: U.S. Department of Environment.

Ferenchak, Nicholson N, and Wesley E Marshall (2016) "The Relative (in) Effectiveness of Bicycle Sharrows on Ridership and Safety Outcomes." In *Transportation Research Board 95th Annual Meeting*. Washington, DC.

Field Museum (2009) "Engaging Chicago Communities in the Chicago Climate Action Plan, Community #1: South Chicago." Chicago, IL: The Field Museum Environment, Culture, and Conservation Program.

Fitzgerald, Joan (2010) *Emerald Cities: Urban Sustainability and Economic Development*. New York, NY: Oxford University Press.

Flatman, Ben (2008) *Birmingham: Shaping the City*. Birmingham, UK: RIBA Publishing.

Florida, Richard L. (2004) *The Rise of the Creative Class: And How It's Transforming Work, Leisure, Community and Everyday Life*. New York, NY: Basic Books.

Freemark, Yonah (2015) "Minneapolis Strikes Again: How Chicago Could Revamp Its Parking Requirements." Metropolitan Planning Council, June 18, www.metroplanning.org/news/blog-post/7162 (accessed July 9, 2015).

Friedman, Milton (2002 [1962]) *Capitalism and Freedom*. Chicago, IL: University of Chicago Press, Fortieth Anniversary Edition.

Gabriel, Keith (2014) "Cycle Revolution Long Overdue in Car-Clogged Brum." *Birmingham Post*, June 12.

Gaffkin, Frank, and Barney Warf (1993) "Urban Policy and the Post-Keynesian State in the United Kingdom and the United States." *International Journal of Urban and Regional Research* 17, no. 1 (1993): 67–84.

Gallun, Ably, and Greg Hinz (2005) "City Floats Tax Hike for Loop." *Crain's Chicago Business*, August 29.

Garcia-Mila, Teresa, and Therese J. McGuire (2002) "Tax Incentives and the City." *Brookings-Wharton Papers on Urban Affairs*, 95–132.

Garrard, Jan, Susan Handy, and Jennier Dill (2012) "Women and Cycling." In *City Cycling*, ed. John Pucher and Ralph Buehler. Cambridge, MA: MIT Press.

Geary, Joanna (2005) "Carbon Trading a Weapon in Battle for the Environment." *Birmingham Post*, July 27.

Geary, Joanna (2006) "Tomorrow's World: Eastside in the Green Spotlight." *Birmingham Post*, November 28.

Gibbs, David, Andy Jonas, and Aidan While (2002) "Changing Governance Structures and the Environment: Economy–Environment Relations at the Local and Regional Scales." *Journal of Environmental Policy & Planning* 4: 123–38.

Gilbert, Richard, and Anthony Perl (2010) "Transportation in the Post-Carbon World." In *The Post-Carbon Reader: Managing the 21st Century's Sustainability Crisis*, ed. Richard Heinberg and Daniel Lerch. Healdsburg, CA: Watershed Media.

Gilfoyle, Timothy J. (2006) *Millennium Park: Creating a Chicago Landmark*. Historical Studies of Urban America. Chicago, IL: University of Chicago Press.

Glaeser, Edward (2011) *Triumph of the City: How Our Greatest Invention Makes Us Richer, Smarter, Greener, Healthier, and Happier*. New York, NY: The Penguin Press.

Go Bronzeville (n.d.) "About." http://gobronzeville.org/about (accessed August 16, 2016).

Goar, Carol (1996) "Asphalt Gardens." *Toronto Star*, August 18.

Goldstein, Jesse (2013) "Appropriate Technocracies? Green Capitalist Discourses and Post Capitalist Desires." *Capitalism Nature Socialism* 24, no. 1 (2013): 26–34.

Goodman Williams Group, and URS Corporation (2005) *Millennium Park Economic Impact Study*. Chicago, IL: Prepared for City of Chicago Department of Planning and Development.

Gordon, David, and Michele Acuto (2015) "If Cities Are the Solution, What Are the Problems? The Promise and Perils of Urban Climate Leadership." In *The Urban Climate Challenge: Rethinking the Role of Cities in the Global Climate Regime*, ed. Craig Johnson, Noah Toly, and Heike Schroeder. New York, NY: Routledge.

Gordon, J. (2007) "Is Your City Green?" *MSN City Guides*. http://cityguides.msn. com/citylife/greenarticle.aspx?cp-documentid=4848590 (accessed October 3, 2007).

Gosden, Emily (2014) "Government Fuel Poverty Strategy 'Meaningless' and 'Inadequate', Campaigners Warn." *Telegraph*, July 22.

Greenberg, Miriam (2008) *Branding New York: How a City in Crisis Was Sold to the World*. New York, NY: Routledge.

Greenfield, John (2011) "Life Cycle: How Did Chicago's Progressive New Transportation Czar Gabe Klein Get That Way?" www.newcity.com/2011/12/07/life-cycle-how-did-chicago%E2%80%99s-progressive-new-transportation-czar-gabe-klein-get-that-way/ (accessed August 16, 2016).

Greenfield, John (2012) "Bike Facilities Don't Have to Be 'the White Lanes of Gentrification'." In *Grid Chicago*. Chicago, IL.

Greenfield, John (2014) "The Pros and Cons of Divvy's New Expansion Map." http://chi.streetsblog.org/2014/08/22/the-pros-and-cons-of-divvys-new-expansion-map/ – more-96287 (accessed August 16, 2016).

Greenfield, John (2015) "CDOT's Sean Wiedel Provides an Update on Divvy Installation, Equity Efforts." http://chi.streetsblog.org/2015/04/24/cdots-weidel-provides-update-on-divvy-installation-equity-efforts/-more-101485 (accessed August 16, 2016).

Greenfield, John (2015) "More Deets on the Divvy Funding Situation." http://chi.streetsblog.org/2015/07/24/more-deets-on-the-divvy-funding-situation/ (accessed August 16, 2016).

Greenfield, John (2016) "Activists Worry CTA-Friendly Housing Will Accelerate Logan Square Gentrification." *Chicago Reader*, April 18.

Greenfield, John (2016) "Little Village Residents Hope Paseo Won't Be a Path to Gentrification." *Chicago Reader*, March 23.

Grimshaw, Jacky (2016) "One Development Ordinance Does Not Serve All Neighborhoods." *Crain's Chicago Business*, July 22.

Grossinger, Annie (2016) "Affordable Divvy for Everyone Enters Second Year." LISC Chicago, www.lisc-chicago.org/news/2679 (accessed August 16, 2016).

Guardian (2011) "Canada Pulls out of Kyoto." *The Guardian*, December 12.

Guardian (2013) "David Cameron at Centre of 'Get Rid of All the Green Crap' Storm." *Guardian*, November 21.

Guardian (2014) "The Scandal of Britain's Fuel Poverty Deaths." *Guardian*, September 11.

Hackworth, Jason R. (2007) *The Neoliberal City: Governance, Ideology, and Development in American Urbanism*. Ithaca, NY: Cornell University Press.

Hager, Mike (2016) "Real Estate Developers Slammed B.C. Over Surprise Foreign-Buyer Tax." *Globe and Mail*, December=13.

Hajer, Maarten A. (1995) *The Politics of Environmental Discourse: Ecological Modernization and the Policy Process*. New York, NY: Oxford University Press.

Hall, C. Michael (2006) "Urban Entrepreneurship, Corporate Interests and Sports Mega-Events: The Thin Policies of Competitiveness within the Hard Outcomes of Neoliberalism." *The Sociological Review* 54, no. Supplement s2: 59–70.

Hall, Tim (2004) "Public Art, Civic Identity and the New Birmingham." In *Remaking Birmingham: The Visual Culture of Urban Regeneration*, ed. Liam Kennedy. New York, NY: Routledge.

Hall, Tim, and Phil Hubbard, eds. (1998) *The Entrepreneurial City: Geographies of Politics, Regime, and Representation.* Chichester, UK: Wiley.

Hammer, Stephen, Lamia Kamal-Chaoui, Alexis Robert, and Marissa Plouin (2011) "Cities and Green Growth: A Conceptual Framework," *OECD Regional Development Working Papers* 2011/08." OECD Publishing.

Harbell, James W. (2002) "Canada Tackles Environmental Problems: There Are Some Differences up North." *Business Law Today* 12, no. 2: 36–41.

Harrison, Kathryn (1996) *Passing the Buck: Federalism and Canadian Environmental Policy.* Vancouver, BC: UBC Press.

Harvey, David (2005) *A Brief History of Neoliberalism.* New York, NY: Oxford University Press.

Harvey, David (1989) "From Managerialism to Entrepreneurialism: The Transformation in Urban Governance in Late Capitalism." *Geografiska Annaler, Series B, Human Geography* 71, no. 1: 3–17.

Harvey, David (1989) *The Condition of Postmodernity: An Enquiry into the Origins of Cultural Change.* New York, NY: Blackwell.

Hatchwell, Paul (2014) "Climate Policies Add Little to Energy Bills, Says CCC." *ENDS Report*, December 11.

Hatchwell, Paul (2014) "Green Deal Uptake Too Slow." *ENDS Report*, February 25, 33–4.

Haughton, Graham, and Aidan While (1999) "From Corporate City to Citizens City? Urban Leadership after Local Entrepreneurialism in the United Kingdom." *Urban Affairs Review* 35, no. 1: 3–23.

Hays, Samuel P. (2000) *A History of Environmental Politics since 1945.* Pittsburgh, PA: University of Pittsburgh Press.

Hendriks, Frank (1999) *Public Policy and Political Institutions: The Role of Culture in Traffic Policy.* New Horizons in Public Policy. Cheltenham, UK: Edward Elgar.

Henriques, Irene, and Perry Sadorsky (2008) "Voluntary Environmental Programs: A Canadian Perspective." *The Policy Studies Journal* 36, no. 1: 143–66.

Heynen, Nik, Maria Kaika, and Erik Swyngedouw, eds. (2006) *In the Nature of Cities: Urban Political Ecology and the Politics of Urban Metabolism.* New York, NY: Routledge.

Hillman, G. Robert (1996) "Return to the National Stage." *Dallas Morning News*, August 25.

Hinz, Greg (1996) "'96 Convention Countdown; the $180-Million Party; City's Primping for Democrats Adds Up." *Crain's Chicago Business*, August 19.

Hinz, Greg (2013) "The Hottest Urban Center in the U.S. – Chicago's Mega-Loop." *Crain's Chicago Business*, March 2.

Hinz, Greg (2016) "City Touches the Brakes on Bike-Lane Expansion." *Crain's Chicago Business*, April 11.

Holcomb, Briavel (1993) "Revisioning Place: De- and Re-Constructing the Image of the Post-Industrial City." In *Selling Places: The City as Cultural Capital, Past and Present*, ed. Gerard Kearns and Chris Philo. Oxford, UK: Pergamon Press.

Howard, Richard (2015) "Warmer Homes: Improving Fuel Poverty and Energy Efficiency Policy in the UK." Policy Exchange.

Howlett, Debbie (2004) "Donors' Cash Turns City Green." *USA Today*, July 15.

Howlett, Michael (2000) "Beyond Legalism? Policy Ideas, Implementation Styles and Emulation-Based Convergence in Canadian and U.S. Environmental Policy." *Journal of Public Policy* 20, no. 3: 205–329.

Hubbard, Phil (1995) "Urban Design and Local Economic Development: A Case Study in Birmingham." *Cities* 12, no. 4: 243–51.

Hubbard, Phil, and Tim Hall (1998) "The Entrepreneurial City and the 'New Urban Politics'." In *The Entrepreneurial City: Geographies of Politics, Regime, and Representation*, ed. Tim Hall and Phil Hubbard. Chichester, UK: Wiley.

Hume, Mark (2015) "Vancouver's Green Shift to Renewable Energy by 2050 Is a 'Realistic Target'." *Globe and Mail*, November 2.

Hunter, Justine (2008) "Vision Prevails in Landslide Victory." *Globe and Mail*, November 17.

Imrie, Robert, and Mike Raco (2003) "Community and the Changing Nature of Urban Policy." In *Urban Renaissance? New Labour, Community and Urban Policy*, ed. Robert Imrie and Mike Raco. Bristol, UK: Policy Press.

IPCC (2014) "Climate Change 2014: Synthesis Report Summary for Policy Makers."

Irish Times (2004) "Civic Regeneration Brings Property Boom to Chicago." *Irish Times*, September 23.

Jackson, Emily (2015) "Transit Ridership Slips in Vancouver Where System Is 'at Capacity': City Report." *Metro News*, May 12.

Jacobs, Jane (1969) *The Economy of Cities*. New York, NY: Random House.

James, Sarah, and Torbjorn Lahti (2004) *The Natural Step for Communities: How Cities and Towns Can Change to Sustainable Practices*. Gabriola Island, BC: New Society Publishers.

Janos, Nik, and Corina McKendry (2014) "Globalization, Governance, and Re-Naturing the Industrial City: Chicago, IL and Seattle, WA." In *The Power of Cities in International Relations*, ed. Simon Curtis. New York, NY: Routledge.

Jefferson, Ian, Chris Rogers, and Dexter Hunt (2006) "Achieving Sustainable Underground Construction in Birmingham Eastside?" *IAEG2006 Paper number 312.*

Jenks, Mike, Elizabeth Burton, and Katie Williams, eds. (1996) *The Compact City: A Sustainable Urban Form?* London, UK: E & FN Spon.

Jessop, Bob (1997) "The Entrepreneurial City: Re-Imagining Localities, Redesigning Economic Governance, or Restructuring Capital?" In *Transforming Cities: Contested Governance and New Spatial Divisions*, ed. Nick Jewson and Susanne MacGregor. New York, NY: Routledge.

Johnson, Craig, Heike Schroeder, and Noah Toly (2015) "Introduction: Urban Resilience, Low Carbon Governance and the Global Climate Regime." In *The Urban Climate Challenge: Rethinking the Role of Cities in the Global Climate Regime*, ed. Craig Johnson, Noah Toly, and Heike Schroeder. New York, NY: Routledge.

Johnson, Craig, Noah Toly, and Heike Schroeder, eds. (2015) *The Urban Climate Challenge: Rethinking the Role of Cities in the Global Climate Regime*. New York, NY: Routledge.

Johnson, Elmer W. (2001) *Chicago Metropolis 2020: The Chicago Plan for the Twenty-First Century*. Chicago, IL: University of Chicago Press.

Johnson, Lisa, and Tamara Baluja (2015) "Transit Referendum: Voters Say No to New Metro Vancouver Tax, Transit Improvements." *CBC News*, July 2.

Johnston, Sadhu Aufochs, Steven S. Nicholas, and Julia Parzen (2013) *The Guide to Greening Cities*. Washington, DC: Island Press.

Johnstone, Craig, and Mark Whitehead (2004) "Horizons and Barriers in British Urban Policy." In *New Horizons in British Urban Policy: Perspectives on New*

Labour's Urban Renaissance, ed. Craig Johnstone and Mark Whitehead. Burlington, VT: Ashgate.

Jonas, Andrew E.G., and Aidan While (2007) "Greening the Entrepreneurial City? Looking for Spaces of Sustainability Politics in the Competitive City." In *The Sustainable Development Paradox: Urban Political Economy in the United States and Europe*, ed. Rob Krueger and David Gibbs. New York, NY: Guilford Press.

Jonas, Andrew E.G., and Kevin Ward (2002) "A World of Regionalisms? Towards a US-UK Urban and Regional Policy Framework Comparison." *Journal of Urban Affairs* 24, no. 4: 377–401.

Joravsky, Ben (2010) "Go On, Smash It." *Chicago Reader*, August 19.

Jordan, Andrew (1998) "Impact on UK Environmental Administration." In *British Environmental Policy and Europe: Politics and Policy in Transition*, ed. Philip Lowe and Stephen Ward. London, UK: Routledge.

Joseph, Mark, and Robert Chaskin (2010) "Living in Mixed-Income Development: Resident Perceptions of the Benefits and Disadvantages of Two Developments in Chicago." *Urban Studies* 47, no. 11: 2347–66.

Judd, Dennis R. (2002 [1995]) "Promoting Tourism in US Cities." In *Readings in Urban Theory*, ed. Susan S. Fainstein and Scott Campbell. Malden, MA: Blackwell Publishers.

Judd, Dennis R., and Randy L. Ready (1986) "Entrepreneurial Cities and the New Politics of Economic Development." In *Reagan and the Cities*, ed. George E. Peterson and Carol W. Lewis. Washington, DC: Urban Institute Press.

Kahn, Mitch (2004) "Book Review: Paradise Lost." *Shelterforce Online*, no. 138.

Kamin, Blair (2004) "Will Chicago's Long-Awaited Millennium Park Be Fine Art or Spectacle? Perhaps a Little of Both." *Architectural Record* 192, no. 5: 61.

Kamin, Blair (2015) "Transit-Oriented Apartment Projects a Positive Development." *Chicago Tribune*, March 21.

Karlenzig, Warren (2007) *How Green Is Your City?* Gabriola Island, B.C.: New Society Publishers.

Kear, Mark (2007) "Spaces of Transition Spaces of Tomorrow: Making a Sustainable Future in Southeast False Creek, Vancouver." *Cities* 24, no. 4: 324–34.

Keil, Roger (2009) "The Urban Politics of Roll-with-It Neoliberalism." *City* 13, no. 2–3: 231–45.

Kennedy, Liam (2004) "The Creative Destruction of Birmingham." In *Remaking Birmingham: The Visual Culture of Urban Regeneration*, ed. Liam Kenned. New York, NY: Routledge.

Kinzer, Stephen (2004) "A Prized Project, a Mayor and Persistent Criticism." *New York Times*, July 13.

Kirby, Sarah (2014) "Press Release: Plans for More than 2,000 New Homes." Birmingham, UK: Birmingham City Council, May 12, http://birminghamnews-room.com/plans-for-more-than-2000-new-homes/ (accessed March 6, 2017).

Koval, John P. *et al.*, eds. (2006) *The New Chicago: A Social and Cultural Analysis*. Philadelphia, PA: Temple University Press.

Koziarz, Jay (2016) "Abandonded Rail Tracks Will See 606-Style Trail Come to Pilsen Neighborhood." *Curbed Chicago*, March 21.

Kraft, Michael E. (2007) *Environmental Policy and Politics*. 4th edn. New York, NY: Pearson/Longman.

Krohe, James Jr.(1990) "Green Streets: Mayor Daley Has a Thing for Trees. He Wants Half a Million of Them Planted Here by 1992." *Chicago Reader*, January 18.

Krueger, Rob, and David Gibbs, eds. (2007) *The Sustainable Development Paradox: Urban Political Economy in the United States and Europe*. New York, NY: Guilford Press.

Kutting, Gabriela, and Ronnie Lipschutz, eds. (2009) *Environmental Governance: Power and Knowledge in a Local-Global World*. New York, NY: Routledge.

Latham, Ian, and Mark Swenarton, eds. (1999) *Brindleyplace: A Model for Urban Regeneration*. London, UK: Right Angle Publishing Ltd.

Latrace, A.J. (2017) "New Logan Square Transit-Oriented Development Quietly Opens." Curbed Chicago, http://chicago.curbed.com/2017/1/23/14363678/logan-square-apartment-for-rent-mode (accessed March 6, 2017).

Layzer, Judith A. (2014) *Open for Business: Conservatives' Opposition to Environmental Regulation*. Cambridge, MA: MIT Press.

Lee, Jeff (2014) "Jury Is Still out on Impact of Downtown Vancouver Bike Lanes." *Vancouver Sun*, September 27.

Lee, Jeff (2014) "Party Moved 'Too Fast' on East Van Towers Bid." *Vancouver Sun*, May 5.

Lee, Jeff (2015) "Citizens' Assembly Releases Grandview-Woodland Report." *Vancouver Sun*, June 19.

Lee, Marc (2014) "Fair and Effective Carbon Pricing: Lessons from Bc." Vancouver, BC: Canadian Centre for Policy Alternatives & Sierra Club BC.

Lee, Phillip (2002) "The Economic and Social Justification for Publicly Financed Stadia: The Case of Vancouver's BC Place Stadium." *European Planning Studies* 10, no. 7: 861–73.

Lee, Taedong (2015) *Global Cities and Climate Change: The Translocal Relations of Environmental Governance*. New York, NY: Routledge.

Lehmann, Steffan (2010) *The Principles of Green Urbanism: Transforming the City for Sustainability*. Washington, DC: Earthscan.

Leitner, Helga (1990) "Cities in Pursuit of Economic Growth: The Local State as Entrepreneur." *Political Geography Quarterly* 9, no. 2: 146–70.

Leitner, Helga, Jamie Peck, and Eric S. Sheppard, eds. (2007) *Contesting Neoliberalism: Urban Frontiers*. New York, NY: Guilford Press.

Lemos, Maria Carmen, and Arun Agrewal (2006) "Environmental Governance." *Annual Review of Environment and Resources* 31: 297–325.

Leone, Roberto, and Barbara W. Carroll (2010) "Decentralisation and Devolution in Canadian Social Housing Policy." *Environment and Planning C: Government and Policy* 28: 389–404.

Levin, Alex, Matt Milkovich, and Gray Turek (2016) "Bicycle Resource Equity in Chicago." Chicago, IL: DePaul University.

Levy, Diane K., Zachary J. McDade, and Kassie Dumlao Bertumen (2011) "Effects from Living in Mixed-Income Communities for Low-Income Families: A Review of the Literature." Washington, DC: Urban Institute.

Ley, David (1996) *The New Middle Class and the Remaking of the Central City*. Oxford, UK: Oxford University Press.

Ley, David, and Cory Dobson (2008) "Are There Limits to Gentrification? The Contexts of Impeded Gentrification in Vancouver." *Urban Studies* 45, no. 12: 2471–98.

Ley, David, Daniel Hiebert, and Geraldine Pratt (1992) "Time to Grow Up? From Urban Village to World City, 1966–91." In *Vancouver and Its Region*, ed. Graeme Wynn and Timothy Oke. Vancouver, BC: UBC Press.

Litman, Todd (2015) "Evaluation Public Transit Benefits and Costs." Victoria, BC: Victoria Transport Policy Institute.

Loftman, Patrick, and Brendan Nevin (1998) "Pro-Growth Local Economic Development Strategies: Civic Promotion and Local Needs in Britain's Second City, 1981–1996." In *The Entrepreneurial City: Geographies of Politics, Regime, and Representation*, ed. Tim Hall and Phil Hubbard. Chichester, UK: Wiley.

Logan Square Neighborhood Association (2017) "Issues and Programs." Logan Square Neighborhood Association, www.lsna.net/Issues-and-programs/index.html (accessed May 23, 2017).

Lopez, Jose (2012) "Jose Lopez Offers the PRCC's Perspective on the Paseo Bike Lanes." In *Grid Chicago*. Chicago, IL.

Longworth, Richard C. (2004) "The Political City." In *Global Chicago*, ed. Charles Madigan. Urbana, IL: University of Illinois Press.

Low, Setha, Dana Taplin, and Suzanne Scheld (2005) *Rethinking Urban Parks: Public Space and Cultural Diversity*. Austin, TX: The University of Texas Press.

Lowe, Philip, and Stephen Ward (1998) "Britain in Europe: Themes and Issues in National Environmental Policy." In *British Environmental Policy and Europe: Politics and Policy in Transition*, ed. Philip Lowe and Stephen Ward. London: Routledge.

Lowe, Philip, and Stephen Ward (1998) "Domestic Winners and Losers." In *British Environmental Policy and Europe: Politics and Policy in Transition*, ed. Philip Lowe and Stephen Ward. London, UK: Routledge.

Lydersen, Kari (2013) *Mayor 1%: Rahm Emanuel and the Rise of Chicago's 99%*. Chicago, IL: Haymarket Books.

Lydersen, Kari (2014) *Closing the Cloud Factories: Lessons from the Fight to Shut Down Chicago's Coal Plants*. Chicago, IL: Midwest Energy News.

Mackie, John (2015) "Tower Proposal Splits Commercial Drive." *Vancouver Sun*, August 6.

Madrid, Jorge, and Bracken Hendricks (2011) "The Recovery Act: The Most Important Energy Bill in American History." Grist, http://grist.org/green-jobs/2011-02-16-the-most-important-energy-bill-in-american-history/ (accessed July 5, 2016).

Malpass, Peter, and David Mullins (2001) "Local Authority Housing Stock Transfer in the Uk: From Local Initiative to National Policy." *Housing Studies* 17, no. 4: 673–86.

Marketing Birmingham (2009) "Annual Review 2008–2009." Birmingham, UK.

Marketing Birmingham (2009) "Birmingham Visitor Economy Overview." Birmingham, UK.

Marlow, Iain, and Brent Jang (2014) "Vancouver's Real Estate Boom: The Rising Price of 'Heaven'." *Globe and Mail*, October 10.

Martin, Steve, and Graham Pearce (1992) "Policy Review: The Internationalization of Local Authority Economic Development Strategies: Birmingham in the 1980s." *Regional Studies* 26, no. 5: 499–503.

Mayor's Bicycle Advisory Council (1992) "The Bike 2000 Plan." Chicago, IL: City of Chicago.

Mayors Climate Protection Center (2010) "Taking Local Action: Mayors and Climate Protection Best Practices." The United States Conference of Mayors.

Mayster, Alex (2016) "5 Up-and-Coming Neighborhoods in Chicago to Buy a Home." *U.S. News & World Report*, August 9, 2016.

Mazmanian, Daniel A., and Michael E. Kraft (1999) "The Three Epochs of the Environmental Movement." In *Toward Sustainable Communities*, ed. Daniel A. Mazmanian and Michael E. Kraft. Cambridge, MA: MIT Press.

McCarthy, James (2013) "We Have Never Been 'Post-Political'." *Capitalism Nature Socialism* 24, no. 1: 19–25.

McElroy, Justin (2016) "One Chart Shows How Unprecedented Vancouver's Real Estate Situation Is." *Global News*, February 21.

McGlone, Conor (2014) "DECC Admits Energy Firms Benefit from ECO Cuts." *ENDS Report*, July 28.

McKendry, Corina (2011) Smokestacks to Green Roofs: City Environmentalism, Green Urban Entrepreneurialism, and the Regulation of the Postindustrial City. PhD Dissertation: University of California Santa Cruz.

McKendry, Corina (2012) "Environmental Discourse and Economic Growth in the Greening of Postindustrial Cities." In *The Economy of Green Cities: World Compendium on the Green Urban Economy*, ed. R. Simpson and M. Zimmermann. New York, NY: Springer.

McKendry, Corina (2016) "Cities and the Challenge of Multiscalar Climate Justice: Climate Governance and Social Equity in Chicago, Birmingham, and Vancouver." *Local Environment* 21, no. 11: 1354–71.

McKendry, Corina (2016). "Participation, Power, and the Politics of Multiscalar Climate Justice." In *The Social Ecology of the Anthropocene*, ed. Richard Matthew, Kristen Goodrich, Connor Harron, Bemmy Maharramov, and Evgenia Nizkorodov: World Scientific Publishers.

McKenzie, Brian (2014) "Modes Less Traveled – Bicycling and Walking to Work in the United States: 2008–2012." In *American Community Survey Reports*. United States: U.S. Census Bureau.

McMartin, Pete (2013) "Down with the Rich! And While We're at It, Bike Lanes!" *Vancouver Sun*, July 30.

Meadows, Donella H., and Dennis L. Meadows (1972) *The Limits to Growth. A Report for the Club of Rome's "Project on the Predicament of Mankinds."* New York, NY: Universe Books.

MEEA (2015) "Retrofit Chicago Celebrated for Helping Residents, Businesses and City Buildings Save Money, Increase Energy Efficiency." Midwest Energy Efficiency Alliance, http://mwalliance.org/conference/inspiring-efficiency-awards/2015-impact-retrofit-chicago (accessed January 16, 2017).

Meek, James (2014) "Where Will We Live?" *London Review of Books*, January 1–9, 7–16.

Middleton, David (2006) "Tomorrow's World: With Flora, Greenery and Wildlife, Revamped Birmingham Is the New Central Park." *Birmingham Post*, November 28.

Mitchell, Chip, and Robin Amer (2013) "Divvy Blues: Bike-Share Program Leaves Some Behind." *WBEZ News*, June 28.

Mitchell, Katharyne (2001) "Transnationalism, Neo-Liberalism, and the Rise of the Shadow State." *Economy and Society* 30, no. 2: 165–89.

Morris, Steven (2014) "Birmingham Joins San Francisco and Oslo in Global Green Cities Club." *The Guardian*, April 3.

NACTO (2015) "Walkable Station Spacing Is Key to Successful, Equitable Bike Share." In NACTO *Bike Share Equity Practitioners' Paper #1*: National Association of City Transportation Officials.

Nathalie P. Voorhees Center for Neighborhood and Community Improvement (2009) "Transit Equity Matters: An Equity Index and Regional Analysis of the Red Line and Two Other Proposed CTA Transit Extensions." Chicago, IL: University of Illinois at Chicago.

Navy Pier (2017) "About Navy Pier." https://navypier.com/about-us/ (accessed May 23, 2017).

Nevarez, Leonard (2003) *New Money, Nice Town: How Capital Works in the New Urban Economy*. New York, NY: Routledge.

New York Times (2010) "After Mayor Daley." *New York Times*, September 9.

Newell, Peter, and Matthew Paterson (2010) *Climate Capitalism: Global Warming and the Transformation of the Global Economy*. Cambridge, UK: Cambridge University Press.

NRDC (2014) "Retrofit Chicago Commercial Building Iniative: Best Practices Report." National Resources Defense Council.

Nyden, Philip, Emily Edlynn, and Julie Davis (2006) "The Differential Impact of Gentrification on Commuities in Chicago." Chicago, IL: Loyola University Chicago Center for Urban Research and Learning.

O'Brien, J. (1999) Autumn Statement: Lobbying Pays off with Curb on Energy Levy. *Birmingham Post*, November 10.

Oke, T.R., M. North, and O. Slaymaker (1992) "Primordial to Prim Order: A Century of Environmental Change." In *Vancouver and Its Region*, ed. Graeme Wynn and Timothy Oke. Vancouver, BC: UBC Press.

Oldfield, Philip (2015) "UK Scraps Zero Carbon Homes Plan." *Guardian*, July 10.

Olds, Kris (1998) "Globalization and Urban Change: Tales from Vancouver Via Hong Kong." *Urban Geography* 19, no. 4: 360–85.

Overview and Scrutiny Committee (2007) "Report of the Sustainability and Climate Change Overview and Scrutiny Committee." Birmingham, UK: Birmingham City Council.

Owen, David (2009) *Green Metropolis: Why Living Smaller, Living Closer, and Driving Less Are the Keys to Sustainability*. New York, NY: Riverhead Books.

Pacyga, Dominic A. (2009) *Chicago: A Biography*. Chicago, IL: University of Chicago Press.

Paehlke, Robert (2009) "The Environmental Movement in Canada." In *Canadian Environmental Policy and Politics: Prospects for Leadership and Innovation*, ed. Debora L. VanNijnatten and Robert Boardman. Ontario: Oxford University Press.

Pain, Steve (2003) "Eastside Will Get Advice on Green Issues." *Birmingham Post*, May 15.

Palmer, John L., and Isabel V. Sawhill (1986) "Foreword." In *Reagan and the Cities*, ed. George E. Peterson and Carol W. Lewis. Washington, DC: Urban Institute Press.

Pander, Sean (2007) "City of Vancouver Climate Protection Progress Report." Vancouver, BC: City of Vancouver.

Parkinson, Michael (1989) "The Thatcher Government's Urban Policy, 1979–1989: A Review." *The Town Planning Review* 60, no. 4: 421–40.

Parsons, Deborah (2004) "Shopping for the Future: The Re-Enchantment of Birmingham's Urban Space." In *Remaking Birmingham: The Visual Culture of Urban Regeneration*, ed. Liam Kennedy. New York, NY: Routledge.

Pasotti, Eleanora (2009) *Political Branding in Cities: The Decline of Machine Politics in Bogotá, Naples, and Chicago*. Cambridge, UK: Cambridge University Press.

Pavel, M. Paloma (2009) "Introduction." In *Breakthrough Communities: Sustainability and Justice in the Next American Metropolis*, ed. M. Paloma Pavel. Cambridge, MA: MIT Press.

Peck, Jamie, and Adam Tickell (1992) "Local Modes of Social Regulation? Regulation Theory, Thatcherism, and Uneven Development." *Geoforum* 23, no. 3: 347–63.

Peck, Jamie, and Adam Tickell (1994) "Searching for a New Institutional Fix: The *after*-Fordist Crisis and the Global-Local Disorder." In *Post-Fordism: A Reader*, ed. Ash Amin. Oxford, UK: Blackwell.

Peck, Jamie, and Adam Tickell (2002) "Neoliberalizing Space." *Antipode* 34, no. 3: 380–404.

Peterson, George E. (1986) "Urban Policy and the Cyclical Behavior of Cities." In *Reagan and the Cities*, ed. George E. Peterson and Carol W. Lewis. Washington, DC: Urban Institute Press.

Peterson, George E., and Carol W. Lewis (1986) "Introduction." In *Reagan and the Cities*, ed. George E. Peterson and Carol W. Lewis. Washington, DC: Urban Institute Press.

Podmolik, Mary Ellen (2015) "Aldermen OK Stricter Affordable Housing Law." *Chicago Tribune*, March 18.

Polanyi, Karl (2001 [1944]) *The Great Transformation: The Political and Economic Origins of Our Time*. 2nd Beacon Paperback edn. Boston, MA: Beacon Press.

Porritt, Jonathon (2005) *Capitalism as If the World Matters*. Sterling, VA: Earthscan.

Porter, Eduardo (2016) "Does a Carbon Tax Work? Ask British Columbia." *New York Times*, March 1.

Porter, Libby, and Austin Barber (2006) "The Meaning of Place and State-Led Gentrification in Birmingham's Eastside." *City* 10, no. 2: 215–34.

Porter, Libby, and Dexter Hunt (2005) "Birmingham's Eastside Story: Making Steps Towards Sustainability?" *Local Environment* 10, no. 5: 525–42.

Porter, Libby, Margaret Jaconelli, Julian Cheyne, David Eby, and Hendrik Wagenaar (2009) "Planning Displacement: The Real Legacy of Major Sporting Events 'Just a Person in a Wee Flat': Being Displaced by the Commonwealth Games in Glasgow's East End; Olympian Masterplanning in London Closing Ceremonies: How Law, Policy and the Winter Olympics Are Displacing an Inconveniently Located Low-Income Community in Vancouver; Commentary: Recovering Public Ethos: Critical Analysis for Policy and Planning." *Planning Theory & Practice* 10, no. 3: 395–418.

Portney, Kent E. (2013) *Taking Sustainable Cities Seriously: Economic Development, the Environment, and Quality of Life in American Cities*, 2nd edn. Cambridge, MA: MIT Press.

Preece, Ashley (2015) "City Cycle Routes Gear up for £2.8m Improvement Scheme." *Great Barr Observer*, December 4.

Price, Gordon, and Patrick Condon (2014) "Debate: Should Vancouver Change How It Zones Big Projets?" *The Tyee*, August 13.

Public Health England (2015) "Birmingham Unitary Authority Health Profile 2015." England, UK: Public Health England.

Pucher, John, and Ralph Buehler, eds. (2012) *City Cycling*. Cambridge, MA: MIT Press.

Punter, John (2003) *The Vancouver Achievement: Urban Planning and Design.* Vancouver, BC: UBC Press.

Purcell, Mark (2006) "Urban Democracy and the Local Trap." *Urban Studies* 43, no. 11 (2006): 1921–41.

Quastel, Noah (2009) "Political Ecologies of Gentrification." *Urban Geography* 30, no. 7: 694–725.

Quastel, Noah, Markus Moos, and Nicholas Lynch (2012) "Sustainability-as-Density and the Return of the Social: The Case of Vancouver, British Columbia." *Urban Geography* 33, no. 7: 1055–84.

Rabe, Barry G. (1997) "The Politics of Sustainable Development: Impediments to Pollution Prevention and Policy Integration in Canada." *Canadian Public Administration / Administration Publique Du Canada* 40, no. 3: 415–535.

Raco, Mike (2007) "Spatial Policy, Sustainability, and State Restructuring: A Reassessment of Sustainable Community Building in England." In *The Sustainable Development Paradox: Urban Political Economy in the United States and Europe*, ed. Rob Krueger and David Gibbs. New York, NY: Guilford Press.

Rawcliffe, Peter (1995) "Making Inroads: Transport Policy and the British Environmental Movement." *Environment* 37, no. 3: 16–36.

Rees, William E., and Mathis Wackernagel (1996) "Urban Ecological Footprints: Why Cities Cannot Be Sustainable and Why They Are a Key to Sustainability." *Environmental Impact Assessment Review* 16: 223–48.

Regelson, Ken (2005) "Sustainable Cities: Best Practices for Renewable Energy & Energy Efficiency." San Francisco, CA: Sierra Club.

Respiratory Health Association (n.d.) "Power Plants: Victory for Clean Air and Healthy Lungs!" www.lungchicago.org/air-quality-power-plants/ (accessed January 28, 2015).

Rhodes, Dawn (2015) "Cabrini-Green Residents, CHA Settle Lawsuit – Adding Public Housing in Area." *Chicago Tribune*, September 13.

Rice, James J., and Michael J. Prince (2013) *Changing Politics of Canadian Social Policy*, 2nd edn. Toronto: University of Toronto Press.

Rice, May (2016) "88-Unit Affordable Housing Complex Proposed for Logan Square." *Chicagoist*, May 19.

Riposa, Gerry (1996) "From Enterprize Zones to Empowerment Zones: The Community Context of Urban Economic Development." *American Behavioral Scientist* 39, no. 5: 536–51.

Robinson, Matt (2016) "Vancouver Leads the Pack for Bike Commutes." *Vancouver Sun*, May 4.

Rodríguez, Arantxa, Erik Swyngedouw, and Frank Moulaert (2003) "Urban Restructuring, Social-Political Polarization, and New Urban Politics." In *The Globalized City: Economic Restructuring and Social Polarization in European Cities*, ed. Frank Moulaert, Arantxa Rodríguez, and Erik Swyngedouw. Oxford: Oxford University Press.

Rome, Adam (2013) *The Genius of Earth Day: How a 1970 Teach-in Unexpectedly Made the First Green Generation*. New York, NY: Hill & Wang.

Rosenthal, Stuart S. (2014) "Are Private Markets and Filtering a Viable Source of Low-Income Housing? Estimates from a 'Repeat Income' Model." *The American Economic Review* 104, no. 2: 687–706.

Rosol, Marit (2013) "Vancouver's 'EcoDensity' Planning Initiative: A Struggle over Hegemony?" *Urban Studies*, 1 18.

Saha, Devashree (2009) "Empirical Research on Local Government Sustainability Efforts in the USA: Gaps in the Current Literature." *Local Environment* 14, no. 1: 17–30.

Sale, Kirkpatrick (1993) *The Green Revolution: The American Environmental Movement 1962–1992*. New York, NY: Hill and Wang.

Sassen, Saskia (2001) *The Global City*. 2nd edn. Princeton, NJ: Princeton University Press.

Sassen, Saskia (2004) "A Global City." In *Global Chicago*, ed. Charles Madigan. Urbana, IL: University of Illinois Press.

Sassen, Saskia (2015) "Bringing Cities into the Global Framework." In *The Urban Climate Challenge: Rethinking the Role of Cities in the Global Climate Regime*, ed. Craig Johnson, Noah Toly, and Heike Schroeder. New York, NY: Routledge.

Sattherwaite, David (2011) "How Urban Societies Can Adapt to Resource Shortage and Climate Change." *Philosophical Transactions of the Royal Society* 369: 1762–83.

Saulny, Susan (2010) "Chicago's 'Mayor for Life' Decides Not to Run." *New York Times*, September 7.

Sawers, Larry, and William K. Tabb (1984) *Sunbelt/Snowbelt: Urban Development and Regional Restructuring*. New York, NY: Oxford University Press.

Schneider, Keith (2006) "To Revitalize a City, Try Spreading Some Mulch." *New York Times*, May 17.

Secter, Bob, and Alex Bordens (2013) "Divvy Opens Strong in White Neighborhoods." *Chicago Tribune*, July 10.

Seyfang, Gill (2004) "Consuming Values and Contested Cultures: A Critical Analysis of the UK Strategy for Sustainable Consumption and Production." *Review of Social Economy* LXII, no. 3: 323–38.

Shaheen, Susan A., Stacey Guzman, and Hua Zhang (2012) "Bikesharing across the Globe." In *City Cycling*, ed. John Pucher and Ralph Buehler. Cambridge, MA: MIT Press.

Shaheen, Susan A., Elliot W. Martin, Nelson D. Chan, Adam P. Cohen, and Mike Pogodzinski (2014) "Public Bikesharing in North American During a Period of Rapid Expansion: Understanding Business Models, Industry Trends and User Impacts." San Jose, CA: Mineta Transportation Institute.

Shecter, Barbara (2017) "Government Intervention on Housing Causes Vancouver to 'Temporarily Freeze in Its Tracks'." *Financial Post*, January 4.

Sheldrake, Lesley (2015) "Affordable Housing DIY." *The Planner*, April 7.

Simmons, Adele (2004) "Introduction." In *Global Chicago*, ed. Charles Madigan. Urbana, IL: University of Illinois Press.

Sinoski, Kelly (2016) "B.C. First to Land Transit Project Cash as Justin Trudeau Unveils Funding Deal." *Vancouver Sun*, June 16.

Slater, T.R. (1996) "Birmingham's Black and South-Asian Population." In *Managing a Conurbation: Birmingham and Its Region*, ed. A.J. Gerrard and T.R. Slater. Studley, Warwickshire: Brewin Books.

Slavin, Terry (2007) "Street Smarts: Cities Rise to Climate Challenge." *Guardian*, December 5.

Slow Roll Chicago. (n.d.) "About Slow Roll Chicago." http://slowrollchicago.org/about/ (accessed May 23, 2017).

Smith, Andrew (2012) *Events and Urban Regeneration: The Strategic Use of Events to Revitalise Cities*. London, UK: Routledge.

Spencer, Kenneth, Andy Taylor, Barbara Smith, John Mawson, Norman Flynn, and Richard Batley (1986) *Crisis in the Industrial Heartland: A Study of the West Midlands*. Oxford, UK: Clarendon Press.

Spinney, Robert G. (2000) *City of Big Shoulders: A History of Chicago*. DeKalb, IL: Northern Illinois University Press.

Stafford, Tom (2013) "The Psychology of Why Cyclists Enrage Car Drivers." *BBC*, February 12.

Stantec Consulting Ltd. (2011) "Vancouver Separated Bike Lane Business Impact Study." Vancouver, BC: Stantec Consulting Ltd.

Stastna, Kazi (2012) "Real Estate Rules Don't Discriminate against Foreigners." *CBC News*, March 19.

Stern, Andrew (2004). "Metal Petals Chicago Reclaims Its Architectural Crown." *Guardian*, July 5.

Stevenson, Hayley, and John S. Dryzek (2012) "The Legitimacy of Multilateral Climate Governance: A Deliberative Democratic Approach." *Critical Policy Studies* 6, no. 1: 1–18.

Strauss-Kahn, Vanessa, and Xavier Vives (2009) "Why and Where Do Headquarters Move?" *Regional Science and Urban Economics* 39: 168–86.

Sustainability West Midlands (2014) "Birmingham City Council – Green Living Spaces Plan." www.sustainabilitywestmidlands.org.uk/resources/birmingham-city-council-green-living-spaces-plan-2/ (accessed May 17, 2016).

Sustainlane (n.d.) "2008 U.S. City Rankings." www.sustainlane.com/us-city-rankings/overall-rankings (accessed December 16, 2010; please note: this URL is now inaccessible).

Sutter, John D. (2016) "There's a Cheap, Proven Fix to the World's Biggest Problem." *CNN*, April 19.

Suzuki, Hiroaki, Arish Dastur, Sebastian Moffatt, Nanae Yabuki, and Hinako Maruyama (2010) *Eco2 Cities: Ecological Cities as Economic Cities*. Washington, DC: The World Bank.

Swarts, Jonathan (2013) *Constructing Neoliberalism: Economic Transformation in Anglo-American Democracies*. Toronto: University of Toronto Press.

Swyngedouw, Erik (2007) "Impossible 'Sustainability' and the Postpolitical Condition." In *The Sustainable Development Paradox: Urban Political Economy in the United States and Europe*, ed. Rob Krueger and David Gibbs. New York, NY: Guilford Press.

Swyngedouw, Erik (2010) "Apocalypse Forever? Post-Political Populism and the Spectre of Climate Change." *Theory, Culture & Society* 27, no. 2–3: 213–32.

Terry, Don (2010) "The Final Farewell at Cabrini-Green." *New York Times*, December 10.

Thomas, Brian C. (2010) "Millennium Park: Thank Mayor Daley for a Chicago Treasure." *Chicago Now*, July 5.

Tilsley, Paul (2008) "Agenda: Why We Need to Lead a New Industrial Revolution." *Birmingham Post*, January 9.

Tilsley, Paul (2009) "Agenda: Time for Change." *Birmingham Post*, January 7.

TransAlt (2003) "Making Chicago 'the City That Bikes'." *TransAlt*, Summer, 14.

TransLink (2017) "About Us." TransLink, www.translink.ca/en/About-Us.aspx (accessed May 23, 2017).

Trust for Public Land (2017) "The 606: Frequently Asked Questions." Trust for Public Land, www.the606.org/resources/frequently-asked-questions/ (accessed February 15, 2017).

Uhlir, Edward K. (2005) "The Millennium Park Effect." *Economic Development Journal* 4, no. 2: 7–11.

UK Secretary of State for Environment, Food, and Rural Affairs (2005) "Securing the Future: Delivering UK Sustainable Development Strategy." Colegate, UK.

UN-HABITAT (2011) "Hot Cities – Battle Ground for Climate Change." In *Global Report on Human Settlement 2011*. Nairobi, Kenya: United Nations Human Settlements Program.

Underwood, Anne (2007) "Mayors Take the Lead." *Newsweek*, April 16.

UNFCCC (2015) "Cities & Regions Launch Major Five-Year Vision to Take Action on Climate Change." http://newsroom.unfccc.int/lpaa/cities-subnationals/lpaa-focus-cities-regions-across-the-world-unite-to-launch-major-five-year-vision-to-take-action-on-climate-change/ (accessed February 24, 2016).

United Nations (1992) "Agenda 21: The United Nations Programme of Action from Rio." New York, NY: United Nations.

United Nations Centre for Human Settlements (1998) *Sustainable Cities Programme: Approach and Implementation*. 2nd edn. Nairobi, Kenya: UNCHS: UNEP.

University of Birmingham (2017) "Birmingham's Global Profile." www.birmingham.ac.uk/university/about/global.aspx (accessed May 23, 2017).

University of British Columbia (n.d.) "UBC-Broadway Line." UBC, http://planning.ubc.ca/vancouver/transportation-planning/transportation-options/transit/ubc-broadway-line (accessed August 13, 2015).

Upton, Christopher (1993) *A History of Birmingham*. Chichester, Sussex, UK: Phillimore.

Ursaki, Julia, and Lisa Aultman-Hall (2016) "Quantifying the Equity of Bikeshare Access in U.S. Cities." In *Transportation Research Board 95th Annual Meeting*. Washington, DC.

U.S. Energy Information Administration (2017) "FAQs: How Much Carbon Dioxide Is Produced When Different Fuels Are Burned?" U.S. Department of Energy, https://www.eia.gov/tools/faqs/faq.cfm?id=73&t=11 (accessed March 5, 2017).

U.S. Energy Information Administration (2014) "Today in Energy." www.eia.gov/todayinenergy/detail.cfm?id=15491 (accessed January 26, 2015).

Usborne, David (2010) "For First Time in Decades, Chicago Faces Life without a Daley in Charge." *UK Independent*, September 9.

VanNijnatten, Debora L., and Robert Boardman (2009) "Introduction." In *Canadian Environmental Policy and Politics: Prospects for Leadership and Innovation*, ed. Debora L. VanNijnatten and Robert Boardman. Ontario: Oxford University Press.

VanWynsberghe, Rob, Bjorn Surborg, and Elvin Wyly (2013) "When the Games Come to Town: Neoliberalism, Mega-Events and Social Inclusion in the Vancouver 2010 Winter Olympic Games." *International Journal of Urban and Regional Research* 37, no. 6: 2074–93.

Viglucci, Andres (2007) "In Chicago's Revival, a Model for Miami?" *Miami Herald*, December 30.

Vivanco, Leonor (2016) "Marchers Take to The 606 Trail to Protest Gentrification." *Chicago Tribune*, May 17.

Vivanco, Leonor (2016) "The 606 Trail, a Study in Contrasts, Celebrates Its First Birthday." *Chicago Tribune*, June 3.

Vogel, David (2003 [1986]) *National Styles of Business Regulation: A Case Study of Environmental Protection*. Washington, DC: Beard Books.

Vogel, Steven K. (1996) *Freer Markets, More Rules: Regulatory Reform in Advanced Industrial Countries*. Ithaca, NY: Cornell University Press.

Wackernagel, Mathis, and William E. Rees (1996) *Our Ecological Footprint: Reducing Human Impact on the Earth*. Gabriola Island, BC; Philadelphia, PA: New Society Publishers.

Walker, Gordon (2012) *Environmental Justice: Concepts, Evidence and Politics*. New York, NY: Routledge.

Walker, Gordon, and Rosie Day (2012) "Fuel Poverty as Injustice: Integrating Distribution, Recognition and Procedure in the Struggle for Affordable Warmth." *Energy Policy* 49: 69–75.

Walker, Jonathan (2015) "Road Charging for High-Pollution Vehicles to Be Imposed in Birmingham by 2020." *Birmingham Mail*, December 17.

Wallsjasper, Jay (2013) "Bike Lanes in Black and White." People for Bikes, www.peopleforbikes.org/blog/entry/bike-lanes-in-black-and-white (accessed December 10, 2013).

Wallstam, Maria, and Nathan Crompton (2014) "Social Housing without Guarantees: The Myth of the 60/40 Ration in the DTES Oppenheimer District." *The Mainlander*, March 12.

Walsh, Edward (1996) "In Chicago, No Daley Double." *Washington Post*, August 24.

Wapner, Paul (2010) *Living through the End of Nature: The Future of American Environmentalism*. Cambridge, MA: MIT Press.

Ward, Kevin (2003) "The Limits to Contemporary Urban Redevelopment: 'Doing' Entrepreneurial Urbanism in Birmingham, Leeds and Manchester." *City* 7, no. 2 (July): 199–211.

Ward, Stephen V. (1998) *Selling Places: The Marketing and Promotion of Towns and Cities, 1850–2000*. London: E & FN Spon.

Ward, Stephen V. (2002) *Planning the Twentieth-Century City: The Advanced Capitalist World*. Chichester, UK: Wiley.

Waterscape (n.d.) "BCN." www.waterscape.com/canals-and-rivers/bcn (accessed February 10, 2011).

Watson, Andrea V. (2016) "Residents Give Wish List for When Englewood Gets Its Own Bloomingdale Trail." *DNAInfo*, January 12.

Watson, Anna (2014) "To What Extent Has Green Deal Policy Facilitated Energy Efficiency Retrofit Supply Chain Development: A Case Study of Birmingham." University of Sussex.

Watts, Duncan (1999) *The Environment and British Politics*. London: Hodder & Stoughton Educational.

Weaver, Matt (2006) "Brown Pledges to Build 'Zero Carbon' Homes." *Guardian*, December 6.

Weber, Rachel (2002) "Extracting Value from the City." In *Spaces of Neoliberalism: Urban Restructuring in North America and Western Europe*, ed. Neil Brenner and Nikolas Theodore. Malden, MA: Blackwell.

Webster, Frank (2003) "Reinventing Birmingham, England, in a Globalized Information Economy." In *Globalization and Society: Processes of Differentiation Examined*, ed. Raymond Breton and Jeffrey G. Reitz. Westport, CT: Praeger.

Weingaertner, Carina, and Austin Barber (2007) "Urban Regeneration and Sustainability: Challenges for Established Small Businesses. Paper Presented at the ENHR International Conference, June 25–28." Rotterdam.

Wernau, Julie (2012) "Fisk, Crawford Coal Plants Had Long History, as Did Battle to Close Them." *Chicago Tribune*, September 2.

Wheeler, Brian (2015) "A History of Social Housing." www.bbc.com/news/uk-14380936 (accessed January 15, 2016).

While, Aidan (2014) "Carbon Regulation and Low-Carbon Urban Restructuring." In *After Sustainable Cities?*, ed. Mike Hodson and Simon Marvin. New York, NY: Routledge.

While, Aidan, Andrew E.G. Jonas, and David Gibbs (2004) "The Environment and the Entrepreneurial City: Searching for the Urban 'Sustainability Fix' in Manchester and Leeds." *International Journal of Urban and Regional Research* 28, no. 3: 549–69.

Wiewel, Wim (1986) "The State of the Economy and Economic Development in the Chicago Metropolitan Region." Chicago, IL: Center for Urban Economic Development, University of IL at Chicago.

Wildlife Trust for Birmingham and the Black Country (n.d.) "Biodiversity Action." www.wild-net.org/wildbbc/index.aspx?id=528 (accessed February 10, 2011; please note: this URL is now inaccessible).

Williams, Katie, Elizabeth Burton, and Mike Jenks, eds. (2000) *Achieving Sustainable Urban Form*. London: E & FN Spon.

Winfield, Mark (2009) "Policy Instruments in Canadian Environmental Policy." In *Canadian Environmental Policy and Politics: Prospects for Leadership and Innovation*, ed. Debora L. VanNijnatten and Robert Boardman. Ontario: Oxford University Press.

Wisniewski, Mary (2016) "New Buildings near 'L' Mostly Aimed at Well-to-Do." *Chicago Tribune*, May 2.

Wolch, Jennifer R., Jason Byrne, and Joshua P. Newell (2014) "Urban Green Space, Public Health, and Environmental Justice: The Challenge of Making Cities 'Just Green Enough'." *Landscape and Urban Planning* 125: 234–44.

World Commission on Environment and Development (1987) *Our Common Future*. Oxford, UK: Oxford University Press.

World Green Building Council, "Rick Fedrizzi, City of Vancouver & Saint-Gobain CEO honoured in WorldGBC Awards," World Green Building Council, www.worldgbc.org/news-media/rick-fedrizzi-city-vancouver-saint-gobain-ceo-honoured-worldgbc-awards (accessed June 4, 2017).

Wyly, Elvin K., and Daniel J. Hammel (2010 [1999]) "Islands of Decay in Seas of Renewal: Housing Policy and the Resurgence of Gentrification." In *The Gentrificaion Reader*, ed. Loretta Lees, Tom Slater and Elvin Wyly. New York, NY: Routledge.

Wynn, Graeme (1992) "Introduction." In *Vancouver and Its Region*, ed. Graeme Wynn and Timothy Oke. Vancouver, BC: UBC Press.

Yaffe, Barbara (2014) "Barbara Yaffe: Vancouver Must Explore Options to Ease Housing Affordability Crisis." *Vancouver Sun*, November 4.

Zavestoski, Stephen, and Julian Agyeman, eds. (2015) *Incomplete Streets: Processes, Practices, and Possibilities*. New York, NY: Routledge.

Zuk, Miriam, and Karen Chapple (2016) "Housing Production, Filtering and Displacement: Untangling the Relationships." In *Berkeley IGS Research Brief*. Berkeley, CA: Institute of Government Studies.

Index

city 73–4; Broadway corridor
186–7; challenge of livability
in 78–80; community amenity
contributions (CACs) 143–4;
Concord Pacific development 75–9,
143; Downtown Eastside (DTES)
area 38, 74, 79, 99–100, 148–50;
Downtown Vancouver Business
Improvement Assoc-iation (DVBIA)
189; "Expo '86" 73–5, 98; failed
promises of social sustainability
97–102; Grandview-Woodland
146, 148; Point Grey Road
189–90; Hornby Street
188–9; "Living First" strategy
66–7; Marpole area 146–8;
megadevelopments and quality
urban design 74–8; neoliberal
environmentalism in 80; Olympic
and Paralympic Winter Games
(2010) 98–100; power of

developers in 143–5; search for a
"sustainable" community in
146–50; securing the city's
green brand 131–4; TransLink
authority 186–7
Vision Vancouver (political party)
100–1, 128, 142–7, 188, 191
voluntary measures for environmental
protection 46–7, 92–3, 104, 113,
122–4, 129–30
volunteers, use of 182

Wackernagel, Mathis 13
Ward, A. Montgomery 60
Washington, Harold 57
Watt, James 30, 105
Whitehead, Mark 22
wildlife habitats 184
World Bank 2

zoning decisions 143–4, 157

Taylor & Francis eBooks

Helping you to choose the right eBooks for your Library

Add Routledge titles to your library's digital collection today. Taylor and Francis ebooks contains over 50,000 titles in the Humanities, Social Sciences, Behavioural Sciences, Built Environment and Law.

Choose from a range of subject packages or create your own!

Benefits for you

>> Free MARC records
>> COUNTER-compliant usage statistics
>> Flexible purchase and pricing options
>> All titles DRM-free.

REQUEST YOUR FREE INSTITUTIONAL TRIAL TODAY

Free Trials Available
We offer free trials to qualifying academic, corporate and government customers.

Benefits for your user

>> Off-site, anytime access via Athens or referring URL
>> Print or copy pages or chapters
>> Full content search
>> Bookmark, highlight and annotate text
>> Access to thousands of pages of quality research at the click of a button.

eCollections – Choose from over 30 subject eCollections, including:

Archaeology	Language Learning
Architecture	Law
Asian Studies	Literature
Business & Management	Media & Communication
Classical Studies	Middle East Studies
Construction	Music
Creative & Media Arts	Philosophy
Criminology & Criminal Justice	Planning
Economics	Politics
Education	Psychology & Mental Health
Energy	Religion
Engineering	Security
English Language & Linguistics	Social Work
Environment & Sustainability	Sociology
Geography	Sport
Health Studies	Theatre & Performance
History	Tourism, Hospitality & Events

For more information, pricing enquiries or to order a free trial, please contact your local sales team:
www.tandfebooks.com/page/sales

 Routledge
Taylor & Francis Group

The home of
Routledge books

www.tandfebooks.com